THE MALE
EXPERIENCE

THE MALE EXPERIENCE

James A. Doyle

Roane State Community College

wcb
Wm. C. Brown Company Publishers
Dubuque, Iowa

To my parents
DOROTHY M. DOYLE AND OWEN E. DOYLE

CONTENTS

Preface

TODAY'S UNCERTAIN MALE   2

1

One Man's Male Experience   4
The Rumblings of Change   9
Technology and the Male Sex Role
Lost Confidences
The Women's Movement
Fears and Tremblings   15
The Horns of a Dilemma   17
Summing Up   17

SECTION 1
PERSPECTIVES ON THE MALE

OF PAST TIMES AND REIGNING   22
MEN: THE HISTORICAL
PERSPECTIVE

2

A New Interpretation of History   23
The Patriarchal Tradition   24
The Epic Male
The Spiritual Male
The Chivalric Male
The Renaissance Male
The Bourgeois Male
Summarizing the Western Roots of
the Male Role Ideal
The American Versions of the Male
Sex Role   36
The Gentleman and His Family
The Horse Trader and the
Suffragette
The He-Man and His Compatriots
Partners at Last
Commenting on the Historical
Perspective   45
Suggested Readings   46

OF PUNY CHROMOSOMES   48
AND POWERFUL HORMONES:
THE BIOLOGICAL PERSPECTIVE

3

Prenatal Events   49
The Role of the X and the Y
Chromosomes
Testosterone's Contribution to
Prenatal Development

Postnatal Events   59
The Changing Male Body
Testosterone and Blue Mondays
Testosterone and Aggression
Testosterone and Nurturant
Behaviors
Commenting on the Biological
Perspective   65
Suggested Readings   65

OF STRANGE PLACES   66   Cultural Variations in Sex Roles   67
AND STRANGER MEN: *Primitive Human Groups*
THE ANTHROPOLOGICAL   *Strange Peoples and Even Stranger*
PERSPECTIVE   *Roles*
4   Male Dominance   73
                                 Matriarchal Rule: Fact or Fiction?
                                 Explanations for Male Dominance
                                 Are There More Than Two Sex
                                 Roles?   82
                                 The Berdache
                                 The Nadle
                                 The Alyha and the Hwame
                                 Commenting on the Anthropological
                                 Perspective   85
                                 Suggested Readings   86

OF PARENT, PEER, AND OTHER 88   Socialization and the Male Sex Role 89
INFLUENCES: THE SOCIOLOGICAL   The Socializing Agents   90
PERSPECTIVE   *The Parents (But, Dear, We Meant*
5   *Well!)*
                                 The Media (The Vast Wastelands)
                                 The Educational System (Johnny, Sit
                                 Up Straight!)
                                 The Peer Group (I Dare Ya!)
                                 Sexism   105
                                 The Socialization of Sexism
                                 The Economics of Sexism
                                 Commenting on the Sociological
                                 Perspective   109
                                 Suggested Readings   110

OF BENT PSYCHES AND BRUISED 112 Sex Differences, or Much Ado
EGOS: THE PSYCHOLOGICAL   About Nothing   113
PERSPECTIVE   *Intellectual Differences*
6   *Social Differences*

Masculine Sex Role Identity   122
*Psychoanalytic-Identification Theory
of Sex Role Identity*
*Social-Learning Theory of Sex-Typed
Behaviors*
*Cognitive-Developmental Theory of
Sex Role Identity*
*Evaluating the Psychological Theories
of Sex Role Identity*
Psychology Looks at the Male Sex
Role   131
*The Male Sex Role Identity (MSRI)
Paradigm*
Two Views of the Male Sex Role
The Sex Role Strain (SRS) Paradigm
Commenting on the Psychological
Perspective   141
Suggested Readings   142

SECTION 2
ELEMENTS OF THE MALE SEX ROLE

OF SISSIFIED MEN AND UNMANLY   148
EMOTIONS: THE ANTIFEMININE
ELEMENT

7

Girls Are Icky!   149
Don't Be a Crybaby!   155
Watch Out for Sissies!   158
Some Closing Comments   161
Suggested Readings   161

OF LARGE OFFICES, FAT   162
PAYCHECKS, AND OTHER PERKS:
THE SUCCESS ELEMENT

8

The Male Sex Role and
a Competitive World View   164
The Male as Good Provider   168
*Historical Sketch of the Provider
Role*
*Contemporary Views on the
Provider Role*
Nice Guys Finish Last   172
Dropping Off the Treadmill   174
Some Closing Comments   179
Suggested Readings   179

OF CLENCHED FISTS AND FLEXED   180
BICEPS: THE AGGRESSIVE ELEMENT

9

The Anomaly of Aggression   181
Men Against Men   184
Men Against Women   188
Rape
Marital Violence
Some Closing Comments   193
Suggested Readings   194

Contents

OF BULGING CODPIECES AND SPENT CONDOMS: THE SEXUAL ELEMENT
10
196

Rites of Passage 198
Boys Need Loving Too
Close Sexual Encounters of a Wondrous Kind
Myths and Male Sexuality
Sexual Dysfunctions and Other Headaches 204
Impotence
Premature Ejaculation
Retarded Ejaculation
The Don Juan Complex
Lack of Sexual Interest
Causes of Sexual Dysfunctions
Are There Any Celibates in the House? 209
Some Closing Comments 211
Suggested Readings 212

OF LITTLE TOUGHIES AND STALWART FRONTIERSMEN: THE SELF-RELIANT ELEMENT
11
214

The Precarious Posture 215
Male Heroes 218
The Athlete, the Soldier, and the Politician 222
Jerseys and Shoulder Pads Make the Man
You're in the Army Now
"My Fellow Americans. . ."
Some Closing Comments 233
Suggested Readings 233

SECTION 3
SOME ISSUES OF CONCERN TO MALES

OF GAY MEN AND OPENED CLOSETS: HOMOSEXUALITY
12
238

From Hatred to Understanding and Back Again 240
The Roots of Antihomosexual Sentiment
A Short-Lived About-Face
Debunking the Myths About Gays 245
The Either–Or Perspective on Sexual Preference
It's All a Problem of Sex Role Identity
Misogyny Is the Answer
It's the Mother's Fault
It's All in the Hormones
Just Like Husbands and Wives
You Can Spot 'Em a Block Away
The Miserable Lot
Protect the Children
They're All Alike

Gay Relationships 253
*The Physical Side of Gay
Relationships*
*The Psychological Side of Gay
Relationships*
Some Closing Comments 258
Suggested Readings 259

OF UNEQUAL POWER AND 260
STRAINED RELATIONSHIPS:
POWER AND MALE-FEMALE
RELATIONS
13

The Name of the Game Is Power 261
Types of Power
The Sexes and the Balance of Power
Male Concerns Over Lost Power
Intimate Male-Female Relationships 266
*Values That Bind and Values That
Separate*
Power and Intimate Relationships
Satisfaction and Well-Being
Some Closing Comments 272
Suggested Readings 272

OF CLASHING VALUES AND A 274
QUESTIONABLE FUTURE: WHERE
TO FROM HERE?
14

Clashing Values and Changing
Times 275
Changing the Guard — or Are We? 279
Are Men Confused and Angry?
*Are C-R Groups Common in Men's
Circles?*
*What About a Men's Social
Movement?*
What About Men's Liberation?
A Closing Comment 290
Suggested Readings 290

Notes 291
Name Index 313
Subject Index 317

Reading a book, any kind of book, is a journey of sorts into the thinking of the author. It seems only appropriate, then, to share with readers of *The Male Experience* a few words about what awaits them in terms of the author's approach.

First of all, I have purposely taken a feminist approach in my treatment of the male experience. Too often people assume that the feminist viewpoint deals only with issues of concern to females. The feminist perspective defined in these narrow terms is too restrictive and decidedly unwarranted. Feminism speaks to the very core of issues and concerns that affect both females *and* males. Power, dominance, nurturance, aggression, competition, and emotional expression are only a few of the issues many males face today. The feminist perspective appears to be one of the better ways in which to focus and analyze such issues.

Second, I am unwilling to support totally any one discipline or academic viewpoint of the male experience over all of the others (see Chapters 2–6). Too often experts from one academic discipline become so enmeshed in their own discipline's viewpoint that they exclude the findings of any other discipline. From time to time biologists close their ears to what sociologists have to say, and psychologists dismiss biology as a reactionary science. For example, some sociologists and psychologists will not even listen to a discussion of hormonal influences on behavior for fear that such an idea may somehow lead to a return to conservative values and social norms. Hormones are apolitical and are treated as such in this book. I have tried to present the various disciplines' ideas and views about what constitutes masculinity and masculine sex-typed behaviors in a fair and nondogmatic way, letting each discipline's evidence speak for itself. However, when I believe that a particular idea from one of the perspectives is unfounded by virtue of current research evidence, I have tried to point this out.

Finally, I would not want readers to think that *The Male Experience* contains the last word on the issues of masculinity and the male sex role. I hope that readers will come away from their reading of the following material with a greater appreciation and understanding of what it means to be a male today. But it is my greater hope that readers, when finished with this book, will begin to think about, to question, and then to analyze for themselves the complex issues surrounding the male experience.

Every book written is more than a collection of words and ideas from a single author or a particular group of authors. I am indebted to so many of my teachers, colleagues, and students for the ideas presented in this book that I cannot begin to name them all for fear of omitting someone. However, I must acknowledge a special debt of gratitude to the many reviewers who read all or portions of the earlier drafts of *The Male Experience* and immeasurably added their expertise to the finished product. They include Robert C. Brannon—City University of New York, Brooklyn College; Michele Paludi—Kent State University; Kay Deaux—Purdue University; Carol Grams—Orange Coast College; James Harrison—Manhattan Psychiatric Center; Alan E. Gross—University of Maryland; Jay A. Mancini—Virginia Polytechnic Institute & State University; Letitia Anne Peplau—University of California, Los Angeles. Besides these unnamed and named collaborators, one other person has been with me every step of the way during the three-year journey that has led to the publication of *The Male Experience*. Thus to my partner Nan, I want to say, "*We* made it happen together."

J. A. D.
April 1982
Oakdale, Tennessee

THE MALE
EXPERIENCE

1

TODAY'S UNCERTAIN MALE

May you live in changing times.   Chinese curse

"It's a boy!" reports the physician to the teenage mother exhausted from her marathon first labor.

"It's a boy!" shouts the wide-eyed cabby to the dazed woman pressed against the Checker's rear seat.

"It's a boy!" croons the midwife to the woman resting in her bed at the rear of the farmhouse.

These dramas of new life may differ in many respects, but the significance of the words "It's a boy!" remains the same. The pronouncement "It's a boy!" immediately sets restrictions, grants privileges, defines status, and lays down expectations. What may appear to be three simple and straightforward words that define sex are probably the most important words spoken over a healthy newborn male.

What lies ahead for these males is what we shall call *the male experience.* To better understand every man's male experience, we can think of the male experience as unfolding on two different but related levels: the public level and the private level.

The public level of the male experience contains all of the expectations and norms, the prescriptions and proscriptions, and the sanctions and stereotypes placed on the male by others. In other words, the public level takes in all of the social *dos* and *do nots, shoulds* and *should nots* that people in general expect of boys and men simply because they are males. Over the centuries, the public level has become rigidly defined and today is quite resistant to any change. The public level of the male experience is often referred to by social scientists as the male's *sex role* or *gender role.*

The second level of the male experience, the private level, can only be inferred or at best speculated about because it is thought to exist within the male's psychological makeup. The private level begins to develop when a young boy starts to identify or label himself as male. In other words, once a boy begins to see himself as male and understands that he is sexually different from girls, then most social scientists reason that he is developing a *masculine gender identity.* (Several authorities on masculine sex-typed behaviors and masculinity have recently argued that the concept of gender identity is an outdated and misleading concept. This viewpoint will be discussed in greater detail in Chapter 6.) From available evidence, most boys begin to perceive themselves as males and consequently begin to express appropriate sex-typed attitudes, behaviors, and interests sometime during their second to fourth year.[1] Furthermore, many social scientists think that once a boy develops a masculine gender identity, little if anything can change it.

It is easy to see how the social definitions of the male experience, that is, the public level, can have a direct impact on how individual men perceive and then define their own sense of masculinity. For example, if a particular society expects or even demands that its men engage in a declared war, then a male member of that society who does not participate in a declared war may come to think that he is less than fully masculine. Here is a case of how society's expectations can influence or shape a man's view of his own masculinity. From the very beginning of our discussion of the male experience, we need to be aware of just how important society's definitions of manhood and masculinity are to every male.

This chapter discusses some of the recent social forces that are only now beginning to undermine the foundations of the traditional male sex role. As noted earlier, the public level of the male experience is resistant to any change in its structure and content. Nonetheless, during the last several decades, society's definitions of manhood and masculinity have been buffeted and challenged by various sectors. We will examine some of the conflicts, strains, and stresses that many men are beginning to feel about their own sense of masculinity. However, before we look at the challenges and changes in the public and private levels of the male experience, let us take a generalized look at the whole of one man's male experience. Possibly, we can gain some insight into the complexities and the conflicts that many males are now experiencing simply because the words "It's a boy!" were pronounced over them.

ONE MAN'S MALE EXPERIENCE

There is no way to write of the male experience without falling prey to the arch-enemy of truth itself, the generalization. To say that society, any society, expects and demands the same from all of its male members or that all men in a particular society experience their sense of masculinity in exactly the same manner would be utterly preposterous. However, in this section we are going to try to capture the spirit of the male experience if not all its unique features. We will do this by creating one life and infusing that life with the expectations, norms, and sense of fragile masculinity that many social scientists report as commonplace among American men today. We will call our man David.

David's male experience actually begins with the fertilization of an egg. His future appearance as a five-foot, eleven-inch, lean human being is determined by the special genetic contributions contained in the forty-four chromosomes that are equally donated by his biological mother and father. That the fertilized egg is destined to be a biological male is determined by the father's contribution of a specialized sex chromosome, designated as a Y chromosome, which joins with the mother's X chromosome. At conception, the biological foundation is laid; if nothing goes wrong, some forty weeks later, the words "It's a boy!" will be spoken.

But before this birth scene can occur, several significant biological events must take place to assure that the fertilized egg does, in fact, turn out to be a biological male. For the first seven or eight weeks of uterine existence, the growing mass of cells called an *embryo* is sexually neutral. Even though the fertilized egg contains a Y chromosome, the growing embryo possesses a common set of sex structures that could develop into either male or female sex structures. Sometime between the sixth and eighth week, a special hormone called *testosterone* spreads throughout the embryo causing the neutral sex structures to develop as male rather than female sex structures. At no other time in David's life, with the possible exception of the beginning of puberty, is his biochemistry as important to his future male experience as during the first three months of uterine existence.

After what probably seems to David's mother an interminable wait, the big day finally arrives and David is born. The words "It's a boy!" greet David and in general foretell to everyone present what kind of life lies ahead for David. During his first hours, David is like a lump of clay waiting to be molded into the person—specifically the male person—others think he should be. The first people to put their imprint on him are, of course, his parents. In all probability, they see in their infant son a firm, strong, and alert boy. We might say that David's parents see a "little toughie" when they look at him. Certainly, David is nothing like the soft, delicate, and sweet little one-day-old female lying in the next hospital crib. Surprisingly, David does not differ that much from his female nursery neighbor in weight, length, color, or muscle tone.[2] No matter; David's parents see him in a very special way, a way conditioned by how society tells adults that newborn boys are supposed to be different from newborn girls.

The first few months are filled with rapid growth for David, and his parents quickly adjust to having a "little man" in the house. The initial joys and excitements surrounding the new family addition slowly settle into the daily routines of taking care of the baby. But all too soon, David's parents begin to treat him differently than they would if he were a little girl. When he is about six or seven months old, his mother starts to withdraw some of her physical attention by not holding him as much as she did when he was younger.[3] She also smiles and talks less to David than do mothers of similar aged female infants.[4] We might say that David's mother is pulling back from him. Possibly, she feels that too much affection and attention may be harmful to a growing boy. The fact of the matter is that many parents think sons need less affection than daughters do.

As the years go by, David quickly learns what his parents expect of him because he is a boy. They probably teach him more with punishment than with rewards.[5] He more often hears the brusque and harsh sound of the word *no* more than the accepting and gentle word *yes*. Many of the child-rearing practices that David's parents use with him may be less than sound parenting practices. David is treated more roughly by his parents than need be simply because he can "take it"; he is pushed into competitive rough-and-tumble games because he is supposed to be "all boy," and he is scolded if he cries when he is hurt because "big boys don't cry." The ultimate criticism is leveled against David when he acts in any way that his father thinks feminine: "No son of mine is going to act like a sissy." Consequently, David soon learns to become somewhat sullen and withdrawn because he fears that his parents may punish him if he does not act like a man. By David's third or fourth birthday, he generally knows what is expected of him as a boy, and more importantly he defines himself as a little man. He knows, for example, that mommies have babies and daddies do not. David's initial awareness of the public and private levels of the male experience are fairly well-grounded in his thinking some time before he gets ready to go to school.

Once David enters the primary grades, his peers begin to influence him, in some ways even more than his parents do. David's male peers strengthen his sense of masculinity and add new expectations and demands to his understanding of the male sex role in general. To attest to how deeply young boys like David know what is expected of males, boys frequently describe men with terms like "strong," "tough," "unafraid," and "ready to fight."[6] Besides his peers, David's teachers also play a part in supporting society's norms and stereotypes for males. Along with peers and teachers, television similarly presents a stereotypic view of the male. For example, on television David sees men dominate women, take bold action, and generally succeed at whatever they do. Thus by the end of his first decade, David's public idea of what it means to be a man and his private feelings of masculinity are pretty well set. But as David begins his second decade, certain biological events and social forces loom on the horizon and soon shake his calm preadolescence.

Few periods in a male's life are as unsettling and unnerving as adolescence. Among the problems the adolescent David must face are mounting peer pressures to conform to an exaggerated view of manhood, a changing body chemistry, an emergent interest in sex, the challenges of competitive sports, and the question of what to do for a job or career. It seems that during adolescence David must face one crisis after another. Let us follow him through these teenage trouble spots.

First of all, David feels the pressures of peer acceptance and approval more strongly during adolescence than at any other time in his life. The peer group determines to a large extent his likes and dislikes, his style of dress and manner of behavior, and his entertainment. It even helps to select his friends. Furthermore, the peer group acts like a kind of mirror in which David can check himself to see how well he fits an exaggerated version of the male sex role. Most young men of David's age seem preoccupied with proving themselves "real men," not only to themselves but also to their peers. To be rejected by the group is one of David's greatest concerns. To avoid such a social and personal disaster, he goes along with the group more often than not, even when he does not fully approve of their activities. However, David does manage every now and then to act independently of his group. And, as the years go by, he will find himself less easily influenced by what his peers say and think. But those days are still some years away.

One of the more unnerving features of David's early adolescence is the distressing changes taking place in his body. Unknown to David, his hormones, especially the one called testosterone, begin to affect the body he once took for granted. It seems that almost overnight he grows several inches, his voice frequently quakes as it deepens, and he broadens through the shoulders. In addition to these changes, some other not-so-public physical changes are also taking place. His penis, scrotum, and testes enlarge, and a definite pubic tuft becomes more prominent. To make matters worse, David's penis begins to act as if it had a mind

Today's Uncertain Male

of its own by becoming erect at the most inopportune times and creating a telltale bulge in his pants. Many a time he walks down the school hall with his books held awkwardly in front of him.

While somewhat amazed at his body's tomfoolery, David becomes more concerned with his appearance. He spends more time in front of a mirror, flexing his muscles, checking for the early signs of facial hair, and just plain primping. David's concern with his body and its looks is related to yet another concern that he must deal with—sex and girls.

During early adolescence, David becomes quite interested in girls and sex. He used to feel indifferent toward girls, actually preferring to avoid them most of the time. Of course, when David was in the fourth or fifth grade, he occasionally participated in "kissing games" at friends' birthday parties. But now David is attracted toward girls and at the same time is perplexed by the emergent sexual feelings that they arouse in him. Sometime during David's twelfth year, he started to masturbate. Frequently, he masturbates four to six times a day, and he needlessly fears that this might damage his resilient organ. Sexual urges, fantasies, and assorted sexual materials are becoming an obsession with David.

As far as girls are concerned, David started to date a girl seriously when he was in eighth grade. He has already overcome much of his initial sexual shyness, and lately he and his girlfriend have started some heavy petting that often ends in mutual masturbation. It is only a matter of time before David loses his virginity. But his awakening sexuality and his interest in girls are only two of the unsettling features competing for David's attention right now.

Few activities play as important a role in an adolescent male's life as do high school athletics. For those gifted with ability, athletics provide attention, recognition, and status among the peer group. However, except for a small number of gifted or natural athletes, there are few other activities that require so much personal commitment and hard work and provide so little payoff in later life as do high school athletics.[7] David is one of those countless young males not blessed with much athletic talent. But he feels the effects of athletic competition when he senses that he is not one of the more popular males in his class simply because he lacks enthusiasm for the school's team sports. And David is starting to feel another pressure. Now that he is getting ready to graduate, he must start thinking seriously about getting a good job or going to college.

After graduating from high school, most of David's friends go off to a state college. David follows suit, leaves home, and moves into a college dorm. He majors in accounting, meets the "right" girl, passes most of his exams, and, four years later, graduates with a bachelor's degree in accounting and public finance. The summer after graduation, David marries his college sweetheart and begins work in an accounting firm.

We might expect that David's life as a newly married man, soon to be a father, and junior accountant to be rather dull and uneventful from now on, especially after all the pressures of his adolescent years. But his adult years will be filled with personal crises, challenging events, and occasions when he will doubt his masculinity and the value of his acquired male sex role.[8]

During his twenties and thirties, David throws himself into his work. He frequently puts in twelve to fourteen hours a day and soon begins to climb the ladder of success. A big office, regular bonuses, and his own secretary are just a few of the signs of that success. David thinks that he must satisfy his family's every need and want if he is to prove to himself and others that he is a real man, a good provider, and so he works even harder. As his salary increases year after year, he often finds himself thinking of his masculinity in terms of the dollar amount printed on his paycheck.[9] In the eyes of David's friends, he has it all—a fine house in the suburbs, a happy family, a good job, and people's respect. But sometime around his fortieth birthday, David begins to feel a knot in his stomach. Something is wrong in his life.

David has accomplished almost everything he set out to do, at least what he thought was expected of him as a man. He has provided for his family and worked hard at becoming a success. He saw that the bills were paid, his daughter's teeth got their needed braces, his son went to the best summer camps, and his wife had all of the home conveniences. David's clients have been happy with the way he has handled their accounts, his boss respects his business judgment, and he has even served as president of a local men's service organization.

Even so, David feels that something is missing. The jogging, tennis, and hair tint do not rid him of the gnawing fears that keep churning inside. When everything is said and done, David feels that his life is rather meaningless. During his early forties, he experiences what some call the male mid-life crisis.[10]

Nevertheless, David is too old to change his ways, or so he thinks. After several anxious years, he quiets his fears with the thought that retirement is approaching. He plans to spend his retirement doing all the things he never allowed himself to do when he was busily climbing the ladder of success—things like getting to know his wife and children better.

As David moves through his fifties, he doesn't work as hard as he used to. There doesn't seem to be much point to putting in the long hours anymore. What can a man his age accomplish anyway, thinks David. He also feels that several of the younger accountants at the office are after his job.

His children are grown now, and only David and his wife are left at home. David does not say much to his wife when they are alone. He reads the paper and watches television almost every evening. He never was very good at communicating with his wife.

Finally, David retires. He and his wife visit their children's families out West. David finds his free time somewhat unsettling. He never quite gets used to not going to work. Retirement, he admits to himself, isn't all that it's cracked up to be. David does not really enjoy his "golden years" because he never took the time to find any other interest besides work.

David died last week of a heart attack. His friends consoled his wife and children with these words: "David was a fine man, and we will miss him."

As suggested at the beginning of David's biography, the unique features of each man's male experience cannot be captured by recounting just a few of the major life events that occurred in David's male experience. Obviously, his male experience—the expectations and norms imposed by society's views of the male sex role and his own definition of his masculinity—was a generalization and thus a simplification of the complexities that make each man's male experience unique. However, this abbreviated account of David's life captures a sense of the public and private levels of the male experience that many men know at various times in their lives.

With this general sense of the male experience, let us look more closely at some of the recent social forces and events that are beginning to challenge the traditional male sex role. The traditional male sex role with its social expectations and demands of what it means to be a "real man" are no longer unquestionably accepted among every circle of our society. To better understand why some men are now finding their own definition of masculinity tenuous, we need to be aware of the new challenges to the traditional views of the male sex role.

THE RUMBLINGS OF CHANGE

Society's views of the male sex role are quite resistant to any significant change. In fact, society has a vested interest in maintaining, supporting, and even defending the definitions and expectations that it associates with the role of each sex. When males know generally what is expected and demanded of them as men, there is less social conflict and less personal strain for all concerned. The same holds true for society's interest in keeping the female sex role within its prescribed and traditional bounds. When changes do occur in these prescribed sex roles, people can become confused and even anxious over their own personal definitions of masculinity and femininity.

Even so, certain features of the male sex role have changed over time for various reasons. However, even minor changes in a social expectation are initially resisted by a majority of people. For example, not too many years ago, most people considered it appropriate for a man to wear his hair short, above the ears and definitely much shorter than women's hair. Beginning in the late 1960s, however, many young men began wearing their hair long, shoulder-length in some cases, much to their parents' dismay. The presence of long-haired musical groups and a growing anti-establishment fervor among many young people partially accounted for the lengthening of men's hair. Nevertheless, a majority of people thought young people in general were losing their minds and that young men in particular were losing their sense of masculinity. More than a few people snidely commented when seeing a long-haired male, "See, you can't tell if he's a male or a female." Society, at least the established or older portion of society, did not take kindly to young men's long hair. Simply put, long hair was considered unmanly. Still, long hair prevailed, and nowadays few people take much notice of a young man with long hair. Interestingly enough, short hair was itself a relatively recent change in the male's prescribed look. Before World War I, long hair was the norm for men. But during the early days of the war, the army instituted the short haircut to eliminate the pesky problem of lice. After the war, the short hair of the returning doughboys quickly became the norm for American men.

Of course, most elements of the male sex role have a long and well-established history and are extremely resistant to any significant change. For example, men have for centuries been expected to dominate women. A central element of the traditional male sex role expressly dictates that men are superior to women in most respects. Any social pressure to alter this particular tenet of the male sex role, such as we have witnessed recently from the women's movement, has been met with considerable and often questionable counterpressure. The reason for such strong resistance to any change in the social prescription of male dominance is simple. To change women's purportedly inferior social position to one of genuine equality with men would cause considerable upheaval in many established social institutions such as the economy, religion, and the family. Furthermore, most men define a large part of their masculinity in terms of their relations with women. If women were to become men's equal, many men would feel their masculinity both threatened and undercut. Thus a major shift toward equality between the sexes would necessitate a change in both sexes' sex role and thereby cause social conflicts in various sectors of society and personal strain in many men.

No matter that changes in the male sex role are resisted; change, albeit slow, is occurring in society's definition of the male mainly because of the combined effects of several social forces. Three specific social forces are pushing the traditional views of what it means to be a man into new areas. These three forces are rapid technological advances, a recent and persistent distrust among many people of established institutions, and the women's movement. Each of these social forces is causing varying amounts of social conflict, and thus each is meeting with varying amounts of resistance.

TECHNOLOGY AND THE MALE SEX ROLE

Most historians of the male sex role suggest that the nineteenth-century industrial revolution did more to affect men's lives than almost any other social change in human history.[11] The movement from an agricultural to an industrial and technological society drastically changed the way men defined their relationships, their status, and their abilities. Throughout the distant centuries, males were expected to prove their worth as men by their physical prowess in providing for the group by killing animals or raising grain. Likewise, males won praise and achieved status for their skillful abilities to produce artifacts with their tools and talents. The industrial revolution replaced the ancient male roles of strong provider and skilled artisan with the role of keeper of the machines. Granted, the industrial revolution provided mass-produced goods and a new and easier way of life, but it also robbed most men of their sense of purpose and creativity.

During the twentieth century, the industrial revolution flowed into the age of technology. Advanced technology, along with its mainstay the computer, has made

Today's Uncertain Male

many of men's long-standing abilities and long-cherished skills almost obsolete. Once men gloried in their ability to think through issues, solve problems, and create new dreams. Today the computer, with its almost limitless storage capacity and millisecond solutions, has in a sense superceded many of men's rational abilities. On the one hand, the computer represents a modern-day pinnacle of human achievement; on the other hand, the computer may be the essential tool of human destruction. Where once human warfare was limited by the numbers of warriors or soldiers, today the whole world totters precariously close to Armageddon mainly because of the ultimate destructive power of the atom and its computer-controlled delivery systems. Even if humanity can avoid its own destruction, there is always the possibility that computers could gain control over humanity. No less an authority than Arthur Clarke suggested such a futuristic scenario in his classic *2001: A Space Odyssey*, in which a computer named HAL defends itself against its human programmers. It may sound like sheer madness, but a world run by computers is no longer unthinkable.

Thus beginning with the industrial revolution and accelerating with the dawn of computers, men have been driven farther and farther away from their traditional male sex role. At one time, men reveled in their physical prowess as they applied their sinewy strength to whatever task required brute force. They were honored for their feats of courage in the face of untamed and uncharted frontiers. Furthermore, men exulted in their wisdom and knowledge gained from years of experience and, consequently, gained pleasure in passing their knowledge to the next generation. Today the abilities that allowed the male to define his place in society as well as his worth as a man are quickly surpassed by machinery and computers.

More and more men are searching for something that they have lost. That something is the very foundation on which the traditional male role was built. The elements of physical strength, creative endeavor, and intellectual ability have been superceded at worst or weakened at best in our technologically oriented world.

LOST CONFIDENCES

If society's institutions (family, religion, political system, military, and so on) support the various traditional elements of the male sex role, the behaviors males are expected to exhibit by virtue of their prescribed sex role provide society's institutions with willing and able participants. In other words, the relationship between society's institutions and the male sex role is one of mutual benefit and support. For example, aggression is an important element of the traditional male sex role (see Chapter 9). Consequently, men are expected to be good fighters and if need be good soldiers. The military requires good fighting soldiers to carry out its designated social function, namely, to aggress or defend against society's enemies. Thus the military needs men to carry out its social mission, and men can perform a part of their expected male role as well as validate their masculinity by being soldiers. The dependent relationships between social institutions like the military and the traditional male sex role require a mutual trust and confidence that both sides will live up to the social expectations inherent in each side. If men do not fight or if the military does not serve its country's needs, a problem or conflict can occur in one, the other, or both sides of the relationship. Such a conflict occurred in the late 1960s and early 1970s and consequently challenged some elements of the traditional male sex role.

The recent Vietnam era provides a prime example of a breakdown in the relationship between specific features in the male sex role and two social institutions, the military and the government. One of the causes for this breakdown was a major rupture in the public's confidence and trust in the leaders of various institutions; that rupture subsequently led many young men to question certain features of their male role.[12]

The Vietnam conflict began in the late 1950s and early 1960s as a purely advisory military operation. However, by the mid-1960s, America was in a full-scale war in Southeast Asia. Initially, most Americans supported the government and the military's stated goals of supporting a besieged democratic Asian country and preventing the spread of communism into the Pacific basin. But as the 1960s drew to an end, the government's handling of dissenters—for example, the beating of demonstrators at the 1968 Democratic National Convention in Chicago and the killing of four students on the Kent State University campus in 1970—turned many previous supporters against the government. Likewise, with the publication of *The Pentagon Papers*, the military as well as the government establishment lost credibility in the eyes of many Americans. The public's trust in its leaders was severely eroded by the early 1970s.

This breakdown in confidence in government and military institutions coupled with a growing antiestablishment sentiment caused many people to question certain social expectations. Among these people were the young men who were expected to act out the role of combat soldier. Many came to question their soldier's role in a war where the leader's motives and behavior were highly suspect. Consequently, many young men either resisted the draft or if drafted avoided combat whenever possible. The incidence of soldier insubordination in Vietnam is a case in point. Many American troops, even in combat zones, deliberately disobeyed their officers' legitimate orders and, in some cases, even killed their "gung-ho" officers.[13] During this period, many young men came to believe that they did not have to be "good soldiers" to prove themselves real men. Thus one of the long-cherished ways in which men historically fulfilled a part of their male sex role and validated their masculinity was seriously undermined.

THE WOMEN'S MOVEMENT

Few recent social movements have had as serious an impact on our society as has the reemergent women's movement of the 1960s. The movement's historical roots extend back to the first women's rights convention, which was held in Seneca

Falls, New York, in 1848. For the next seventy-two years, a group of dedicated women and some few men worked tirelessly against staggering odds to win for women the right to vote. In 1920, the passage of the Nineteenth Amendment to the Constitution guaranteed women that right. In 1923 the National Women's party succeeded in getting the Equal Rights Amendment (ERA) introduced in Congress. Subsequently, the amendment that reads "equality of rights under the law shall not be denied or abridged by the United States or by any state on account of sex" was introduced before Congress every year from 1923 until 1972, when Congress finally proposed it to the states. Between 1920 and 1960, the women's movement faltered because of the division among the different women's groups.[14]

After its forty-year sleep, the women's movement awoke and developed into what most people now call the women's liberation movement. Several events contributed to the awakening. In 1961 President John F. Kennedy created a national Commission on the Status of Women that investigated the role women play in American society. The commission concluded that women were relegated to a "second-class" status in society. In 1966, after several years of little action on the commission's recommendations, Betty Friedan and several others founded the National Organization for Women (NOW).[15]

It is difficult to categorize the participants of the contemporary women's liberation movement. Their diversity of backgrounds, life-styles, politics, and goals defy simple labeling. However, the movement as we know it today emerged from the creative energies of two major groups. Both groups were primarily white, middle-class, and college-educated, but the similarities ended there. The first group, the one we call the *traditional group,* was mainly composed of older women who resurrected the women's movement through their involvement in national organizations like NOW, the Women's Equity Action League, and the Federally Employed Women organization. This traditional group formed a cohesive, highly structured social-political force. Governed by a hierarchical structure with national and state officers, the traditional group skillfully lobbied, campaigned, and maneuvered for redress of women's unequal status in the male-dominated systems of politics, business, and religion.

The second group, referred to here as the *experimental group,* was a younger group (most members were under thirty) that came to the women's liberation movement from other social activist groups like the civil rights movement and the New Left movement of the 1960s. This experimental group shunned the formal organizational structure of the traditional group, preferring instead to meet in small, autonomous gatherings in living rooms, church basements, and YWCA meeting rooms around the country. The experimental group succeeded in developing a large, grass-roots following of women who came together to share their female experience. The experimental group's most notable contribution to the women's liberation movement was the development of a resocialization technique called the *rap group.*[16] The rap group was a dynamic learning experience—although most women probably did not think of it in these terms—in which a small number of women shared their concerns, feelings, and problems as women in an atmosphere of concern and trust. By means of the rap group, large numbers of women across the country shed their feelings of aloneness and alienation and found their "consciousness raised" in terms of establishing a new definition of sisterhood.

The traditional group provided a nationally based pressure organization that brought about changes in society's legal, economic, and political structures, while the experimental group fostered a new sense of pride and self-worth among countless thousands of women. Even though these two groups have never totally merged, they have influenced each other's development and course of action. The issues of women's oppression and the effects of sexism would not have become the pressing concerns that they are today if it were not for the energy, drive, and dedication of both groups.

Most people will agree that the women's liberation movement has had a significant impact on our society during the last decade or so. But what does a social movement that set for its goal the elimination of the twin social evils of women's oppression and blatant sexism have to do with the male sex role? The English poet Alfred Tennyson may have provided an answer to this question when he wrote, "The woman's cause is man's. They rise or fall together."

For the most part, the expectations and demands of the male role are essentially the flip side of the expectations and demands forced on women by their own sex role. In other words, the features of the male and female sex roles are interdependent and reciprocal. Men, for example, are taught to behave in ways characterized as dominant, independent, and active. Women, on the other hand, learn to act in submissive, dependent, and passive ways. Thus any change in the characteristics of one sex role sets off a chain reaction in the characteristics of the other sex role.

As more and more women come to question and then to change their traditional sex role behaviors and attitudes, men are forced to look at their own sex role behaviors and attitudes and deal with the very real possibility that they, too, will have to change their traditional ways. Consequently, the resocialization aimed at women and brought about by the women's liberation movement not only influences women's lives but men's as well.

There we have it: three separate social forces—the escalation of technology, a breakdown in confidence in established social institutions, and the women's liberation movement—all coming together and, we might add, interacting with each other at around the same time. The outcomes of these forces on society are varied, but one thing is clear: they have all influenced the sex role that men have traditionally been expected to play in society. These changes and challenges have caused many men to experience in very personal ways a heightened sense of uncertainty. With the social or public level of the male experience undergoing scrutiny and even challenge, many men have found themselves questioning their own sense of masculinity.

FEARS AND TREMBLINGS

How have the social pressures noted above forced many men to feel threatened and anxious over their masculinity? Obviously, we are not as certain about the private side of the male experience as we are of the public side. On the one hand, we can see that certain long-standing social expectations have changed in recent years with respect to the male sex role. For example, men are no longer expected as they once were to settle disagreements among themselves by fighting. Today men are expected to resolve their differences by discussion rather than by physical blows. On the other hand, we must be cautious when we speak of men's private feelings about their masculinity. Because a man's sense of his own masculinity may not be easily viewed or measured, we can look to specific public expressions to see if men's sense of their masculinity has been influenced by the recent changes in the public side of the male sex role. Two such public expressions of men's changing and somewhat threatened masculinity stand out.

First of all, in the last several years, we have seen a dramatic rise in the number of men who have entered sex therapy programs. Various sexual problems like impotence and retarded or premature ejaculation are common complaints mentioned by many men.[17] The fact that many men are undergoing sex therapy today is significant because throughout the centuries men have come to view their sexual prowess and functioning as an important and never-failing feature of their masculinity. Women may have problems with sex and sexual functioning, but men never—or so tradition goes.

Besides seeking sex therapy, large numbers of men today are seeking professional counseling for various personal and situational problems. The rise in the number of male clients has caused the mental health professions to take special notice of some of the specific psychological concerns and problems that afflict men who feel their masculinity threatened by the changing times.[18] More and more men are looking to therapy for the answer to the question, "What does it mean to be a man today?"

A second indication of the problems some men are facing in regard to their definition of masculinity can be found in today's popular literature. For decades writers have captured the essence of the times long before the scientific community has. In the last decade, authors like Avery Corman, Gail Parent, and Philip Roth have written of troubled men facing personal dilemmas over their definitions of masculinity.[19] Take for example, Joseph Heller's best-selling novel *Something Happened,* in which we meet Bob Slocum. Slocum is typical of many white, middle-aged, and middle-class males. By external appearances, Slocum is a successful family man and worker who is liked by almost everyone. But Slocum has a problem. The problem is that he fears everyone in his world: his boss, his boss's boss, his coworkers, his secretary, his wife, his two normal teenagers, and even his retarded son. Slocum's fear centers on the fact that he thinks he is not seen as a real man by these other people. Many men suffer the same fear that Heller writes about with such insight. If we listen to men talking, we can quickly discover just how fearful they are. Some of the things men fear include aging,

*"Diane, bring in my paper on 'identity crisis,' I want what's-his-name here to see it."**

assertive women, balding, bills, boredom, clinging women, death, emotions, failures, homosexuals, impotence, loneliness, rejection, and retirement. These are just a few of the fears that novelists have sensed in contemporary men and have been writing about with increasing frequency.

From the increase in the numbers of men in various kinds of therapy and the public's acceptance of the "troubled-male" image in literature, there seems ample evidence to suggest that many men are experiencing conflict and doubt over their definition of masculinity. The problem for these men becomes even greater when we consider that we are in the midst of changing our definition of the male sex role. Society has neither totally abandoned its traditional view of the male role nor has it adopted a completely new version of what it means to be a male in a society where oppression of women and sexism are on the wane. Consequently, men are pulled from many directions. One side says be strong and dominant, and the other says be gentle and warm. Theoretically, one can be both strong and gentle, but the problem remains that most men's socializations do not include the training for this. Following are a few of the conflicting messages that many males are presently experiencing and that compound their problems.

THE HORNS OF A DILEMMA

Just what is expected and demanded of most males in our society to prove that they are real men? Although this question defies a simple answer, we can list several major expectations and demands that are considered sex-appropriate for men to exhibit.

First, men are usually seen as the opposite of women. Consequently, whatever is expected of women or whatever is seen as typical in women's behavior should be the opposite in men. For example, women are often characterized as emotional, illogical, timid, and indecisive. Thus men are expected to be unemotional, logical, assertive, and decisive. Furthermore, men should be highly competitive and successful in most of their dealings, especially in work-related activities. To a lesser extent than in the past men are still expected to be combative or aggressive, especially when threatened by others. In addition, men are not only thought to be naturally interested in sex but also able to satisfy even the most sexually demanding woman. Finally, men should be tough and self-reliant. Characteristics such as these are so ingrained in our society's expectations of men that even many mental health professionals view such stereotypic characteristics as forming the basic description of a mentally healthy adult male.[20]

As is so often the case in a rapidly changing social climate, men are asked, even expected, to act in ways in which they have had little or no training in their male sex role. For example, many women, especially those women who have openly challenged their own traditional female sex role, expect men to be open, gentle, warm, compassionate, and communicative. In other words, these women expect men to act in ways contrary to a man's socialization. This would not be impossible to accomplish if all of society or at least most of its members were in agreement about what is expected of men. But agreement on this issue seems some decades in the future. In fact, some women who are in the forefront of wanting men to change their traditional ways are inconsistent in their expectations of men. More than a few "liberated" women have candidly noted that they prefer men to be gentle and warm *as well as* physical, dominant, and protective.[21] This inconsistency has caused many men to become confused and even angered over what they see as a "no-win" situation. The matter comes down to such basics as should I open the door for a woman? If I do, will I be thought a gentleman or a chauvinist? Clearly, the male experience is fraught with more uncertainty and conflict today than at any other time in our recent history.

SUMMING UP

We have covered considerable ground in this first chapter. We have noted how the male experience can be interpreted as having two sides or levels. The first level, with its social expectations and demands, determines what social scientists call the male sex role. The second level is the more private level of the male experience and is referred to here as the male gender identity or a man's sense of masculinity. Next, we presented a fictional biography of one man's life in which we covered in very general ways some of the major events encountered by many men. We have reviewed several recent social forces that taken together have caused people to question and even to challenge many of the traditional features of the male sex role. We described how many men are beginning to feel their sense of masculinity threatened by these recent social pressures for change. As evidence of the uncertainty in men's sense of masculinity today, we noted the recent increase in the numbers of men in therapy and the number of popular authors who are focusing on the issue of the male's fragile sense of masculinity. Finally, we suggested that many men are presently caught between opposing social forces that push and pull them in ways that run contrary to their socialization.

Now we turn our attention to several disciplines to see how they view various features of the male experience.

1

PERSPECTIVES ON THE MALE

*The frontiers are not east or west, north or
south, but wherever a man fronts a fact.*

Henry David Thoreau[1]

In a far-off land, there was a remote village totally inhabited by blind people.
One day nearby the village a mighty king camped with his army and an enormous
elephant.

The blind inhabitants had little experience with armies and even less experience with ponderous pachyderms. The unknown creature that shook the earth
caused great fear among the villagers. To calm their fear, the village council
decided to send three scouts to discover the form of the thunderous beast. When
the blind scouts returned, each spoke confidently of the elephant's form.

The first scout, who had felt the elephant's ear, reported to the village assem-
bly that the elephant was like a large, rough fan that moved about creating great
currents of air that almost knocked the scout off his feet.

The second scout, who had held the elephant's trunk, scoffed at the first scout's
report and related how the elephant was like a long, bristly snake that had coiled
and lifted him into the air.

The third scout, who had weaved amid the elephant's legs, dismissed the previous narratives as so much poppycock and proceeded to describe the elephant
as four massive, moving pillars that could shake the ground, causing all nearby
to tremble.

Now it is clear that each scout thought he had experienced the complete elephant. The problem was, however, that each scout had focused on only a single
portion of the animal's anatomy. Because the scouts reported conflicting versions
of the colossal creature, the villagers remained confused and fearful of the king's
elephant.

What connection do the exploits of three blind scouts and an elephant have
with our discussion of the male experience? Well, in the next five chapters we
are going to look at the male experience from five different perspectives: historical, biological, anthropological, sociological, and psychological. Each perspective casts a different light, presents a different version, so to speak, of the male
experience. Each perspective emphasizes certain features and downplays certain
other features of the male experience. Analogously, each perspective resembles
one of the blind scouts. Each perspective deals with particular features of the
male experience and thinks, all too often, that it has grasped the total picture.
For the moment, let us briefly preview each perspective and highlight one or two
main issues in each.

How we define the male sex role and how men experience their masculinity
today are better understood in the context of how these features were defined a
hundred, a thousand, or even ten thousand years ago. The *historical perspective*
focuses on those stable features that have been a part of the male experience over
the centuries, and at the same time it draws our attention to recent changes. A
knowledge of the past makes the present and future possibilities concerning the
male experience more understandable.

Recent advances in microscopic enlargement and breakthroughs in genetics are extending the frontiers of our knowledge of human biology. At last, the information contained in the microscopic sex chromosomes is being decoded. Testosterone, dubbed by many the "male hormone," is now seen as responsible for much of the male's physiology as well as a possible basis for certain male behaviors. This is only one of the areas we will cover in the *biological perspective* of the male experience.

For centuries people have asked questions about their existence, meaning, and purpose. These questions and the answers that people accepted became the ingredients for the most human of all creations: culture. In the broadest sense of the word, culture gives meaning to people's lives. Insight into and understanding of the richness and variation of the male experience can be gained from a knowledge of the ways, beliefs, and values of other peoples, both distant and near. The *anthropological perspective* views the male experience through eyes that at first appear exotic and alien but through which we can gain a greater appreciation of the male experience.

All of us from our very earliest days experience the impact of a miniaturized society, the family. The family group comprised of parents, siblings, and relatives interacts with the infant in ways that help the developing child to define itself, first as a human and then as a male or a female. Groups large and small mold the infant in ways deemed acceptable by the larger society. The *sociological perspective* focuses on the socialization process of the young male child.

For well over half a century, psychologists have spent thousands of hours in research on how the sexes differ from each other. Elaborate theories of unconscious urges, external rewards, and mental images have been developed to explain how males come to perceive themselves as masculine and females as feminine. However, some in the psychological community are beginning to challenge long-established views of masculinity; thus our discussion of the *psychological perspective* includes an examination of recent changes in the interpretation of the male sex role and masculinity.

Just as the three blind scouts in our earlier example perceived the elephant from three different vantage points, each of the perspectives covered in the following five chapters brings to the study of the male experience its own built-in assumptions about what features to look for, what questions to ask, how best to study it, and sometimes even what answers are most acceptable to the particular perspective. We must also keep in mind that each perspective is the work of humans, and the work of humans is often less than completely objective.

Therefore, we should not be put off by some contradictory stances among the perspectives (for example, the male experience is largely a product of biological factors versus the male experience is the end result of social forces). When we find opposing views, we should recall how physicists find it quite helpful sometimes to regard light as a continuous wave and sometimes to regard it as a series of particles. If physicists are comfortable with their seemingly contrary perspectives of the form of light, we need not be too perplexed about the infrequent differences among the various perspectives of the male experience.

2

Of past times and reigning men:

THE HISTORICAL PERSPECTIVE

. . . most history is guessing, and the rest is prejudice. Will Durant[1]

A major task of a historical study of the male past is to find the roots of maleness and determine how profound they are. Peter Stearns[2]

The history of masculinity is a relatively new subject of inquiry with a small but growing literature. Elizabeth and Joseph Pleck[3]

Many define history as the written record of the cultural, social, economic, religious, and political dealings of the human race. But if we take the time to examine a number of history books, we come away with the impression that recorded history is slanted in favor of the male portion of the human race. Many history books describe only the deeds of kings, generals, presidents, dictators, bishops, and philosophers. History as most of us have come to know it from our books deals almost exclusively with the lives of notable and powerful men. We must look long and hard to find mention of women and the powerless. But history is or at least should be more than a collection of dates, battles, intrigues, and reigns of great and near-great men. People's lives—male *and* female, the powerful *and* the powerless—are the fabric that makes up the rich tapestry of human history.

Why, then, do we include a chapter on the history of the male sex role and masculinity? This chapter is not about great men's deeds or accomplishments but rather about a stable and long-standing feature of the male sex role, namely, *patriarchy,* or the supremacy of the father. We trace patriarchy back to those ancient societies in which males began to exert more influence and power over females than vice versa. Next we move through the centuries and see the power invested in the male sex role grow more prominent, especially during the Greco-Roman period. Then we discover the almost total power that is placed in the father's hands during the Middle Ages. Finally, we discuss patriarchy and the male role in American history. But first let us take a small detour into the recent past and note how several social movements have brought about a reinterpretation of the content of history.

A NEW INTERPRETATION OF HISTORY

During the late 1920s, several French historians set out to correct what they felt was an incomplete portrayal of human history. Two historians in particular, Marc Bloch and Lucien Febvre, were instrumental in developing a school of historical investigation that has since become known as the *Annales.* The purpose of the Annales school was to move away from the traditional historical analysis of the notable and the powerful throughout history and to focus rather on the lives of ordinary people and everyday events. This particular approach to historical analysis became known as "social history."[4] Social customs, traditions, marriage patterns, fertility rates, death records, and other facets of common people's lives provided a wealth of historical material that forced historians to take another look at human existence.

Until recently, most students in American history courses read little or were exposed to few of the contributions of groups such as blacks, Mexican Americans, and women. During the late 1960s and 1970s, several groups called attention to these glaring omissions. Furthermore, feminists like Elizabeth Gould Davis charged that the prevalent view of world history was decidedly male-biased and that historians had for centuries, consciously or unconsciously, left out the significant role women had played in the development of the human race.[5] Consequently, scholars—mostly females—corrected this one-sided, male-dominant historical perspective with several excellent works on the role of women in human history.[6]

On a hot July night in 1969, an incident in New York City sparked the birth of the gay liberation movement. A group of police raided the Stonewall, a popular gay bar, and many of the clients fought back after being harrassed by the police. Since what has been dubbed the Stonewall Rebellion, large numbers of gays have come out openly to defend their life-style and to demand an end to the discrimination that has plagued gay people down through the ages. Not only has the gay movement of the 1970s permitted countless gays to take pride in themselves as human beings, but it has also caused an awakening of interest in an accurate account of gays in American history.[7]

The concerns and questions generated by the women's movement and the gay liberation movement also spawned an interest among some men during the 1970s in the male sex role and conceptions of masculinity. These men began to question the socialization process that caused little boys to grow into "macho" men. An analysis of the costs as well as the privileges of being male in a male-dominated society prompted some men to look twice at what they had taken for granted, namely, their male experience. One area of investigation that grew out of these men's interest was that of the historical roots of the male role and how it took shape in American history.[8] And this is the subject of our chapter.

Because it would be impossible to cover every aspect of the traditional male sex role, we shall concentrate on the historical development of *patriarchy,* or father-rule. Patriarchy is in many ways one of the founding concepts of Western civilization and thus has influenced the lives of nearly every male and female in Western society for the last several thousand years. Let us begin our discussion by looking back almost three thousand years to the time when the male role as we presently know it was being shaped in Greece.

THE PATRIARCHAL TRADITION

It is hard to say exactly how long there has been a distinct set of expectations and demands for each sex. The basis for different sex roles as we understand them today appears to have been established long ago in an attempt by early humans to divide essential labor between those individuals who could best accomplish specific tasks. It seems certain, however, that throughout most of recorded history the male's power and influence within the group has been greater than the female's. This feature of male dominance within the group we interpret here as the basis of patriarchy. Some feminists contend that prior to recorded history some evidence in myth and legend suggests an earlier period in human history when woman-rule or *gynocracy* was the norm.[9] Furthermore, some archeological evidence suggests women's prominent and strong presence in early society, especially in terms of the influence of female goddesses in the everyday lives of common folk.[10] Rather than extend our discussion of the history of the male sex role back into the more shadowy periods of human history, we will confine our discussion to that of recorded time, beginning with Greece in the eighth century B.C.

During roughly the last three thousand years, there have been at least five distinct male models or ideals that Western men were expected to imitate. As with all ideals, each of the five is a larger-than-life exaggeration impossible for any man to achieve in its entirety. Even so, the males who lived during the period of each ideal knew of the ideal's distinctive features and were influenced by it in their daily lives. One feature, however, permeated all five ideals; that feature was the support of a patriarchal social order in which the male, especially the father, was seen as the dominant force in all male-female relations.

We have given the following names to the five male models or ideals: the epic male, the spiritual male, the chivalric male, the Renaissance male, and the bourgeois male.

THE EPIC MALE

The male ideal depicted in the ancient Greek and Roman periods comes down to us primarily through the epic sagas written by men like Homer and Virgil. In these sagas, we enter a decidedly masculine world, a world inhabited by soldiers, adventurers, warriors, kings, and gods. Men were the "doers," the conquerors and rulers, of a threatening and barbaric world. Women were peripheral to the action and accorded importance only to the degree that they served men's needs.

The epic male hero was first and foremost a fighter and a leader. The essential characteristics of this period's male role were prowess and skill in battle, physical strength and courage, and loyalty—first to leader and king, then to male comrades, and finally to clan and family. Essentially, the epic male role embodied the features of the warrior-ruler.

The female figure of epic times was honored more for her physical beauty, charms, and dedication to men than for any endeavor based on talent or ability. The female was viewed as a passive object of men's desire. Most people, for example, know of Helen of Troy not because of any achievement or special talent but rather because her exquisite and compelling beauty drove men to wage the Trojan War. When we do read of powerful women in the epics, they are usually goddesses who derive much of their power from a male figure. A case in point is the goddess Athena—born out of the head of the god Zeus—who stands more for patriarchal values than for matriarchal concerns. Recall it was Athena who defended Orestes for killing his mother Clytemnestra. Clytemnestra had killed her husband-king, Agamemnon, after his return from the Trojan War. Out of revenge for his father's murder, Orestes killed his mother. To the Greeks, killing a husband-father was more serious than killing a wife-mother. According to our medical knowledge of the day, the father was seen as the true parent of the child,

Table 2.1 Five Historical Male Role Ideals

Ideal	Source(s)	Major Features
Epic Male	Epic sagas of Greece and Rome (800–100 B.C.)	Action, physical strength, courage, loyalty, and beginning of patriarchy.
Spiritual Male	Teachings of Jesus Christ, early church fathers, and monastic tradition (400–1000 A.D.)	Self-renunciation, restrained sexual activity, antifeminine and antihomosexual attitudes, and strong patriarchal system.
Chivalric Male	Feudalism and chivalric code of honor (twelfth-century social system)	Self-sacrifice, courage, physical strength, honor and service to the lady, and primogeniture.
Renaissance Male	Sixteenth-century social system	Rationality, intellectual endeavors, and self-exploration.
Bourgeois Male	Eighteenth-century social system	Success in business, status, and worldly manners.

whereas the mother was viewed as a mere incubator. In Athena's defense and Orestes' acquittal, we see the foundation of patriarchy well establishd in fifth-century B.C. Greek society.

The same epic proportions are carried over to the classical Roman period. In Virgil's *Aeneid,* we read of the masculine world of Aeneas and his journey from Troy to Italy and the founding of Rome. Once again, the male is as an adventurer and doer of great deeds. Likewise, the female of the Roman epic is portrayed as a bystander to men's actions or a helpless victim of men's relentless pursuits.

Before leaving the epic period, we must mention one last feature of the male role, a feature that has drawn considerable attention and subsequent condemnation down through the ages. Both the Greek and the Roman societies showed wide acceptance of homosexual and pederast (man-boy) sexual relationships. From the fifth century onward, we can vividly see in various works of art the degree to which homosexual relationships were an acceptable and even noble social practice among a majority of men.[11] The Greek philosopher Plato, speaking in the *Phaedrus,* calls the love between men "nobler and more spiritual than the love between men and women." We see here striking evidence of the belief that the male is thought superior to the female. Even in sex, many males preferred homosexual to heterosexual activity.

THE SPIRITUAL MALE

The dawn of Christianity brought about a radical change in basic human values that influenced the course and development of Western civilization. The Christian faith and its teachings added new features to and changed some features of the classical epic ideal of the male role. The life and teachings of Jesus Christ provided the basic tenets of Christianity, but it was the early church fathers who largely influenced the male role ideal.

The image Christ gave to humanity was one of nonviolence (Matthew 26:52) and service to others (John 13:12–16). The poverty, purported celibacy, and self-renunciation of Jesus' life provided a singular role model for both men and women that radically differed from anything witnessed in classical times or even in the teaching of the Hebrew's Old Testament. However, the ideal male role under Christianity did not take complete form as we have come to know it until several centuries after Christ's death.

The Christian view of the male and the female roles came from the writings of the early church fathers and the monastic tradition of the fourth and fifth centuries. In fact, contrary to the indivisible human ideal contained in Christ's original message, the early church fathers followed the classical view of the separation of the sexes and reinforced the traditional version of two distinct roles, one for each sex. Underlying these two roles was the church fathers' belief in the causal link between sexuality and sin. The ideal Christian man, especially one called to the clergy, was expected to renounce the flesh, in other words, to avoid all sexuality. Thus the ideal male role endorsed celibacy, or at least infrequent sexual experiences, and a turning away from earthly pursuits. In the Christian ethos, the ideal male was one in whom the spiritual was preeminent over the worldly.

Patriarchy found itself a highly favorable niche in the Christian church. The male, portrayed as the image of God the Father, was seen as the ultimate authority in all matters, both spiritual and secular. Women were to subjugate themselves to all males' rulings, their priest's, father's, husband's. To support this strict patriarchal world view, the church fathers were quick to quote from Paul's letter to the Corinthians:

> For a man indeed ought not to cover his head, forasmuch as he is the image and glory of God: but the woman is the glory of man. For the man is not of the woman; but the woman of the man. Neither was the man created for the woman; but the woman for the man (1 Cor. 11:7–9).

Not only did Christianity portray men as women's ultimate authority, men were also expected to disdain the female. Under Christianity, women especially suffered from the link between sexuality and evil. By virtue of their presumed insatiable sexual nature, women were cast as the embodiment of all that was evil. Following the earlier traditions of viewing women as the source of all evil (for example, the Hebrew's conception of Eve and the Greek's view of Pandora), the early church fathers portrayed women as the reason for men's and humanity's downfall and subsequent sinfulness. Pope Clement, an early church father, captured the antifeminine sentiment by pronouncing, "Every woman should be overwhelmed with shame at the very thought that she is a woman."[12]

One other feature relating to the spiritual male ideal was the stance the church fathers took against homosexuality. They viewed the widespread acceptance and practice of homosexuality among the Greeks and Romans as further evidence of the moral degeneracy of those pagan societies. To be a man, a spiritual man, a male was expected to renounce his sexual desires and activities. But for those men too weak to follow the manly celibate life, the only acceptable sexual outlet was to be found in heterosexual activity. To have sex with another man was a degradation of human nature and an abhorrence before God. Thus the antihomosexual sentiment that has been so prominent a feature of Christian societies owes its legacy to the preachings and exhortations of the early church fathers.

THE CHIVALRIC MALE

Beginning in twelfth-century Europe, a new social order called *feudalism* developed and ushered in a new stability for the people of Western Europe. During the previous six centuries, the Roman church stood almost alone as the unifying authority in Western Europe. However, with the rise of feudalism, authority spread out from the church to include a cultured aristocracy and a military class. Feudalism spawned the growth of towns, expanded trade, and developed a money economy and the cult of the Virgin Mary. The rise of the soldier or knightly class provided a new ideal for the male role, one that transformed the asexual spiritual male into a sensual chivalric or knightly male.

The male role during the feudal period focused on the model of a fighter, a soldier, although not just a common soldier but a very special soldier—the knight-errant. No longer did the male ideal include the spiritual male's sense of asexual self-renunciation and nonviolence; rather, the chivalric male ideal emphasized physical strength, prowess in combat, loyalty to the king or liege lord, and devotion to a lady. We see in the chivalric ideal a return to many of the same qualities of the epic male figure of classical times. But there were also some differences between them. The most apparent difference lay in the chivalric's fantasized sensual relationship between the man and the lady.

The view of womanhood in the guise of the lady is a significant feature of the feudal period. Recall that in the centuries that followed the Christianization of Europe, women were singularly portrayed as the source of temptation and evil because they were the daughters of Eve. Even the purity and sinless nature of the Virgin Mary, the mother of Jesus, was played down in the early church. (Although the cult of Mary did flourish for a short time among some early Christian communities, the church fathers squashed this veneration of Mary because of the similarity between Mary's veneration and certain pagan practices of worshipping a mother goddess.[13]) But under feudalism a new view of womanhood developed, one that included a dualistic version of woman's nature. Women were seen as either pedestaled virgins or lusty temptresses and prostitutes.

The lady of the feudal period was a secularized version of the Virgin Mary. She existed more in men's fantasy than in reality. The knight devoted his strength and skills to her service. The love between the knight and his lady although sensual was not usually consummated. To consummate such a relationship usually brought about tragedy for both parties as we see in the Arthurian legend of Lancelot and Guinevere. In the other view, women were portrayed as insatiable creatures who pleased men with their lusty sexuality. Feudalism's dualistic view of womanhood has come down through the ages and contributed to the present-day conception of woman's nature.

Patriarchy continued to grow in importance under feudalism. A prime example of this can be seen in the practice of *primogeniture,* which became well established during this period. The right of primogeniture assured that the wealth and property that made up the father's estate passed directly to his eldest male heir. Thus the power of the eldest male over his siblings and his mother was guaranteed under this patriarchal arrangement.

THE RENAISSANCE MALE

England of the sixteenth century witnessed the rise of the Renaissance male ideal. Feudalism with its two social extremes, the rich aristocracy and their subjects the serfs, made room for a growing middle class. The knight riding his horse in quest of glory and his lady's approval changed into a man searching for knowledge. The once powerful Roman church lost much of its authority over what people could believe and think. The Renaissance rekindled the virtues of knowledge that were prominent during the late classical period. No longer was authority vested in a few church leaders or kings. Consequently, men and some few women began to think for themselves—about the wonders of the world and its mysteries.

The Renaissance male ideal stressed the rational and intellectual abilities of men. Men were still expected to be doers, active and in control, but the goals of their activity had changed. Classical or epic man sought physical perfection, spiritual man was motivated toward an afterlife, but Renaissance man sought intellectual goals that would free him from the restraints of a dogmatic church authority. An archetypal example of Renaissance man was Michelangelo, whose intellectual achievements in both the arts and sciences could not have been accomplished under the restrictions of the powerful Roman church two or three hundred years earlier.

There was yet another side to Renaissance man, a dark, forbidding, and even tragic side. He discovered many secrets of nature long thought to be only the domain of gods and goddesses. He also explored the secrets of his personality, and these secrets sometimes led to personal anguish and internal conflict. The great English playwright William Shakespeare captured the essential tragedy in man's hidden secrets through Hamlet, Macbeth, and Lear.

Patriarchy during the Renaissance continued to be the norm for Western society. The power of men over women's lives continued along the established paths of the preceding periods. However, some few women escaped the yoke of total male domination. Women like Elizabeth I, daughter of Henry VIII, were powerful in their own right; but even in Elizabeth's case, the male influence on the queen's decisions was ever present.

THE BOURGEOIS MALE

By the eighteenth century a strong and powerful middle class had become well established in England. The previous aristocratic goals and manly pursuits of territorial conquest, spiritual fulfillment, and acquisition of knowledge were replaced by the middle class's more mundane goals of money, status, and prestige. The middle class of urbanized Europe and England helped to create the new bourgeois male ideal.

The middle-class man of the eighteenth century was driven to achieve what he saw as the ultimate symbol of power: money. This bourgeois man was seeking status and prestige and the way to gain these was through success in business dealings. The entrepreneur or business adventurer was his model. To risk and then to succeed in business was the final proof of a man's worth.

The female role in the eighteenth century continued to be one of subjugation to man. The ideal of the young virgin as a reward for the hard-working and successful male played a dominant role in eighteenth-century literature.

SUMMARIZING THE WESTERN ROOTS OF THE MALE ROLE IDEAL

We now come to the end of our brief survey of the male role ideals that have existed during the history of Western civilization. Obviously, many of the expectations typically linked to the contemporary male role have their roots in earlier historical periods. For example, the emphasis on man as a doer and the expectations of physical strength, courage, and loyalty owe their heritage to the epic male role of classical Greek and Roman times. The view of man as the priestly link to God, his assumed authority in religious matters, and the rejection of the behaviors associated with females and homosexuals extend back to early Christianity. The conception of man as the champion of women and protector of the weak owes its legacy to the chivalric male ideal of the feudal period. The belief in man's superior rational and intellectual abilities owes much to the Renaissance male model. The expectation of success in the competitive world of business is a more recent male characterization that reaches back only two or three hundred years to the bourgeois period. By combining these elements, we have a fair composite of the complete man as most know him in the twentieth century.

The one consistent theme that runs through all of these distinctive periods is patriarchy. We saw how father-rule was already fairly well established during the epic period, although the classical societies did allow for a definite female presence in their religions. But the early Christian church fathers' belief in the causal links among sex, evil, and women removed all vestiges of female influence from religion and substituted a singularly stern and unforgiving father figure. Consequently, a total patriarchal system flowered during the early Christian era. Even though the cult of the Virgin Mary allowed for a certain feminization of the social order during the feudal period, patriarchy became stronger with the advent of primogeniture, the passage of wealth from father to eldest son. Patriarchy continued unabated during the subsequent Renaissance and bourgeois

The epic male. *Source: Historical Pictures Service, Inc.*

The spiritual male. *Source: The Bettmann Archives.*

The chivalric male.   *Source: Historical Pictures Service, Inc.*

The Renaissance male. *Source: Bronzino,* Portrait of a Young Man. *The Metropolitan Museum of Art, New York. Bequest of Mrs. H. O. Havemeyer, 1929. H. O. Havemeyer Collection.*

periods. In fact, patriarchy did not go challenged until the middle of the nineteenth century, when certain social movements began their assault on the established male-dominated social order in England and America. We will have more to say about the erosion of male dominance in America in the next section.

Thus far we have covered the European roots of the male role ideal. Now it is time to discuss the imprint of American history on the male ideal. Even though the early immigrants brought with them the major features of the male role of which we have already spoken, the unique combination of cultures and the distinctive frontier spirit of American society produced a hybrid version of the male role. As we found in the history of Western civilization, America during its short history has also produced several male role models.

The bourgeois male. *Source: Hals,* Balthasar Coymans. *The National Gallery of Art, Washington, D.C. Andrew Mellon Collection,* 1937.

THE AMERICAN VERSIONS OF THE MALE SEX ROLE

After just spanning a period of more than twenty-five hundred years (from 800 B.C. to the eighteenth century), we might think that America's relatively short history would provide little change in the male role ideal. Nothing could be further from the truth. In just three and a half centuries, the United States has provided a rich social climate for several male role transitions. But how shall we divide the American historical scene and its perspectives on the male role? Elizabeth and Joseph Pleck write that the history of the sexes in America is best conceived and divided into specific "periods that correspond to much broader and far-reaching changes in American politics and warfare and to new directions in economic, religious, and family life."[14] The Plecks have thus separated the history of the male sex role and masculinity in America into four periods: agrarian patriarchy (1630–1820), the commercial age (1820–1860), the strenuous life (1861–1919), and companionate providing (1920–1965).

In the following discussion we will use these four periods. Furthermore, we will pay particular attention to the economic, legal, and social changes that influenced women during these periods because changes in the female's role directly influenced the male's role. And, we will continue to focus on the influence of patriarchy over both men's and women's lives.

THE GENTLEMAN AND HIS FAMILY

According to history, the Puritans sailed to America to escape persecution and to express their particular brand of stern religious beliefs. Being a contentious minority, the Puritans saw themselves as vastly superior to the liberal majority of seventeenth-century England because of their strict moral code and belief in a rigid patriarchy. The Puritans especially disdained the "feminization" of English society that had come down from the earlier chivalric period. Central to Puritan belief was the view that men were intended by God to be superior to women, who were to defer and subjugate themselves to the male in all matters.[15] Possibly, the Puritan's strict and unbending moral fiber was a factor in their survival of those first inhospitable years in the American wilderness. Thus, with the Puritans, a strict patriarchal tradition was planted early and deep in the American colonies.

As the American wilderness was settled, the colonists became less preoccupied with mere survival and turned their energies to establishing a new way of life, a life based on English patriarchal standards. In the colonies of the late seventeenth century, for example, English common law played a significant role in the colonists' daily lives. Under common law, the father as head of the household was the only one permitted to enter into contracts, buy or sell land, and represent the family in civil matters. Consequently, women had no legal rights in the early colonies.

Land or rather its ownership became a significant feature in colonial men's lives. A landowner was thought to have greater power, influence, and status than

Table 2.2   The American Male Role Ideals

Ideal	Source(s)	Major Features
Aristocrat	Eighteenth-century English aristocratic values	Self-confidence, intellectualism, strong patriarchal tradition, individualism.
Common Man	The values of the new Republic	Common sense, success in business, personal ingenuity, heightened sexual interests and activity.
He-Man	Westward expansion and the rise of feminism	Strenuous activity, involvement in sports, two-fisted preparedness.
Partner	Loosening of nineteenth-century Victorian values	Good provider, hard work, concerned about family matters.

a man without land. Over time, American landowners formed a nucleus of what can be considered an American "aristocracy." The American aristocrat soon became the image or model by which early colonial men measured their masculinity. Furthermore, certain features became associated with the landed aristocrat, features such as independence, self-confidence, intelligence, and a spirit of individualism.

During this period, the role of the father in most family matters was that of an unquestioned authority figure. The father controlled his sons' education, choice of careers, and future economic status by passing down his land and wealth through the long-established practice of primogeniture. Daughters were equally under their father's control, even to his choice of their future husbands. And, by virtue of the law, the wife was totally dependent on her husband's goodwill.

As this period drew to a close with the American Revolution and the formation of the new Republic, the woman's role began to change. The mother took a more active and influential role in the rearing of her children.[16] The family model took on a quasi-democratic appearance with the husband and wife splitting responsibilities; the father became even more involved in the worldly matters of business, and the mother assumed family responsibilities such as the education of her children.[17] The beginning of the nineteenth century brought about a decline in the aristocratic ideal for men and a turn toward specific social concerns for women.

THE HORSE TRADER AND THE SUFFRAGETTE

During the early colonial years, the male was the center of the social order and the ultimate authority in most matters. The female was almost a nonentity, a passive figure in the background whose womanly mission was to bear children in silence and keep to herself in loyal submission, first to her father and later, as an adult, to her husband. But the first half of the nineteenth century witnessed a new social order, a new pattern of living for each sex, commonly referred to as the "doctrine of the spheres."

In the fervor and upheaval of the new Republic, we find the ingredients for a social revolution wherein two separate but theoretically equal spheres or cultures became evident; one sphere was for the males and the other for the females. The two were divided according to presumed sex differences. The male, who was viewed as more aggressive and competitive by nature, was thought more fit for the masculine pursuits of politics and economic ventures. The ideal of the colonial period's male aristocrat gave way to the ideal of the "common man." The model of the common man not only looked the part of the opportunistic hard worker but he was expected to possess common sense and an eye for practical matters that made him especially well suited for the give and take of hard bargaining in the business world. The female, on the other hand, by virtue of her presumed genteel and emotional nature, was thought best suited for "womanly" activities involving home and religion.[18] The ideal wife was pictured as possessing a high degree of domestic ability and was expected to create an inviting shelter to which her husband could return after a hard day of business dealings in the unfriendly male world.[19]

A dramatic turnabout occurred in the commercial period with respect to the sexual element of the male role. Recall that ever since the early Christian period women, not men, were thought to be oversexed. For centuries women were portrayed as the source of passion and sensuality. Of course, men were sexual creatures also, but it was women's nature that was given to carnal desires and, as the church taught, was the cause of the male's downfall. However, during the early nineteenth century, men were portrayed as having a stronger sexual bent than women, who were viewed as being above sex or at least put off by it. For this reason, men were encouraged to exert themselves in their work, to become successful in their business ventures because through work a man could expend a large portion of his sexual energies on tasks more worthwhile than mere sexual release. After a hard day's work, the passionate husband had little energy or spirit left for baser things, which was perfectly all right with his "cool" wife.

Although the woman's role during this period revolved around the home, she also became involved in the most pressing issue of the day, slavery. Large numbers of Northern women became advocates of the growing abolition movement. Furthermore, concern over the plight and oppression of the slave caused some Northern women to focus on their own sex's inequality. The legal subjugation of the wife to her husband was finally rescinded by a series of laws collectively known as the Married Women's Acts. (The first such law was passed in Mississippi in 1839.) Under these laws, women gained the rights to enter into contracts, to sue or be sued in their own name, to control the property they brought into their marriages, and to take on paid employment without their husband's consent.[20]

As the Republic grew more stable, women in growing numbers reacted against their second-class citizenship. The Declaration of Independence had proclaimed the lofty ideal that "all *men* are created equal," and women found themselves left out, with few rights or privileges other than those granted them by their husbands. Furor over the patriarchal social system and women's oppressed status caused some women to band together to fight for their rights as equal citizens under the law. The energy and indignation these women felt came together at the first feminist convention in Seneca Falls, New York, in 1848. Even though the convention focused on women's oppression and their lack of the vote, a third of the signers of the Seneca Falls' Declaration of Principles were men.[21]

Thus the commercial age, although it lasted only forty or so years, left an indelible imprint on the roles of both sexes. Men were thought highly sexed, and in order to control their lusty passions, they were exhorted to turn their energies to work. The patriarchal tradition was under attack, and men found their esteemed privileges slowly eroding. Women, on the other hand, ruled the house and were encouraged by a reformist religion to fight for equal rights and justice for blacks and women alike. The commercial period found men and women living in two almost completely separate worlds, and the sexes were not to come together again for another half century. On a larger scale, the Republic was about to divide over the issue of states' rights. With all of these forces, the stage was set for the third period in the history of the male role, a period in which men turned to physical exertion and battle to bolster the sagging male role.

THE HE-MAN AND HIS COMPATRIOTS

The Plecks refer to the years between 1860 and 1919 as the period of the "strenuous life." This period began with a war in which brother fought brother and ended with the Great War, which was heralded as the war to end all wars. Sandwiched between these bloody conflicts, men struggled with changing times that provided them few opportunities to bolster their masculinity. With the erosion of patriarchy and the Victorian attack on men's sexuality, men answered the challenges to their manhood by turning to all-male activities in which they could play at being rough and tough. Teddy Roosevelt set the tenor of this period in an address before a men's group in Chicago:

> I wish to preach, not the doctrine of ignoble ease, but the doctrine of the strenuous life, the life of toil and effort, of labor and strife; to preach that highest form of success which comes, not to the man who desires mere easy peace, but to the man who does not shrink from danger, from hardship, or from bitter toil, and who out of these wins the splendid ultimate triumph.[22]

The decades directly preceding the twentieth century found large numbers of men migrating from farms to cities. America was fast becoming an industrial giant, and the factories needed strong backs to stoke the furnaces of progress. Opportunities for individual male enterprise and success were becoming scarce, and men needed other ways to validate their flagging sense of masculinity. To counter the depersonalized regimentation and routine drudgery of factory work, the American working male organized team sports like football and baseball.

Where else could men pit their strength, release their pent-up aggressiveness, and once again feel the masculine stirrings prompted by a hard-fought victory as well as on the football field? The popularity of organized sports spilled over to include large numbers of male spectators who could vicariously live through some aspect of their manhood with the mock battle of their team against another.[23] Along with team sports, men frequented all-male saloons and clubs to find a shelter from the female presence and to revel in masculine comraderie. We can appreciate the strength of men's need to be with other men when we note that membership in fraternal lodges in America grew to an estimated 5.5 million members by 1901.[24] Thus large numbers of working-class and middle-class men turned to other men for companionship on the playing fields and in saloons and clubs for reassurance that they were still, in fact, real men.

Few formal organizations captured the spirit of the strenuous life and men's attempt to validate their masculinity by physical means better than the Boy Scouts of America.[25] In 1910 Ernest Thompson Seton, one of the founders of the Boy Scout movement in the United States, noted how scouting with its emphasis on the outdoors and strenuous physical activities was a desirable way to achieve manhood. To make his point, Seton emphasized the physical aspects of manhood over most others (for example, the intellectual) in the introduction to his book *Boy Scouts of America:*

> Realizing that *manhood,* not *scholarship,* is the first aim of education, we have sought out those pursuits which develop the finest character, the finest physique, and which may be followed out of doors, which, in a word, *make for manhood.*[26]

The scouting movement was only one in a long line of social movements that attempted to give disenchanted males another chance at being real, muscular men. Where the scouting movement succeeded, others failed. One of the most ambitious and costly ventures in promoting the strenuous life occurred in East Tennessee.[27] During the 1870s, the English author Sir Thomas Hughes felt compelled to assist the latter-born sons of England's aristocracy to develop their physical stamina and proper manly character. The "Will Wimbles," as Hughes dubbed them, were not entitled to their fathers' estate or titles because of primogeniture. Many of these men squandered their lives on frivolous activity and were a blight to many families. Hughes, a believer in a creed known as "muscular Christianity," thought honest labor and fresh air were the only salvation for the Will Wimbles. With a group of Boston capitalists, Hughes purchased some 40,000 acres in the East Tennessee wilderness and founded the village of Rugby. The transplanted Will Wimbles began a new life based on hard work and the principles of Christianity. Not surprisingly, the social experiment failed after only a few years, perhaps because the land was ill fit for farming but more probably because the Will Wimbles were ill fit for the strenuous life they found in the mountains of East Tennessee.

Men were not alone in the search for appropriate ways to express their sex role during this period. Women also were moving into new areas and trying new roles. Women who had been prevented from taking paid employment outside of the home during the early years of the nineteenth century were, by the middle of the century, a visible part of the work force. For example, between the years 1850 and 1870, the number of female factory workers jumped from 225,992 to 323,370.[28] Besides factory work, women were moving into previously all-male occupations like teaching, clerical work, and librarianship in increasing numbers.[29] The feminist movement that began at Seneca Falls continued to grow as women from different backgrounds became more vocal in their demands for an end to the separate and unequal spheres that kept the sexes apart.[30]

The period of the strenuous life finally ended with men validating their masculinity in the ageless way of warfare and bloodshed. For almost sixty years, men had turned to sports, exclusive male enclaves, the glories of the Wild West, and even a few short-lived battle campaigns, all in an attempt to bolster their feelings of manliness. During these years, more and more women continued to fight for their basic right as citizens of this country—the right to vote. Most men feared the defiant suffragette movement because they knew that with this change in women's status, other more significant changes in the sex roles were sure to follow. Almost as if providence had stepped in, the Great War began and once more men were called upon to fulfill their manly destiny, that of warrior-soldier, and all was well in the separate spheres, at least for a few more years.

PARTNERS AT LAST

With the end of World War I, the separate worlds of the sexes turned topsy-turvy. The passage of the Nineteenth Amendment to the Constitution gave women the right to vote and the war years showed that they could take over in a man's world when the doughboys had gone "over there." During the early 1920s, social customs and traditions changed drastically with the advent of the flapper, the speakeasy, the Charleston, and sexual dalliances in the backseats of mass-produced Fords. The old props of the male role quickly became cultural dinosaurs. The modern era of sex roles or the period of "companionate providing" was ushered in.

The separate cultural spheres began to crumble as men spent more time in women's company. For companionship, men turned to women rather to other men, who now were seen as competitors and not as companions. With technology and specialization, men no longer validated their manliness in purely physical activities but turned to providing for their families as evidence of their manhood. The role of breadwinner or good provider became the primary element in the definition of masculinity.

During the 1920s, as the discharged soldiers traded in their rifles and shoulder patches for steady jobs and bimonthly paychecks, an economic disaster of monstrous proportions loomed on the horizon. In 1929 the disaster struck with the

The aristocrat and his family. *Source: Joseph Blackburn,* Isaac Winslow and His Family. *The Abraham Shuman Fund. Museum of Fine Arts, Boston.*

stock market crash that set off the Great Depression, which affected countless men, women, and children. The male role of breadwinner became an anachronism almost overnight. A man without a job not only lost status in his own eyes but also in the eyes of his family.[31] Even though the ordinary jobless man had little to do with the causes of the depression, "[t]he suddenly-idle hands," wrote Studs Terkel, "blamed themselves, rather than society. . . . No matter that others suffered the same fate, the inner voice whispered, 'I'm a failure.' "[32] Men once again found themselves caught in the dilemma of not being able to live up to the social expectation that counted, that of being a breadwinner. Rather than laying the blame for their emasculation on the rightful social sources, in this case the male role itself and the economy, these angry men blamed themselves and felt the stinging self-indictment of being failures.

Either by chance or some sinister international plot, the American economy and the American male's damaged manhood were revitalized by yet another war. The age-old masculine attributes of courage, endurance, toughness, and "guts" were once again unfurled, and men found themselves playing at being real men, this time by dint of the combat role.[33] After World War II, American men returned to take up the breadwinner role in earnest, and women were forced to abdicate their wartime jobs and return to their kitchens and nurseries.

Perspectives on the Male

The common man. *Source: William S. Mount,* Bargaining for Horses. *The New York Historical Society, New York City.*

During the 1950s and early 1960s, American men reasserted their superior role over women. Being a man meant raising career aspirations and accumulating status symbols as proof of his masculinity. Being a women meant shuffling the kids to school and supporting her husband's driving ambition to make it to the top. Many women found themselves trapped in a monotonous life-style that some years later Betty Friedan would call the "feminine mystique." The "normalcy" of this period ended abruptly with the chaotic social movements of the late 1960s. The decade of the 1970s brought an end to cheap energy, and women joined the work force in unprecedented numbers. Once again men faced new challenges to their superior male role and were finding fewer opportunities to prove themselves real men. Finally, some men began to ask themselves questions such as, "What does it really mean to be a man today?" or "What do other men and women expect of me simply because I have a penis between my legs?" Questions like these do not lend themselves to easy answers.

The he-man and his friends.   *Source: The Library of Congress Collection.*

Partners.   *Source: Oskar Kokoschka,* Hans Tietze and Erica Tietze-Conrat. *Abby Aldrich Rockefeller Fund. The Museum of Modern Art, New York.*

COMMENTING ON THE HISTORICAL PERSPECTIVE

We began this chapter with a discussion of the Greeks and their concerns over physical strength and courage in battle, and we ended with a contemporary male's questioning of what it means to be a real man. We might think that after all of these centuries men would finally have an answer. But many men nowadays seem as puzzled over their masculinity and their male role as probably were some of the early Greek males who did not quite measure up to the ideal epic male figure. Before we leave our discussion of the history of the male sex role we need to ask even more questions. Sometimes it seems that history provides more questions than answers!

First of all, what value does a historical perspective of the male sex role provide? We could answer this question in a general way by paraphrasing the words of the philosopher George Santayana and stating that ignorance of history dooms one to repeat the same mistakes over and over. One mistake that we can avoid as the result of a greater understanding of the history of the male role is the erroneous belief that what society expects of males today has always been expected down through the ages. For example, many males today believe that they must appear to be strongly sexed and completely competent in sexual relationships in order to prove to themselves and to other men and women that they are, in fact, truly masculine. But we know from our historical survey that the expectation that men be more highly sexed than women is a relatively recent addition to the male role. Likewise, many men today feel that aggressiveness is an essential and long-standing feature of the male role. Again, however, we know that during the Christian era the ideal male was nonviolent. The practice of "turning one's other cheek" rather than striking back in anger was expected of the spiritual man. Thus one of the significant values of a knowledge of the historical perspective is that we can see the contemporary male role for what it really is— *a changing social phenomenon.*

Second, are there any features to today's male sex role that do extend back to the beginnings of recorded history? The answer to this question is a straightforward "yes." The patriarchal social system in which the male in the role of father or husband dominates the female does appear throughout recorded Western history. Of course, there exists the possibility that in some prehistoric period the relationship between the sexes was egalitarian or possibly even gynocratic. However, since the Greek and Roman eras, the prevalence of father-rule appears to be a consistent phenomenon in Western civilization.

Certainly other questions can be raised by our discussion of the history of the male sex role and masculinity, but we will end our discussion of the historical perspective here and move on to an examination of the male experience from the biological perspective.

Dubbert, J. *A Man's Place: Masculinity in Transition.* Englewood Cliffs, N.J.: Prentice-Hall, 1979.

Filene, P. *Him/Her/Self: Sex Roles in Modern America.* New York: Harcourt Brace Jovanovich, 1974.

Kirshner, A., ed. *Masculinity in an Historical Perspective.* Washington, D.C.: University Press of America, 1977.

Pleck, E., and Pleck, J., eds. *The American Male.* Englewood Cliffs, N.J.: Prentice-Hall, 1980.

Stearns, P. *Be a Man! Males in Modern Society.* New York: Holmes & Meier, 1980.

3

Of puny chromosomes and powerful hormones:
THE BIOLOGICAL PERSPECTIVE

> . . . the biological disadvantages accruing to the male are not so much due to what is in the Y chromosome as to what is not in it.
>
> Ashley Montagu[1]

> When it comes down to the biological imperatives that are laid down for all men and women, there are only four: Only a man can impregnate; only a woman can menstruate, gestate, and lactate.
>
> John Money and Patricia Tucker[2]

At one time or another, we have all admired a curvaceous female or a muscular male. Clearly, we can all see that the sexes *are* different. But some people have gone beyond the obvious physical differences and concluded that the sexes differ in other less notable ways as well. For instance, some scientists theorize that male and female sex roles and traditional sex-typed characteristics like male aggressiveness and female nurturance are largely the result of genetic differences.[3] Even the controversial double standard of sexual conduct that condones male promiscuity and restricts female sexual activity is thought to be programmed by genetic material.[4] However, others find little or no research evidence for the idea that biology is the cause of either sex roles or sex-typed behaviors or characteristics.[5]

For our purposes here, we need not belabor the controversy between the "biology is destiny" and the "environment is everything" groups. Nevertheless, it does seem that the biological perspective has become a sort of scapegoat in the discussion of sex roles. Those who see red at any mention of biology seem to dismiss a fundamental truth: Humans *are* biological creatures. Rather than present traditional sex roles and sex-typed behaviors as the inevitable outcomes of some biological imperative, we will try to present the biological perspective as but one component—albeit an important component—in the male experience.

In this chapter we will first outline certain biological events that shape the physical development of the male fetus. Here we will concentrate on the functions that the Y chromosome and certain hormones play during crucial prenatal periods. Then we will examine the influence that testosterone, a powerful hormone, has on adult characteristics. Specifically, we will discuss testosterone's role in certain physical and behavioral areas.

PRENATAL EVENTS

We are biological creatures first, and only later does the enviornment begin to play a part in our development. To understand the significance of the biological events that shape us, we need to review some of the basic biological principles that pertain to genetic development.

Every human body contains billions of cells that we can think of as the building blocks of the body. Most cells in the human body contain twenty-three *pairs* of chromosomes, which under a powerful microscope look like tiny, threadlike strands of colored beads. Packed with their genetic materials, the chromosomes are chiefly responsible for either physical features such as height, hair texture, eye color, skin pigmentation, and so on or the genetic sex of the body.

During pregnancy, cell bodies first grow and develop as an embryo and later on as a fetus, which grows at a phenomenal rate. But how does cell growth occur? When we speak of cell growth, we usually mean the division of a cell's chromosome materials. When a cell divides, its twenty-three pairs of chromosomes first double to forty-six pairs, and then the cell divides into two separate cells, each again containing twenty-three pairs of chromosomes. Thus the original fertilized cell becomes two cells, then later four cells, then eight cells, and so on. Within a matter of weeks, there are literally millions of cells.

We said that most cells contain twenty-three *pairs* of chromosomes. The sex cells, however, contain *only* twenty-three chromosomes. These sex cells are the unfertilized egg or ovum produced in the woman's ovaries and the sperm produced in the man's testes. Sex cells are an exception to the rule of division. The division of an unfertilized egg or sperm takes place without first doubling its chromosome materials; consequently, both egg and sperm have only half of the necessary chromosome materials for a complete human being. In fact, the only way an egg cell can survive is to mate or be fertilized by a sperm cell. If unfertilized, the egg dies in a matter of days.

Now that we have briefly noted some of the biological principles relating to cells, chromosomes, and the division of cells, let us look more closely at how the male experience begins with a special sperm cell.

THE ROLE OF THE X AND THE Y CHROMOSOMES

For this discussion of biological sex development, we will divide the prenatal period into fives stages (see Table 3.1). The first two stages are discussed in this section and the last three in the next section.

Conception occurs when a male's sperm penetrates a female's unfertilized egg. Of the twenty-three chromosomes in each, twenty-two govern the physical characteristics, and the twenty-third is a sex-determining chromsome, which is labeled either X or Y. The female's egg always contains an X chromosome, whereas the male's sperm can have either an X or a Y chromosome. With an XX combination, the genetic sex is female, and with an XY combination, the genetic sex is male. Therefore, the father's sperm determines the genetic sex of the embryo (see Figure 3.1).

The sex-determining characteristics of male sperm are only one of the interesting features coming to light in various laboratories across the country. For example, at the New York Fertility Foundation, researcher Landrum Shettles has shown in the pictures taken by a scanning electron microscope that all sperm are not equal (see Figure 3.2). Sperm bearing a Y chromosome are what scientists call *androsperm,* and they are different in size and structure from sperm carrying an X chromosome or *gynosperm.*[6] Androsperm have a sharp, spearlike head, while gynosperm have a rounder, more blunted head. The androsperm's longer, more energetic whiplike tail allows it to move faster than a gynosperm— a fact that Shettles has tested by racing the two in his laboratory. Furthermore, the androsperm appear to move better in an alkaline environment, whereas the gynosperm better tolerate an acidic environment. These different characteristics have led Shettles and other researchers to suggest ways in which couples may enhance their chances of having either a boy or a girl (see "Dr. Shettles's Ways to Improve Nature's Odds").

Table 3.1 The Five Stages of Male and Female Development

Stage I.	**Chromosome Sex: XY = genetic male, XX = genetic female.**
	During the first weeks of the embryo's growth, the same internal and external sex tissue, or anlagen, develop in both genetic sexes.
	A. Internal anlagen
	1. Sex gland
	2. Wolffian duct
	3. Mullerian duct
	B. External anlagen
	1. Genital tubercle
	2. Urethral fold
	3. Labioscrotal swelling
Stage II.	**Gonadal Sex: testes = male, ovaries = female.**
	After the eighth week of gestation, the sex gland develops as either testes or ovaries. The factor responsible for this difference is a genetic message contained in the Y chromosome.
Stage III.	**Hormonal Sex: In males, testosterone and the Mullerian-inhibiting substance are both produced by the testes.**
	A. Testosterone causes the Wolffian duct to develop as
	1. Vas deferens
	2. Seminal vesicles
	3. Prostate gland
	B. The Mullerian-inhibiting substance prevents the Mullerian duct from developing into the female structures:
	1. Fallopian tubes
	2. Uterus
	3. Upper part of the vagina
Stage IV.	**External Sex: In males, testosterone causes the external sex anlagen (Stage IB) to develop into the male form rather than the female form.**
	A. The genital tubercle becomes the penis rather than the clitoris.
	B. The urethral fold becomes the shaft of the penis rather than the labia minor.
	C. The labioscrotal swelling becomes the scrotum rather than the labia major.
Stage V.	**Assigned Sex: At birth, the announcement, "It's a boy!"**

The fact that the androsperm are faster than the gynosperm raises an interesting point. Androsperm impregnate more eggs than do gynosperm, accounting for what scientists believe to be a ratio of between 145 and 160 male conceptions for every 100 female conceptions.[7] Of course, this male-biased imbalance does not last for long. Given the male embryo's greater chance of spontaneous abortion, some nine months later, the male-female ratio has dropped to approximately 105 male live births for every 100 female. The androsperm's greater speed in the race for the egg appears to be a biological "hedge" against their susceptibility to abort.

Moreover, when we take a closer look at the size difference between an X and a Y chromosome (Figure 3.1), it becomes clear that the Y chromosome contains much less genetic material than the more robust X chromosome. We might even

DR. SHETTLES'S WAYS TO IMPROVE NATURE'S ODDS

Male babies: 1. Before intercourse, the female should douche with a solution of water and baking soda to create an alkaline environment.
2. The couple should have intercourse during ovulation, having abstained during the previous cycle.
3. The female should have an orgasm, thus increasing a favorable environment for the androsperm.
4. Emission of sperm should occur during deep penetration.

Female babies: 1. Before intercourse, the female should douche with a solution of water and vinegar to create an acidic environment.
2. The couple should have intercourse two to three days before ovulation.
3. The female should refrain from having an orgasm.
4. Emission of sperm should occur during shallow penetration.

say that the Y chromosome looks "puny" when compared to the X. The difference in an X's and a Y's genetic materials becomes crucial in sex-linked diseases. A *sex-linked disease* is one that is directly attributable to a defect in a particular gene. Males have less genetic material in their Y chromosome and thus are prone to a greater number of sex-linked conditions than are females. In *The Natural Superiority of Women,* Ashley Montagu lists over sixty specific sex-linked conditions that primarily afflict males.[8] Now let us turn our attention to one such sex-linked disease and see how the Y chromosome's lack of genetic material causes harmful, if not lethal, consequences for the male.

Hemophilia or the bleeder's disease is an inherited illness caused by a defective recessive gene located in the mother's X-bearing sex chromosome. If the father's contribution is a *normal* X-bearing sex chromosome—causing an XX genetic female—his X chromosome will suppress the effects of the mother's defective gene. However, such is not the case for an XY genetic male. In this case, the Y-bearing sex chromosome contributed by the father does not contain the necessary genetic material to suppress or override the mother's defective gene. Thus the Y chromosome's lack of genetic material accounts to a great degree for most of the inherited sex-linked conditions noted by Montagu.

However, not all problems associated with a male's genetic endowment relate to the Y chromosome's smallness or sparsity of genetic material. In some rare instances, the problem is just the reverse: A male has a surplus of sex chromosomes. Recall that normally the male has two sex chromosomes, an X and a Y.

Figure 3.1 Arrangement of human chromosome cells, (a) for a male and (b) for a female. Notice that the twenty-third pair differs — XX for a genetic female and XY for a genetic male. *Source: Courtesy of the March of Dimes.*

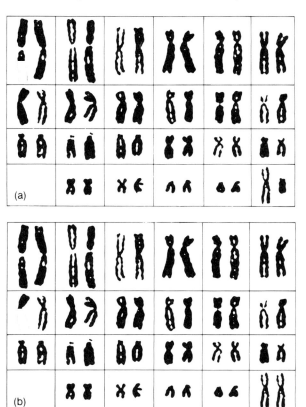

Sometimes, however, a male has an additional X chromosome or an XXY genetic pattern (Klinefelter's syndrome) or an extra Y chromosome or an XYY pattern (the "supermale"). The Klinefelter male has an unusually small penis, sterile testes, and usually some sign of mental retardation.[9] As for the supermale, when a group of researchers found a higher than expected number of XYY genetic patterns among prison inmates, speculation grew that the additional Y sex chromosome predisposed these men to a life of crime.[10] However, subsequent research found that the supermale is not prone to crime, although he is thought more likely to lose his control and "fly off the handle," thus coming to the attention of authorities more often than the normal XY genetic male.[11]

The vast majority of XY conceptions, however, do not end in spontaneous abortions, sex-linked diseases, or subsequent developmental complications caused

Figure 3.2   Androsperm, *right*, and gynosperm, *left.*   *Source: Manfred Kage, Peter Arnold, Inc.*

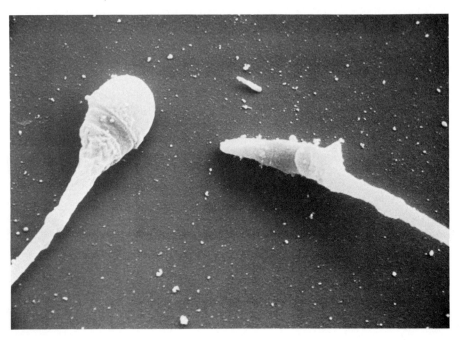

by a surplus of genetic material. We now turn our attention to the majority of cases in which conception produces a normal XY genetic male and follow his course during the remainder of the prenatal period.

During the first several weeks after conception, the XY embryo goes through an explosive growth period in which the original fertilized egg divides and redivides into millions of cells. Throughout this period, both internal and external sex structures begin to take shape. One point that is frequently overlooked is that for the first six to eight weeks after conception, the embryo is *ambisexual,* meaning that it has specialized internal and external sex tissues, or *anlagen, for both sexes* (see Table 3.1, Stage IA and B). For example, the embryo has a general, all-purpose sex gland that could develop into either testes or ovaries. Although scientists do not as yet fully understand what makes an XY embryo's sex gland develop into testes rather than ovaries, growing evidence suggests that a specialized chemical substance called *H-Y antigen* located in the Y chromosome causes the sex gland to develop into testes and not ovaries.[12] However, one thing is clear; sometime during the third month, the male embryo's sex gland develops into testes (see Table 3.1, Stage II). This development causes the powerful hormone testosterone to begin its crucial work on the remaining internal and external sex structures. In the next section we will focus on testosterone's contribution to the development of a normal male.

Perspectives on the Male

The male embryo's newly formed testes produce *testosterone,* one of a group of hormones commonly referred to as *androgens.* Strictly speaking, testosterone's major role is to masculinize the already formed genetic male embryo. It may sound strange that a hormone is needed to accomplish the work already begun by the Y chromosome. However, the fact remains that without sufficient amounts of testosterone—or if the male embryo's sex tissues (that is, anlagen) are somehow immune to testosterone's masculinizing effects—the male embryo will develop as a female, albeit a sterile female.[13]

The Internal Sex Structures As noted in Table 3.1 (Stage III), sometime during the third or fourth month, the male embryo's testes begin to produce testosterone, which subsequently directs the developmental course of the Wolffian duct. The *Wolffian duct* is an important part of the male embryo's sex structures for it will, with the help of testosterone, develop into three separate sex-related structures: the vas deferens, the seminal vesicles, and the prostate gland (see Figure 3.3). We will describe the workings of these three structures in detail in a later section of this chapter. For the moment, we should note that the sole purpose of these structures is to move the sperm produced in a mature male's testes outward, all the way to the end of the penis. Working together, these three structures form a type of transportation system that allows mature sperm to fulfill their primary purpose, impregnation.

The testosterone-induced Wolffian duct's evolution into separate male sex structures leaves the fetus with one other internal sex tissue, the *Mullerian duct.* The Mullerian duct is also programmed to develop into three structures: the female's fallopian tubes, uterus, and upper part of the vagina. If by some quirk of nature the Mullerian duct were to develop in a male fetus along with the post-Wolffian structures, the male would have both male and female internal sex structures and be classified as a *hermaphrodite.* But most often, nature's way is to prevent this from happening. To accomplish this, the testes produce a chemical substance that prevents the Mullerian duct's development and subsequently causes the duct to shrivel up. The exact chemical ingredient responsible for this is not known. For obvious reasons, scientists call this inferred chemical the *Mullerian-inhibiting substance.*[14]

The External Sex Structures When most people speak of external sex organs, they normally mean a male's penis and scrotum and a female's clitoris. Many people are unaware that a male's penis and a female's clitoris both develop out of an identical or ambisexual sex tissue known as a *genital tubercle* (see Figure 3.4). During the first six to eight weeks after conception, both genetic male and female fetuses have three identical or ambisexual sex organs, namely, a genital tubercle, an *urethral fold,* and a *labioscrotal swelling* (see Table 3.1, Stage IB). Once again, the development of a penis instead of a clitoris is dependent on the presence or absence of the hormone testosterone. If testosterone is

Figure 3.3   The prenatal developmental sequence of the male and female internal sex structures.   *Source:* Money, J. and A. Ehrhardt, *Man and Woman, Boy and Girl.* Copyright © 1972 by The Johns Hopkins University Press.

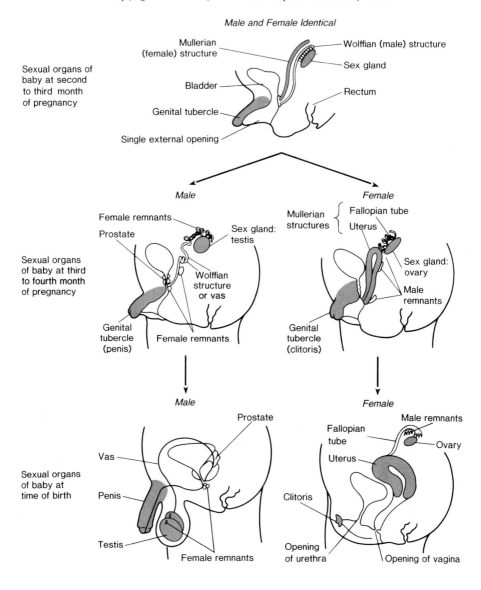

Figure 3.4 The prenatal developmental sequence of the male and female external sex structures. *Source:* Money, J. and A. Ehrhardt, *Man and Woman, Boy and Girl.* Copyright © 1972 by The Johns Hopkins University Press.

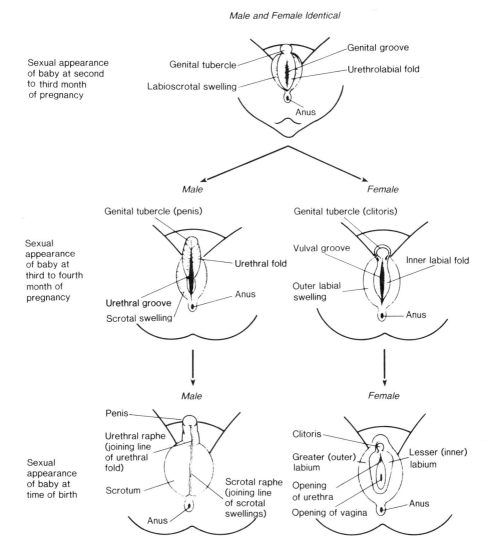

present during the third or fourth month, as we would expect in a genetic male fetus with normal testes, then the genital tubercle will develop as a penis. If, on the other hand, a genetic male's testes do not produce enough testosterone, then the genital tubercle will develop as a clitoris or as an immature and poorly developed penis. Clearly, testosterone plays the significant role in the development of a male's external sex organs. With testosterone, each of the original ambisexual sex tissues develops as a specific male sex organ: the genital tubercle becomes a penis, the urethral fold develops as the shaft of the penis, and the labioscrotal swelling forms the scrotal sack that holds the male's testes.

Thus far we have seen how testosterone causes the original ambisexual internal and external sex tissues to develop into their respective male sex structures or organs. But testosterone's effects on the developing fetus is not limited only to sex structures. It also affects certain portions of the brain.

Testosterone and the Brain Most people recognize a very basic sex difference in the fact that women menstruate and men do not. A woman's menstrual cycle is controlled by certain hormones secreted by the pituitary gland. For a woman, certain glands located in the brain secrete specialized hormones that cause menstruation if she is not pregnant and lactation if she is pregnant. For a man, however, there are no clear-cut external signs of an interaction between certain glands located in the brain and his sex organs. But scientists are now convinced that testosterone causes the male's brain or more specifically certain glands in the male's brain to secrete specific hormones that influence his sex organs and their functions. Let us see how this happens.

As already noted, testosterone is chiefly responsible for the masculinization of the internal and external sex tissues. However, some testosterone finds its way through the blood system to the hypothalamus located deep in the brain. Under the influence of the hypothalamus, the pituitary gland secretes a second hormone called the *interstitial cell stimulating hormone* (ICSH) back to the testes. Within the testes, ICSH stimulates the Leydig cells to produce more testosterone and the entire cycle starts over (see Figure 3.5). In the mature male, the pituitary gland secretes a second hormone called the *follicle stimulating hormone* (FSH). The major function of FSH is to produce sperm in the testes. Testosterone is therefore essential during certain critical periods of fetal development to establish an important link to parts of the brain, which then secrete other hormones thought to be necessary for male development.[15]

Testosterone is the crucial ingredient that assures that the genetic male will develop normally. Because of testosterone, the words, "It's a boy!" are spoken at birth (Table 3.1, Stage V).

For the first three to four months after birth, the testosterone level remains high, after which it drops off for the next ten to twelve years. Testosterone production dramatically increases with the onset of puberty, and once again several physical changes occur in the male's body.

Figure 3.5   Testosterone's effects on the hypothalamic-pituitary glands and the resultant hormones.   *Source: Adapted from S. Levine, "Sex Differences in the Brain,"* Scientific American, *April 1966, p. 84.*

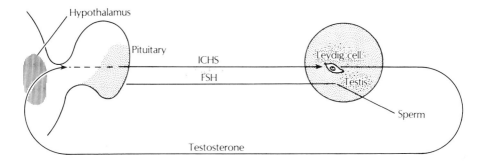

POSTNATAL EVENTS

During adolescence, the period between childhood and early adulthood, family ties weaken and the adolescent male begins to move toward a more diverse and extended network of friends and acquaintances. Consequently, he is often beset with new social demands as he tries to fit in with his peer group. As if the social aspects were not unnerving enough, his body also begins to play strange tricks on him. For years, the young boy took his body for granted, but no longer.

In this section we will focus first on the physical changes brought on by a resurgence of testosterone in the body. Next we will discuss some of the research that deals with emotions and mood changes that appear to be related to testosterone level. Finally, we will examine the evidence linking hormones with male aggression and nurturing behaviors.

THE CHANGING MALE BODY

Adolescence begins with the onset of puberty. Puberty is normally considered as that period when a male's and a female's internal sex organs (testes and ovaries) are capable of producing the means for reproduction (sperm and eggs). For the female, puberty is ushered in rather dramatically with the beginning of a regular monthly menstrual cycle. For the male, however, puberty sneaks up; no single sign tells the boy when his sperm are viable or capable of reproduction. Puberty for the young adolescent male is marked rather by a series of physical changes known as *secondary sex characteristics,* which develop slowly. Following are some of the major physical changes that mark a boy's passage into puberty.

During the early teen years, a biological mechanism somehow programs the hypothalamus and the pituitary glands to begin producing quantities of FSH and ICSH to stimulate the testes to produce viable sperm and large amounts of testosterone, respectively. As the production of testosterone increases, the testes become larger and the scrotal sack takes on a wrinkled look. The shaft of the penis

The Biological Perspective

59

becomes larger, and sprouts of coarse pubic hair appear at the base of the shaft. Besides the appearance of pubic hair, other parts of the body begin to show alterations in hair distribution, for example, the armpits, the chest, the upper lip, and the hairline around the temples. The larynx or voice box grows larger and causes the voice to deepen. The skin coarsens and becomes oily, causing skin problems such as acne. The male's overall physique changes as his shoulders broaden, his musculature increases, and he gets taller and heavier. The male's physical strength dramatically increases as his bones harden and his muscle tone increases.

Adolescence is also a time when a young male's thoughts turn to sex. His first sexual stirrings may come unexpectedly in *nocturnal emissions*—what most people call "wet dreams"—or in the first serious exploration of sexual feelings, thoughts, and experiences through *masturbation*. Whatever the activity, most adolescent males begin to feel their interest in and urges toward sex at this period, when testosterone levels are again on the increase. For the male, the sex drive is probably the strongest during adolescence.

For centuries people have identified the testes as the center of the sex drive in animals and humans alike. Before scientists discovered the role of the testes as the producers of testosterone, many people believed that the testes cause the male to act sexually. Farmers have castrated their male animals to prevent them from breeding. In some countries, male sex offenders have been castrated to prevent their further sexual activity.[16] In some Eastern countries, potentates and emperors have castrated those selected to guard harems and special concubines. People have even castrated homosexual men to prevent their "sinful" sexual behaviors.[17] But does testosterone cause the sex drive?

A definite answer to this question is not yet possible. One of the problems researchers encounter is that of obtaining an accurate measure of the level of testosterone available to the body. In other words, just because a high level of testosterone is found in the bloodstream, one cannot assume that all of the testosterone can be used by the body or that it causes, say, the sex drive itself. Some of the testosterone is bound or locked up by other hormones, especially one hormone called the *sex hormone binding globuline*.[18] In fact, in one study of college women, a researcher measured the women's sex drives and their levels of testosterone (keep in mind that a woman's adrenal glands also produce testosterone) and found no relationship between testosterone and sex drive.[19] Further research is necessary to answer the question about the relationship between a male's sex drive and his testosterone level.

One fact seems certain, however. As we have already noted, testosterone causes the young male's body to change. In a sense, testosterone makes the boy over and a young man emerges. But testosterone may cause other changes in the male besides the obvious and not so obvious physical changes. There is growing interest in the effects testosterone may have on the moods and the emotions that males experience throughout their lives.

TESTOSTERONE AND BLUE MONDAYS

Many people believe that women are given to bouts of elation, happiness, or plain good feelings on one day and may be sullen, morose, or even depressed a week later. One of the most prevalent stereotypes of women in general is the extreme changes in their emotionality. Ask almost anyone the cause of a women's changeable emotional state and he or she will probably answer that it is because of her menstrual period. Translated that simply means that a woman's emotional life is supposedly controlled by the cyclic nature of her hormones. For centuries, people have believed that a woman's menstrual cycle and the flow of menstrual blood were chiefly responsible for all sorts of negative female characteristics, ranging from volatile personality to being thought unclean and therefore to be avoided.[20]

When asked about men's emotionality, many people recite another popular stereotype, that men are not particularly emotional. Furthermore, most people believe that men are not influenced by their hormones, at least not to the extent that women are. Because men do not have an obvious sign of a regular cyclic event like menstruation, most people do not believe that men are as likely to be influenced emotionally by their hormones. But we have already noted how testosterone affects a male's body. Can it be that testosterone also affects a male's emotionality? Similarly, does testosterone in men's bodies go through periodic rising and falling cycles as the hormones estrogen and progesterone do in women's bodies? The answers to these questions have only recently been sought by researchers, and the initial studies are quite enlightening.

In 1972 endocrinologist Estelle Ramey wrote an article for *Ms* magazine in which she reviewed and reported that males have definite and regular hormone cycles.[21] Since then, a small number of studies about the various lengths of men's hormone cycles have been published. For example, C. A. Fox took daily blood samples from one male for a period of eighty-six days and found large fluctuations in testosterone levels. Interestingly, Fox reported that high levels of testosterone were not associated with the man's desire for sex.[22] Fox's research would suggest that high levels of testosterone are not the cause of an adolescent male's interest in sex.

Although Fox found large daily fluctuations in testosterone, he found them only in one man. Some may argue that we cannot infer the same fluctuations for all men. Furthermore, Fox did not report any fluctuating cycles of more than a day. What about the possibility that testosterone may fluctuate in increasing and decreasing cycles from week to week or even longer, much like the female's normal twenty-eight-day menstrual cycle? An extensive study conducted by Charles Doering may shed light on these questions.

Doering and several colleagues studied the testosterone levels of twenty men for sixty days.[23] He found that a majority of these men had identifiable testosterone cycles ranging from three to thirty days, with several of the cycles clustering around twenty-one to twenty-three days. Based on the research reported thus far, testosterone levels definitely fluctuate daily and also reveal longer cycles of from several days to several weeks in length. But is there a relationship between a man's testosterone level and his emotional state?

Once again, Doering's research has provided some interesting findings. Every other day, when the twenty men had their blood samples taken, they also completed a psychological test called the *Multiple Affect Adjective Checklist* (MAACL). The MAACL measures several different emotional states, including anxiety, hostility, and depression. Doering found that testosterone levels did not relate to either hostility or anxiety measures. Surprisingly, however, testosterone levels did relate in a significant way to reported feelings of depression. As the males' levels of testosterone increased, they were more likely to report that they were feeling depressed. Generalizing from Doering's research, we might infer that a male's feeling of being sad or mildly depressed may be linked to an increase in his testosterone. In another study Mary Brown Parlee found evidence of regular cycles in men's emotional states.[24] Parlee did not measure the testosterone levels of her fifteen males, however. Nevertheless, men, like women, seem to have regular fluctuating hormone cycles, and there is some evidence that a male's testosterone level affects his emotional state, at least with respect to depression.

TESTOSTERONE AND AGGRESSION

One of the most prevalent and persistent beliefs about males is that they are predisposed toward aggression. *Aggression* is defined here as the *intentional* inflicting of physical or psychological pain on another.[25] In looking to the animal

Perspectives on the Male

kingdom, we find evidence that the males of most species are more aggressive than the females, although there are several exceptions to this sex difference; for example, among hamsters and gibbons, the females are more aggressive than the males.[26] Not surprisingly then, with the weight of countless animal studies, social scientists have looked to biology for the basis of human aggression. After reviewing well over fifty studies of human aggression, psychologists Eleanor Maccoby and Carol Jacklin concluded, "Aggression is related to levels of sex hormones, and can be changed by experimental administration of these hormones."[27] But before we too quickly close the book on male aggression and testosterone, let us review some of the studies.

One of the most frequently cited human studies purported to show a relationship between testosterone levels and male aggression was conducted by Persky, Smith, and Basu.[28] Two groups of males were selected to take a series of psychological tests and to have their testosterone levels measured. One group was made up of eighteen college students (ages seventeen to twenty-eight), and the second was made up of older adults (ages thirty-three to sixty-six). Persky and his colleagues found that testosterone levels related significantly only with the hostility scores of the Buss–Durkee Hostility Inventory and then only in the younger group. Even though this study found that testosterone levels were higher among those young men who scored high in aggression, we must keep in mind that this aggression was only a score on a paper-and-pencil test. What about the testosterone levels among men who actually get into fights?

This question was put to the test in yet another study. Kreuz and Rose studied the testosterone levels of prison inmates who were classified as either "fighters" or "nonfighters" on the basis of the number of times they had been put into solitary confinement for fighting.[29] Kreuz and Rose found no difference between the testosterone levels of their "fighters" and "nonfighters." These two groups were also given the Buss–Durkee Hostility Inventory—the same test used by Persky— and no relationship between testosterone levels and hostility scores was found. Furthermore, other researchers who have repeated Persky's study have failed to find a relationship between male aggression and testosterone level.[30] After reviewing the research on male aggression and hormones, Joseph Pleck thinks the relationship somewhat tenuous. Pleck writes,

> Given the social importance of aggressive behavior, it is clear that research on its possible biological sources will continue to receive serious attention. At the present time, the evidence in animals for hormonal factors in male aggression is strong (albeit complex). But comparable evidence for human male aggression is much weaker and less consistent.[31]

Thus the claim that researchers such as Maccoby and Jacklin make, that the male hormone testosterone is definitely linked to male aggression, is at the very least an equivocal issue in the minds of other researchers.[32] For the moment, it seems clear that male aggression and its causes will remain a serious issue for further research. Let us now move to yet another area of adult behavior in which researchers see the possible influence of male hormones.

In many people's minds, men are not cut out to take care of infants. After being asked to hold their baby or to change its diaper, more than a few men have responded, "That's woman's work! Anyway, women know how to do it better." Many men believe that something in women—possibly an instinct or their hormones—naturally predisposes them to bathe, powder, diaper, and feed little ones better than men can. But the facts do not support such thinking.

In many animal species, males perform a number of the so-called maternal behaviors, such as building the nest, incubating the eggs, and later on protecting the young while the mother is off in search of food. Even among primates, there is considerable evidence of strong childrearing behaviors among males.[33] Therefore, we cannot say that the male in all species does not take an active and responsible role in raising the young. But what of the research evidence among humans?

In a study conducted by Ehrhardt and Baker, seventeen young females who had been prenatally exposed to high levels of androgen were found to exhibit few socially prescribed "maternal" behaviors.[34] For example, these young girls showed little interest in playing with dolls and taking care of infants, and in general, they did not prefer to play the role of mother in fantasies or games. However, we cannot generalize from this study that normal males with their exposure to prenatal androgens are predisposed against acting in nurturant ways. In Ehrhardt and Baker's study, ten young males who were prenatally exposed to excessive amounts of androgens were actually *more* interested in taking care of infants than were their normal brothers.[35] After reviewing this study, Pleck concludes that "the presence of male sex hormones during prenatal development appears to suppress nurturant interest in females but not in males."[36] In fact, the only barriers preventing males from behaving in nurturant ways seem to be the longstanding prejudices on the part of society and many men's reluctance to share in the daily activities of raising their children.

We have covered several topics in our discussion of testosterone's influence on the male after birth. First we saw how the male hormone sets off a series of physical changes in the adolescent male. Next we examined some research and found little basis for thinking that the male hormone causes the male's sex drive. Then we reviewed some evidence that suggests that high levels of testosterone may play a role in depression among males. Last we could find little conclusive evidence that testosterone either causes aggression or limits nurturant activity among males. One thing we can safely say, however, is that interest in the biological basis of behavior will continue to be a controversial issue for years to come.

COMMENTING ON THE BIOLOGICAL PERSPECTIVE

In this chapter we have presented the male experience from the biological perspective. After reviewing the biology of conception, we discussed several important prenatal events in which the Y chromosome and the hormone testosterone play crucial roles in forming fetal males. We then examined the postnatal impact of testosterone on a young male's body. Finally, we described some of the research relating testosterone to certain emotions, to aggression, and to nurturant behaviors.

Most people would agree that a powerful hallucinogenic drug like lysergic acid diethylamide (LSD) can cause a person to act in unusual ways. Even so, few people would condemn *the study* of drugs and their effects on people's behaviors. However, whenever the effects of hormones are discussed, many feminists immediately react negatively, often labeling the discussion reactionary or politically motivated. Hormones are neither political nor biased in favor of traditional, egalitarian, or ultrafeminists definitions of male and female behaviors. The fact is hormones produce and control certain biological functions. Testosterone causes a penis rather than a clitoris to develop in a fetus. How the penis is used or what symbolic significance is attached to it has nothing to do with the workings of the hormone on the basic sex tissue. Likewise, testosterone causes a young male to develop broad shoulders and large muscles. How the young male uses his strength depends on the environment in which he finds himself, not on the amount of testosterone circulating in his bloodstream. It is hoped that we can move beyond the rhetoric that condemns the biological perspective as being the enemy of change in outdated and culturally determined sex roles and begin to appreciate and understand more fully the mysteries locked in puny chromosomes and powerful hormones.

SUGGESTED READINGS

Diagram Group. *Man's Body: An Owner's Manual.* New York: Paddington Press, 1976.
Julty, S. *Men's Bodies, Men's Selves.* New York: Delta, 1979.
Money, J., and Tucker, P. *Sexual Signatures.* Boston: Little, Brown, 1975.
Montagu, A. *The Natural Superiority of Women.* New York: Collier Books, 1974.

4

Of strange places and stranger men:
THE ANTHROPOLOGICAL PERSPECTIVE

Gender has been the most important basis for assigning rights and obligations and determining the division of labor within the family and within societies. Gender has been a very significant source of differences in the way people responded to and brought up human societies.
                                                    Betty Yorburg[1]

In the preceding chapter, we examined the ways in which certain biological features cause the sexes to differ in their genetic, hormonal, and anatomical makeup. With this chapter, we begin our discussion of how specific social and environmental forces shape specific human behaviors. Too often, we think that biological forces affect people in inflexible ways, leaving them little room for changing biology's givens. The idea that "anatomy is destiny" is a prime example of such rigid thinking. However, history is filled with human discoveries that have overcome many biological factors. For example, a man's biology may cause his pancreas to fail, bringing on the debilitating and often lethal disease of diabetes mellitus. But modern-day medical knowledge permits the diabetic man to live a normal life by means of a daily injection of insulin. In a less critical area, we can point to the man who feels anxious about being bald (another condition caused by biology) and so wears a toupee. In both examples, cultural products are used to overcome biological factors. We dare say that culture has as much (if not more) impact on a man's behavior as his biology does.

In this chapter we will review the impact of culture on people's lives and behaviors. *Culture* is defined here as a particular group's systematic knowledge and behaviors that are passed from one generation to the next. We will begin our discussion of culture and the anthropological perspective by first examining the wide variations among groups in what is defined as appropriate behaviors for the sexes. Next we will discuss the nearly universal phenomenon of male dominance and several of the theories that have been proposed to explain it. Finally, we will describe several American Indian societies in which there are more than two sex roles.

CULTURAL VARIATIONS IN SEX ROLES

For centuries, philosophers and scientists alike have tried to unravel the mysteries surrounding human nature. What are the basic elements of human nature? How do humans differ from other animals? Are humans more a product of their biology or their culture? These are only a few of the questions people ask when they try to understand what it means to be a human being.

The prevailing view of human nature was drastically changed in 1859 when Charles Darwin published *On the Origin of Species*. Therein Darwin theorized that all living species evolved from a common ancestry over countless millions of years. Before Darwin, scholars held the view that all species had been created in their final form by a Divine Creator. Since Darwin, scientists have searched for evidence that would show a gradual evolution of the human species—homo sapiens—from other more primitive humanlike or hominid species.[2]

Physical scientists speculate that the early hominids' upright posture, bipedal (two-footed) walking ability, and exceptionally large brains were significant features in the evolution of the human species. These features, along with opposable thumbs, permitted early hominid groups to become highly adaptive and creative creatures in a changing environment. Thus one basic feature of human nature is its adaptability to a wide range of environmental situations.

Among most Western societies, human nature is often defined as selfish, self-centered, competitive, and aggressive. The problem with such a definition is that not all human groups evinced such "Western" behaviors. The fact of the matter is that in many primitive societies cooperation and harmony among group members were the major features, not selfishness and competition. For example, the Arapesh of New Guinea, the Ituri pygmies of Central Africa, and the Shoshone Indians of the western United States all exhibited a strong predisposition toward group harmony and cooperation. And the recently discovered Tasaday people of the Philippines do not even have words for hatred and warfare.[3] Thus the belief that human nature is basically self-centered, competitive, and violent seems more characteristic of Western societies' values than of the values of the entire human race. What we can say with certainty as we look at various human groups down through the ages is that human beings are a highly adaptive species with an almost limitless capacity to create.

PRIMITIVE HUMAN GROUPS

Too often people base their views of human nature on the types of behavior that they see around them. If we were to generalize about the human race while focusing only on the human behaviors found in large twentieth-century, technologically oriented metropolises like New York City, London, Paris, and Moscow, we could easily conclude that human beings are indifferent to other people's sufferings, are given to violence, and are highly competitive for their society's scarce goods. But if we are to get a more accurate picture of basic human nature, we must also look at primitive groups. In this section we will focus on the interactions and behaviors of primitive human groups.

In addition to bipedalism, a large brain, and opposable thumbs, two other biological features also played significant roles in the evolution of the human group, namely, year-round mating and a long period of childhood dependency. Mating among most animal species occurs during biologically defined periods when the female is in heat. Even among the great apes like the chimpanzee and the gorilla, mating takes place only when the female is biologically receptive. Among humans, however, sexual mating can occur at any time. This year-round mating ability is responsible for the greater stability of male-female relations and is the basis for a more permanent bond between the sexes.

Along with year-round mating, humans have a significantly long period of childhood dependency. Because a mature human brain cannot pass through a mother's birth canal, humans are born with a prematurely developed brain that continues to develop during the first several years after birth. Consequently, a human infant remains dependent on adult care for a much longer period than do most other animal species. This dependency and the necessity for the mother to remain nearby to nurse the infant curtailed the mobility of early women.

These two features taken together promoted a stable social organization commonly thought of as a family and fostered what has come to be known as the

Perspectives on the Male

"Your aptitude tests indicate that you'd make a good hunter or gatherer."

basis for a divison of labor. Throughout most of history, humans have formed into small social groups based on family or kinship ties; here adult males were chiefly responsible for hunting, and adult females were obligated to childrearing duties and to foraging for fruits and vegetables close to the campsite. The basic hunter-and-gatherer social organization has existed for the greater part of human history; even today, it can be found among the Aranda aborigines of Australia.

Despite this evidence of a basic division of labor between the sexes, there is actually great diversity in the kinds of work that males and females are expected to perform in the vast majority of primitive societies (see Table 4.1). The predominant Western view that biology plays a prominent role in the activities expected of males and females receives little support in a cross-cultural analysis of the divisions of labor in primitive societies. If biology were the sole determinant of male and female roles, we would then expect little if any variation among the groups. But such is not the case.

STRANGE PEOPLES AND EVEN STRANGER ROLES

When we examine various primitive societies, it becomes evident that their male and female roles are exceedingly different from those that we are familiar with in Western society. Probably few studies point out the extreme variations in sex roles more graphically than the field work conducted by anthropologist Margaret Mead. Between 1931 and 1933, Mead conducted an anthropological and sociological study of three primitive groups living in northeastern New Guinea. After

Table 4.1 Division of Labor in 224 Societies by Sex

Activity	Number of societies in which activity is performed by				
	Males always	Males usually	Either sex equally	Females usually	Females always
Pursuing sea mammals	34	1	0	0	0
Hunting	166	13	0	0	0
Trapping small animals	128	13	4	1	2
Herding	38	8	4	0	5
Fishing	98	34	19	3	4
Clearing land for agriculture	73	22	17	5	13
Dairy operations	17	4	3	1	13
Preparing and planting soil	31	23	33	20	37
Erecting and dismantling shelter	14	2	5	6	22
Tending fowl and small animals	21	4	8	1	39
Tending and harvesting crops	10	15	35	39	44
Gathering shellfish	9	4	8	7	35
Making and tending fires	18	6	25	22	62
Bearing burdens	12	6	35	20	57
Preparing drinks and narcotics	20	1	13	8	57
Gathering fruits, berries, nuts	12	3	15	13	63
Gathering fuel	22	1	10	19	89
Preserving meat and fish	8	2	10	14	74
Gathering herbs, roots, and seeds	8	1	11	7	74
Cooking	5	1	9	28	158
Carrying water	7	0	5	7	119
Grinding grain	2	4	5	13	114

Source: G. Murdock, "Comparative Data on the Division of Labor by Sex," *Social Forces,* May, 1937, pp. 551–53.

her field work, Mead wrote the classic *Sex and Temperament*.[4] Therein we read of the gentle Arapesh, the cannibalistic Mundugumor, and the head-hunting Tchambuli.

The mountain-dwelling Arapesh live in the area bounded by the sea to the north and extending back into the coastal mountains and grassy plains to the south. Mead characterized the Arapesh life as "organized . . . in a common adventure that is primarily maternal, cherishing, and oriented away from the self toward the needs of the next generation."[5] Arapesh men and women are best described as cooperative, unassertive, and gentle. Whether caring for the crops or for the children, both sexes work cooperatively for the good of all. Aggressive behaviors and seductive sexual advances are prohibited in Arapesh society. An

Perspectives on the Male

Arapesh male who displays aggressive behavior is ostracized from the group or at least shunned for any such display of "deviant" behavior. Competition in any form brings with it shame and disgust for the participants. In Arapesh society, status and prestige come to those who share and cooperate within their group. Mead best explained the Arapesh in terms that we in the West have come to associate with the feminine role:

> To the Arapesh, the world is a garden that must be tilled, not for one's self, not in pride and boasting, not for hoarding and usury, but that the yams and the dogs and the pigs and most of all the children may grow. From this whole attitude flow many of the other Arapesh traits, the lack of conflict between old and young, the lack of any expectation of jealously or envy, the emphasis upon cooperation. Cooperation is easy when all are whole-heartedly committed to a common project from which no one of the participators will himself benefit. Their dominant conception of men and women may be said to be that of regarding men, even as we regard women, as gently, carefully parental in their aims.[6]

Thus Mead concluded that the traits expected of Arapesh men show them to be caring, cooperative, gentle, kind, loving, nurturant, sharing, and concerned not with self-interest but rather with others' interests. The ideal Arapesh male appears diametrically opposite the ideal we set for males here in the west. Mead's observations of the Arapesh people permit a glimpse of a society built on mutual trust and cooperation. For a people who come closer to our culture's ideal male, we must travel further inland to meet the Mundugumor.

Traveling up the Sepik river, Mead encountered the Mundugumor people, who were known especially for their cannabilistic practices and their fondness of warfare. For the Mundugumor male, life is a constant battle:

> The Mundugumor man-child is born into a hostile world, a world in which most of the members of his own sex will be his enemies, in which his major equipment for success must be a capacity for violence, for seeing and avenging insult, for holding his own safety very lightly and the lives of others even more lightly. From his birth, the stage is set to produce in him this kind of behavior.[7]

Because the Mundugumor mother sees her maternal responsibilities as burdensome, the child quickly learns to fend for itself within the village. The early experiences of neglect and rejection foster a degree of self-reliance that leads to the child's development of the prized traits of competition and aggression. Mundugumor society is filled with prohibitions against any show of tenderness, kindness, or other gentle emotional expressions. The submissive and reticent Mundugumor native is deemed a misfit and shunned by others. Life among the Mundugumors is a trial, and only those most fit—the aggressive and unyielding ones—are viewed with honor and respect.

Mead found in both the Arapesh and the Mundugumor societies a fundamental similarity; males *and* females are both molded toward identical trait patterns. The Mundugumor's emphasis is on a harsh self-centeredness, and the Arapesh's pattern is toward a gentle other-centeredness. Basic sex differences in the personality traits are not encouraged in either group. To find a society in which basic personality differences between the sexes are clearly defined and encouraged, Mead traveled west of the Mundugumor to a people called the Tchambuli.

Living around Lake Aibom, the Tchambuli are a head-hunting society in which the usual sex roles as we know them in Western society are reversed. Tchambuli *women* are responsible for the business of the village. They earn the money used by the family to purchase goods. They are responsible for the farming, fishing, and manufacturing required by the village. When it comes to important events like marriage, the women's approval is necessary. Temperamentally, the Tchambuli women are easygoing and reliable. Generally, an air of affability exists among the women of the village. Tchambuli men are another matter. Men are considered to be the weaker sex. They seem interested only in their own adornment and self-aggrandizing pursuits. Their days are spent in other men's company, where they compare costumes and other body adornments. The men are especially adept at artistic skills. Their relationships among themselves can only be described as catty and suspicious. Around women, Tchambuli men become timid, and they appear in awe of the opposite sex:

> . . . the Tchambuli [man] may be said to live principally for art. Every man is an artist and most men are skilled not in some one art alone, but in many: in dancing, carving, plaiting, and so on. Each man is chiefly concerned with his role upon the stage of his society, with the elaboration of his costume, the beauty of the masks he owns, the skill of his own flute-playing, the finish and *elan* of his ceremonies, and upon other people's recognition and valuation of his performance.[8]

Although Mead's interpretations of the Arapesh's basic "feminine" sex roles, the Mundugumor's "masculine" sex roles, and the Tchambuli's "reversed" sex roles have been criticized as too subjective, we cannot doubt that her field research shows that sex roles vary greatly among cultures. Other anthropologists have found additional primitive societies in which particular features of sex roles vary in extreme ways. For example, anthropologist Mervyn Meggitt studied the Mae Enga and Kuma peoples, two New Guinea highland cultures, and found extreme cultural differences in their attitudes and behaviors toward sexuality.[9] Meggitt found that Mae Enga men shun almost all contact with women, going to such lengths as constructing separate sleeping huts for each sex. Among men, menstrual blood is thought of as a pollutant that causes those males who come in contact with it to become gravely sick. Furthermore, sexual intercourse is considered harmful for the male, who afterwards must retire to a smoke-filled hut to purify himself and to regain his strength. Not surprisingly, among Mae Enga people, all sexual activity is prohibited between unmarried people. On the other hand, Meggitt found the Kuma's sexual attitudes and practices almost the complete opposite of the Mae Enga. Kuma males and females regularly sleep together with no concern over menstrual blood. Kuma males gain honor and status with other males by bragging about sexual conquests and prowess. Kuma girls

Perspectives on the Male

frequently attend festivals where they choose sexual partners from among the married and unmarried males. Meggitt and Mead's research emphasizes that what are considered to be appropriate sex role behaviors by Western society are extremely varied in many non-Western cultures.

MALE DOMINANCE

In general, the unique roles that males and females play vary from one social group to another. However, whether one is looking at the sex roles of modern Western society or at those of some primitive tribe in New Guinea, males appear to play a controlling role over females in many social spheres. Ernestine Friedl, professor of anthropology at Duke University, sees male dominance as a nearly universal cultural feature of the male experience. Friedl even goes so far as to say that "Male dominance is so widespread that it is virtually a human universal; societies in which women are consistently dominant do not exist and have never existed."[10] Assuming that Friedl's assumption is correct, what is it that causes males to dominate females, and what about the current thinking among some feminists that females dominated men in prehistoric times? Let us begin our discussion of male dominance with the latter question, that of the purported period in human history when females dominated males.

MATRIARCHAL RULE: FACT OR FICTION?

Recently, there has emerged a view of human history that is referred to by certain feminists, most notably Elizabeth Gould Davis and Merlin Stone, as the "golden age of matriarch."[11] The basic outline of this historical account is that approximately 8,000 to 10,000 years ago women ruled over a highly advanced civilization. During this age, women ruled with justice, love, and sensitivity. Fertility was controlled by women through natural and harmless methods. Religion centered on the worship of the Great Mother Goddess, and her priestesses glorified the inherent beauties and sensual nature of the female sex. The civilized world was a peaceful and serene place for all inhabitants, females and males alike.

Somehow the harmony of the matriarchal world was disrupted by a small group of discontented and rebellious men who seized power and set out to destroy all evidence of matriarchy. First of all, men prevented women from using contraception and thus forced women into an oppression brought on by continuous pregnancy. The religion of the Great Mother Goddess was replaced by the worship of a stern and unforgiving father figure who allowed only males to worship in the temples. No longer were love, peace, and harmony dominant themes in human relations but rather warfare, conflict, and aggression. Down through the ages, historians—another role males usurped for themselves—purposely rewrote the historical records to exclude any mention of that time when women ruled the civilized world. The only vestige of this peaceful period in human history can be found in certain mythical legends.

Even though most feminist and nonfeminist anthropologists discount the evidence of a golden age of matriarchy based solely on legend and a few artifacts of female religious figures found in certain ancient ruins,[12] Rohrlich-Leavitt suggests that Minoan Crete "women participated at least equally with men in political decision making, while in religion and social life they were supreme."[13] However, we should be skeptical of Rohrlich-Leavitt's claim about Minoan Crete's matriarchal social structures because her evidence can be interpreted to mean that Minoan Crete society was an egalitarian society at best, if not basically a patriarchal society. In the words of anthropologists Michelle Rosaldo and Louise Lamphere,

> Whereas some anthropologists argue that there are, or have been, truly egalitarian societies . . . and all agree that there are societies in which women have achieved considerable social recognition and power, none has observed a society in which women have publicly recognized power and authority surpassing that of men.[14]

Part of the problem concerning the questionable existence of a matriarchal society lies in the confusion between matriarchy and matrilineality. *Matrilineality* refers to the descent system based on the ancestral line's being reckoned through the female's side of the family rather than through the male's, whereas *matriarchy* refers to a society ruled by females. Several American Indian nations were matrilineal, the most notable being the Choctaw, Creek, Iroquois, and Hopi. For example, a Hopi male typically moved in with his wife's family. The older woman and her husband, her daughters and their husbands, and the unmarried sons made up the average Hopi family unit. The Hopi had an interesting way of settling a family dispute. If for some reason a Hopi woman became disenchanted with her husband, all she needed to do was to put his belongings outside of the dwelling and the marriage was dissolved. The same privilege did not extend to the husband. In Hopi society, the female had a great deal of power within the *domestic* sphere, but in the ceremonial, religious, and political spheres, the Hopi male retained control.

The Iroquois nation is often mentioned as a society in which the female had considerable political power over the male. And in some ways the Iroquois women were exceptional when compared to most other women in terms of social and political status. The basis of Iroquois women's power centered on their being able to elect the men who served on the nation's governing council. By influencing the election, the women indirectly had a voice in the decisions of tribal importance. However, the women themselves were not permitted to sit on the council, and once elected the men could dismiss much of their female backers' advice. Thus the Iroquois nation was definitely not a matriarchal society.[15]

At the present time, there is no conclusive anthropological evidence to show that a matriarchy once existed in the Western world.

Women in a male-dominated society. *Source: FAO photo by P. A. Pittet.*

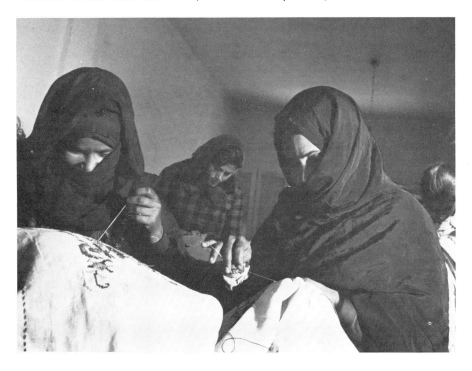

EXPLANATIONS FOR MALE DOMINANCE

Over the past several years, anthropologists have focused much of their attention on the issue of male dominance. Why have males for so long and in virtually every society dominated the political and economic spheres, for the most part leaving women to dominate the domestic sphere? There are several explanations for this state of affairs, four of which we will consider in this section. The first is the Judeo-Christian explanation of divine origin, one given little credence by social scientists but one that holds considerable sway in many people's minds. The other three explanations for male dominance are the center of much controversy among different scientific perspectives; these include the genetic, the socioeconomic, and the psychological.

Judeo-Christian Explanation for Male Dominance Genesis describes how human creation took place. According to Genesis, Yahweh, the God of Moses and the Jewish people, formed the first man (called Adam) from the earth's slime. In time, God saw that Adam was lonely. God then created the woman Eve out of Adam's rib to be his companion. They were childlike in their pastoral Eden until one fateful day when Eve, the more gullible of the two, believed a serpentine promise of supernatural knowledge if she would eat of the forbidden fruit. Eve lured Adam into sharing the fruit with her. Later, God saw the shame of sin on each of His creations and cast them out into the world's travail. To impress woman of the depth of her luring sinfulness, He sealed woman's subordinate fate with these words: "You shall bear children in intense pain and suffering; yet even so, you shall welcome your husband's affections, and *he shall be your master*"[16] (italics added).

For those for whom a literal reading of the Bible is the basis for "the way things are," this biblical command is sufficient explanation for male dominance. For many males and females alike, especially in the current resurgence of fundamentalism, male domination has been God's way ever since that day when Eve led Adam into a land of toil and tears.

The Biological Explanation for Male Dominance During the 1960s, a number of books that promulgated the idea of a biological basis for various human behaviors became quite popular among educated laypeople. For example, in *On Aggression,* Nobel-prize laureate, Konrad Lorenz wrote that aggressive behavior was a positive "life-preserving" feature rather than a "diabolical" or "destructive" human activity. Zoologist Desmond Morris wrote in *The Naked Ape* of how contemporary human relations could be explained in terms of our evolutionary link with the great hairy apes. In *The Territorial Imperative,* playwright-turned-historian Robert Ardrey, compared the human inclination to defend property and possession to that of a dog's tenacious defense of a meatclad bone. Each of these authors stirred controversy with his particular brand of biologically based explanation of human behavior. But none caused the furor that Lionel Tiger, an anthropologist from Rutgers University, created with his book *Men in Groups.*

In *Men in Groups,* Tiger dealt with two issues. First, he hypothesized that certain cultural and social features are more simply explained in biological terms. Second, he was convinced of a biological predisposition among human groups to establish exclusive all-male groups. Tiger speculated that the inclination to form all-male groups, a feature he called *male bonding,* has "underlying biological . . . roots in human evolutionary history." According to Tiger, male bonding led inevitably to an inequality between the sexes and the eventual exclusion of women from the sources of power within the group:

> Males dominate females in occupational and political spheres. This is a species-specific pattern and is associated with my other proposition: that males bond in a variety of situations involving power, force, crucial or dangerous work, and relations with their gods. They consciously and emotionally exclude females from these bonds. The significant notion here is that those various different expressions of male dominance and male bonding in different communities are what one would expect from a species highly adaptable to its physical and social environments. . . .[17]

Tiger's idea of a male bond has been criticized on several counts, not the least of which was Tiger's tendency to report on only those societies with highly visible male organizations, while excluding others with well-established female groups. Tiger's secondary task of demonstrating the biological basis for a male bond

Perspectives on the Male

proved overly ambitious for the available ethnographic data. Even so, Tiger's primary task of grounding specific social and cultural behaviors within a biological framework has become the basis for the new hybrid science of sociobiology. Let us move from the questionable male bond principle to the sociobiologists' belief in a genetic foundation for male dominance.

Sociobiology rests on the basic belief that biological principles can be applied advantageously to the social sciences and their subject matter. Just how the sociobiologist accomplishes this goal is quite simple. He or she first identifies a cultural pattern found in most societies (for example, male dominance) and then examines this social feature with an eye to how it enhances human survival. If the feature appears to enhance the odds of the species' survival, then the sociobiologist hypothesizes a genetic basis for it and develops ways to test the hypothesis.

Incest provides a good example of how the sociobiologist sets out to prove a link between a cultural pattern and a biological element such as the genes. *Incest* (that is, sexual intercourse between close family members such as father and daughter, mother and son, or brother and sister) is prohibited in most societies. The survival-enhancing feature of this cultural prohibition is well known. Specifically, children born of incestuous relationships are more likely to carry defective or mutant genes that predispose them to various forms of mental retardation and physical afflictions and even to premature death. Consequently, such children are less likely to develop normally and later on to mate successfully, thus preventing their genes from being passed on to the next generation. On the other hand, children born of a nonincestuous relationship are more likely to succeed in passing along their genes because of fewer mental and physical problems. Hence sociobiologists argue that people with a genetic predisposition *against* incest are more likely to pass their genes to subsequent generations.

To test the hypothesized predisposition against incestuous relationships, sociobiologists point to the marital arrangements found in an Israeli kibbutz. Beginning in the late 1940s and 1950s, the kibbutz was a social experiment in collective living where all of the inhabitants would be free of traditional social and sex roles found in most other social groups.[18] The children in a kibbutz are raised in extremely closeknit, mixed-sexed groups. What can only be called a strong family spirit pervades each children's group. When the children grow up, marriage between a twosome from the same kibbutz is unheard of even though no social prohibition exists against such a marriage. The sociobiologist argues from such naturally acquired data that people must have a built-in aversion to mating with someone with whom they have a close familylike relationship.

Edward Wilson, a proponent of the sociobiological perspective, argues that male dominance can be explained as an extreme social pattern that developed out of the basic division of labor found among primitive hunter-gatherer societies. First of all, early groups who divided the work of subsistence between males who ranged far from the camp for game and females who stayed close to camp to gather vegetation and care for the young provided an optimal social arrangement for the group's survival. Over time, these early genetically based social patterns became even more rigidly fixed by tradition and custom. As groups grew larger and more elaborate in their political, economic, and social patterns, the male's preeminence in external affairs (away from the camp) transferred to other areas, including those relating to women's lives. In Wilson's words,

> When societies grow still larger and more complex, women tend to be reduced in influence outside the home, and to be more constrained by custom, ritual, and formal law. As hypertrophy [extreme development of a preexisting social structure; in this case, male domination over external affairs] proceeds further, they can be turned literally into chattel, to be sold and traded, fought over, and ruled under a double morality. History has seen a few striking local reversals, but the great majority of societies have evolved toward sexual domination as though sliding along a ratchet.[19]

The Socioeconomic Explanation for Male Dominance Some anthropologists believe that male dominance is an outcome of certain social and/or economic forces rather than a survival-enhancing, genetic arrangement. For example, Marvin Harris argues that warfare and infanticide have occurred throughout human history because people are driven toward these actions by social pressures and/or economic scarcity.[20] Specifically, Harris links male dominance, or what he calls male supremacy, with the institution of warfare; he believes that warfare has been the major social institution that societies have used down through the ages to control population and preserve natural resources:

> The practice of warfare is responsible for a widespread complex of male supremacist institutions among band and village societies. The existence of this complex is a source of embarrassment and confusion to advocates of women's rights. Many women fear that if male supremacy has been in existence for so long, then perhaps it really is "natural" for men to dominate women. But this fear is groundless. Male supremacist institutions arose as a by-product of warfare, of the male monopoly over weapons, and of the use of sex for the nurturance of aggressive male personalities. And warfare, as I have already shown, is not the expression of human nature, but a response to reproductive and ecological pressures. Therefore, male supremacy is no more natural than warfare.[21]

For Harris, then, male dominance developed as a primitive human response to certain life-threatening social and environmental conditions. Harris's view is more optimistic than those presented by the sociobiologists in that he allows for the possibility of an egalitarian relationship between the sexes given the absence of certain negative social and economic conditions.

Not all anthropologists who favor a socioeconomic explanation are willing to grant that male dominance stems from such a brutal history. Ernestine Friedl provides a more benign view of the causal basis of male dominance. She thinks that the primitive male's physique and strength lent themselves to the role of roving hunter of large game and the female's maternal and nursing capabilities restricted her more or less to a fixed campsite. Beyond these basic physical sex differences, two specific socioeconomic features played a significant part in the male's influence and status in the early family group. First, on the far-ranging hunts, males made contact with other human groups. Over time, these chance encounters grew into formal meetings where bartering scarce items such as flint rocks could take place. Control over the traded goods and the intermediary function between the family and other groups provided the male with new power. Second, the hunter had control over the distribution of the meat brought back from the hunt. Meat was a desirable addition to a diet of nuts, berries, and other natural foods. The one who dispensed meat gained definite status in the early human groups. Friedl takes note of these two features of the early male role and suggests that they led to a social pattern of male dominance:

> Patriarchies are prevalent, and they appear to be strongest in societies in which men control significant goods that are exchanged with people outside the family. . . . The greater the male monopoly on the distribution of scarce items, the stronger their control of women seems to be. . . . The source of male power among hunter-gatherers lies in their control of a scarce, hard to acquire, but necessary nutrient—animal protein.[22]

Studies of a number of primitive societies have shown that, even though meat made up a little more than a quarter of the group's diet, the person who brought in and distributed meat from the hunt was cast in a superior role within the group.[23] Other researchers have found a pattern of socialization among primitive societies that supports Friedl's thesis. In societies where the group's economy is supported primarily on the male's superior strength and stamina, the sex roles emphasize large sex differences that in most cases lead males to dominate females.[24]

Psychological Explanations for Male Dominance Psychiatrists and psychologists have long studied male dominance, and several have developed intriguing theories that suggest various psychological mechanisms to explain the basis for male dominance. We will focus here on three psychological explanations, namely, envy of women's creative power, fear and dread of women, and avoidance of feminine identification.

Sigmund Freud, the founder of psychoanalysis, proposed that males were superior to women by virtue of having a penis. Furthermore, Freud contended that the male personality was more fully developed and, consequently, that the male was the more creative of the two sexes.[25] But not all who followed Freud believed in the natural superiority of males or in their inherent creative powers. For example, Karen Horney, a psychoanalyst herself, rejected Freud's biological determinism and suggested that females were the more creative members of the species, especially when one takes into account the ultimate creative act of human birth:

> At this point I, as a woman, ask in amazement, and what about motherhood? And the blissful consciousness of bearing a new life within oneself? And the ineffable happiness of the increasing expectation of the appearance of this new being? And the joy when it finally makes its appearance and one holds it for the first time in one's arms? And the deep pleasurable feeling of satisfaction in suckling it and the happiness of the whole period when the infant needs her care?[26]

But is there any evidence that males envy this naturally creative potential that women possess? Bruno Bettelheim thinks there is because of the existence of certain highly formalized male rituals in some primitive tribes.[27] Especially noteworthy are the practices of couvade and subincision. *Couvade* is a social ritual whereby a male whose wife is about to give birth is suddenly stricken with abdominal pains and is rushed to a specially prepared hut where a mock delivery occurs. After the mother's actual delivery, the newborn is taken to the father's hut where the baby becomes party to yet another birthing process, this time the ritualized one of the father. Bettelheim contends that couvade is a symbolic way for males to invest themselves with the creative power of the female. Another ritual that has feminine overtones is *subincision*. Generally, the practice of subincision is carried out in the context of puberty rites when a young man passes into adulthood. The practice involves slitting the underside of the male's penis, thus creating an opening similar to a vagina. The blood from the incision is treated as the symbolic equivalent of the first menstrual blood.

In many cultures, women have been portrayed as evil, sinister, and a force to be dreaded.[28] Some psychologists, Karen Horney among them,[29] have suggested dread of women as a plausible explanation for male dominance. Yolanda and Robert Murphy studied the Mundurucú people and found some striking evidence supporting just such a contention.[30]

The Mundurucú are a forest-dwelling people who live near the upper Tapajós region of north central Brazil. Mundurucú men and women live most of their lives apart from each other. Not only do the sexes work in separate groups, they live in separate houses. Women work together doing chores around the village, while men spend much of their time hunting. The extreme sex division is justified because men believe themselves superior to women. Blatant male supremacy is a ritualized part of Mundurucú society.

However, on the basis of their analysis of the folklore surrounding ancient Mundurucú male-female relations, the Murphys reported a mythlike quality about the Mundurucú practices of male supremacy. The folklore relates that the Mundurucú women once dominated the men. To account for this female domination, the women supposedly had acquired the men's magical, sacred flutes (possibly a lightly veiled symbol of the male penis) and this caused the men to subordinate themselves to the women. The men were subjected to a constant series of demeaning chores around the village, and they were made into sex objects for women's sexual gratification. The men's lives of drudgery, servitude, and sexual abuse lasted until the men stole back the sacred flutes and safely hid them in their segregated houses. The moral of the story is abundantly clear, at least to Mundurucú men: Unless women are kept subordinate, they may once again steal the sacred flutes and subjugate men. Thus the Mundurucú patriarchal social order, according to the Murphys' analysis, sits atop a precarious series of psychological defense mechanisms that help to allay the Mundurucú male's basic fear of women.

Perspectives on the Male

A third psychological explanation for male dominance is the avoidance of feminine identification. The theory states that because the mother is the primary model for the infant son in most cultures, he is likely to develop a feminine identity (that is, to perceive himself as a girl rather than as a boy) as he grows older unless he does something to counteract this feminine identity. What he does, according to this theory, is to subjugate and control those very people with whom he identified as a little boy—women. As Nancy Chodorow sees it,

> A boy, in his attempt to gain an elusive masculine identification, often comes to define his masculinity largely in negative terms, as that which is not feminine or involved with women. There is an internal and external aspect to this. Internally, the boy tries to reject his mother and deny his attachment to her and the strong dependency on her that he still feels. He also tries to deny the deep personal identification with her that has developed during his early years. He does this by repressing whatever he takes to be feminine inside himself, and, importantly, by denigrating whatever he considers to be feminine in the outside world.[31]

The anthropological evidence for the avoidance of a feminine identity is slim but interesting. In those primitive societies where little boys' identification with their mothers is strongest and strong attachments are presumably formed between mothers and sons, severe and painful initiation rites involving genital operations are more common than in those societies where little mother-son identification takes place.[32] The idea here is that boys who identify with their mothers need some form of "shock treatment" in the guise of a painful pubertal rite to counteract their unconscious feminine identity. In these societies, male dominance is an additional way in which males can support their "fragile" masculine identity.

Putting Male Dominance in Perspective Several interesting features run through the foregoing psychological explanations for male dominance. Women, in the final analysis, are to blame for their own domination. If women were not so creative, fear-provoking, dreadful, or easy to identify with, men would not have a psychological need to dominate them. In a sense, the psychological perspectives are little better than the divine-origin explanation that squarely lays the blame for male domination on Eve's shoulders. We should also question the notion of a psychological need for male dominance. The assumption of an unseen or unconscious psychological need is in many ways similar to suggesting that male dominance originally was a biological feature that allowed all humans to better adapt or survive in a hostile environment. Thus the psychological explanations for male dominance suffer from many of the same flaws that undercut the divine-origin and the biological explanations.

The socioeconomic view appears to offer a much better explanation of male dominance in that it suggests that male power developed out of social and economic conditions. Once the advantages and privileges of power became known, men continued to ritualize their dominant status in other cultural ways. Few would deny that having power over others feels good. Perhaps the best explanations for the practices of male dominance is simply this: Long ago men discovered that dominating women won them all kinds of privileges that were too good to give up.

ARE THERE MORE THAN TWO SEX ROLES?

Throughout this chapter, we have noted the variety of sex roles that females and males have played in various primitive cultures. Not surprisingly, these sex roles have fallen into one of two categories normally built around the different activities expected and prescribed for each sex. The fact is that in the majority of societies we find only two sex roles, two formalized patterns of behavior that males or females supposedly fit by virtue of talent, temperament, and sex. But what about the possibility of more than two sex roles? Might there be other socially prescribed categories that a person could adopt? There are a few societies that allow a person to live her or his life in a way that is considerably different from the ways in which the majority of females and males live. Before we discuss these societies, we want to describe two situations that emphasize the changeable quality of sex roles as some see them. Unlike most groups in Western society, some groups view a person's sex role as something that can be changed if the situation warrants it.

Imagine a couple growing old with several daughters and no sons. Because of his age and limited strength and stamina, the father is having great difficulty feeding his family with the little he brings back from the hunt. The daughters stay home to learn the ways of women and to wait for the young men who will take them in marriage. The couple's future appears bleak with no son to help them in their declining years. Then the couple decides to take drastic action. Their youngest daughter, a mere child, is dressed like a boy. The father teaches "him" how to make arrowheads and how to shoot a bow. The "boy" accompanies the father on the hunt and learns the ways of the forest. The "boy" is given a pouch that contains the dried ovaries of a bear. This is considered powerful medicine that will prevent the "boy" from becoming pregnant. The couple is happy now for they have a strong son who will provide for them in the future and the village has another fine male hunter.

Imagine yet another village in which a couple worries about their youngest son. The boy acts differently from the other boys his age. He does not play the games that other boys play. The boy spends most of his days in the company of the village's young girls. His parents are gravely concerned about what kind of man their son will grow up to be. To settle their minds, they decide to test their son. They build an enclosure and one day they place their son in it. In the enclosure they also place a bow and arrow and some weaving materials in a wooden box. Next they set fire to the enclosure. Nervously, they await their son's escape; they are especially curious about what he may be clutching as he runs from the flames. After several anxious moments, their son bolts out of the fiery pen holding the weaving materials. Now the parents understand and accept the way their son is to be. He is to become another woman of the village.

These accounts are not fanciful stories but prescribed ways in which some American Indian tribes dealt with what they considered a changeable aspect of human life.[33] For several Indian tribes, sex roles were not a biological given but rather a creation of sociocultural conditions and thus subject to change over time. Therefore, it was not uncommon among some American Indian tribes for a young person of one sex, usually a male, to take on the role prescribed for the opposite sex. Some other tribes had additional categories of sex roles that were neither male nor female. The berdache is the best example of such a special sex role.

THE BERDACHE

The Crow Indians looked upon the *berdache* as a special human being in that he was viewed as neither a male nor a female. The Crow Indians, as well as certain other native American groups, did not categorize sex roles into two mutually exclusive groups. The berdache was a biological male who simply chose not to follow the ideal Crow male role of warrior. The berdache suffered neither shame nor scorn for his role.[34] We should not confuse the berdache with a homosexual as did many early non-Indian writers.[35] Some berdaches chose to live with men, but others did not. A Crow warrior who took a berdache for a wife suffered neither scorn nor ridicule from other males of the tribe.

One of the most colorful portrayals of a berdache is presented in Thomas Berger's novel *Little Big Man*.[36] Berger gives a graphic description of a berdache called Little Horse, who comfortably interacted with both males and females of the tribe. Choosing not to be a warrior and to live up to the warrior ideal, Little Horse took on the attire and many of the mannerisms of a female, but even so he was not considered a female.

THE NADLE

Anthropologist Michael Olien reported on two other Indian tribes, the Navajo and the Mohave, that allowed for very special sex roles.[37] When a Navajo infant was born with ambiguous genitals, the child was assigned the role of a *nadle*. In addition to those assigned this role at birth, the Navajos allowed others to assume the role later on. The nadle was treated with extreme deference. When engaged in women's work, the nadle dressed as a woman; when involved with men, the nadle appeared as a man. The only activities denied the nadle were hunting and warfare. The nadle was allowed to intervene in delicate tribal problems such as marital disputes and to choose either a male or female sexual partner.

A Crow Indian berdache.   *Source: The Museum of the American Indian, Heye Foundation, #34256.*

THE ALYHA AND THE HWAME

The Mohave Indians of the Far West recognized four distinct sex roles: the traditional male and female roles and the alyha and the hwame. A male who chose to live as a woman was called an *alyha*. The male-turned-female underwent a special initiating ceremony that conferred the alyha status. From that time onward, the individual was treated as a woman. The alyha dressed as a woman, worked with women, and even mimicked a woman's menstrual flow by cutting the upper thigh. When the alyha married a man (and again this carried no shame), the alyha performed all of the duties expected of a wife. After a suitable period, the alyha would get pregnant and prepare for the birth of a child. Near the end of the pregnancy, the alyha would drink a strong potion that would cause cramps associated with the beginnings of the birth process. The baby born to an alyha was always stillborn and would have to be buried immediately by the mother as was customary among the Mohave people. In this way, the alyha mother saved face with her husband and the tribe. After the burial and a suitable period of grief, the alyha resumed her normal wifely duties.

It was also possible for a Mohave female to become a male. As with the Mohave male-turned-alyha, the female who wished to become a male was ceremoniously ushered into a special role known as a *hwame*. The hwame dressed and acted in every way expected of a man. The hwame was prevented from only two activities, going into battle and assuming a leadership role within the tribal structure. As for marriage, the hwame married a female and set up residence much like other Mohave males.

It is important to emphasize that the hwame, the alyha, the nadle, and the berdache were not considered deviant or abnormal by their own tribe's standards. Each had chosen a role that was different from that of the majority, but he or she was not stigmatized for assuming that role.

COMMENTING ON THE ANTHROPOLOGICAL PERSPECTIVE

In this chapter we suggested that sex roles are not inflexible and immutable behavior patterns prescribed among rigid biological lines. In fact, we found that the specific behaviors and roles prescribed for each sex vary greatly from one culture to another. We did note, however, that the basic division of labor in most early primitive societies appeared to develop along certain general biological lines; for example, men generally were responsible for hunting large game, and women were primarily in charge of childrearing activities. One feature that appeared to be nearly universal among various cultures was male dominance over females, although in most primitive cultures, men did not dominate women in every sphere. For the most part, women exerted considerable influence and power in domestic areas, and there are examples in a few cultures where women's influence extended into political and economic areas as well. Finally, we examined several exceptions to the prevalent dualistic nature of sex roles. We found that a few American Indian tribes permitted their members to take on other than the normally defined traditional male and female sex roles.

What can we learn from the anthropological perspective on the male experience? One striking feature that should be apparent is that the male role in Western society in the latter part of the twentieth century is unique to our own society and its history. Other non-Western societies define the male experience in quite different ways. To say that ours is the ultimate or best way would be foolish. For the thousands and thousands of years that humans have lived in groups, the male and female roles have changed because social situations and pressures warranted change. In our contemporary society, where brute strength has been superceded by machines and where meat does not come from a dangerous hunt but from the local supermarket, it is ridiculous to hang onto the view that the male role must emphasize certain biological features that have little meaning other than to keep the sexes separate. The anthropological perspective presents us with the valuable insight that the contemporary Western male role is not universal and that change is an inevitable part of cultural features.

SUGGESTED READINGS

Harris, M. *Cannibals and Kings*. New York: Random House, 1977.
Martin, M., and Voorhies, B. *Female of the Species*. New York: Columbia University Press, 1975.
Mead, M. *Sex and Temperament*. New York: Morrow, 1935/1963.
Rosaldo, M., and Lamphere, L., eds. *Woman, Culture, and Society*. Stanford, Calif.: Stanford University Press, 1974.

5

Of parent, peer, and other influences:
THE SOCIOLOGICAL PERSPECTIVE

. . . it is by no means obvious that attempts to foster sex-typed behavior (as traditionally defined) in boys and girls serve to make them better men and women. Indeed, in some spheres of adult life such attempts appear to be positively handicapping. We suggest that societies have the option of minimizing, rather than maximizing, sex differences through their socialization practices.

Eleanor Maccoby and Carol Jacklin[1]

The previous chapter focused on the profound influence that culture has on the definition of sex roles. This chapter centers on the impact that specific groups and social institutions *within* a culture have on a person's definition of his or her appropriate sex role. We will begin our discussion by examining the process of socialization whereby a male learns the ways to be a man in his particular group or society. Next we will take a close look at several socializing agents (the family, the media, the educational system, and the peer group) that help to form a young male's definition of manliness and masculinity. Finally, we will discuss the social problem of sexism and its impact on our society.

The sociological perspective offers several insights into the male experience with its focus on the important shaping influences that groups have on the individual. No matter if the group is impersonal and large like the media or educational system or personal and small like a family or peer group, the male experience is directly affected and molded along certain lines by these socializing forces. Whereas the anthropologist draws attention to the often strange and novel ways men act in other cultures, the sociologist studies the social influences on males in their own society. In many respects, the research of the anthropologist and the sociologist complement each other because both pay attention to the social forces that fashion sex roles.

SOCIALIZATION AND THE MALE SEX ROLE

A human infant at the moment of birth is a totally dependent and helpless creature. Born with a few reflexes like sucking and orienting its head, the newborn could not survive for more than a few hours without the assistance of other people. In contrast, the young of most animal species are born with innate and complex behavior patterns called *instincts* that allow the animal to adjust quickly to its environment. Humans, on the other hand, are born ignorant of the ways of their environment. The primary means that a helpless and dependent human infant has to acquire the necessary skills and talents to adapt effectively to its environment is socialization. Socialization is the process by which humans, beginning in infancy and extending throughout life, learn the ways of their group.

Societies have their own distinctive features, including certain behaviors, traditions, values, and beliefs. By means of the socialization process, these features are passed from one generation to another. For example, in our society, children learn to eat with forks, knives, and spoons; in Japan, children learn to eat with chopsticks. We are not only taught what utensils to eat with but also other, more complex behaviors such as how we should interact with others. For example, in social interactions, Arabs stand much closer together in conversation, touch more often, and lean toward each other more than Americans do. Socialization even accounts for the values that a particular society espouses. For example, children in the United States are taught to share primarily with members of their immediate family; children in an Israeli kibbutz learn to share with many other people outside of the immediate family. Socialization accounts for a variety of behaviors and values that distinguish one society from another.

Learning skills such as dressing, eating with utensils, and toileting are important tasks for every young child, but one of the most important goals of socialization is teaching the young their appropriate sex role. Society has a vested interest in teaching its members sex-appropriate behaviors. For example, a social institution such as the family depends for its continuance on a little boy's growing up and taking on the role of the father and on a little girl's learning the role of the mother.

The way in which children learn their sex role and its appropriate behaviors is a complex task. Learning that males are supposed to act in a self-reliant, aggressive, and unemotional fashion—all important elements in the traditional male sex role—is much more difficult than, say, learning to eat with a fork rather than with the fingers. The socialization of the male sex role is accomplished primarily because so many separate socializing agents take part in the learning process.

THE SOCIALIZING AGENTS

In this section we will examine the way in which the socialization process molds the young male into what his society deems essential for manhood. We will concentrate on those socializing agents that have the greatest impact on the young boy: his parents, the mass media, the educational system, and his peers. Although we will concentrate on the early years of the male's socialization process, we should not forget that this process continues throughout his life.The male is continually being socialized to adapt to age-related expectations and demands such as marriage and paid employment.

THE PARENTS (BUT, DEAR, WE MEANT WELL!)

The sociology of the family is undergoing a reexamination of its past, present, and future.[2] Topics such as the feminist movement, varying sexual patterns, new family structures, changing sex roles, and inherent role conflicts within the traditional family unit are being examined in countless sociology courses around the country, some of which are utilizing innovative teaching materials.[3] In this section we will examine how parental expectations and treatments affect both sexes, especially the male.

Even before a child is born, society's values influence couples who plan on having children. In countless ways, males are more valued in our society than are females. For example, a majority of couples when questioned answered that they wished their first-born child to be a male.[4] Before social security and company pension plans, having males rather than females may have provided parents with an economic hedge against their old age. But today, preferring a male over a female seems at least an anachronism if not a foreboding of possible future problems. Amitai Etziona, a highly respected social scientist at Columbia University, pointed to this problem when he noted that with the expanding field of prenatal technology, the day is fast approaching when parents will be able to select their child's sex, and if males are still preferred, we will run the risk of males outnumbering females.[5] One can hope that before the day of "select-a-sex," society will have progressed beyond its biased favoritism of one sex over the other.

In general, parents have a different set of expectations for each sex.[6] The sex-linked expectations can be seen even before birth. For example, many pregnant women remark that they must be carrying a boy because of their fetus's excessive movements. Why a boy and not a girl? These women are simply expressing what is commonly accepted by many adults, that boys are more active and energetic and girls are more gentle and sedentary even *in utero*.

Aside from the expectant parents' frequent references to the probable sex of the growing fetus, the socialization process begins in earnest at birth. Others besides the parents are quick to differentiate between the sexes. After a quick check of the genitals, the attending doctor and nurses often describe a male newborn as robust and strapping and a female as petite and adorable. Even in the delivery room, society views the sexes in very different ways. It is not surprising, then, that parents follow suit and view their newborn infant as robust or adorable.

In a classical study conducted by Rubin, Provenzano, and Luria, parents were asked to describe their newborn infant on the day of its birth. The fathers were interviewed after each had observed his infant in the nursery, and the mothers were interviewed later on the same day after each had handled and fed her infant. Furthermore, the parents were asked to rate their infant on an eighteen-item bipolar scale containing items such as *active* versus *passive, strong* versus *weak,* and *noisy* versus *quiet.* Parents of male infants tended to describe their sons as "firmer, larger, better coordinated, more alert, stronger, and hardier."[7] Parents of females described their daughters as softer, smaller, prettier, and more delicate. Fathers were more likely to describe their infants of either sex in more extreme ways than were mothers. Surprising in light of the different physical descriptions given by the parents was the fact that the infants of both sexes were not appreciably different in their average heights, weights, and Apgar scores, which are ratings of color, muscle tonicity, reflex irritability, and heart and respiratory rates assigned by the attending physician within ten minutes of birth.

Obviously, parents do more than just attribute one set of characteristics to one sex and another to the opposite sex. Parents also encourage sex-typed activities. For example, when a group of mothers were told that they were playing with a nine-month-old male, they offered "him" a toy train to play with. When a different group of mothers played with the same infant, this time identified as female, these mothers offered "her" a doll.[8] In the minds of these mothers, it seems, little boys should enjoy trains more than dolls.

It is clear that if little boys are to grow up to be "real men," they need more than toy trains to play with. Little boys need to learn certain male-appropriate behaviors. But how do parents teach their sons to act differently from girls? At least part of the answer is provided by the findings of a longitudinal study conducted by Susan Goldberg and Michael Lewis.[9] Goldberg and Lewis observed thirty-two males and thirty-two females and their mothers in free-play activities and a frustration-producing situation. At thirteen months of age, the girls were found to be more dependent on their mothers, clung to them more, showed less exploratory behaviors, and displayed a quiet play style. The boys, on the other hand, showed considerable independence of their mothers, were more vigorous and exploratory, and displayed frequent gross motor activities such as jumping, banging on objects, and running around the play room. To produce frustration in the children, the researchers placed a barrier between the child and his or her mother. In this situation, girls generally stood at the barrier and cried for their mothers, and most of the boys tried to get around the barrier. In both the play and the frustration settings, the children showed striking sex differences in their behaviors.

When Goldberg and Lewis examined these sex differences, they found a link between the behaviors of the thirteen-month-old children with different mother-child interactions when the children were six months old. In general, the mothers of females touched, talked with, and handled their daughters significantly more than the mothers of the males did. Therefore, Goldberg and Lewis concluded that the early differential interaction accounted for a part of the children's later behaviors.

Parents also create different environments for each sex. In a study of pre-schoolers' bedrooms, Rheingold and Cook found obvious differences in the decor and the toys provided for males and females.[10] Boys' rooms were more likely to be furnished in a "masculine" motif with sports' equipment, trucks, and military paraphernalia. Girls' bedrooms showed a preference for a "feminine" decor with dolls and domestic materials very much in evidence.

In the research cited thus far, we see that parents generally attribute different characteristics, present different sex-typed activities, interact differently, and create different environments for each sex. What do parents wish to accomplish with these different parenting practices? They obviously want their sons to become men and their daughters to become women. But is there a single feature that parents expect more of in their male children and less of in their female? Apparently, yes; the much sought feature appears to be independence.[11] A young boy must be taught to be independent or self-reliant if he is to become a real man in our society. Of course, parents want both their sons *and* daughters to be independent, but independence in the male is considered more important, a *primary* requisite for manhood. Some of the research in differential parenting practices points out that parents strive to push their sons toward independence more than they do their daughters.

Recall that in Goldberg and Lewis' research, thirteen-month-old boys clung less to their mothers and explored more (both early examples of independence) than similarly aged girls did. This sex difference was found to relate to the boys' mothers' withholding contact or touch at an earlier age. In another study, a group of mothers were asked at what age they would allow their child to use a pair of scissors unsupervised and when their child could play away from home without them.[12] Mothers of boys gave much earlier ages for both activities than did mothers of girls. Furthermore, in a study conducted in Canada, parents of boys reported that they would be less likely to offer comfort to their son if he complained of a minor injury than they would if their daughter so complained.[13]

Granted that withholding contact and comfort and allowing a child to play unattended encourage a type of independence, the single most powerful determinant of independence appears to be the type of punishment used to teach desired behaviors in a child's early years. One can punish a child in a variety of ways. Here, again, parents use different types of punishment for each sex. Lenore Weitzman, a sociologist at the University of California at Davis, points out that

> Boys are subjected to more physical punishment, whereas psychological punishments, such as the threat of withdrawal of love, are more frequently used for girls. *Children trained with physical punishment have been shown typically to be more self-reliant and independent.* The other method of childtraining—the love-oriented or psychological method—usually produces children who are more obedient and dependent. As girls are most often trained with psychological methods they are exposed to more affection and less punishment than boys.[14] (Italics added.)

If, as Weitzman suggests, physical punishment is more likely to create a sense of independence—a "desired" goal for the young male—it seems only reasonable to ask if physical punishment may produce some undesirable traits as well. In an analysis of the male sex role, Ruth Hartley suggests along with Weitzman that boys are subjected to more physical punishment than are girls but adds that physical punishment brings on some negative consequences, not the least of which are bouts of anxiety:

> . . .more stringent demands are made on boys than on girls and at an early age, when they are least able to understand either the reasons for or the nature of the demands. Moreover, these demands are frequently enforced harshly, impressing the small boy with the danger of deviation from them, while he does not quite understand what they are.To make matters more difficult, the desired behavior is rarely defined positively as something the child *should* do, but rather, undesirable behavior is indicated negatively as something he should *not* do or be—anything, that is, that the parent or other people regard as "sissy." Thus, very early in life the boy must either stumble on the right path or bear repeated punishment without warning when he accidently enters into the wrong ones. This situation gives us practically a perfect combination for inducing anxiety—the demand that the child do something which is not clearly defined to him, based on reasons he cannot possibly appreciate, and enforced with threats, punishments, and anger by those who are close to him.[15]

Much of the research cited so far has focused on the mother-child relationship. But in the past decade or so, there has been a growing interest in the father-child relationship. This interest has captured the attention not only of social scientists but also of the public. Movies like *Kramer vs. Kramer* and *Tribute* and books like *Father Power, How to Father,* and *What's a Father For?* have all focused

"Herbie, this is all part of becoming a man."

on different issues related to "fathering."[16] This new interest in the father-child relationship had even spawned a grassroots social movement of men who are seeking their paternal rights in child-custody cases.[17] These men are challenging the age-old assumption that only mothers can inherently give more love and care to a child and thus should automatically obtain custody of the child in a divorce.

Social research has begun to shed light on the father's role in his child's sex role development. For example, fathers have been found to be much stricter than mothers in their definitions of appropriate sex-typed expectations and behaviors."[18] Fathers, it appears, are especially intolerant of any hint of their son's deviations from sex-appropriate behaviors. More often than not, it is the father and not the mother who encourages the son to stand up against the neighborhood bully and exhorts the son to be a man and not a sissy.

In addition to a father's verbal encouragement, other facets of his life can influence a young boy. David Lynn, a psychologist at the University of California at Davis, points out that a father's work status and his child's perception of that status can shape a young boy's perception of masculinity:

> The way in which a father's children develop masculine or feminine characteristics seems to be related to the status of his work. The father's work status helps determine whether children cling to narrow masculine and feminine definitions and at what age they begin to differentiate themselves by sex. In contrast to the high-status father, the working man presents a masculine model that is more clearly differentiated from the feminine one; for example, he is likely to condone aggression, a

Perspectives on the Male

traditionally masculine attribute. His work is especially attractive to young boys, who understand and find intrinsically interesting such activities as building a house or repairing a car. The high-status father, although he presents a subtler model of masculinity, becomes more attractive as a standard for the boy as he matures and becomes aware of his father's status and prestige."[19]

If a father's work status can affect a son's notion of masculinity, as Lynn suggests, what effects are likely to occur for the young boy who has no father or whose father is absent a majority of time? The issue of father absence has sparked some interest among social scientists during the past few years and has generated some debate as well. On the one hand, Henry Biller, a psychologist at the University of Rhode Island, contends that "Paternal deprivation can lead to conflicts and rigidities in the individual's sex role adjustment, which in turn are often related to deficits in emotional, cognitive, and interpersonal functioning."[20] However, Joseph Pleck, in his analysis of Biller and others' work on father absence, suggests that much of this research suffers from misleading and unfounded interpretations of the data.[21] Pleck sees no reason based on the data for the extreme claims of detrimental effects occurring to a boy whose father is not present during the boy's formative years. Even though the experts disagree on this, one study is worth noting because it points up the issue of peer influence on a boy whose father is absent.

In a study of black and white boys between the ages of nine and twelve years, E. Mavis Hetherington segregated the boys into three groups: those whose fathers were present, those whose fathers were absent when the boys were four years old or younger, and those whose fathers were absent when the boys were six or older.[22] None of the boys whose fathers were absent had a father substitute living with him at the time of the study. The most striking difference between the father-present boys and *all* of the father-absent boys was that the latter were significantly more dependent on their peers. Thus it appears from Hetherington's study that, in order to learn and practice their sex role during their formative years, boys whose fathers are absent use other socializing sources (peers) to a greater extent than do boys whose fathers are present.

Before we look at some of the other socializing agents, let us quickly review some highlights of the parents' socializing effects on young males. First of all, parents do perceive the sexes differently and consequently interact with them differently. In general, boys are handled less, punished more, and given greater freedom earlier by their parents than girls are. In our culture, boys are socialized earlier into their sex role and pushed away from parental dependencies earlier than girls are.[23] A striking feature in the parent-child literature is the relative lack of information about the father-child relationship as compared to that of the mother-child relationship. The dirth of material on the father's role may be the result of traditional views of the father as solely concerned with the economic well-being of the family and not as involved or concerned with childcare.[24] The father-child relationship should receive more attention in the future as more couples begin to share childrearing responsibilities.[25]

Fathers today are playing an increasingly larger role in their children's lives.
  Source: Richard L. Good.

Let us now turn to another source of sex role learning for young boys, the mass media.

THE MEDIA (THE VAST WASTELANDS)

A few years ago, the saying, "You are what you eat," made the rounds among dieting circles. Of course, eating is important, but food isn't everything. We could just as well substitute the idea that "You are what you see and read." Europeans and Americans are a visual people who take in their world, by and large, through documentaries and sitcoms, and articles and books. The values, beliefs, and behaviors of a majority of young people are shaped by the various media. Let us begin our discussion of the media and their socializing impact on the young with a look at television.

Television Programming Several years ago, Newton Minnow, then chairman of the Federal Communications Commission, indicted television as being a "vast wasteland." Possibly following Minnow's lead, many people today take pleasure in vilifying television. However, television still remains a popular entertainment form and a powerful educational source, as well as a primary means that young people have for defining their respective sex roles.

Perspectives on the Male

For preschool children, television, or the "flickering blue parent" as some disparagingly call it, is a primary socializing agent second only to parents. Several television shows are produced especially for preschool children. *Mr. Rogers and His Neighborhood* and *Sesame Street* are two popular and frequently praised children's programs. *Sesame Street,* for example, has long been recognized for its innovative educational material and its respect for social and ethnic differences. However, *Sesame Street* does present sex roles in rather traditional and stereotypic ways. In a study of *Sesame Street's* content, Jo Ann Gardner points out how the program's major characters portray a restrictive view of male and female sex roles.

> On one program, Big Bird (having said that he would like to be a member of a family and having been told that Gordon and Susan would be his family) is told that he will have to help with the work and that since he is a boy bird, he will have to do men's work—the heavy work, the *"important"* work and also that he should get a girl (bird) to help Susan with her work of arranging flowers, redecorating, etc. There was more and virtually all of it emphasized that there is men's work and then there is women's work—that men's work is outside the home and women's work is in the home. (This in spite of the fact that *17 million* children under eighteen have mothers who are employed outside the home; of these, 4.5 million are under six.)[26]

Besides showing traditional sex role patterns, children's television shows portray the sexes in a biased and somewhat unrealistic fashion.The males are usually presented as aggressive, dominant, and engaged in exciting activities from which they receive rewards from others for their "masculine" accomplishments. Females, on the other hand, are presented in auxiliary roles; they are usually deferential to boys and men and receive little reward or feedback for their activities.[27] Thus many social scientists believe that children's television programming has a decided male bias in the fare that it serves its young preschool audience.

Obviously, children do not limit their viewing only to "children's" programs. Young children watch prime-time shows as well. The television industry allegedly exhibits sensitivity to the young viewer's presence during the late afternoon and early evening by presenting situation-comedy and family-oriented shows. Adult fare with its violence and sex is reserved for later hours when children are supposedly in bed. But the demarcation between family and adult hours is something of a prefabrication on the part of the television programmers. It is also estimated that approximately three-quarters of a million young children are in the television audience between midnight and 2 A.M.[28] Thus it is legitimate to ask how the sex roles are portrayed during prime time.

Michele Long and Rita Simon in a study of twenty-two family programs found that women were generally portrayed as dependent on men, and men were generally portrayed as independent of women and in control of the situation.[29] In another study, male characters were shown in ambitious, adventuresome, strong, and dominant roles, while females were cast in dependent, submissive, and weak roles.[30] Overall, television depicts men as either heroes or villains and women as either adulators or victims.[31] The conclusion drawn from these and other studies is that men are expected, at least in the minds of the producers, to act independently and aggressively, and to be in charge, while women are the bystanders in life's drama.[32]

Television Commercials Television commercials have also been studied for their prevailing messages about sex roles. Thirty- or sixty-second advertising spots contain potent messages not only about a product but about life as well. Frequently, the product is wrapped in social values, a particular life-style, or some other ploy, such as sex, to capture the viewer's interest. Children learn much about sex roles from commercials.

Commercials are usually aimed at women—the primary purchasers at grocery and retail counters. Keenly aware of the traditional female sex role of housewife and mother, Madison Avenue generally shows women alarmed over the waxy buildup on the floor, recoiling from unpleasant odors emanating from toilet bowls, reeling from a head-thumping migraine, or vexed over the softness of toilet tissue. In general, women are portrayed as domestics who are concerned only with household problems. Interestingly, the voice-over in a majority of these "for women only" commercials is male—authoritative and always ready to ease a woman's burden with the cure-all product.

However, Madison Avenue presents a completely different picture of men in commercials. Men are shown as involved with cars and tools and as sharing the natural reward after a trying day at office or plant—a beer. In television commercials, males are aggressive, competitive, independent—always macho. The only time men are portrayed as less than "real men" is when they are trapped in the house. Bardwick and Schumann take note of this feature in television commercials:

> The image of the American man in TV commercials as muscular, knowledgeable, dominating, independent, sexy, cosmopolitan, athletic, authoritative and aggressive exists only when he is seen away from his family. In embarrassing contrast the American father and husband is portrayed as passive, stupid, infantile and emasculated. . . . But outside the house trouble is what he's looking for. Swift as a panther, stealthy as a cougar, free as a mustang he speeds to his rendezvous with status, independence and violence.[33]

Research on the relationship between various products and the portrayal of the sexes supports the ascertion that commercials present the sexes in stereotypic ways. For example, women—young, attractive, and seductive—appear in cosmetic commercials; men—strong, decisive, and virile—appear in car and beer commercials.[34] The underlying message is that women are concerned only with their physical attributes, preservation of their beauty, and delay of the aging process, and men are interested only in power, status, and achievement.

Children learn from commercials. They not only pester parents for a specific cereal touted by a favorite cartoon character, they also see women on their knees in the kitchen or perplexed over which brand of laundry soap to use while men are flying planes, playing baseball, and drinking beer. The commercial as potent educator is a force to be reckoned with, at least in the mind of one second-grade teacher. When asked to spell the word "relief", one of this teacher's pupils promptly answered, "Relief is spelled R-O-L-A-I-D-S."

Children's Books Children's books are another source for socializing young children into society's image of appropriate sex roles. Again Lenore Weitzman writes,

> Through books, children learn about the world outside their immediate environment: they learn what other boys and girls do, say, and feel, and they learn what is expected of children their age. Picture books are especially important to the preschool child because they are often looked at over and over again at a time when children are in the process of developing their own sex role identities. In addition, they are read to children before other socialization influences (such as school, teachers, and peers) become important in their lives.[35]

In the past decade or so, several studies have been conducted on the content of children's picture books especially with an eye to the representation of and activities engaged in by male and female characters.[36] One study that typifies the research in this area was conducted by Weitzman and several of her colleagues.[37] Weitzman analyzed those children's books that had been awarded the prized Caldecott Medal for excellence in children's literature. The analysis was revealing about how the sexes were portrayed and what social expectations were placed on each sex. The majority of the prize-winning books were about males and their adventures; for the most part, females were remarkably absent. Furthermore, the male characters were involved in a variety of challenging roles that required skill, competence, and independent action; the few female characters presented were generally portrayed in passive or auxiliary roles. The message of most of these first readers is quite clear: Boys and men lead exciting lives in which they are expected to overcome difficult obstacles and eventually achieve the sought-after goal; girls and women—when they are shown—are presented as secondary to the plot and usually performing monotonous and less demanding tasks. It is no wonder that so many young girls see boys' lives as more exciting and fulfilling. We should not be surprised to hear a young girl wish out loud to be her brother or some other boy she feels has a more exciting life.

One other noteworthy feature of the portrayal of the boy's life in these books is the absence of his caring for others. There is a glaring scarcity of boys and men caring for small children. For the most part, a boy's world is outside climbing trees, building clubhouses, chasing other boys, and playing sports. The home, domestic chores, and especially caring for little children are almost exclusively reserved for girls.

Beginning in their most impressionable years, boys learn from various media what it means to be a real man. The message presented serves males in only limited ways. Given the one-dimensional, stereotypic view of the male sex role, Newton Minnow could have broadened his disparaging remark to include more than just television.

THE EDUCATIONAL SYSTEM (JOHNNY, SIT UP STRAIGHT!)

Generally speaking, the educational system is responsible for preparing the young for adulthood. In earlier times, the young learned all that they needed to know from their family. Formal education was a privilege reserved primarily for the wealthy. Nowadays, the young must acquire many skills in order to fit into our specialized world; consequently, no single family can provide all of the necessary education. Many young people enter school at around three or four years of age and continue through college and beyond. Given the importance of education in today's world, one would like to think that the educational system approaches each child with a minimum of bias and preconceived expectations. Nothing could be further from the truth.

Academic, Career-Orientation, and Athletic Programs We should be somewhat skeptical of the platitudes dispensed by the educational system about the weights given a student's intellectual potential, socioemotional development, or even the student's own preference for one career or another. Statistics on different careers—a major by-product of the educational system—suggest that a student's sex determines in large part what careers await him or her. For example, in 1979 males comprised 97.1 percent of civil engineers, 89.3 percent of physicians, 87.6 percent of lawyers, and 81.1 percent of chemists. In those careers considered less prestigious and lower down on the pay scale, males comprised only 2.6 percent of preschool teachers, 21.9 percent of librarians, 12.1 percent of cashiers, 3.3 percent of typists, and less than one percent of all secretaries.[38]

How can one account for the wide disparity in career options between the sexes? The answer appears to be the educational system's "tracking program." Students are counseled into programs that lead to specific careers on the basis of test results, student preferences, and more often than most would openly admit, on the basis of the student's sex. Females—considered deft with their fingers and temperamentally suited to routine and monotonous tasks—make ideal "girl Fridays." Males—judged to excel in math and science—are "natural" candidates for professional careers.

Varied academic and career-oriented programs are not the only areas in education where males have been granted more favored status. Historically, athletic programs, especially team sports, have been a male preserve at all educational levels. In the minds of many, team sports are seen as the adolescent male's *rite de passage* through which boys become men. From grade school through college, team sports are considered the crucible in which boys learn the values of competition and cooperation that will serve them later on in the business world. With the passage of Title IX of the Education Amendment of 1972, the obvious forms of sex discrimination in school athletic programs were outlawed. However, in a report published in 1978 by the Department of Health, Education, and Welfare on the implementation of Title IX, the authors noted that the ". . . rules and policies that perpetuate unequal treatment of males and females—which are now clearly illegal—are still going uncorrected in the nation's schools."[39]

We should not jump to the conclusion, however, that the educational system is completely enamored of the male from his first day in preschool until the final cap-and-gown ceremony many years later. There are some pitfalls that beset the male during his school years. For example, quite often in the classroom, the male who shows a tendency toward lack of concentration and an inclination toward unruliness may find himself victimized by a negative label. If the boy with such behaviors becomes troublesome to his teacher, he is likely to be diagnosed as hyperactive—a label that is attached to boys more than nine times more frequently than to girls.[40] Once diagnosed as hyperactive, the boy will probably be given a drug such as Ritalin, which induces a form of chemical docility. Although boys have ample career options and generous and self-serving athletic programs, they also are more likely to be tagged with negative psychological labels that often bring with them the consequences of drug-induced personality changes.

Setting aside a debate about whether boys benefit or suffer more than girls do in school, some take the extreme position that boys in general suffer undue debilitating psychological consequences in school. One of the most outspoken proponents of this view is Patricia Sexton. In *The Feminized Male,* Sexton argues that the educational system severely undermines a young male's developing masculinity. Sexton's thesis is simply that the educational system generally rewards those students who display "feminine" attributes such as conformity, orderliness, and self-discipline and at the same time penalizes "masculine" characteristics such as independence, aggressiveness, and high levels of activity. In Sexton's view, the major culprit is the female teacher who punishes the boy for his boyish ways. Sexton also dismisses the suggestion that more male teachers would offset the female teachers' feminizing influences on young boys. According to Sexton, male teachers are themselves feminized and thus would provide little help to their male students.

> Putting a man, any man, in place of women in the school will not do. A man who is less than a man can be more damaging than a domineering mother. The chances of getting feminized men in the school are fairly good because those eligible and willing, given the present hiring codes and salaries, are usually those who made it through a feminine school system without conflict or failure.[41]

Even if we were to grant, for the sake of argument, Sexton's charge that male teachers are "feminized," does having a male teacher negatively affect a boy's academic performance or his social and emotional development as Sexton suggests? In a review of the literature, Joseph Pleck finds little evidence supporting the contention that male teachers either improve or lower a boy's academic performance or hinder his social and emotional development.[42] However, Pleck does note one benefit the male student has as a result of having a male teacher. Boys who have a male teacher report a more positive educational experience than do boys who have female teachers. Thus Sexton's claim that so-called feminized male teachers "can be more damaging than a domineering mother" appears unwarranted and more than a little informative about Sexton's own view of how mothers should act toward their male children—definitely not domineering.

Teachers Until now we have focused on the educational system's tracking programs, the preferential treatment given males in athletic programs, and sweeping charges that female teachers subvert a male's developing masculinity. But what of day-to-day student-teacher interactions? Do teachers treat their students differently on the basis of sex? According to the literature, the latter question can be answered with a resounding yes. Let us focus on one study that highlights the degree to which teachers treat the sexes differently and the behavioral consequences of this treatment on shaping boys' and girls' behaviors.

Psychologist Lisa Serbin and several of her associates observed fifteen preschool teachers in their classrooms.[43] Serbin was interested in how these teachers handled problem behaviors among their students, especially aggressive and dependent behaviors. Overall, boys displayed more aggression and girls more dependence in the classroom. Serbin found this difference linked to how the teachers treated the sexes and not to some innate sex difference.

In the classroom the teachers responded to each sex with a definite pattern. Simply put, the teachers responded to the boys' aggression but not to the girls'. In fact, the teachers reprimanded the boys more than three times more frequently for their aggressiveness than they did the girls for their aggressiveness. Common sense would suggest that aggressiveness that leads to reprimands should have caused the boys' aggression to decrease. If this were so, the boys should have been less aggressive than the girls. But common sense fails us in this matter. Paying attention, even a negative kind of attention such as a reprimand, does not decrease aggression but rather *increases* it.[44] Aggression that is ignored, as it was with the girls, is less likely to continue. Boys' more frequent aggressiveness may therefore be the result of the teacher's attention to it rather than to some natural inclination among boys to act aggressively.

In regard to dependency, remember that Serbin found that girls are more dependent on their teachers than boys are. Again Serbin found teachers' actions influencing this sex difference. When a boy asked for help with some task, his teacher gave aid no matter where he was in the room. On the other hand, when a girl requested help, the teacher complied only when the girl was nearby. The message is clear. Boys may venture away from authority and still receive help from an adult, but girls must stay nearby if they are to learn from an adult (an early form of dependency on others). Thus preschool teachers may unwittingly foster stereotypic behaviors in their students and add still more pressure to the socialization of young children into traditional sex roles.

Textbooks Textbooks also have a definite socializing influence on young students. The materials presented in textbooks can and often do encourage traditional sex-typed attitudes and behaviors.[45] Quite often the picture of the sexes given in textbooks does not mirror the reality as experienced by students. For example, in a study of the content of textbooks, Marjorie U'Ren found women in only fifteen percent of the illustrations. U'Ren remarked that "The significance of this imbalance is obvious. We tend to forget the simple fact that the female sex is half the species, that women are not merely a ladies' auxiliary to the human race."[46]

Perspectives on the Male

Not everyone, however, is willing to conclude that textbooks favor boys and men. Some critics suggest that textbooks discriminate against males.[47] Once again we hear charges of "feminization," this time leveled against textbooks. Texts that show boys reading books, helping with household chores, or playing musical instruments are criticized as being damaging to a boy's sense of masculinity. But rather than stifling a young boy's developing masculinity, the early readers appear to go to considerable lengths to offer boys a much wider variety of career options than they do girls. One study of early school textbooks found that boys and men were shown in almost 150 different activities and jobs, whereas girls and women were portrayed in only twenty-seven "feminine" activities.[48] In spite of the charges of "feminized" textbooks, textbooks like teachers appear to reinforce traditional sex-typed behaviors and attitudes among young students.

Thus the educational system in general and teachers and textbooks in particular direct male and female students into traditionally prescribed sex roles. Boys are "tracked" into programs leading to jobs and careers that will enable them to become good providers for their future wives and children. The same socializing agents "track" girls into programs that will enable them to become good wives and mothers.[49]

THE PEER GROUP (I DARE YA!)

As children grow older they begin to spend more time with one very special group made up of other people of about their own age and background—the peer group. School-aged children spend considerably more time with their peers than they do with their family.[50] Children learn from one another, and what they learn from other socializing agents (parents, television, books, teachers) they often practice with other children. The peer group provides a unique social situation in which children can rehearse new behaviors and a variety of roles with relative impunity from adult authority figures. As children become more independent of their parents, they grow more dependent on their peers. Peer acceptance and approval become highly valued personal needs that motivate most young people. Beginning in a child's preschool years and continuing well into adolescence, peer pressure is a powerful socializing agent for shaping sex roles.

As suggested earlier, peer influence plays an important role in teaching and maintaining sex-typed behaviors. In fact, peer influence can override the influence of significant adults. For example, Beverly Fagot and Gerald Patterson observed boys in a preschool nursery playing with trucks, cars, and building materials, while girls played with dolls and artwork.[51] When the teachers encouraged the boys to join in some "feminine" activities, the boys resisted. According to Fagot and Patterson, the boys appeared to ignore the attention and reinforcement from their teachers and preferred the company and approval of other boys. The fact that the boys resisted their teachers' influence points up an interesting feature of peer influence. It seems that boys try to influence others' behaviors more than girls do.[52] Boys not only try to control others, but they are

Figure 5.1 Children's activities attributed to one sex or the other and to both sexes. Note the degree of sex role stereotyping in the activities attributed to just one sex. *Source: R. Schell and E. Hall,* Developmental Psychology, *3rd ed. (New York: Random House, 1979), p. 305.*

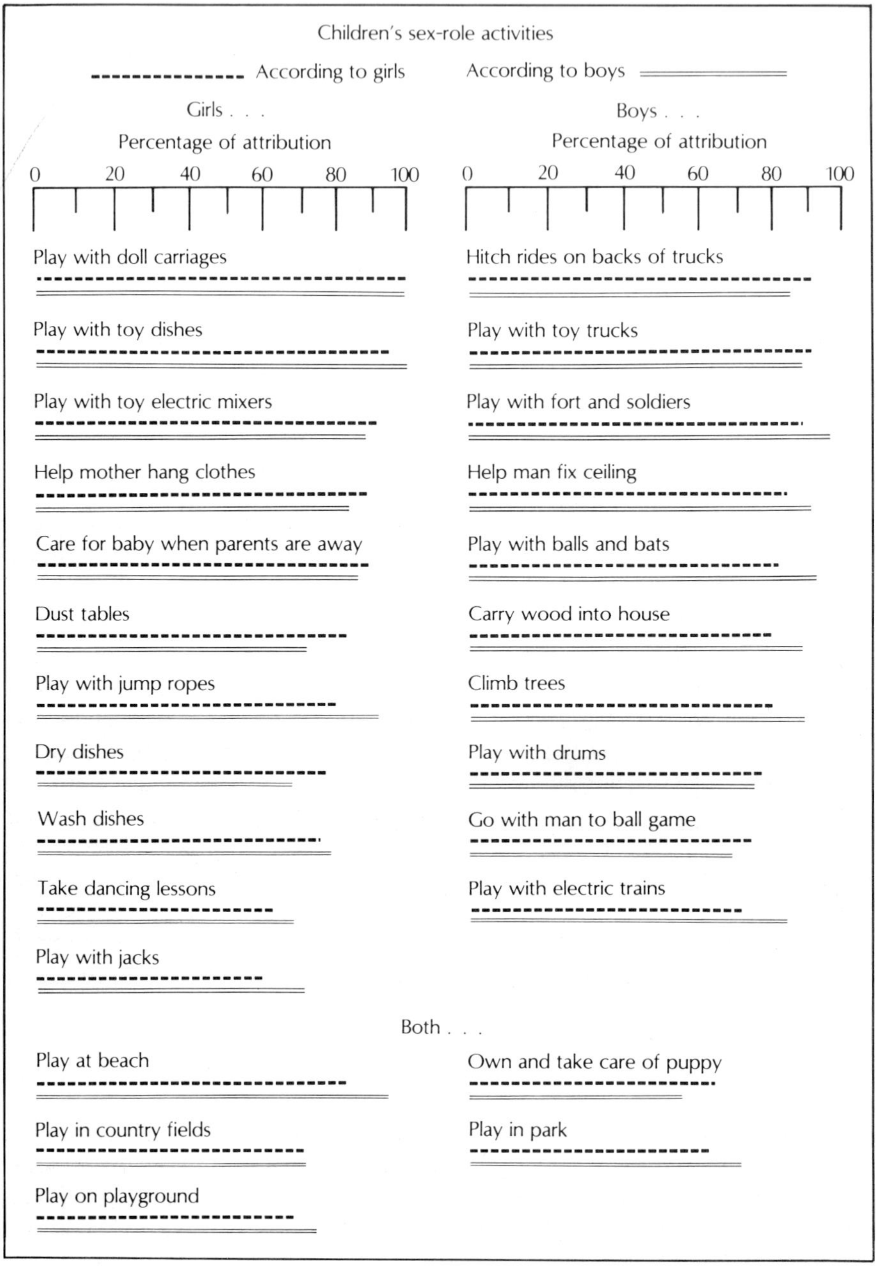

Children's sex-role activities

------------ According to girls   According to boys ==========

Girls . . .   Boys . . .

Percentage of attribution   Percentage of attribution

0   20   40   60   80   100   0   20   40   60   80   100

Play with doll carriages   Hitch rides on backs of trucks

Play with toy dishes   Play with toy trucks

Play with toy electric mixers   Play with fort and soldiers

Help mother hang clothes   Help man fix ceiling

Care for baby when parents are away   Play with balls and bats

Dust tables   Carry wood into house

Play with jump ropes   Climb trees

Dry dishes   Play with drums

Wash dishes   Go with man to ball game

Take dancing lessons   Play with electric trains

Play with jacks

Both . . .

Play at beach   Own and take care of puppy

Play in country fields   Play in park

Play on playground

probably more likely themselves to be controlled by other boys. We might therefore suggest that peer pressure is a more powerful influence in a young boy's life than in a young girl's.

Peer groups tend to be sex-segregated throughout the childhood years. The interests and activities of these sex-segregated groups are clearly defined, at least in the minds of young children. Interestingly, when Hartley and Hardesty asked a group of eight- to eleven-year-old boys and girls what activities they believed were appropriate for boys and girls, both sexes showed a high degree of agreement[53] (see Figure 5.1). For example, both sexes believed that playing with dolls and toy dishes was more appropriate for girls and that playing with trucks and toy soldiers was more appropriate for boys.

When we examine the activities that boys and girls attribute to each sex, there is a continuity of sorts between the girls' activities and the traditional adult female activities (for example domestic chores and childcare), whereas there is an apparent lack of continuity between the boys' activities and traditional adult male activities. Girls, it seems, have a more accurate view of the traditional female roles, whereas boys show an "ignorance" of traditional adult male roles. Gregory Stone noted this feature of children's play in the following anecdote.

> . . . a colleague noticed a boy and girl playing house in the front yard. The little girl was very busy sweeping up the play area, rearranging furniture, moving dishes about, and caring for baby dolls. The boy, on the other hand, would leave the play area on his bicycle, disappear to the back of the (real) house, remain for a brief while, reappear in the play area, and lie down in a feigned sleep. The little girl had a rather extensive knowledge of the mother role, but for the boy, a father was one who disappeared, reappeared, and slept, *ad infinitum*.[54]

Probably at no other time in a male's life are the demands to conform to peer group pressures greater than during adolescence. Costanzo and Shaw found young people between eleven and seventeen years of age more likely to conform to peer pressures than at any other age.[55] In many ways, a young male's acceptance and approval by his peer group is contingent on his acting out traditional features of the male role in exaggerated ways. For example, proving oneself a man through acts of aggression and toughness is a necessary part of peer acceptance among many adolescent male groups.[56] The male who acts like a "chicken" or a "sissy" quickly finds himself spurned by his male peers. Overall, the adolescent male finds himself confronting numerous demands from his peers. He discards certain roles and activities associated with childhood and tries on newer ones related to his newly acquired status as a young male adult.

SEXISM

In the last chapter we noted that male dominance was a nearly universal feature in most cultures. When one group of people dominates another group, a set of beliefs usually justifies such unequal social statuses. The dominant group normally speaks of some natural difference or some divine plan underlying the dominance of their group over the other group. For example, some white people believe that blacks are naturally intellectually inferior or that God destined whites to rule over blacks. The set of beliefs that support such social arrangements is called an *ideology.* The ideology that supports the belief that males are naturally superior to females is called *sexism.*

Sexism is an integral feature of our culture. We are not born with sexist beliefs but rather are taught them by others. Thus sexism is one of the more sinister ideologies that people in our culture are socialized into accepting.

THE SOCIALIZATION OF SEXISM

Almost every segment of society is infused with sexist beliefs and attitudes. When children turn the pages of their favorite picture books, they are apt to see little boys playing outside in tree houses and chasing their friends, while little girls are helping their mothers with the dishes and dusting or taking care of their little brother or sister. When these children watch television, they see men telling other people what to do, while women are listening. When children go to church on Sunday, they watch a man up front talking, while everyone else is listening quietly. Little children learn the message quickly: Men do things, important things, and women sit by quietly.

The socialization of sexism is so thorough that even women come to believe themselves inferior to males.[57] And why not? Women have been taught since their childhood that males are preeminent in the world and females are almost forgotten. The language girls learn in school teaches them to say "man" or "mankind" rather than "human being" or "humanity." If they read the New Testament they hear St. Paul telling the Corinthians that "A man . . . is the image of God and reflects God's glory; but woman is the reflection of man's glory. For man did not come from woman; no, woman came from man; and man was not created for the sake of woman, but woman was created for the sake of man."[58] Many girls grow up to believe that their highest accomplishment can only be achieved by raising children and keeping a good home for husbands and children alike.[59]

Of course, women do many other things besides housework. Women are engaged in a variety of fields and professions, but even here the work done by a woman is often seen as less valuable and worthwhile than the same work done by a man. When a female and a male do identical work, both males *and* females are more likely to view the male's work as having more value. An interesting study highlights this feature of sexism very effectively. Philip Goldberg gave two groups of college females identical copies of several scholarly articles to evaluate.[60] For one group, the articles were attributed to a "Joan T. MacKay," and for the other group, the same articles were attributed to a "John T. MacKay." In general, the articles attributed to the female author were evaluated as less persuasive and competent in their style and content than those articles attributed

Perspectives on the Male

to the male author. Research conducted by Goldberg and countless other researchers graphically shows that the socialization of sexism effectively infects women and men alike in our society.

One of the most pernicious effects of sexism is how it has prejudiced people to believe that women cannot act effectively in a leadership position. In a national Gallup poll, people were asked, "If you were taking a new job and had your choice of a boss, would you prefer to work for a man or for a woman?" Among the males sampled, sixty-three percent favored working for a man, four percent favored a woman, and thirty-two percent stated that it made no difference. When women responded to this question, sixty percent reported that they would choose a man, ten percent favored a woman, and twenty-seven percent stated that it made no difference.[61] Nearly two-thirds of the males and females sampled reflected the sexist belief that men are preferable as bosses. Why do so many females and males think that men are better leaders in the working situation? The answer is simply that people are socialized to think of men in positions of power and control and women in relatively powerless positions. Even when we look at elected officials, the prejudice against women as leaders once again shows up. In the ninety-sixth Congress, there were only sixteen female representatives and only *one* female senator.[62]

THE ECONOMICS OF SEXISM

Most people believe that a person should receive a fair wage for a day's work. Even those who are opposed to the passage of the Equal Rights Amendment, argue that a women should be paid the same wage as a man for the same kind of work. But no single area attests to the unequal status of women and the pervasiveness of sexism in our society as much as that of paid employment. For example, in 1978 the median income for a civilian, full-time employed male was $15,730 as opposed to $9,350 for a comparable woman. In other words, for every dollar a full-time employed male earned, a comparable female earned fifty-nine cents.[63]

Women suffer from wage discrimination in varying degrees depending on their age (see Table 5.1). For example, the average full-time employed teenage female earns eighty-nine cents for every dollar earned by the average full-time employed teenage male. However, full-time employed females between thirty-five and forty-four years of age earn *only* fifty-six cents for every dollar earned by the same aged male. The injustice of this gross wage difference is compounded when one considers the millions of middle-aged women who are the sole breadwinners in their families. The argument that women do not need as much money as men do is rather groundless, especially for those divorced, separated, and widowed women who have children to support.

But what about education and the wages earned by females and males? Many people still believe that for every year of education salaries rise comparably. On the average, wages do increase with education, but again we see a significant

Table 5.1 Median Income, By Age and Sex, United States, 1979[a]

Age group	Female Col. A	Male Col. B	Female income as percent of male income (A ÷ B)
14–19 years	$ 6,715	$ 7,518	89%
20–24 years	8,571	11,480	75
25–34 years	11,155	16,824	66
35–44 years	11,184	20,069	56
45–54 years	10,934	20,464	53
55–64 years	10,873	19,436	56
65 years and over	10,664	16,107	66

[a]Data refer to year-round, full-time civilian workers.

Source: U.S. Bureau of the Census, *Statistical Abstract of the United States, 1980* (Washington, D.C.: U.S. Government Printing Office, 1980), p. 463.

disparity between the salaries earned by male and female high school and college graduates (see Table 5.2). For example, an average college-educated female with a full-time job can expect to earn approximately fifty-nine cents for every dollar earned by the average college-educated male with a full-time job.

How can a society such as ours justify such inequality and discrimination in paid wages that women suffer? Phyllis Schlafly, a vocal proponent of the STOP ERA movement, contends that women choose to earn less than men. Schlafly believes that if women earned the same wages as men the institution of the family would crumble. In her testimony before a congressional committee on sex discrimination in the workplace, Schlafly stated,

> The 59-cent figure is the average wage paid to all women, as compared to the average wage paid to all men. We certainly do not want a society in which the average wage paid to all women equals the average wage paid to all men, because that would be a society in which all women work the same long hours of every week, the same 12 months out of every year, the same lifetime of work on the job, and do the same heavy, dangerous, backbreaking jobs that men do. That would be a society which would have eliminated the role of motherhood.
>
> We want a society in which the average man earns more than the average woman so that his earnings can fulfill his provider role in providing a home and support for his wife, who is nurturing and mothering their children.
>
> There are many valid reasons why the average man earns more pay than the average woman. He works longer hours, works more years on the same job, has more experience and education, and does harder or more dangerous work. Millions of men do dangerous, heavy, he-man jobs that most women cannot do. *The average woman voluntarily declines the added responsibilities, the long hours, and the lifetime commitment required for the high-paying positions in the professional and business world.*
>
> The reason why women are in jobs that are less demanding with shorter hours and less pay is not sex discrimination. *It is career choice. The overwhelming majority of American women make the career choice to give priority to homemaking and motherhood and to the maintenance of an intact family.*[64] (Italics added.)

Perspectives on the Male

Table 5.2 Median Income, By Education and Sex, United States, 1978[a]

Years of school completed	Female Col. A	Male Col. B	Female income as percent of male income (A ÷ B)
Less than 8	$ 6,648	$10,474	63%
8	7,489	12,965	58
9–11	7,996	14,199	56
12	9,769	16,369	60
College, 1–3	10,634	17,411	61
College, 4	12,347	20,941	59
College, 5 or more	15,310	23,578	65

[a]Data refer to year-round, full-time workers age 25 and over.

Source: U.S. Bureau of the Census, *Current Population Reports* (Washington, D.C.: U.S. Government Printing Office, 1980), P-60, No. 120.

Schlafly's statement that a majority of women choose low-paying and less prestigious jobs because they are unwilling to take on the added responsibilities of better-paying jobs is ridiculous. Would Schlafly also say that black men choose low-paying jobs, less prestigious jobs, or no jobs at all because they are too unmotivated to get better jobs or just plain enjoy standing on street corners rather than working? Probably not, because such a statement would be seen as evidence of blatant racism. Why then do all not see Schlafly's statements about women for what they are—blatant sexism?

We socialize females and males alike from their earliest years to think of females as inferior to males. We reinforce this belief by paying women less for the same jobs that men do. We talk of motherhood and the maintainer of the family as the proper roles for women, and all the while what we really mean is that women's work in the home and outside is not as valuable as men's.

COMMENTING ON THE SOCIOLOGICAL PERSPECTIVE

In this chapter we examined the impact of four socializing agents—parents, mass media, education, and peers—on the development of the male sex role. Much of what a man thinks, the attitudes that he holds, the behaviors that he exhibits, and the emotions that he expresses are molded to a great extent by these socializing forces. The outcome—the roles men play—forms a kind of social drama wherein men interact with other men, women, and children, using the scripts that are provided by society and that man have committed to memory (son, athlete, husband, father, worker, and so on).[65] One of the most insidious facets of the socialization process is sexism. Sexism, the belief that females are naturally inferior to males, limits the developmental potential of more than half of the population. Are the roles that males play and sexist beliefs and practices an aid or a hindrance to males? Social scientists are beginning to question the usefulness of men's roles and the inherent inequality of male-female relations in contemporary life.

The sociological perspective presents the male experience as the end product of the socialization process. Need we socialize boys and men to think of themselves as better than girls and women? What good comes from this? Some may argue that the traditional sex roles are an inevitable outcome of roles that early human groups developed over countless centuries. But we no longer live in a society where a man's worth is determined by his physical strength and a woman's by the number of children she can bear. If we are to survive into a twenty-first century, perhaps we should consider the merits of raising children free of the restrictions of sex role labels.

SUGGESTED READINGS

Chetwynd, J., and Hartnett, O., eds. *The Sex Role System.* London: Routledge & Kegan Paul, 1978.

Dahlstrom, E., ed. *The Changing Roles of Men and Women.* Boston: Beacon Press, 1971.

Greenberg, S. *Right from the Start: A Guide to Non-Sexist Child Rearing.* Boston: Houghton Mifflin, 1978.

Kaplan, A., and Bean, J., eds. *Beyond Sex-Role Stereotypes.* Boston: Little, Brown, 1976.

Stoll, C. *Female & Male.* Dubuque, Ia.: Wm. C. Brown, 1978.

Weitz, S. *Sex Roles.* New York: Oxford University Press, 1977.

6

Of bent psyches and bruised egos:
THE PSYCHOLOGICAL PERSPECTIVE

The great enemy of the truth is very often not the lie — deliberate, contrived and dishonest — but the myth — persistent, persuasive and unrealistic. Too often we hold fast to the clichés of our forebears. We subject all facts to a prefabricated set of interpretations. We enjoy the comfort of opinion without the discomfort of thought. John F. Kennedy[1]

Thus far we have looked at the historical roots, the few biological differences, the various cultural ideals, and the socializing agents that shape the male experience. This last perspective, the psychological, focuses on the individual outcomes of these other forces on the total person. However, to fully understand the individual male and his development, we must take into account and build on the knowledge and the findings of other disciplines. Consequently, the psychological perspective borrows heavily from these other disciplines in its perspective on the male experience.

In this chapter we will first consider some of the common stereotypic sex differences and see if, in fact, these assumed differences stand up to the scrutiny of research. Next we will examine three psychological theories of how the sexes learn their respective sex roles. Finally, we will present Joseph Pleck's analysis of the male sex role.

SEX DIFFERENCES, OR MUCH ADO ABOUT NOTHING

Obviously, the sexes differ in their genital structures and secondary sex characteristics. But do the sexes also differ in the ways they think and act? For decades, researchers have found that most people describe the typical male and female in very different ways.[2] For example, people believe males to be more aggressive and ambitious and less expressive than females are, and females are believed to be more dependent, warm and emotional than males are (see Table 6.1). Not only do a majority of people attribute different descriptive traits or sex role stereotypes to the sexes, they also believe that the sexes differ in certain psychological processes. For example, many people think the sexes differ in their intellectual and creative abilities. Thus social scientists have been particularly interested in the field of sex differences.

Studies in sex differences are commonly faulted for what researchers call *the fallacy of the average*. The meaning of this fallacy becomes clear with a simple example. The apparent sex difference in men's and women's height—a biological feature that is determined by one's genes—will do. The average height of the American male is five feet, nine inches, whereas the average height of the American female is five feet, four inches. Consequently, we can reason that "on the average" American men are significantly taller than American women. But we cannot say that *all* American men are taller than *all* American women. The reason we cannot make such a statement is simple: Many American women are taller than five feet, four inches, and many American men are shorter than five feet, nine inches. The fact that many early studies reported significant sex differences in a variety of abilities based solely on average scores has been similarly misleading. Contemporary social scientists are beginning to question many of these studies and to point out that by and large males differ among themselves more than the average male differs from the average female.

Table 6.1 Common Sex Role Stereotypes

Males	Females
Aggressive	Submissive
Ambitious	Modest
Cold	Warm
Independent	Dependent
Strong	Weak
Unemotional	Emotional
Unexpressive	Expressive
Worldly-wise	Home-centered

Psychologists have long been in the business of compiling vast amounts of data revealing the nature and scope of sex differences. In the 1920s Lewis Terman conducted one of the first large-scale, in-depth studies of psychological sex differences, using over 600 boys and girls with superior IQs (IQs over 130).[3] Some years later Terman teamed up with Leona Tyler to produce another report on sex differences.[4] These and other reports generally suggested that the sexes differed in a wide number of abilities, many of which coincided with popularly held beliefs. A turning point in the study of sex differences came in 1974 when two Stanford University psychologists, Eleanor Maccoby and Carol Jacklin, published *The Psychology of Sex Differences,* which soon became a classic text in the field.[5]

Maccoby and Jacklin reviewed over 2,000 articles and books, most of which were published after 1966. In their attempt to analyze the field of sex differences, Maccoby and Jacklin reported not only those studies that found sex differences but also those that did not, which are often conveniently omitted from the literature. Maccoby and Jacklin's study of sex differences is, for the present, the most thorough and comprehensive report on sex differences.

To make our discussion of sex differences more manageable, we will treat two general areas, namely, intellectual and social differences. Each of these contains a large store of common-sense wisdom underlying the belief in sex differences, but for the most part, scientific evidence is sorely lacking. The two areas selected here are not exhaustive but are especially noteworthy with respect to the male experience.[6]

INTELLECTUAL DIFFERENCES

Throughout the ages, a large number of highly valued skills, talents, and abilities always appeared to be the property of males. In hunting societies, brute strength was essential, and men were the epitome of the brute. With the addition of domesticated animals and cultivated crops, men became the par excellence herdsmen and farmers, even though women probably invented the digging stick and trained the first wild canines. Following industrialization, men found that they were suited for the machine by dint of their mechanical talent, while women

Perspectives on the Male

stood by perplexed with all of the pulleys and levers. In the technological age, we discover men programmed to interface with computers, while women are only keypunch operators. It seems that whatever talent is valued in a society men have an uncanny amount of that particular talent. Granted that women have some talent, there always seems to be some drawback. "Women have great talent," wrote the German philosopher Arthur Schopenhauer, "but no genius, for they always remain subjective."[7]

Men have been known to gloat over the self-flattering belief that they are smarter than women. Look around or back through history; who are or were the leaders, inventors, philosophers, and scientists? Why, men of course! Any mark of women's intellectual abilities was either absent or possibly dismissed by historians with selective attention. Nevertheless, based on scientific studies using various measures of general intelligence, Maccoby and Jacklin note that the one "reliable generalization" about the sexes and intelligence is that there is no difference between the sexes.

Verbal Ability Women have long been thought to excel at talking—endlessly. Comedians have made women's verbal output part of their stock materials, and audiences laughingly have approved of the image. Notwithstanding this unflattering portrait, studies have shown that women are superior to men in verbal abilities such as vocabulary size, spelling, sentence complexity, creative writing, and many other elements of general verbal fluency. Even though studies conducted in the 1930s and 1940s found young girls exhibiting verbal skills earlier than young boys did, Maccoby and Jacklin caution that girls' verbal superiority actually begins around the time of early adolescence and continues onward into early adulthood. Given the fact of female superiority in verbal skills, one wonders how men have been able to overcome their deficit and end up as the world's greatest orators!

Visual-Spatial Ability When it comes to what psychologists call *visual-spatial abilities,* boys excel over girls. Visual-spatial abilities are those that allow one to pick out and make sense of objects in one's field of vision. For example, the bird-watcher who spots a scarlet tanager on a distant tree limb is said to have a keen visual-spatial ability. To spot the tanager, the birdwatcher has had to ignore a large amount of irrelevant visual material, such as moving tree limbs and different shaped leaves, and to pick out the silhouette of the beautiful tanager against the backdrop of the forest mural.

Psychologists in their quest to measure visual-spatial abilities have moved into darkened rooms rather than out into forest and field. Herman Witkin and several colleagues have compiled a great deal of information about visual-spatial abilities based on their use of a device called a *rod-and-frame test.*[8] In a rod-and-frame test, a person typically sits in a dark room facing an illuminated rectangular frame that encloses a rod (see Figure 6.1). The frame and rod are both adjustable, and the viewer's task is to tell when the rod appears in a true vertical position. The difficulty comes from the frame's position, which can confuse the

Figure 6.1 Various positions for the rod-and-frame test.

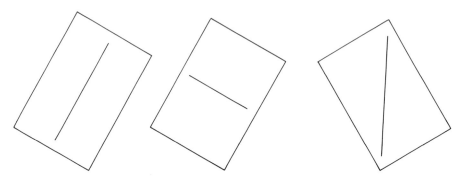

viewer's judgment of the rod's verticality. To align the rod in a true vertical position, the viewer must ignore the frame. Generally, the studies in Maccoby and Jacklin's review of the rod-and-frame test found that beginning in adolescence and continuing into adulthood, males have a keener visual-spatial ability than do females.

In his research Witkin noted that males' ability to ignore the frame and concentrate on the rod in judging its verticality was linked to a specific thinking process called an *analytical cognitive style.* According to Witkin, the possession of an analytical style predisposes males to ignore and avoid the irrelevant aspects of a task and any impulse that may lead them to an incorrect solution. Put more simply, males with their purported analytical ability are thought to be better able to focus on the task at hand and to come up with the correct solution regardless of other competing demands. Because females used the frame to assist them in their judgment of the rod's verticality, they were considered to possess a *global cognitive style.* Consequently, females purportedly have difficulty disregarding extraneous material and are quick to rely on impulse and possibly to make more mistakes. The bottom line in Witkin's notions of analytic and global cognitive styles was that men think differently from women. Following this line of reasoning, men it would seem are better suited for some jobs than women are. For example, men with their analytical ability are disposed to be better organizers, whereas women with their global style make better followers than leaders. Even though some will argue that men and women think differently,[9] Maccoby and Jacklin could find no substantive evidence for such an alleged sex difference in thinking styles.

Quantitative Ability History and tradition would have us believe that men are superior to women in mathematical ability. The research into quantitative abilities does indicate that beginning in adolescence, males show a slightly superior quantitative aptitude.

Perspectives on the Male

"Sure I can count up to 10 . . . But not from memory."

In the minds of most people, the belief that males are superior in math carries over to include the idea that males are similarly gifted in science, especially in the natural sciences. Visit almost any university or industrial research facility, and you will come away with the notion that the natural sciences are an almost exclusively male preserve. (In 1978 ninety-one percent of all physical scientists in the United States were male.[10]) But numbers alone should not lead us to the conclusion that males are somehow predisposed toward the natural sciences. Maccoby and Jacklin argue that although males seem drawn to science, it may not be on account of their superior mathematical ability but rather some other ability, for example, their visual-spatial aptitude.

> During adolescence, boys' superiority in math tends to be accompanied by better mastery of scientific subject matter and greater interest in science. The two disciplines are of course closely linked in that science relies heavily upon math in formulating its problems and finding their solutions. One may ask whether male superiority in science is a derivative of greater math abilities or whether both are a function of a third factor. In this connection, some findings of the Harvard Project Physics are interesting. Physics achievement tests were given to a large sample of high school students. On the portion of the test calling for visual-spatial skills, the male physics students did better; on verbal test items, females physics students obtained higher scores. It would appear that verbal and spatial factors account for some of the variance in science achievement.[11]

Creativity Creativity is both an elusive and a desired ability. One who can discover a unique solution or produce a novel work of art or machinery or whatever is usually thought to be creative and finds the public's attention turned his or her way. Because the majority of well-known creative people were and are male, the assumption is that males somehow are predisposed to creative acts. Probably because of the lack of female names in the annals of creativity, females are thought to be less prone to creative insights. Research on the proprietors of creative abilities portrays a somewhat different image. In their summary of some thirty studies of both verbal and nonverbal creativity, Maccoby and Jacklin concluded,

> . . . on verbal tests of creative ability no sex differences are found in the preschool and the earliest school years, but from about the age of 7 girls show an advantage in a majority of studies. On nonverbal measures, no clear trend toward superiority of either sex can be discerned. In general, then, it may be said that tests of creativity reflect the already documented difference between the sexes in verbal skills; clearly, girls and women are at least as able as boys and men to generate a variety of hypotheses and produce unusual ideas. Thus the underrepresentation of women in the ranks of the outstanding creative figures of earlier and present times would not appear to arise from any general deficiency in "the production of associative content that is abundant and unique."[12]

We have reviewed several abilities, most of which are presumed to be found more readily in one sex or the other. But more often than not, the research in sex differences either finds no evidence for a supposed sex difference or the difference unexpectedly favors the sex stereotypically thought deficient. For example, research finds no difference between the sexes in their general intelligence, styles of thinking, or nonverbal creative abilities. For reasons yet unknown, beginning in early adolescence, boys excel in visual-spatial abilities and girls excel in verbal abilities. Although boys seem to have a slight advantage in math, their presumed edge in science may be related to factors other than mathematical ability. Girls, on the other hand, outperform boys in creative tasks that involve words. Overall, the sexes do not seem radically different in their abilities, at least not in the ones that count when one considers the ingredients for a productive life.

SOCIAL DIFFERENCES

Sex differences in social behaviors are especially noteworthy to our discussion of the male experience. The common sex role stereotypes portray males, for example, as much more likely to act more aggressively, coldly, reservedly, and self-assuredly toward others than are females. Before we discuss the evidence relating to several commonly assumed sex differences in social behaviors, we should keep in mind one important fact. In those instances where sex differences are shown, they are more likely the result of society's pressures than some innate biological sex difference.

Perspectives on the Male

Self-Disclosure Most people like to talk to others about themselves. It often makes a person feel good to share something personal or intimate with another person. "To get something off one's chest" is supposedly a helpful and practical aid for one's mental health. Social scientists refer to this sharing as *self-disclosure*.

The late Sidney Jourard conducted much of the early research on self-disclosure. Much of Jourard and others' research pointed to a sex difference in self-disclosure, namely, that most males reported that they not only disclosed less about themselves to others but also that when they did disclose they did so to fewer people than females did.[13] Furthermore, while some studies found no sex difference in self-disclosure, no study reported males disclosing more than females.[14] This does not mean that males never disclose personal information about themselves. However, when males do disclose, they usually do so with women and not other men. The females to whom males choose to disclose are usually close relatives or friends (mothers, girlfriends, or wives). In fact, males generally look upon males who are disclosers with some skepticism.[15] Why most males keep their personal feelings from others is a matter of speculation. Possibly they do so because males are taught very early in life to hide their feelings from others. "If others know how you really feel," notes Marc Fasteau, "you can be hurt, and that in itself is incompatible with manhood."[16]

Dependency Napoleon Bonaparte is credited with saying, "Nature intended women to be our slaves . . . they are our property; we are not theirs. They belong to us, just as a tree that bears fruit belongs to a gardener."[17] Many people still believe this today, and their belief is portrayed in the common stereotype of the dependent and clinging woman.

In the last chapter we noted that much of a young boy's socialization revolves around efforts to make him independent. Dependency-independency is a multi-faceted concept and thus somewhat difficult to define. In the following paragraphs we will look at three facets of dependency: proximity, susceptibility to peer pressure, or conformity, and a special form of dependency, that of using others to help define one's sex role.

When a child clings to or stays close by a parent or an adult caretaker, the child is exhibiting what psychologists call *proximal behaviors*. Observing proximal behaviors in young children is both a common method and a valid behavioral measure for defining dependency. Recall that Goldberg and Lewis found that thirteen-month-old females showed more proximal behaviors than did thirteen-month-old males.[18] Furthermore, these researchers found that the higher incidence of proximal behaviors among female children was linked to how their mothers treated them earlier on. Therefore, do the sexes differ in proximal behaviors naturally or are they a product of differential treatment by parents or other adult caretakers? As of the moment, we do not have a definite answer. However, after reviewing more than twenty-five studies dealing with touching and proximal behaviors, Maccoby and Jacklin concluded that ". . . the number of studies finding no difference in proximity outnumber the 'girls higher' studies by more than three to one, and hence the picture as a whole is quite clearly one of sex similarity rather than sex difference."[19]

As children grow older, they begin to turn more toward peers for acceptance and approval. The kinds of peer groups females form are quite different from those formed by males. Girls are more likely to form "chumships," which are exclusive two-person or three-person groups. Boys, on the other hand, tend to congregate in larger groups, which by their very size come to exert considerable pressure on their members. In their respective groups, there is no evidence that either males or females are more or less susceptible to peer pressure.

However, a number of early conformity studies found that females tended to conform more readily to group pressure in certain situations than did males.[20] For example, in an Asch-type situation, a person is asked to select two lines of equal length after hearing a number of other persons first give obviously incorrect answers. The early research of this type found females more easily swayed by the group to give incorrect answers (that is, to conform to group pressure) than males were.[21] But subsequent researchers began to question the nature of the Asch situation with respect to its content (visual-spatial ability) as possibly being male-biased. Several people began to suggest the possibility that females might be expected to conform to group pressure in those situations calling for visual-spatial judgments, while males might just as likely conform to situations calling for female-biased tasks.

Frank Sistrunk and John McDavid set out to study the nature of the task on the level of a person's conformity.[22] First, they compiled three sets of topics purportedly divided into topics of male interest, female interest, and of interest to both sexes. Next, they had male and female students give their opinions on each of the three sets of topics after they had first been given the opinions of a fictitious majority for each topic. Not surprisingly, males conformed more to the majority's opinion on the topics of female interest, and females conformed more to the majority's opinion on the topics of male interest. For the neutral topics, there was no difference between females and males in the amount of conformity to the majority's opinions. From this research, we can assume that females are no more likely to conform in all situations than are males. Females tend to resist conformity to group pressure when they are sure of the situation to about the same degree that confident males do.

We come now to a third type of dependency, which some people may argue is not really dependency in the traditional sense of the word. Recently, Joseph Pleck outlined a unique male-female situation in which some men depend on women to validate certain features of their masculinity. Pleck writes that "In traditional masculinity, to experience oneself as masculine requires that women play their prescribed role of doing the things that make men feel masculine."[23] For example, a clinging woman makes some men feel very masculine in the sense of being protective and powerful in the relationship. Furthermore, Pleck describes how men who act traditionally need women to act as an emotional outlet.

Perspectives on the Male

Thus some men experience emotions such as compassion, joy, and ecstasy only through their relationships with women. These men are almost fearful, it seems, to feel these emotions for themselves. In a sense they experience their emotions vicariously through women. This leads us to suggest that men who define their masculinity in the traditional manner are dependent on women not only to act as a support for their masculinity but to be a bridge for some emotional experiences that they may think of as too feminine for them to express.

Nurturance Women have traditionally been thought to possess a certain predisposition for providing aid to others. Their supposed natural concern and ready willingness to help others have made them natural candidates for nursing, teaching, and social work careers, as well as a career as wife and mother. Men, on the other hand, are thought more prone to withhold assistance from others and to show what may be called indifference in the face of other people's adversity. Maccoby and Jacklin's review of some twenty studies reveals little evidence of sex differences in nurturant behaviors.

However, one study reported by Maccoby and Jacklin is worth noting because of its antistereotypic conclusions regarding adult men and nurturant behaviors. Ross Parke and S. E. O'Leary observed parents' interactions with their newborn infants with an eye especially on the number of nurturant behaviors (holding, rocking, looking, fondling, and smiling) engaged in by each parent.[24] When both parents were together, fathers engaged in *more* nurturant behaviors (with the exception of smiling) than mothers did. When the fathers were alone with their babies, they engaged in as many or more nurturant behaviors as did mothers when they were alone with their babies. Interestingly, Parke and O'Leary's sample of fathers consisted of two significantly different groups of men. The first group was mainly well educated and interested in natural childbirth. (Several from this group had been in the delivery room during the birth of their baby.) The second group was primarily working-class, and no members of this group were in the delivery room during the birth of their baby. Even with two such different groups of men, finding that fathers can and do provide as much nurturance as mothers do should put to rest the notion that men are incapable of nurturant behavior.

Aggressiveness The picture of the male as aggressor and the female as pacifier is a stereotype ingrained in many people's minds. As shown in Maccoby and Jacklin's review of sex differences in aggression, males are clearly more *physically* aggressive than are females at every age and in every situation.[25] From preschool years through adulthood, males are more apt to intentionally inflict pain on others than are females. But we should not be too quick therefore to assume that females are somehow inhibited from being aggressive toward others. One can be aggressive in many other ways besides physically. For example, researchers have found little or no differences between males and females in verbal aggressiveness (yelling, screaming, and swearing), in nonverbal aggressiveness (glaring, frowning, and making obscene gestures), or when others encourage or provoke either sex to be aggressive (for example, use rewards or shocks).[26] Even though there is clearly a sex difference with respect to physical aggression, the sexes do not differ in others kinds of aggression.

We have examined a number of common stereotypic sex differences in social behaviors. Surprisingly, researchers have found little evidence to support many of these commonly accepted stereotypes. Granted, most males seem to be less willing than most females to disclose their intimate feelings to others, with the possible exceptions of a few close females. Males are more physically aggressive than are females, but little can be found to suggest a sex difference in other forms of aggressiveness. The stereotypic portrayals of females as dependent, conforming and nurturant are grossly unfounded. Thus, with respect to sex differences regarding the social behaviors and intellectual abilities that we have examined, the sexes appear more similar than the common sex role stereotypes would have us believe.

MASCULINE SEX ROLE IDENTITY

Although the sexes are not so different in certain intellectual abilities and social behaviors, the sexes are different in some other very important ways. For example, each sex learns its own unique sex role, and its members come to define themselves in terms of what society deems a masculine or feminine sex role identity. Recall that by sex role identity we mean that a person is thought to identify psychologically with and conform to his or her same sex group. Furthermore, keep in mind that sex role identity is an implied or hypothetical idea that cannot be observed or measured directly but only indirectly by a person's behavior. Thus a male is thought to have a masculine sex role identity if he describes himself and acts in those ways his society labels as masculine.

How a masculine sex role identity develops is a point of some debate among psychologists. In this section we will examine three theoretical positions on the development of sex role identity: the psychoanalytic-identification theory, the social-learning theory, and the cognitive-developmental theory.

PSYCHOANALYTIC-IDENTIFICATION THEORY OF SEX ROLE IDENTITY

Few people in recent history have had the impact on contemporary thought, than has the founder of psychoanalysis, Sigmund Freud. Freud's views on human nature and the underlying causes of human behavior challenged the earlier assumption of the preeminence of rational thought and conscious control over behavior. Freud contended that human nature is beset by animal instincts and urges and that most human activity is determined by unconscious forces. Although Freud's theory of human nature encompasses a great deal more than the development of a masculine or feminine sex role identity, we shall restrict our discussion to the psychological stages and interpersonal relationships that foster the development of a person's sex role identity.

Perspectives on the Male

Freud's theory of psychosexual development was first outlined in 1905 with the publication of *Three Essays on the Theory of Sexuality*.[27] Although Freud's psychosexual theory deals with universal patterns of both male and female development, his understanding of the female's psychosexual development remained an "impenetrable obscurity" to him, causing many to criticize his theory as being overly male-biased.[28] Freud's psychosexual theory encompasses five distinct stages; oral, anal, phallic, latency, and genital.

During the first year of life, the infant is totally dependent on others for its survival. Because the mouth, lips, and tongue are the basic structures associated with nourishment, various pleasurable sensations, and release of instinctual urges, Freud labeled this period the *oral stage*. During this stage, the infant becomes strongly attached to its mother because she is the one most likely to provide oral pleasure in the guise of breast or bottle feeding.

During the second and third years of life, the focus of pleasure moves from the oral area to the anal region, and thus Freud called this period the *anal stage*. The child experiences pleasure from the retention and expulsion of feces, and eventually he or she comes to learn how minor withholding of the sphincter muscle can intensify the subsequent pleasure of bowel movement. Toilet training generally takes place during the anal stage. Freud hypothesized that depending on how parents handled this initially painful experience for the child, the outcome would have lasting effects on the child's later personality.

According to Freud's theory, boys and girls go through the oral and anal stages in generally parallel ways. Beginning in the fourth year and continuing into the fifth year, however, the psychosexual development of boys and girls diverges. Freud called this period the *phallic stage*.

For a boy, the major conflict during the phallic period is called the *Oedipus complex*. In Freud's theory, the Oedipus complex contains the features that Sophocles described in his tragic Greek play *Oedipus Rex*. In the play, the king of Thebes unknowingly kills his father and later enters into an incestuous marriage with his mother. Based on his own self-analysis, Freud believed every boy unconsciously relives this age-old conflict of desiring his mother and wishing his father's demise.

As the phallic period unfolds, the boy begins to fear that somehow his father may discover the son's unruly desires and consequently punish him or, more specifically, his penis. The boy's fear of the father's retaliation Freud called *castration anxiety*. The devastating anxiety created by the fear of castration forces the boy to renounce his mother and to identify with his former rival, his father. With the new allegiance or bond to his father, the boy begins to identify with his father by adopting the attitudes, morals, values, and— of particular importance to the present discussion—his father's sex-typed behaviors. Freud speculated that once the son identifies with his father, the son's masculine sex role identity emerges.

The female version of the phallic period Freud called the *Electra complex*. As with the boy, the girl develops a strong attachment to her mother during her first two to three years. But when the girl discovers that she has no penis like her brother or father, she blames her mother for her lost penis. After renouncing her mother, the girl vies with her mother for her father's attention and love. At the heart of the daughter's new relationship with her father is what Freud called *penis envy.* The resolution of the girl's phallic period comes about when she realizes that she cannot have her father as a lover and thus identifies with her mother. By identifying with her mother, the girl learns the attitudes and behaviors appropriate for the female and consequently forms a feminine sex role identity.[29]

The resolution of the phallic period finds each sex identifying with his or her same-sex parent, thereby assuring the continuance of appropriate sex role behaviors for the next generation. The phallic period is not only crucial in the formation of each sex's masculine or feminine sex role identity, but it is also thought to be the starting point at which each sex becomes attracted to the opposite sex in the guise of parents. Consequently, the fourth period, the *latency stage,* finds each sex repressing sexual fantasies and wishes out of consciousness. Freud believed that the latency stage lasts from about the seventh year and to the beginning of puberty. During these years, children tend to move away from parental control and contact and begin to spend more time with the same-sex peers.

At puberty each sex enters the *genital stage.* During this period, young people begin to become interested in sexuality and are attracted to the opposite sex. According to Freud, the adolescent male and female learn to inhibit childhood fantasies in favor of more responsible and reality-oriented adult activities. The focal point of the genital stage is the directing of the person's sexual energies into an appropriate heterosexual relationship (marriage) and responsible work practices.

Freud's theory of the development of a sex role identity is entangled with several extremely controversial concepts, such as unconscious mental processes, Oedipus and Electra complexes, and castration anxiety and penis envy. There is virtually no way to test the validity of these ideas because of the difficulty—some would say the impossibility—of measuring unconscious events. We are left with an interesting theory but one that is virtually impossible to substantiate.

SOCIAL-LEARNING THEORY OF SEX-TYPED BEHAVIORS

Although Freud's theories have captured the minds and interests of a wide circle of intelligent laypeople, American psychologists, for the most part, have been influenced more by what is called *behaviorism.* John Watson, an early proponent of behaviorism, debunked the idea of unconscious processes in favor of the notion that all behavior is learned. Behaviorists like Watson saw no need to hypothesize an innate psychological construct such as sex role identity but rather suggested that masculine and feminine behaviors (sex-typed behaviors) were all learned. In the 1930s and 1940s, B. F. Skinner expanded on Watson's ideas and suggested that most behaviors are learned through the process of *reinforcement,* which simply means that a behavior that is followed by a reward is more likely to continue.

Perspectives on the Male

Skinner's theory of learning has stimulated countless social scientists to look at human behavior as caused not by unconscious urges and wishes but rather by their consequences. Psychologists like Albert Bandura and Richard Walters have taken Skinner's theory of learning and added a social identification component to it to come up with a social-learning approach to human development in general and sex role development in particular.[30] Probably the most comprehensive presentation of the social-learning approach to sex role development was presented by Walter Mischel.[31]

The social-learning approach is relatively straightforward in its explanation of sex role development. Most early learning of simple behaviors can be explained by traditional learning principles. Take the example of a little boy who is given a model train for his birthday. His father offers to help set up the train, and father and son spend hours playing together. In this example the young boy is likely to develop an interest in trains (a sex-typed interest) because of the rewards that come with playing with trains (his father's approval and sometimes his presence).

Young children also learn sex role behaviors that are too complex to be explained solely on the basis of the reward principle. The social-learning approach allows for the learning of more complex activities on the basis of what is called *observational learning*. Accordingly, one learns by observing and imitating others, that is, models. The example comes to mind of a five-year-old boy perched on the bathroom sink in front of the mirror, face lathered with shaving cream, precariously about to shave with his father's safety razor. How can we account for all of the behaviors that have gone into this complex activity? Certainly, his parents have not rewarded him for playing with shaving cream or safety razors. No, he has observed his father while shaving and now is about to perform the male ritual of the first shave, albeit without the stubble.

The key to observational learning is the choice of a model to imitate. In general, children tend to imitate a model who meets four criteria: The model is perceived as similar, as warm or friendly, as powerful and/or having high status, and is rewarded for performing the specific action being imitated. We can use the example of our "little shaver" to see how his model for shaving (his father) meets these criteria.

First of all, the little boy sees his father (and other men on television) with shaving cream on his face going about the business of shaving. The little boy views himself as a little man and thus sees no reason why he should not shave also. Second, if the father is warm and loving toward his son, including him in activities such as shaving, the son is more likely to imitate the behaviors observed in a friendly atmosphere. Third, the father is certainly powerful and strong in the eyes of a five-year-old son, but even more important than physcial strength the boy may see his father as more powerful than his mother. Sensing his father's dominant role or status within the home, the little boy is more likely to imitate the father's behaviors rather than the mother's. Fourth, if the son has watched

Children learn many sex-typed behaviors that are carried into adulthood. *Source:* top, © *Jean-Claude Lejeune;* bottom, © *Burke Uzzle, Magnum Photos.*

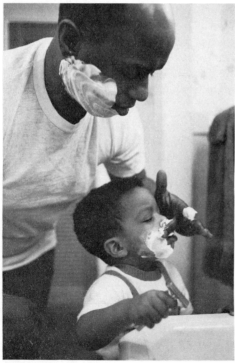

his father shaving and heard him comment on how good it feels to shave, later on the son is more likely to imitate the activities for which his father is rewarded. Given all of these conditions, it is no wonder that we find our five-year-old about to slice off these pesky little whiskers.

Essentially, social-learning theory states that early sex-typed behaviors are learned because of the rewards that a child receives or the punishments that he avoids for performing certain sex-typed behaviors. Later more complex sex-typed behaviors are learned by the observation and imitation of others. Social-learning theory does not limit a child's model to only his or her same-sex parent. Television characters, sports heroes, teachers, older siblings, and many others are imitated by impressionable children.

COGNITIVE-DEVELOPMENTAL THEORY OF SEX ROLE IDENTITY

The theory of cognitive development was proposed by the Swiss zoologist Jean Piaget. Piaget theorized that the human ability to think logically is genetically determined and unfolds in a strict, sequential, stagelike fashion. Psychologist Lawrence Kohlberg has taken Piaget's views on cognitive (intellectual) development and applied them to sex role development.

Kohlberg disagrees with Freud's views on the sexual basis of sex role identity (the Oedipus and Electra complexes) and with the singular emphasis on the importance of reinforcement and modeling of social-learning theory. Instead, Kohlberg's theory ". . . stresses the active nature of the child's thought as he organizes

The Psychological Perspective

his role perceptions and role learnings around his basic conceptions of his body and his world."[32] Kohlberg contrasts his views of sex role development with that of the social-learning model in the following way:

> [In social-learning theory,] sex-typed behavior and attitudes are acquired through social rewards that follow sex-appropriate responses made by the child or by a relevant model. The social-learning syllogism is: "I want rewards, I am rewarded for doing boy things, therefore I want to be a boy." In contrast, a cognitive theory assumes this sequence: "I am a boy, therefore I want to do boy things, therefore the opportunity to do boy things (and to gain approval for doing them) is rewarding."[33]

The first step in the cognitive-developmental approach is the boy's self-labeling of himself as a "boy" or the development of what Kohlberg calls a *masculine gender identity*. But how does a male child come to learn the label "boy" and to attach it and all of its properties to himself? He learns the label "boy" in much the same way as he learns any other label, such as "mommy," "daddy," "doggie," and so on. Others teach him that he is a "boy." As a boy grows older and his thinking process develops, he learns to associate more complicated relationships with his sex and thus he learns the principle of gender constancy. For example, a little boy who states that he is going to be a daddy when he grows up is showing by the association of himself and the label "daddy" that he has developed a masculine gender identity and that he has learned that being a daddy is part of (that is, is consistent with) being a boy. With the following example, Kohlberg suggests that gender identity is dependent on an age-related cognitive developmental sequence.

> The following comments were made by Jimmy, just turning four, to his four-and-a-half-year old friend Johnny:
> Johnny: I'm going to be an airplane builder when I grow up.
> Jimmy: When I grow up, I'll be a Mommy.
> Johnny: No, you can't be a Mommy. You have to be a Daddy.
> Jimmy: No, I'm going to be a Mommy.
> Johnny: No, you're not a girl, you can't be a Mommy.
> Jimmy: Yes, I can.[34]

Some evidence of a relationship between age and the development of a child's gender identity comes from clinical cases reporting the outcomes of sex-reassignment procedures. Simply stated, *sex reassignment* means that a child of one biological sex is raised as the other sex. The necessity for sex reassignment of a child normally occurs only in the most extreme circumstances. John Money and Patricia Tucker describe just such a case, when an accident prompted sex reassignment for a male child.

> A young farm couple took their sturdy, normal, identical twin boys to a physician in a nearby hospital to be circumcised when the boys were seven months old. The physician elected to use an electric cauterizing needle instead of a scalpel to remove the foreskin of the twin who chanced to be brought into the operating room first. When this baby's foreskin didn't give on the first try, or on the second, the doctor

stepped up the current. On the third try, the surge of heat from the electricity literally cooked the baby's penis. Unable to heal, the penis dried up, and in a few days sloughed off completely, like the stub of an umbilical cord.[35]

After several months of fruitless searching for some way to save their son's masculinity, the parents decided to reassign their son to the role of a daughter. Money and Tucker state that if the parents had waited until their son's gender identity had formed, there would have been little hope for the success of the reassignment procedure.

Kohlberg cites Money's research in sex reassignments as evidence of the age-related aspect of a child's gender identity. A child of one biological sex can learn behaviors and attitudes of the opposite sex only if the child's gender identity is not yet developed. According to the cognitive-developmental theory, once a child adopts a sex-specific gender identity, he or she will behave in ways that are appropriate or consistent with his or her gender identity regardless of external forces.

EVALUATING THE PSYCHOLOGICAL THEORIES OF SEX ROLE IDENTITY

We have presented three psychological theories that attempt to explain the development of the male's sex role identity, namely, psychoanalytic-identification, social-learning, and cognitive-developmental (see Figure 6.2). We now will briefly evaluate each of these theories in terms of how well it explains the concept of sex role identity.

As we have already mentioned, Freud's psychoanalytic-identification theory of sex role identity is a rather complex set of ideas which postulate that sex role identity develops out of a child's unconscious conflict and subsequent identification with his or her same-sex parent. A serious drawback to this perspective is its inability to explain adequately female development. (This does not imply that the theory necessarily explains male development accurately.) Furthermore, the suggestion that sex role identity develops out of certain dramatic events that take place in a five- or six-year-old child's unconscious mind is impossible to verify. The psychoanalytic-identification model of sex role identity may have caught the attention and interest of a few clinical psychologists and psychiatrists, but most others place greater credence in more observable and measurable explanations of sex role development.

Social-learning theory borrows heavily from both traditional-learning and observational-learning theories to explain sex role development. The traditional learning principle of reinforcement purportedly explains how children learn specific sex-typed behaviors. The basic idea here is that children are reinforced (that is, rewarded for performing certain sex-typed behaviors) by their parents, other adults, and peers. Some research suggests that parents are more likely to reinforce sex-typed behaviors with boys than with girls[36] and that peers tend to reinforce sex-typed behaviors more strictly than do adults.[37]

Figure 6.2 Three psychological theories of masculine sex role identity.

	Psychoanalytic-identification theory	Social-learning theory	Cognitive-developmental theory
Stage I.	♂ Son / ♀ Mother — Desire for mother (Oedipus complex)	♂ Son / ♂ Father — Son's attachment to father as major rewarder (and punisher-controller)	♂ Son — Sex-typed identity
Stage II.	♂ Son / ♂ Father — Fear of father's retaliation (castration anxiety)	♂ Father / ♂ Son — Identification modeling of father	♂ Father / ♂ Son — Modeling of father
Stage III.	♂ Father / ♂ Son — Identification with father (Oedipus resolution and masculine sex role identity)	♂ Son — Sex-typed behaviors and attitudes	♂ Father / ♂ Son — Attachment to father

Observational learning may be a more important element of social-learning theory because it attempts to explain how children learn complex sex-typed behaviors. The basic feature of this component suggests that a child learns an entire sequence of sex-typed behaviors (for example, putting on shaving cream, playing with a razor, and going through the motions of shaving) by imitating others (models) even without their reinforcement.

The social-learning theory goes far in conceptually explaining how both sexes learn their sex-typed behaviors. This perspective explains the development of *both* sexes' sex role development to a much greater degree than does the psychoanalytic-identification theory. However, there is little substantive evidence to support the idea that the sexes are exposed to the levels of differential reinforcement that this theory proposes. Furthermore, there is less evidence than we might suspect at first that imitation of same-sex parent accounts for many of a child's sex-typed behaviors.[38] Thus the social-learning theory of sex role development does not appear to be the sole answer for a child's sex role development.

The cognitive-developmental theory of sex role development suffers in much the same way as the psychoanalytic-identification theory in that it accounts for the male's sex role development much better than the female's development. The basic idea of this theory is that a young boy must first form a cognitive picture of himself as a male rather than a female, after which he goes on to learn appropriate sex-typed behaviors mainly by imitating his same-sex parent and other male figures. This perspective subscribes to many of the same principles of learning—and their pitfalls as well—outlined in the social-learning theory. Again, the cognitive-developmental theory has not generated convincing research to support its major thesis.[39]

Perspectives on the Male

PSYCHOLOGY LOOKS AT THE MALE SEX ROLE

As is evident from previous chapters, researchers from various disciplines have debated the issue of what comprises the essential features of maleness and what forces mold the male sex role. For decades, psychologists have played an important part in shaping many people's thoughts about the male sex role and masculinity. In this section we will examine what psychologists have theorized about the male experience. The psychology of the male sex role has gone through several transitions in a relatively short period of time.

THE MALE SEX ROLE IDENTITY (MSRI) PARADIGM

Before we take up the history of psychology's research into masculinity and the male sex role and its contributions to popular belief, turn to "Sex Roles Quiz #1" (pages 132–33) and answer *true* or *false* to each statement. How many did you answer *true?* More than half? Joseph Pleck, Program Director of the Wellesley College Center for Research on Women, developed this quiz as a check to see how much a person's thinking is influenced by what psychologists have been saying about masculinity during the past forty to fifty years. The more statements that you answered true, the more you have been influenced by prominent psychological theories about what masculinity is and how it develops.

The sixteen statements in this quiz are based on assumptions about masculinity that psychologists have been making for years. Pleck outlined these assumptions in a careful analysis of what he calls the *male sex role identity* (MSRI) paradigm. (A *paradigm* is a set of ideas or assumptions that scientists make in order to better understand their subject matter.[40]) According to Pleck, the basic assumptions of the MSRI are as follows:

1. Sex role identity is operationally defined by measures of psychological sex typing, conceptualized in terms of psychological masculinity and/or femininity dimensions.
2. Sex role identity derives from identification-modeling and, to a lesser extent, reinforcement and cognitive learning of sex-typed traits, especially among males.
3. The development of appropriate sex role identity is a risky, failure-prone process, especially for males.
4. Homosexuality reflects a disturbance of sex role identity.
5. Appropriate sex role identity is necessary for good psychological adjustment because of an inner psychological need for it.
6. Hypermasculinity in males (exaggerated masculinity, often with negative social consequences) indicates insecurity in their sex role identities.
7. Problems of sex role identity account for men's negative attitudes and behaviors toward women.
8. Problems of sex role identity account for boys' difficulties in school performance and adjustment.
9. Black males are particularly vulnerable to sex role identity problems.
10. Male adolescent initiation rites are a response to problems of sex role identity.
11. Historical changes in the character of work and the organization of the family have made it more difficult for men to develop and maintain their sex role identities.[41]

SEX ROLES QUIZ #1

	True	False

1. Developing a secure sense of one's masculinity (for males) or femininity (for females) is one of the most important tasks in personality development.

2. A secure sense of masculinity or femininity comes primarily from one's relationships with the parent of the same sex in childhood and adolescence.

3. Excessive masculinity on the outside often indicates that a man is unsure about his masculinity on the inside.

4. Growing up in a household without a father is likely to cause serious sex role identity problems for boys.

5. Many things can go wrong in personality development to cause people to be insecure in their sex roles. As a result, a relatively large proportion of people, especially males, have sex role identity problems.

6. Homosexuality reflects a profoundly disturbed sense of one's masculinity or femininity.

7. Two problems faced by men today compared to a hundred years ago that make it hard for them to feel really masculine are that their jobs are more passive and sedentary and their authority over their wives diminished.

8. Having a secure sex role identity, as shown by sex-appropriate traits and characteristics, is one of the most important contributors to good psychological adjustment.

9. One of the main sources of male violence, crime and delinquency is that many men need to compensate for their insecure sense of masculinity.

10. The reason for the initiation ceremonies for the male adolescent in many cultures is that they serve to help the boy develop a secure sex role identity, especially in societies where the boy has lived or associated primarily with women earlier in life. _____ _____

11. Because of his intense early identification with his mother, a boy develops an early feminine sex role identity, which later he must overcome to have a secure masculine identity. _____ _____

12. Black males are especially vulnerable to sex role identity problems because of the high rate of paternal absence and lack of good male role models among blacks. _____ _____

13. Many men participate in bodybuilding and sports to compensate for an inner insecurity in their masculinity. _____ _____

14. We need more men in daycare centers and elementary schools to provide boys with male sex role identity models. _____ _____

15. The reason for the hostility and violence that some men show toward women is men's fear of the psychological femininity in themselves deriving from their early relationships with their mothers. _____ _____

16. The current blurring of women's and men's sex roles is making it hard for children to develop healthy sex role identities. _____ _____

Source: J. Pleck, *The Myth of Masculinity* (Cambridge, Mass.: MIT Press, 1981), pp. 1–3.

Several basic psychological ideas underlie the MSRI paradigm. First of all, most scientists interested in the subject of masculinity have accepted as fact that sex role identity develops out of an innate psychological need. Consequently, masculinity or femininity is thought to be a basic part of a person's personality structure, not something a person learns or acquires from social agents. Another idea holds that the more a male fits society's stereotypes of masculine behavior, the more psychologically healthy he is. Conversely, the more distant a male's behaviors are from the male sex role, the less psychologically healthy he is. Still another component of the MSRI is the belief that many things can go wrong, and often do, during sex role development, especially for males. For example, if a boy's mother is domineering and strong-willed and his father is weak and passive, the boy's developing sense of masculinity may become disturbed, opening up the possibility of the boy's growing up to be a homosexual. Or, if a boy has an insecure and poorly developed sense of masculinity, he may try to overcompensate for this condition by exaggerating certain features of the male sex role like performing acts of violence and aggression against others, especially women. Furthermore, Pleck suggests that because many social scientists and laypeople alike think of masculinity and femininity as innate features of personality, these people believe that traditional conceptions of masculinity and femininity should not be tampered with. In fact, they believe that proposed changes in the overall conceptions of sex roles and specific sex-typed behaviors can only lead to harmful consequences for both society and the individual.

How the MSRI developed and what psychological theories of masculinity and femininity account for it provide a revealing analysis of the trends of psychological research over the past forty years. Pleck outlined three specific research trends that account for the present-day view of masculinity: the bipolar, the multilevel, and the androgynous theories of masculinity.

The Bipolar Perspective on Masculinity From the 1930s until the 1950s, psychologists turned their attention to measuring masculinity and femininity by means of various psychological tests.[42] A major concern of many psychologists of this era was how best to measure what was basically thought of as mutually exclusive categories of sex-appropriate traits, behaviors, and preferences. For example, if a man stated that he liked to play football, work on a car, and read sports magazines—all traditionally defined sex-typed masculine activities—it was assumed that he would not like to play croquet, do needle work, and read romance stories—all traditionally defined sex-typed feminine activities. In terms of this approach, masculinity was defined simply as the score a male earned on any number of masculinity-femininity (m-f) tests. The more masculine sex-typed items on a m-f test that a male agreed with, the more masculine he was presumed to be. However, a male who scored low on the masculinity items and thus obtained a high femininity score was thought to have a poorly developed or inadequate masculine identity. The important features of this perspective were that masculinity was thought to be an intricate part of personality, the opposite of femininity, and could be measured, that is, defined, by various psychological tests.

The Multilevel Perspective on Masculinity During the 1950s and 1960s, a second theoretical perspective emerged; this one incorporated Freud's views on the dual nature of consciousness and unconsciousness and the bipolar perspective on masculinity and femininity. Freud had theorized that personality contains both conscious and unconscious levels, and thus several psychologists speculated that masculinity must also have both unconscious and conscious levels.[43] Sex role identity was thought of in terms of two distinct levels, either of which could be masculine or feminine in its makeup. Theoretically speaking, a male's sex role identity could take on one of four possible combinations: (1) unconscious and conscious masculinity, (2) unconscious and conscious femininity, (3) unconscious femininity and conscious masculinity, and (4) unconscious masculinity and conscious femininity. As psychologists grew more skillful in constructing ambiguous tests, which are generally called *projective tests,* attention focused on those tests that purportedly measured the deeper, more unconscious features of masculinity.[44]

The Androgynous Perspective on Masculinity The third and most recent theoretical perspective of the MSRI is referred to as *androgynous;* it dismissed the notion of an unconscious level in a person's sex role identity. Furthermore, the androgynous perspective suggested that masculinity and femininity are not opposite ends on a single continuum—as proposed in the bipolar perspective—but rather that masculinity and femininity are actually two independent dimensions of personality.[45] Thus a person may exhibit both masculine and feminine characteristics (androgynous sex role identity) or highly masculine sex-typed characteristics (masculine sex role identity) or highly feminine sex-typed characteristics (feminine sex role identity).

Interestingly, each of the three perspectives viewed the relationship between mental health and sex role identity from the vantage of how it conceived masculinity and femininity. The bipolar theory suggested that because masculinity and femininity were opposite poles on a single dimension, the more masculine a male's behaviors were (exhibiting masculine sex-typed characertistics), the more mentally healthy he was. The multilevel theory suggested that an adult male's mental health was related to his having both an unconscious and a conscious masculine identity. And the androgynous perspective suggested that a male should exhibit both masculine and feminine sex-typed characteristics to be considered mentally healthy. The androgynous perspective maintains that a proportion of masculine and feminine sex-typed characteristics are essential in order that a person can deal with the complex nature of a changing world.

Even though these perspectives vary in how they describe the dimensions of masculinity and femininity, they share some common elements, including the beliefs that personality traits (for example, toughness, warmth, aggressiveness) can be described as either masculine or feminine sex-typed characteristics and that masculinity and femininity are innate features of personality that can be tapped or measured by psychological tests. These commonalities suggest that the bipolar, multilevel, and androgynous perspectives are more similar than might first be apparent.

TWO VIEWS OF THE MALE SEX ROLE

A common complaint recorded in much of the literature on masculinity is that many contemporary males are experiencing more conflict in their lives nowadays than ever before.[46] Much of the conflict appears to be caused by a clash between

Table 6.2 Comparison of Traditional and Modern Versions of the Male Sex Role

Traditional Male Sex Role	Modern Male Sex Role
Is found in primitive non-Western cultures and lower socioeconomic groups.	Is most obvious in contemporary middle-class society.
Is validated primarily by physical strength and aggression.	Is validated by economic success, achievement, and power over others, especially in the business world.
Shuns emotional expressions, especially those emotions indicative of weakness and vulnerability.	Expects male to be sensitive and emotionally expressive with women but not with other men.
Approves of emotions that indicate strength and power such as anger.	Discourages emotions such as anger and hostility.
Approves sexual double standard where sex is a male prerogative.	Downplays sexual double standard and expects male to satisfy female's sexual needs.
Supports strong male-male relationships but not of an intimate nature.	Encourages men to seek company of women as emotional and romantic partners.
Views women as either whores or madonnas, but in either case as inferior to men.	Views women as different but not inferior, although not men's equal in the business world.

two different male sex role models, namely, the traditional and the modern (see Table 6.2). Many of the features contained in these two models are at odds with each other; consequently, the inconsistencies expressed by these models' opposing expectations cause many males to feel that they are being pulled in two different directions. For example, men are taught very early in life to control their emotions and the expressions thereof. On the other hand, men are often rewarded for expressing feelings of, say, anger, which is considered acceptable for males but not for females. Another example of the opposing expectations in the two versions occurs when males are expected to have close attachments or deep relationships with other men, but at the same time male relationships are expected never to go beyond the point at which emotional expressions of concern and intimacy could be interpreted as having homosexual overtones. The problem is not one of the sex-typed expectations comprising a single male sex role but rather of their constituting two different versions of the male sex role. Let us review both of these in terms of the built-in inconsistencies between them, inconsistencies that can lead to confusion and conflict for many males.

The Traditional Male Sex Role Model Many middle-aged and older men in America grew up believing that a real man had to be strong, unafraid, ready to fight, in control of his emotions, and sexually self-centered. Images of John Wayne or some other physically impressive macho male come to mind. Because of the image of the self-reliant, pioneer-hero who built America, the physical male role has a relatively long-standing history and comprises the essential elements of the traditional male sex role.

Perspectives on the Male

The traditional male role emphasized physical prowess and brute strength as essential ingredients for a man's conception of masculinity. Weakness and vulnerability, especially obvious in the so-called tender emotions, were to be avoided at all cost. Men turned to other men for companionship and friendship seeking masculine relationships in men's clubs and saloons or in strenuous physical sports. Women were objects to be used or kept. Men were the rulers, the patriarchs, and women were to defer to men in almost all matters except those of the home, where women were permitted a certain degree of power and influence in domestic matters.

The traditional male role viewed sexuality as primarily a male activity. In an extreme sense, all men were thought of as insatiable in their sexual needs, and all women were thought to fall into one of two categories: madonnas (mothers, sisters, and wives) or whores (fallen women who were of little virtue and available for sex). Men thought sex was a birthright that they should engage in at will, while women—good women, that is—should remain virginal, saving themselves for their husbands only.

The traditional male sex role placed men in a superior category over women. Women were thought to possess few skills or talents that would serve them anywhere outside of the home. (Of course, a fallen woman had one asset that any man could use, her body.) Furthermore, men believed themselves to be intellectually and physically superior to all women.

As America moved into the twentieth century and society became more technologically oriented, a new male sex role emerged.

The Modern Male Sex Role Model The modern male sex role downplayed the male's physical assets in favor of his intellectual abilities. Men were no longer expected to settle their differences by physical force but rather through communication and reason. Men were still expected to conquer others, but under the new male image, conquest came through knowledge, skillful use of manipulation, and other less physical means. No longer was the rough-and-ready, give-'em-hell type of male idealized; the urbane and cool image now came to be the male ideal. The good-looking and sensitive Paul Newman or Robert Redford type replaced John Wayne in the minds of millions of young men.

The modern male sex role confined male-male relationships primarily to the workplace. Rather than being portrayed as companions and close friends, the newer version of the male role painted other men as competitors in the business world and as rivals in the sexual world. Thus the presumed close bonding between males, which had been a central feature in the traditional model, was replaced with men turning to women rather than other men for companionship and emotional involvement.

Male-female relationships changed drastically in the modern version of the male role. Women were no longer seen as living in an essentially separate world from men. Rather, women and men shared a common world, and men were expected to form deep involvements with women, opening themselves up and sharing their feelings more freely than ever before. In a sense, the new relationship between women and men was one of partnership in which each could draw on the other's strengths and share the other's feelings. However, men were still expected to show no signs of weakness or vulnerability.

According to the modern view, sexuality was no longer a male pastime and prerogative but rather an encounter between two equal, pleasure-seeking creatures. Males were expected to perform intricate, withholding sexual acrobatics, all in the name of satisfying the multiorgasmic female. Much of man's worth depended on the pleasure he brought and the orgasms he caused rather than on the number of women he had sex with. A male who could not please and satisfy a woman's sexual needs was no man at all.

As we have seen, the view of womanhood also changed in the twentieth century's version of the male sex role. Women were no longer expected to automatically defer to men in all matters. A partnership called for input from each partner, who had his or her own perspective to bring to all questions of mutual concern. Women were seen as having certain abilities and skills that could be helpful and complementary to men. Even so, the modern male role envisioned women's presumed more emotional nature as not appropriate to the competitive and success-oriented world of high-level business.

Obviously, remnants of the traditional male sex role linger in this last fifth of the twentieth century, and many men still compare themselves to the expectations of the physical male ideal. At the same time, the achievement-oriented and success-driven ideals of the modern male sex role prompt men to question their masculinity.

THE SEX ROLE STRAIN (SRS) PARADIGM

Although psychologists have been enamored of the propositions and tenets of the MSRI paradigm for several decades, research findings have forced many to seriously question its validity. In the last decade, several social scientists have begun to look anew at the male sex role. Most notable among them is Joseph Pleck, who has proposed a new paradigm that presents the male sex role in a new light. Before we describe Pleck's *sex role strain* (SRS) paradigm, turn to "Sex Roles Quiz #2" (page 139). Again, read each statement and answer *true* or *false*. How many did you answer *true* this time? The more statements you thought were *true,* the more you agree with some of the basic propositions of Pleck's SRS approach to the male sex role.

To highlight the features of the SRS paradigm, Pleck has outlined ten propositions:

1. Sex roles are operationally defined by sex role stereotypes and norms.
2. Sex roles are contradictory and inconsistent.
3. The proportion of individuals who violate sex roles is high.
4. Violating sex roles leads to social condemnation.
5. Violating sex roles leads to negative psychological consequences.
6. Actual or imagined violation of sex roles leads individuals to over-conform to them.

Perspectives on the Male

SEX ROLES QUIZ #2	True	False
1. Society has very definite ideas about what men and women should be like.	___	___
2. There is no way that people can do all the things expected of them as men and women.	___	___
3. People who flaunt society's expectations about how men and women should act are usually ostracized.	___	___
4. There is greater tolerance of tomboys than sissies.	___	___
5. Many masculine and feminine traits are undesirable.	___	___
6. Many people have ideas about masculinity or femininity that they cannot live up to.	___	___
7. Many men who seem too masculine are concerned about living up to society's expectations.	___	___
8. Probably most people fail to live up to society's expectations for men and women.	___	___
9. Masculinity need not exclude emotionality.	___	___
10. Masculinity and femininity would be less stressful if less stereotyped.	___	___
11. Masculinity need not include aggressiveness.	___	___

Source: J. Pleck, *The Myth of Masculinity* (Cambridge, Mass.: MIT Press, 1981, pp. 133–34.)

7. Violating sex roles has more severe consequences for males than females.
8. Certain characteristics prescribed by sex roles are psychologically dysfunctional.
9. Each sex experiences sex role strain in its work and family roles.
10. Historical changes cause sex role strain.[47]

If we compare Pleck's ten propositions of the SRS paradigm with his eleven propositions contained in the MSRI paradigm (see page 131), we can discern a definite shift or change in the basic assumptions underlying the male sex role.

First of all, recall the MSRI paradigm insists that psychological masculinity or femininity is an innate feature of personality that can be measured by certain psychological tests. However, in the SRS paradigm, sex roles and what are thought of as masculinity and femininity are viewed as complex sets of widely shared beliefs about sex-typed traits that are typical (sex role stereotypes) and desirable (sex role norms) for males and females (Proposition 1). In other words, the SRS states that masculine sex-typed behaviors and what people commonly refer to as psychological masculinity are not innate features of a male's personality but rather are sex-typed behaviors learned by a male in order to adapt to situational demands and social pressures. In the MSRI viewpoint, masculinity is a basic psychological feature of a male's personality, but in the SRS perspective, masculinity is a result of social demands and pressures. Here we see the basic difference in how each paradigm looks at and defines masculinity.

Second, the MSRI paradigm states that sex role identity is a risky and failure-prone feature of personality development, especially for males. In other words, many things can go wrong in a male's developing sex role identity and often do; by and large, the end result of a poorly developed or inadequate masculine sex role identity is the cause of many other psychological problems experienced by the male. However, the SRS paradigm states that because of the built-in inconsistencies and contradictions among various elements of the male sex role, many males think of themselves as inadequate and insecure, and they experience personal role strain as a result of not living up to society's male sex role (Propositions 2–7). For example, when a male feels he is not as aggressive, successful, or tough as he thinks other males are, he may feel that it is his fault rather than sensing that the problem lies not in himself but in the contradictory social expectations placed on him by the male sex role. In a sense, the MSRI paradigm places the blame for many of the male's problems on his supposedly underdeveloped or inadequate masculine sex role identity, whereas the SRS paradigm blames society for supporting contradictory sex role expectations that make many males feel less masculine than they think other males are.

A third feature of the SRS paradigm points out that many males in their attempt to live up to the male sex role actually develop unhealthy or dysfunctional behaviors (Proposition 8). For example, a male who believes that he must be aggressive or emotionally constricted in order to be masculine may find himself behaving in an unhealthy fashion. Such a male may develop serious psychological problems or behave in antisocial ways simply by trying to live up to unrealistic sex role expectations.

A fourth feature of the SRS paradigm notes that many men feel personal strain because they cannot realistically accomplish all of the demands placed on them by virtue of their family and work roles (Proposition 9). Because a man is expected to be successful in the competitive world of work and also a dutiful and sensitive husband and father, many men literally feel inadequate in their masculinity because they are not able to accomplish all of their goals and objectives in these roles.

Fifth, the SRS paradigm suggests that because society is changing so rapidly and available opportunities to prove oneself to be a real he-man seem to be shrinking, many males feel themselves less masculine than men in previous generations (Proposition 10). Granted, society is changing, and many men do not feel that they can prove themselves and their masculinity in the ways that frontiersmen did. The SRS paradigm cites society's contradictory masculine standards (the contradictions between the traditional and the modern versions of the male sex role) as the culprit in these men's masculinity problems, not the individual male himself or his supposed inadequate male sex role identity. The question the SRS perspective asks is how a man can feel like John Wayne when there are no more physically demanding frontiers to conquer.

Pleck's SRS paradigm presents a new perspective on a number of troubling questions that many men are asking themselves today: "Why do I feel so inadequate as a husband and father? Why am I not as competitive and successful as the other men in the office? Why do I want to have sex with every beautiful woman I see on the street? Why do I get so upset when I can't get an erection? Why am I not content with myself as a man? Why do I feel so many other men are more masculine than I am? Could it be that something is wrong with me? Could it be that I am not really a man's man?" Many psychologists and psychiatrists would have the man who asks these questions look inside and examine his masculine identity for the root of the problem. Pleck's analysis would have the man who asks these questions look at society's standards and expectations for males and question their reasonableness. The problem rests not inside the man and his masculine sex role identity but rather in society and its definitions of what it means to be a man today.

COMMENTING ON THE PSYCHOLOGICAL PERSPECTIVE

Psychology presents an interesting perspective on the male experience. Many researchers have observed, measured, and theorized about all types of presumed sex differences in various intellectual and social behaviors. The fact of the matter is that much of this research has borne few results and found the sexes more similar then different. Psychologists have also gone to great lengths to answer the question, "How do the sexes learn their sex-specific, sex-typed behaviors?" Again, the prevalent models of the psychoanalytic-identification, the social-learning, and the cognitive-developmental theories have spawned more questions than answers about presumed sex-typed behaviors. Over the years, psychologists have grown accustomed to thinking of what they refer to as masculine sex role identity and to presenting this as an innate part of a male's personality. In fact, a new perspective developed by Joseph Pleck questions many of the venerable ideas of sex role identity and presents a new approach that views masculinity as primarily a personal adaptation of social pressures.

As more and more contemporary women and men begin to question and challenge their respective sex roles, psychology can best assist them by systematically debunking those persistent myths that have grown up and supported the unrealistic, contradictory, and, often times, debilitating aspects of sex roles. Rather than helping people to adjust to or fit into outmoded sex roles, clinical psychologists, counselors, and psychiatrists would do better to assist people in their strivings for *self-actualization* (the development of a person's full capabilities and potentialities). Once we all learn to see ourselves and others as basically capable, competent, and growing individuals with considerable potential rather than as people trying to cope with the restrictive demands and stereotypes of our sex roles, we might find the world a better place to live in.

SUGGESTED READINGS

Maccoby, E., ed. *The Development of Sex Differences.* Stanford, Calif.: Stanford University Press, 1966.

Maccoby, E., and Jacklin, C. *The Psychology of Sex Differences.* Stanford, Calif.: Stanford University Press, 1974.

Pleck, J. *The Myth of Masculinity.* Cambridge, Mass.: The MIT Press, 1981.

Sargent, A. *Beyond Sex Roles.* St. Paul, Minn.: West Publishing Company, 1977.

Tavris, C., and Offir, J. *The Longest War: Sex Differences in Perspective.* New York: Harcourt Brace Jovanovich, 1977.

2

ELEMENTS OF THE MALE SEX ROLE

What are little boys made of?
Snips and snails, and puppy dogs' tails;
That's what little boys are made of. Anonymous

What makes for a really light chocolate soufflé or a really hearty loaf of yeast bread? Why the ingredients, of course, and the cook's skill in mixing and baking them so that the finished product tastes like we expect it to taste.

Well, what makes a biological male into a complete psychosocial man? A male is a man if he acts like his society expects him to act in accordance with the male sex role. In other words, a male is a man to the degree that he exhibits the socially prescribed traits, characteristics, and behaviors of what is expected of men in a particular group or society at large.

In the next five chapters we are going to discuss several elements that are thought to encompass the male sex role. As in all delicate creations, the recipes for what constitutes a real man may vary somewhat. Not everyone agrees with the specific elements, their proportions, or for that matter, even whether all of the ingredients are necessary for the finished product. Let us take a brief look at what some social scientists believe to be the essential elements of the male sex role.

After reviewing several studies in which people noted the stereotypic traits of the "typical male," psychologists Michael Cicone and Diane Ruble found that certain traits occurred more often than others. Traits such as ambition, unemotionality, strength, interest in sex, courage, and aggressiveness were frequently associated with the designation of "typical male." The researchers then discovered that these traits fit into three general descriptive categories, which they outlined as follows:

1. How a man handles his life *(active* and *achievement-oriented)*. This group includes the qualities adventurous, ambitious, independent, courageous, competitive, leader, and active. The common denominator is a kind of go-getting, dynamic attitude toward life in general, with the possibility of worldly accomplishment and success.
2. How a man handles others *(dominant)*. This group includes aggressive, powerful, dominant, assertive, boastful. It is the putting of the self over and against other people which characterizes these traits.
3. How a man handles his psyche *(level-headed)*. Here we put logical, realistic, stable, unemotional, and self-control. The "typical man" is seen as cool and self-contained.[1]

Another "blueprint" for what constitutes the male sex role was elaborated by psychologist Robert Brannon. Brannon drafted his version of the male sex role in terms of four major themes, to which he gave the following headings:

1. No Sissy Stuff: The stigma of all stereotyped feminine characteristics and qualities, including openness and vulnerability.

Elements of the Male Sex Role

2. **The Big Wheel:** Success, status, and the need to be looked up to.
3. **The Sturdy Oak:** A manly air of toughness, confidence, and self-reliance.
4. **Give 'Em Hell!:** The aura of aggression, violence, and daring.[2]

In these two descriptions of the elements of the male sex role, the analyses are quite similar. In the following chapters we will borrow heavily from both analyses, especially from Brannon's. Before we begin, however, a quick preview of each element is in order.

One of the first lessons little boys learn is to avoid anything that may make them appear feminine or sissified. Little boys quickly pick up the message that they should never under any circumstance be caught acting like girls. The lessons can be cruel and even terrifying. A little boy found playing quietly with one of his sister's dolls may hear his father yell as he yanks the doll away, "Damn it, no son of mine is going to play with dolls like a girl!" If his father's outburst causes the boy to cry, the father may try to soothe his son by saying, "Now, now, son, stop your crying, only girls cry, and for damn sure you don't want to act like a girl, now do you?" Of course, the question is only rhetorical. The little boy is expected to want to be anything but a girl. The first element in the male sex role is designated here as the *antifeminine element* because after awhile boys learn not only to avoid anything identified as feminine, but as they grow older, they actually begin to dislike everything even vaguely connected with what society calls "feminine."

The second element in the male sex role is called the *success element*. Early in a boy's life, he is taught to get out there and be a winner, a champ, numero uno, in other words, a success. The introductory lessons usually revolve around competitive sports and may even include his achievements in school. As a boy grows up, the initial lessons translate into other expectations normally related to his first job and later on into his long-term aspirations for a career. Success in work usually allows a young man to prove himself successful in terms of another expectation: the role of breadwinner for his family. Failure at any of these male sex role expectations may bring some of the harshest criticisms directed at a man. The bottom line reads that a man who is not successful at what he does is thought unmanly.

The third element in our discussion of the male sex role is the *aggressive element*. Today most men do not see themselves or wish others to see them as quarrelsome bullies. The time when a man was frequently expected "to step outside and prove himself a man" is pretty much limited to television's portrayal of the Wild West. Even so, most young men are expected to stand up and fight, especially if someone else starts it. This male lesson is simple and straightforward: If goaded or bullied by another, a man must fight. To run away or avoid a fight casts a male in a cowardly and unmanly light.

Men are commonly thought insatiable when it comes to sex, and this view brings us to the fourth element in the male sex role, the *sexual element*. Many a young woman is told by her concerned mother never to trust men because they are out for only one thing—sex. Young men out on a date are likely to remember their father's jocular quip, "Don't do anything I wouldn't do." The end result of these early messages and many others is that most people believe that men are virtual satyrs in their relations with women. Whether men are driven by their biology, by social pressures, or by a combination of both, most men believe that sex and an interest in sexual matters are essential features of the male sex role.

The final element in our discussion of the male sex role is the *self-reliant element*. Of all the manly expectations, the self-reliant element is probably the most difficult one to analyze. One of the problems here is that a man does not show others how self-reliant he is just by what he says or by what he does. No, being self-reliant is a matter of style, a particular personal bearing in the way a man talks and behaves. A second problem is that this element encompasses many additional attributes that a man is expected to exhibit. For example, under the heading of self-reliance, also fall toughness, courage, confidence, independence, determination, and coolness.

There we have the five elements that appear central to the American conception of the male sex role. It should be obvious that no man can exhibit all five elements at one time. There is simply no way a man can be antifeminine, successful, aggressive, sexual, and self-reliant on any one given occasion. However, even though a man need not display all of the elements simultaneously, he must be able to exhibit each of them when the situation warrants it if he is to be considered a "real man."

It should be equally obvious that various groups place different weights or values on each of the five elements. Not every group a man identifies with requires that he act out each of the elements in the male sex role in order to be seen as manly. For example, among a group of academics, the achievement of success through publications or promotion to a high academic rank may be one of the more important ways a male college professor can substantiate his masculinity. For a street gang, however, a young man may be expected to mug a pedestrian or shoot a rival gang member in order to prove his masculinity. College professors are not usually seen as aggressive or violent people, and so the aggressive element would undoubtedly play a lesser role in their overall male sex role than it would in a street-gang member's.

Thus we must be cautious in our generalizations of the five elements of the male sex role. Each and every man cannot exhibit all of them in every facet of his life, neither do all of the elements carry equal weight in regard to every man's life.

7

Of sissified men and unmanly emotions:
THE ANTIFEMININE ELEMENT

*Primitive society practices its misogyny in terms
of taboo and mana which evolve into explan-
atory myth. In historical cultures, this is transformed into ethical, then literary, and in the
modern period, scientific rationalizations for
the sexual politic. Myth is, of course, a felici-
tous advance in the level of propaganda, since
it so often bases its arguments on ethics or theories of origins. The two leading myths of
Western culture are the classical tale of Pandora's box and the Biblical story of the Fall. In
both cases earlier mana concepts of feminine
evil have passed through a final literary phase
to become highly influential ethical justifica-
tions of things as they are.* Kate Millet[1]

*My temper represented a grave threat to me;
it signified a loss of control by the reason and
will and a surrender to ungovernable emotion.
I felt as if there were a terrible creature within
me whom I must never let escape or he'd destroy blindly — friend, foe, and innocent bystander alike.* G. Gordon Liddy[2]

The first and possibly the strongest element in the entire fabric of the male sex role is a negative or prohibitive injunction that states in its most basic form, "Boys, whatever you do, don't be like or do anything like a girl." Even before boys learn the other major lessons of their sex role, they are taught to avoid anything that even vaguely smacks of femininity.

If the first lesson on the male sex role contained a simple statement to the effect that boys are different from girls by virtue that boys cannot do some things that girls can do (for example, "Johnny, when you grow up you can't have a baby; only girls like Mommy and your sisters can have babies") that would be all right. But this first lesson does not end with a simple explanation of basic biological differences and some elementary sex education. No, it goes on to demean females. The first lesson of "don't be like a girl" is followed by several misogynist (hatred of women) postscripts. The complete first lesson goes something like this: "Don't be like a girl because . . . well, girls are bad, stupid, inferior, subordinate, and . . . well, girls are just plain icky!"

Along with the prohibition of "don't be like a girl because . . ." the first lesson contains other messages that add still other negative dimensions. For example, boys are taught never to express, at least not publically, certain emotions that might be seen as signs of weakness and vulnerability. Emotions such as joy, love, compassion, tenderness, and fear are all to be avoided by boys. The message to boys is once again quite clear: Only girls show these emotions, and boys would appear unmanly if they were to show the same emotions. And, of course, boys should never express their gentle or affectionate feelings toward other boys. Girls can express affection for other girls because that's what girls do anyway. But the lesson is straightforward with respect to boys: Boys should beware of other boys who are overly expressive of their tender feelings. You know, they may not be real men!

In this chapter we will analyze the blatant misogyny or sexism that is an outgrowth of a boy's first sex role lesson of "don't be like a girl because. . . ." We also will discuss the lengths to which boys and men go in order to avoid certain "troublesome" emotions and the consequences of such emotional constriction. Finally, we will take a look at certain prohibitions surrounding male–male relationships.

GIRLS ARE ICKY!

Males and females are different. For most people, the obvious anatomical differences are the icing on the cake and cause for the exclamation of *vive la différence!* But there is one experience that both male and female children share equally. In most instances, both sexes are raised by women. Even if the woman is not the biological mother but rather a female relative or some other maternal surrogate, it will be a woman in almost ninety-nine out of a hundred cases. Thus both girls and boys spend their first impressionable years in close proximity to a woman and not a man. Having an adult female for her primary caretaker allows a young female ample opportunity to learn from another same-sex person the ways of womanhood in a realistic fashion. The young male, on the other hand, spends relatively little time in the company of his father or other same-sex adults, and thus he must rely on other means (for example, television and male peers) to learn the ways of manhood. The inherent problem facing most young boys who learn their male sex role from television and peers is that these sources tend to exaggerate and separate the activities of each sex into strictly stereotypic sex role categories. The way that television and peers present the male sex role has a definite air of unreality about it. Take for example television. Television portrays the sexes in rigid and unrealistic sex roles. Men are shown as dominant, forceful, and in control of themselves and others (that is, females), and women are portrayed as support systems for the male. According to most television programs, males do only stereotypic manly things, females do only stereotypic feminine things, and never the twain shall meet. The little boy sitting on the floor in the living room absorbs the intended message all too well: Don't be like a girl. Whatever girls do, boys don't. If girls play with dolls, boys don't; if girls help around the house, boys don't; if girls cry when they fall and skin their knees, boys don't; and so on and on.

If all that young boys learned was "you're not like girls in certain ways," that would be one thing. But a rider is attached to the lesson. The additional message is that girls/women and all that is associated with females are not only different but they are also unequal to whatever is associated with males. The notion of different is quickly translated in many young males' minds to mean bad and inferior. Thus the total first lesson in the male sex role is "don't be like girls/women because they are unequal, bad, and inferior." The outcome of such training is that "one half of the human race regards the other at best with condescension and suspicion, at worst with hatred and fear."[3] For those who think we overstate the case, a small sampling of notable quotations may testify to the depths of some men's (that is grown-up boys') misogynous or sexist beliefs.

> I thank thee, O Lord, that thou hast not created me a woman.
>> Daily Orthodox Jewish Prayer (for a male)
> When a woman thinks . . . she thinks evil.
>> Seneca
> How can he be clean that is born of a woman?
>> Job 4:4
> Let the women learn in silence with all subjection . . . I suffer not a woman to usurp authority over men, but to be in silence.
>> St. Paul
> God created Adam Lord of all living creatures, but Eve spoiled it all.
>> Martin Luther
> Regard the society of women as a necessary unpleasantness of social life, and avoid it as much as possible.
>> Count Leo Tolstoy
> And a woman is only a woman but a good cigar is a smoke.
>> Rudyard Kipling
> The only position for women in SNCC is prone.
>> Stokely Carmichael, 1966

"Boy, if I ever stop hating girls, she's the one I'm going to stop hating first."

It would be preposterously naive to suggest that a B.A. can be made as attractive to girls as a marriage license.
    Dr. Grayson Kirk (former President, Columbia University)
The only alliance I would make with the Women's Liberation Movement is in bed.
    Abbie Hoffman
Women? I guess they ought to exercise Pussy Power.
    Eldridge Cleaver, 1968[4]

These are not the insignificant ramblings of a few inconsequential men but rather definite value statements from several notable men whose ideas have influenced millions of people. If we are to understand fully the male sex role, then we must face the ignoble fact that sexism and misogyny are definite parts of the first crucial lessons a boy learns about what it means to be a man. No less an authority on male–female relations and sex roles than Jessie Bernard sums up the issue of men's feelings toward women in this statement:

> . . . there is clear evidence that although individual men may love individual women with great depth and devotion, the male world as a whole does not. Terms like "hatred" or "hostility" may be too strong to describe this response, so the term "misogyny" has been invented. As long as women know their place and keep in it, misogyny need not rear its ugly head. Women are "dears" and "lovelies." But when they intrude on the male world, they become "damfool women."[5]

To get a better appreciation of the depth and magnitude of sexism as an integrated feature of the first lessons in the male sex role, let us briefly review the roots and historical traditions of sexism and misogyny and the pervasiveness of sexism in present-day society.

The antifeminine perspective, or sexism, owes its heritage to the institution of patriarchy. Patriarchy, or the rule of the father, with its own distinct system of values, beliefs, laws, religions, and economics, can be traced back to the beginnings of the Greco–Roman civilizations. The religious traditions of the Judeo–Christian perspective likewise initiated a strict patriarchial cosmology and world view and instituted the belief that women were "the source of all male difficulties."[6] Down through the ages, patriarchy became the norm for all "civilized" societies. When in the seventeenth century the Puritans fled England to the New World with its promise of religious freedom, the basic human freedoms were withheld from women, who worked alongside of men in building a new nation. When the Americans struck out on a rebellious road, the constitutional document that outlined the sought-after freedoms for its independent citizenry stated that "all *men* are created equal." Women and blacks were intentionally left out of the document's protection. Since that time, America has come a long way in granting freedoms and rights to those who were at first disenfranchised. Even so, with the defeat of the Equal Rights Amendment (ERA), women still do not have a constitutional guarantee of their full and equal rights under the law.[7]

But that's all history, all in our past, some will insist. Surely, women are not discriminated against now, not in these enlightened times. The problem is, however, that sexism is alive and well in these final years of the twentieth century. Even in prominent institutions of higher learning, young men confess that although they espouse egalitarian attitudes in public, down deep they feel threatened by and somewhat hostile toward women of equal or superior intelligence.[8] Negative attitudes toward women are also found at less prestigious colleges as well and more strikingly among some groups of college males than others.[9] College males' attitudes toward women's roles may have improved (become more accepting of women's roles and rights) relative to previous generations of college males,[10] but the prevalence of negative stereotypic attitudes toward women is as entrenched in the male sex role today as it ever was before.[11] The sad truth is that most men talk a good line about sex equality, but when push comes to shove, they think women should stay in their place and not make "damfools" of themselves.

Nowhere is the virus of sexism more obvious and more debilitating to women than in the workplace. Differential pay scales, common myths and fallacies about women's abilities and potentialities, and men's attitudes toward women's managerial capabilities are just a few of the seemingly insurmountable obstacles women face.

Historically, a woman's work has been valued less than a man's. No matter what it was that a woman produced, compared to what a man produced, her product was of less merit.[12] Especially in terms of pay, women's work is much less valued than a man's. Author and human relations expert Stan Kossen elaborated on the problem of unequal pay for women's work in the following passage.

In spite of legislation stipulating equal pay for equal work regardless of sex (the *Equal Pay Act of 1963*), a substantial amount of discrimination against women remains. The gap between incomes of men and women has actually widened in recent decades. Although the income of full-time, year-round working women rose from $2,827 in 1956 to $7,719 in 1975, their income as a percentage of men's earnings actually *declined from 63 percent to 59 percent over the same period.*[13]

Some have suggested that women's average pay is less than men's not because of sexism but rather because women choose low paying and less responsible jobs such as waitressing. However, no matter what type of work women perform, they are usually paid less than men who do the same work. Even those few women in prestigious positions are likely to be paid less than men in comparable positions. Psychologist Rhoda Unger documents the charges of sexism in institutions of higher learning:

> A number of findings support these women's perceptions that sexual inequality exists between men and women employed at institutions of higher education. For example, in 1973 the Task Force on the Status of Women in Psychology reported that although women account for 25 percent or more of the doctorates currently awarded in psychology and about the same percentage of members of the American Psychological Association, they (1) form a disproportionately small fraction of those employed by high-status institutions, (2) are most frequently found in low (instructor–assistant professor) academic ranks, (3) have lower salaries than comparable men even when rank and number of years of employment are equated, (4) account for an extremely small fraction of those administering programs or supervising graduate training, and (5) are less often found in regular tenure track appointments as opposed to part-time quasi-positions.[14]

Equal pay for equal work will continue to be a hotly debated issue in the 1980s. The recent Supreme Court decision that ruled in favor of equal pay for work of "comparable worth," will only fire the contest between those in favor of and those opposed to women's rights.[15]

There is no shortage of myths and half-truths about women's inherent abilities or the lack thereof for the competitive workplace. For the most part, the stereotypic notions about women act as a deterrent keeping them from gaining a meaningful foothold in the business world.[16] Paul Samuelson, one of this country's leading economists, details some of the more common myths about women:

> Women are built by nature to tend babies in the home. They are emotional. They have monthly ups and downs. They cannot carry heavy weights. They lack self-confidence. Men will not work under a woman. Man-to-man talk will be inhibited by the presence of women. Even women prefer a male physician to a female one. Women lack imagination and creativity. If you mix men and women on the job, they will carry on to the detriment of efficiency and good morals. By the time you have trained a woman, she'll get married and leave you; or have a baby; or alternatively, you won't be able ever to get rid of a woman once you've hired her. If a woman does turn out to be a superlative economic performer, she's not feminine, she's harsh and aggressive with a chip on her shoulder against men and the world (and she's killing her chances of getting married). Women workers, seeking pin money, take bread from the mouths of family breadwinners.[17]

HOW TO TELL A BUSINESSMAN FROM A BUSINESSWOMAN

A businessman is aggressive; a businesswoman is pushy.

A businessman is good with details; a businesswoman is picky.

He loses his temper because he's so involved in his job; she's a bitch.

When he's depressed or hungover, everyone tiptoes past his office. If she's moody, it must be her time of the month.

He follows through; she doesn't know when to quit.

He's confident; she's conceited.

He stands firm; she's hard.

His judgments are her prejudices.

He is a man of the world; she's been around.

If he drinks it's because of job pressure; she's a lush.

He's never afraid to say what he thinks; she's always shooting off her mouth.

He exercises authority diligently; she's power mad.

He's close-mouthed; she's secretive.

He's a stern taskmaster; she's hard to work for.

He climbed the ladder of success; she slept her way to the top.

The myths about women act as a kind of Catch–22. First, we are told, women won't stay in a job because of the lure of wedding bells or the purported urges of the maternal instinct. Then if she does stay, she can't be gotten rid of, we are told. If she does her job too well, it must be because she is not really a woman. Women, it seems, are in a no-win situation; no matter what they do, it is interpreted negatively (see "How to Tell a Businessman from a Businesswoman").

Many women have learned that there is no place for them on most companies' management teams. Many women who have filled out an application for a managerial position have been confronted with the comment, "You've gotta be kiddin'." Somehow, management is seen as an exclusively male activity, and the sign in the personnel office might as well read, "Women need not apply." The problem in many companies is that male managers hold sexist attitudes about women's abilities in general and especially with respect to a woman's being able to handle managerial responsibilities.[18] This point is borne out in the research of industrial psychologist Virginia Schein.

Schein asked 300 middle level *male* managers to describe the requisite personality characteristics, attitudes, and temperaments needed to fulfill the responsibilities of a middle level managerial position.[19] Furthermore, she asked these managers to describe the characteristics of men in general as well as of women in general. Not surprisingly, the managers described almost identical personality profiles for successful managers and men in general. On the other hand, they saw women as *not* having the requisite personality characteristics or temperament for management. Schein concluded that men in managerial positions see the male, but not the female, as having the necessary personal characteristics for the demands of a management position. No wonder that we find so few women in management and those who are there generally receiving a smaller salary than men in comparable positions. The few women in management are often there by the grace of a token system, which can be viewed as yet another form of sexism.[20]

We could go on to describe the depths of sexist ideology and its prominence in other institutions, but that would be the same story. Suffice to say, sexism is indigenous in our society, and few people are spared its infectious symptoms.[21]

DON'T BE A CRYBABY!

If we were to ask a group of people, say, a group of college students whether they would describe males as emotional or unemotional, most of the students would probably answer unemotional. The perception of men as stereotypically unemotional is a fairly consistent finding in many social psychological studies dealing with sex role stereotypes.[22] But the fact of the matter is that men are emotional, albeit in a rather circumspect way. Men do express emotions, ones that appear harsh, raw, and often harmful to themselves and others. Emotions such as anger, disgust, hostility, contempt, and cynicism are just a few of the emotions that men express quite openly in public. However, the reason that so many people consider men unemotional is that the word "emotion" is linked with the notion of femininity. Of course, women, too, show the emotions of anger and hostility, but the emotions women are most often associated with are the more gentle emotions such as love, joy, compassion, ecstacy, and fear. Thus when people are asked about emotions, they often think of the "feelings of the heart"—of women swooning with love—and not of men pounding their fists on the table and yelling obscenities at their neighbor. To think of a man swooning or expressing concern over a lost puppy is almost unthinkable for many people and especially for men. Overall, males tend to think that the fewer female sex-typed traits they possess— and this especially holds true of emotionality—the more masculine they are.[23] Remember the male's first lesson: "Don't be like a girl." Girls are emotional and so boys must not be.

Some men go to all kinds of lengths to hide or rid themselves of what they consider "troublesome emotions." These are emotions that leave a person open and vulnerable to others. For example, when one expresses one's love for another person, there is no way of knowing that the other person will return that love. If Jim tells Jack that he fears something, Jack may ridicule Jim and say what a fool he is for fearing something that Jack himself does not fear. Love, fear, and compassion are just a few of the more troublesome emotions that many men try to rid themselves of. Now and then, we even find a man like convicted Watergate conspirator, G. Gordon Liddy, who considers any emotion whatsoever (even anger and disgust) that competes with "reason and will" to be troublesome. For Liddy, a real man should be cold, calculating, unemotional, inscrutable, and totally in control of all his faculties. Researchers have found that more than a few men agree with Liddy's analysis of masculinity. Many males believe that the more they control or hide their emotions, the more inscrutable and cool and manly they appear to others.[24]

In this section we will discuss some of the consequences men face when they repress their troublesome emotions and why men diligently defend themselves from their own emotional experiences.

Warren Farrell, author of *The Liberated Man,* writes of the debilitating outcomes many men experience when they avoid or try to rid themselves of their troublesome emotions. First, Farrell describes a condition he calls *emotional incompetency.* The emotionally incompetent man in Farrell's analysis is one who is unable to handle or deal with other people's emotions. For example, many men find themselves extremely uncomfortable around other people who are expressing their emotions freely and openly. It is as if these men do not know how to act, how to respond to other people's emotional expressions. Many women who have expressed their feelings of, say, sadness or hurt with tears have heard their husband or lover say, "Please, honey, stop crying; you know how that makes me feel." Yes, most women know all too well how men feel around a woman who is crying—either insensitive or awkward! These men are really saying, "I can't deal with these emotions, so stop it!" The other side of the coin turns up when a man complains to one of his male friends, "You know any time my wife wants something from me, all she has to do is open the old floodgates, and—wham—she gets it." Here a man is saying that he distrusts a woman's emotions. In his eyes, emotions are a form of blackmail. The fact is that many men just do not permit themselves the human luxury of shutting up long enough to let another person have an emotional release; they cannot seem to resist opening their big mouths and showing just how very little they know about the emotional experience. Many men are truly emotionally incompetent.

The second condition men face with their troublesome emotions is what Farrell calls *emotional constipation,* a man's inability to express his own troublesome emotions.[25] Although males do feel love, pain, tenderness, sadness, sorrow, compassion, joy, and so forth, by the age of five or six, they learn not to show these emotions, at least not in public. The rule among many males is simple: Don't show any emotion that may make you appear weak, vulnerable, or feminine. Many a father has chastised his son for crying: "Now stop it! No son of mine is going to be a crybaby and act like a sissy. Get up to your room, and don't come down till you can act like a man!" There we have it again, the concern among men for not being thought of as a woman. Crying is something girls and women do, not boys and men, no matter how much they hurt. A classic example of the consequences men suffer when they show their troublesome emotions in public happened in the 1972 presidential race. After a newspaper editor printed slanderous remarks about his wife, presidential candidate Edmund Muskie broke down and cried in public while defending his wife's name. After the news services ran a picture of Muskie weeping, standing out in the cold New England weather,

Elements of the Male Sex Role

his chances for election were about as good as the proverbial snowball's chance in hell. Defending his wife's honor is perfectly all right for a man to do, but to break down and cry—no real man would do that! Muskie had committed an unpardonable sin in the minds of many people. He showed his troublesome emotions, and for many males and females alike, the question of his manhood and masculinity were in doubt from that moment on. It seems that many people do not want their leaders to show any sign of weakness.[26] Farrell relates an incident wherein one of his friends paid dearly because he allowed himself to express some "unmanly" emotions in the office:

A friend explained to me that he broke down and cried in front of a colleague at the office after some personal tragedies and office frustrations. He explained, "The news of my crying was all over the office in an hour. At first no one said anything. They just sort of looked. They couldn't handle the situation by talking about it. Before this only girls had cried. One of the guys did joke, 'Hear you and Sally been crying lately, eh?' I guess that was a jibe at my masculinity, but the 'knowing silence' of the others indicated the same doubts. What really hurt was that two years later, when I was doing very well and being considered for a promotion, it was brought up again. My manager was looking over my evaluations, read a paragraph to himself and said, 'What do you think about that crying incident?' You can bet that was the last time I let myself cry."[27]

Some emotions are more troublesome for men to deal with than others. One emotion that many men deny even to the point of its being harmful to their personal relations is fear. Fear is something women are given to, and that is enough to make it something men should not even admit to. When men fear, say, the possibility of losing their job, they often will not even admit their fear to their wife: "No sense in bothering the little woman with things she can't do anything about anyway." Keeping fears hidden from others, especially those who care a great deal, is one way in which many men keep others at a distance.

The late psychologist Sidney Jourard referred to the condition of a person's openly sharing his or her personal or intimate thoughts and feelings with another person as *self-disclosure*. Men tend to self-disclose less than women, regardless of age, education, or economic status. Jourard suggested that men suffer a sort of psychological isolation because of their self-imposed restriction against self-disclosing to others. He leveled one of his harshest indictments against men when he noted that

[If] a man is reluctant to make himself known to another person, even to his spouse— because it is not manly thus to be psychologically naked—then it follows that *men will be difficult to love*. That is, it will be difficult for a woman or another man to know the immediate present state of the man's self, and his needs will thereby go unmet. Some men are so skilled at dissembling, at "seeming," that even their wives will not know when they are lonely, bored, anxious, in pain, thwarted, hungering for affection, etc. And the men, blocked by pride, dare not disclose their despair, or need.[28]

Charging that "men will be difficult to love" is a strong statement. And yet with so many men working so hard to guard their emotions and feelings for fear that they will appear weak, vulnerable, feminine, or less than a real man, no wonder so many men live lives of desperate isolation. When a man refuses to admit his love, or fears, or anxieties, or joys, the other people in his life may well interpret his reserve as a signal that all is well when in fact it may not be so.

We have noted the deep antipathy many men feel about women in general and about their own troublesome emotions. We now want to discuss one last prohibition that men live with in order to live up to their male sex role, a prohibition that restricts the kinds of relationships men have together. Again, the antifemale bias lurks in the shadows wherever and whenever men congregate.

WATCH OUT FOR SISSIES!

Men have always seemed to enjoy one another's company. Historically, men were expected to enjoy one another's company more than the company of women. In the distant past, men ventured into the bush or onto the savannah after large game in all-male groups. Hunting parties, drinking bouts in all-male saloons, athletic clubs, fraternities, service clubs, and the proverbial "boys' night out" are just a few of the social rituals attesting to men's attachments to one another. The prevalence of all-male groups over the ages and in many disparate cultures led anthropologist Lionel Tiger to hypothesize a genetic "male bond."[29] Although the evidence for a male bond is highly questionable, the phenomenon of men spending more time in women's company than with men is a relatively recent social expectation (see "Partners at Last" in Chapter 2). Even with the recent addition of male–female social relationships, there is no lack of activities wherein men can be with other men.

One would think that with all of the time men spend together—at work, at the neighborhood bar, at the ballpark, at the bowling alley, around the barbecue pit, or under the hood of a car—the resultant relationships would be deep, sharing, and emotionally open. Who better to turn to than to another man, another man who knows firsthand the pressures, anxieties, fears, and, yes, the joys of what it means to be a man. One might think that there are just some things another man would understand better than a woman would. Women have these types of relationships with each other. What about men? Many male–male relationships are anything but emotionally satisfying and personally gratifying. Again, the major stumbling block is the difficulties men have with their emotions, especially in expressing the caring emotions. There is also another impediment to male–male relations. Constantly lurking in the shadows of men's minds is the fear, and for some men the horror, that other men may think them less than a real man.

As we suggested earlier, men have trouble expressing their own or dealing with others' more gentle emotions. Women, on the other hand, often are able to share these emotions with other women. Women, in fact, are allowed and encouraged to comfort one another, to show concern and love for one another, to share one another's sadnesses and joys. But these emotional experiences are almost never encouraged among men. Boys are taught to hold back, to close off, to negate their feelings toward other boys. If a boy slips and shows concern or compassion for another boy's pain, he must be taught a lesson so that he will not do so in the future. Author Marc Feigen Fasteau relates just such an incident that happened to him when he was eight years old:

> What is particularly difficult for men is seeking or accepting help from friends. I, for one, learned early that dependence was unacceptable. When I was eight, I went to a summer camp I disliked. My parents visited me in the middle of the summer and, when it was time for them to leave, I wanted to go with them. They refused, and I yelled and screamed and was miserably unhappy for the rest of the day. That evening an older camper comforted me, sitting by my bed as I cried, patting me on the back soothingly and saying whatever it is that one says at times like that. He was in some way clumsy or funny-looking, and a few days later I joined a group of kids in cruelly making fun of him, an act which upset me, when I thought about it, for years. I can only explain it in terms of my feeling, as early as the age of eight, that by needing and accepting his help and comfort I had compromised myself, and took it out on him.[30]

The older male camper had transgressed, had broken a provision in the lesson of the male sex role. He had showed concern for another male's plight. Fasteau, as the young camper, likewise broke a male sex role expectation; he had shown himself weak and in need of comfort. That also is forbidden to men. Why are caring behaviors so powerfully prohibited to males? Well, again, remember the first lesson in the male sex role: Don't be like a girl. If girls show compassion one for the other and openly express their hurts in each others' company, then boys must not do the same. But there is also another dimension to this prohibition against boys and men showing other boys and men their positive and caring feelings one for one another. An extra taboo overshadows male relations, a veritable Sword of Damocles hangs over them, the constant specter of homosexuality.

Few words strike as much horror or fear in a man's mind as does the word "homosexuality." Even though there have been historic periods and other cultures in which homosexuality was more or less just another sexual preference, in most American men's minds, homosexuality is a potential threat hovering over young men. Parents fear it, clergy denounce it, politicians campaign against it, and men in general control each other with the threat of it. Gregory Lehne in an article about *homophobia,* or the irrational fear of homosexuality, states that the major function of homophobia is to act as "a device of social control, directed specifically against men to maintain male behavior appropriate to the social situation."[31] To see what Lehne means, watch almost any group of boys or men in almost any situation. If one of the group members acts in a way that makes the other males uncomfortable in their sex role, the others will usually make some disparaging remarks about the one male's masculinity. When men make remarks about another male's masculinity, even in jest, the message is clear: "You'd better shape up, conform to what is expected or else we might think you're one of those . . . one of those queers." Quickly, then, most men fall in line to the drumbeat of the male sex role.

One of the consequences of the fear of homosexuality and the constant concern over what other men think about one's masculinity is that men have very few close male friends. Men have plenty of buddies with whom they drink and talk over politics, sports, work, and sex. But other men with whom they can share their fears and anxieties as well as their pleasures and joys is another matter. Quite often the fact that a man has no real male friends becomes painfully clear only when he needs someone to lean on:

> After my divorce I realized that I had allowed all of my friendships to drop, and I had no one to talk to. It was pretty lonely, I began sleeping around a lot just to be with someone. And I started hanging around this one bar on nights I didn't have a date. I'd always be with people, but I never got what I wanted. It was like a sieve—the loneliness was a bottomless pit.[32]

Listen to the painful loneliness of this man's cry for another human being. He found no one because like so many other males he had allowed his friendships to drop. Probably he had never allowed himself to have a real friendship with another man or perhaps with a woman either, not even his former wife. Men cannot allow themselves to get too close, to form deep and intimate friendships with other men because they may have to deal with the gnawing fear of homosexuality. Even if a man begins to feel something positive for another man, he must, according to the male sex role, hold himself in check before something happens that may be misinterpreted by other men. Psychologist Robert Brannon points out this feature of male relationships most poignantly in an incident that happened to him in college:

> Like the majority of men (as I was greatly relieved to find out later!), I secretly feared at one time in my life that I was a "latent homosexual." In college the affection and caring I felt for my three roommates worried me, because I could sense that it wasn't really *all that* different from the affection I felt for the girlfriends I knew best and liked most. If the truth be known, I cared more genuinely for my male friends at this time than for any female I knew. What's worse, when we were sprawled out somewhere watching T.V. or reading, and our legs or arms would touch comfortably, it was . . . well, pleasant! Once one of my roommates and I were lying on our old sofa, talking and drinking beer. For some reason—as I recall there wasn't much room—he put his head in my lap with some wisecrack about getting comfortable. We continued talking. But I felt a closeness, a sort of emotional bond that hadn't been there before. And . . . after a while, I felt a very real desire to lightly stroke his hair, the way I would have done had he been a woman. Finally, I said something brilliant like "Get off me you lazy sonofabitch, you're gettin' heavy."[33]

Two people at ease, comfortable, and sharing their thoughts of the moment; one feels the impulse to stroke the other's hair, a simple gesture of togetherness and human communication. And what happens? "Get off me you lazy sonofabitch!" Men can be so insensitive to each other because of a fear that one or the

Elements of the Male Sex Role

other may be a homosexual. Another missed opportunity to cement a relationship, to firm up a friendship. Men have many ways of subverting their own relationships. No wonder Jourard thought them difficult to love. Most men go out of their way to keep people, men and women alike, at an emotional arm's distance. This emotional distancing is one of the heaviest prices males pay for trying to live up to the first lesson in the male sex role.

SOME CLOSING COMMENTS

Throughout this chapter we have avoided an in-depth analysis of misogyny. In earlier chapters we eluded to the connection between patriarchy and misogyny; even so, why should physically powerful men feel it necessary to demean and degrade women, their emotions, and caring relationships among men? Men from earliest times could see that they were different from women. Why carry the obvious physical differences to such absurd lengths?

We could suggest some deep psychological basis, such as an unconscious feeling of inferiority that men feel toward women's creative ability (birth and natural feeding) and that men feel they must compensate for by putting down women and all that is thought of as feminine. Or we could note that because men are usually raised by women, men must go to extreme psychological lengths to rid themselves of an early feminine identification with their mothers, and so they attack women. Or perhaps misogyny had its roots in some earlier economic system and arose by virtue of who handed out the meat. Maybe misogyny is nothing more than the obscene outgrowth of one group's need to feel superior over another. When it comes to the human group, there are only two basic categories, females and males. Why men seem to have a penchant for prejudice and discrimination against women and not vice versa is a matter of speculation. But to argue for or against these or other possible causes of misogyny is beyond the scope of this book. What is obvious is that boys learn their first lesson in the male sex role very early and from several different sources: "Don't be like a girl."

This first lesson that boys must learn about what it means to be a real man is a negative one, with plenty of threats and accusations. In the next chapter we will turn our attention to a prescriptive rather than prohibitive lesson: "No matter what you do, be a success, make something of yourself, make us proud of you, son!"

SUGGESTED READINGS

Bullough, V. *The Subordinate Sex*. New York: Penguin Books, 1974.
Eisler, R. *The Equal Rights Handbook*. New York: Avon, 1978.
Marine, G. *A Male Guide to Women's Liberation*. New York: Avon, 1972.
Rogers, K. *The Troublesome Helpmate*. Seattle: University of Washington Press, 1966.
Snodgrass, J., ed. *For Man Against Sexism*. New York: Times Change Press, 1977.

8

Of large offices, fat paychecks, and other perks:
THE SUCCESS ELEMENT

> . . . *success and status are the bedrock elements of the male sex role, and no man in America escapes from the injunction to succeed.*
> Robert Brannon[1]

> *A strange juggling of ethical perspectives takes place under the influence of a competitive standard. When a man competes, it seems winning becomes his primary objective; other concerns grow dim. As he struts toward pinnacles of success, too often he forgets the whole spectrum of rectitude and integrity which should, hopefully, line his avenue to the top.*
> Jack Nichols[2]

> *The toughest thing about success is that you've got to keep on being a success.*
> Irving Berlin[3]

Next to the negative injunction, "don't be like a girl," no other element is as important and universal for defining a male's sex role as the one that positively charges a male to be a SUCCESS.

To begin our discussion of success, we will first focus on the idea that most American males see the world or, better yet, social reality in a very different way than most American females do. For many males, the world consists of a series of limited goods and rewards that must be competed for and won at any cost. Winning the goods and gaining the rewards become proofs of a man's success, which consequently bolsters his sense of being a real man. In contrast to manly competition, American males generally view cooperation as a stereotypically feminine trait, an unmanly approach to problem solving.

In the second section we will examine what has been and still is for many men the single most definitive feature of the male sex role, the element of success. Since the beginning of the industrial revolution, men have focused much of their energy on fulfilling the bread*winner* role in the nuclear family. As the chief breadwinner, a man's success and ultimately his definition of masculinity has been primarily judged by himself and many others by how well he provides for his family's needs and wants. As we might suspect, severe consequences can befall a man who puts all of his proofs of masculinity, so to speak, in one basket, especially a basket so precariously woven with the strands of a changing and volatile economy.

No discussion of men and success would be complete without an obligatory "how-to" section. The "secrets" of success are big business, and men put considerable stock in what other supposedly successful men have to say about success. In the third section we will focus on one "expert's" prescription for success in the business world.

Finally, we will deal with what for a majority of men may come as a disquieting fact: Some men are turning their backs on the "success-at-all-costs" game. For a growing number of men, being a success no longer has the appeal it once did. The idea of "not making it" or settling for less rather than more is beginning to make inroads into the changing male sex role, and some men are proclaiming a variety of advantages in such a life-style.

An early American psychologist, famed Harvard professor William James, referred to men's obsession with success as a "bitch-goddess" plaguing their lives. (Why James thought it necessary to refer to success in this way may reveal more about James's nineteenth-century antifemale bias than about his insight concerning men and the element of success.) For most men, success is difficult to achieve and once achieved difficult to hold onto. However, many American men still seem driven to worship success as if it were all that mattered in their lives. The sad truth is that for many men success *is* all that matters.

Competition and winning are considered masculine characteristics in our society. *Source:* © *Jean-Claude Lejeune.*

THE MALE SEX ROLE AND A COMPETITIVE WORLD VIEW

Almost any man, no matter if he be a company president, a foreman on the second shift, or a janitor who picks up after others, shares with most others a common, burning passion "for the thrill of victory," for being the best at something. Being a winner is very masculine. Men recognize the qualities of a winner and spend vast amounts of time and energy trying to become winners in their own and in others' eyes. Vince Lombardi summed up the obsession when he said, "Winning isn't everything; it's the only thing."

To become winners most men believe that they must compete, and compete they do. (In its most general sense, competition occurs when a person seeks something of value for *only* himself or herself.) Not too long after the diapers come off, boys learn that competition is an important feature of life. If they are ever going to amount to anything, if they are ever going to be real men, they quickly learn that they must beat out the other guy. In the early school grades, boys begin in earnest to grasp the competitive spirit; the school insists on ranking everyone's performance and hands out stars, favorable nods and smiles, and good grades for the few who come out on top. Competition is also fostered on the playground and the sandlot. Boys who might enjoy just throwing the ball around or hitting some balls just for the fun of it are quickly organized into a team, suited up in official uniforms with the local hardware store's name on the back, and coached into being part of the best team in town. Then on hot summer nights, their parents line the bleachers and scream at their sons to get out there and slam the ball over the fence. Boys see their parents agonize over a missed play or a strikeout and know deep down that losers aren't loved.[4] So it goes that boys grow into manhood knowing that if they are to be loved, if they are to be winners, if they are to be real men, they had better play the game *to win*.

One of the major problems of the emphasis on competition is that males begin to see everything in their world in terms of competition. Too often, when males are given a choice between competing or cooperating with another person, they usually choose competition even if it costs them more in the long run.[5] For example, think of two seven-year-old boys meandering down a street on a summer day on their way to who knows where. Before long one or the other throws out the challenge, "Race ya to the corner!" And they're off. Moments later at the corner, the winner, somewhat out of breath, shrieks, "Yea, I beat ya!" The other boy shoots back between gasps, "Oh yeah, well you had a head start and you cut me off back there." The result is that one boy feels smug in the knowledge that he beat his friend in a "fair" race and the other boy tastes the agony of defeat at the hands of a male friend. Of course, they will continue to be friends, but now there is an unspoken element in their friendship. The winner knows that he beat his friend, and the loser wishes that just once he could beat his friend at something and let him sense how it feels to be a loser.

When competition becomes a major perspective, as it does for most males, it brings with it a distorted view of the world, a set of assumptions about what the world is really like. We will briefly examine several of these assumptions.

First, the competitive spirit forces men to think that everything of value or worth in the world is *limited* or comes in *fixed quantities*. In other words, if something has value, it must be limited and can be measured. A man's valued masculinity can be measured as if it were a quantifiable element. Consequently, many males translate their sense of masculinity into how much money they earn, the size and number of windows in their office, the number of workers they have under them, the cost and horsepower rating of their new car, how far they live from the city, how many children they have, and the cost of their wife's new coat. If you can't win, buy, bargain, or steal it, it has no value in terms of a man's masculinity. That's the competitive way. Men begin to think in terms of quantifying even something like love. When at the breakfast table a wife mentions to her husband that he hasn't said "I love you" to her for over a year, he snaps, "What the hell are you talking about? Didn't I get you that new dishwasher that you've been wanting for over a year? What more do you want from me?" All that she wants is to hear three words, and he gives her a cost analysis of his purchases for the home! The competitive spirit makes men think that all of life's values come in prepackaged and measured forms.

A second assumption grows out of the first. If "valued" things are limited, there are just so many of them to go around. This brings up a problem in male–male relationships. If there are just so many testaments to a man's success—a very valued element in the male sex role—then every other man out there is a potential rival for the limited and available proofs of manly success. There are, for example, just so many large offices with windows, so many promotions, so many perks, or so many gold rings on the merry-go-round of life. If a man's friend gets a promotion at the office, all too often a man may think that promotion could have been his if his friend hadn't brown-nosed the boss so much. Men quickly learn ways to make their own track record look better than other men's. They produce more products, sell more products, write more reports, or complete the project sooner. The race for success is on, and every man soon learns the cardinal rule: "Don't trust the other guy, even your best friend, because he's after the same limited prizes that you are."

A third assumption that most men make is that competition is always good, not bad or neutral but always good. Fathers scream at their sons to get out there and beat the other boys no matter what the cost. On the playground or in the classroom, the important thing, the valued thing, the *good* thing is to be a competitor who wins. Competition is what made America great, and what's good for America is good for every man.

Thus competition forces many men to define part of their male sex role in terms of their acquiring "limited" goods as proof of their masculinity, to view every other man as a potential rival for these goods, and to believe that competition is always good for men.

An outgrowth of this preoccupation with competition and winning is that men come to view these features as exclusively male characteristics. Many men think that women do not have the same drive, ambition, or push to compete and win that men supposedly have. Boys and men compete, whereas girls and women cooperate. Granted, *all* women do not have the same desire for competition for competition sake that many men have, but many women do value competition and winning.[6] Possibly, males think of themselves as more readily accepting of competition than are women because of the popular belief that competition spurs action and achievement.[7] In the minds of these same men, action and achievement may be synonymous with masculinity. However, the belief that competition spurs action or achievement is questionable and not universally supported by research.[8] One problem we encounter with an assumed competitive-cooperative sex difference is that many men may feel that any attempt on their part toward cooperation would make them appear unmanly, while many women may think that competition robs them of their femininity. Consequently, some men denigrate cooperation as a viable way of solving problems or gaining valued goals.

The fact of the matter is that some tasks are better handled in a competitive way and others are more amendable to a cooperative problem-solving approach.[9] Tasks with definite rules and limits and unequivocal and measureable outcomes lend themselves to competition. For example, in a field and track meet, individual sporting events like the 400-meter race or the pole vault fit nicely into a competitive format. Pitting one athlete against another or against the clock is one way to decide who covered the distance fastest or vaulted highest. However, there are many other tasks for which cooperation rather than competition works better. Specifically, in situations where there are few rules and regulations determining the limits of the problem, or where the outcome is less certain or more equivocal, or where there is a multitude of possible solutions for the task, or where the goal of harmonious personal relations is desired, a cooperative rather than a competitive approach may prove more beneficial.[10] Raising children, dealing with the problem of crime in the street, fighting inflation, rectifying the lowered productivity in American industry are all problems that present ambiguous situations where the outcomes of separate approaches are not always predictable. With such problems, husbands and wives, politicians and citizens, and labor and management would accomplish more by cooperating with each other than by pulling against each other to see which side will win.

But that brings us back to the issue of the male's competitive world view and the "we" versus "they" approach. A husband and father often views his wife's or children's ideas about family concerns as an affront to his role as husband and father. Too often men approach family problems as yet another test of their patriarchal mandate. Consequently, there is little room for open discussion and mutual cooperation among all members of the family. Father is right and everyone else is wrong. The same competitive mentality can be found in many labor–management disputes. Each side (comprised mostly of males) sees the other side as competing for more than its rightful share of the scarce goods (wages, benefits, and so on). Instead of sitting down and communicating with each other, each side tries to outmaneuver the other and come away the victor. We find the same competitive spirit, the "we" versus "they" syndrome, in politics. No matter whether it is republicans, democrats, or independents, politicians look upon one another as the enemy who must be beaten in the next election. No matter what serious problems face our country, politicians (again, mostly males) try to get as much political mileage as they can out of how their opponents are the ones to blame for all of the country's ills. Many politicians seem more concerned with fixing blame then with fixing problems and working for solutions.

Psychologist Judith Bardwick, in a study of businessmen, asked one man why he worked so hard; he replied,

> I don't know. I guess I enjoy it to a great extent. . . . I really hate to be a failure. I always wanted to be on top of whatever I was doing. It depends on the particular picture but I like to be on top, either chairman of the committee or president of an association or whatever.[11]

This businessman's reply could as easily have been made by a politician. Success is the name of the game in politics as well as in business, and winning brings success, or so most males think.

If the truth be known, many of the problems men face daily are self-induced by virtue of men's competitive world view. We noted in the last chapter how lonely and isolated many men are by virtue of their not having many genuine male relationships. But given their deeply ingrained suspicious and competitive approach, how can men have such relationships? How can a man develop a genuine, open, and sharing friendship with another man when the other man is seen as being after the same promotion or the same woman or the one to beat in a "friendly" game of tennis? Men cannot let up; they must constantly be on guard lest they be beaten and shown to be a loser. One never knows when the fellow next to them will yell, "Race ya to the corner!"

THE MALE AS GOOD PROVIDER

The male sex role's insistence on success creates certain new expectations for the male as well as certain problems. One such expectation is that of his being viewed as a good provider. Simply put, the expectation of being a good provider stipulates that the more goods a male provides for his family's material well-being, the more successful (that is, masculine) he is. Let us begin our discussion of the male's provider role with a brief history of its roots.

HISTORICAL SKETCH OF THE PROVIDER ROLE

In the distant past, males were judged successful in relation to their hunting skills. Later on, with the discovery of agriculture, males found success measured in relation to their farming skills. Essentially, as long as a male brought in his share of the primary group's subsistence—in fact, males brought in considerably *less* than females—he was viewed a success by others. This perspective on the male as provider held sway throughout most of history only to change with the rise of the industrial revolution.

With the advent of the industrial revolution's factory system, a radically new economic and social order came into existence.[12] For countless centuries, there had been little distinction between those who produced goods and those who consumed them. Most people were quite self-sufficient in terms of their material needs. During the industrial revolution, however, specialization became commonplace, and a gulf grew between producers and consumers.

The relationship between the sexes also changed during this period. Whereas for centuries the sexes had lived and worked in close proximity, the factory and its centralized location forced men to leave their homes and journey some distance to work. Males and females became divided in their life-styles more than ever before. Industrialization caused a separation of the producer and the consumer functions as well as new sex role definitions that called for separate work environments for the sexes.

For centuries men had shared the provider role with women, but with industrialization men were expected to become the *sole* provider for their family's material needs. Men soon found themselves closeted for most of the day in foul-smelling factories rather than in open fields, cottages, or small shops. From an agriculture-artisan-based definition of masculinity, the industrial revolution re-tooled masculinity to fit the needs of a factory system with a voracious appetite for strong workers. Quickly, the provider role was transformed into the "good-provider role," which then became a prominent standard among men for the achievement of success. Even though the industrial revolution provided more people with a higher standard of living, there were definite costs. Sociologist Jessie Bernard notes the cost to men:

> The most serious cost [of the good-provider role] was perhaps the identification of maleness not only with the work site but especially with success in the role. "The American male looks to his breadwinning role to confirm his manliness" (Brenton, 1966, p. 194). To be a man one had to be not only a provider but a *good* provider. Success in the good-provider role came in time to define masculinity itself. The good provider had to achieve, to win, to dominate. He was a breadwinner. He had to show "strength, cunning, inventiveness, endurance—a whole range of traits henceforth defined as exclusively 'masculine' " (Demos, 1974, p. 436). Men were judged as men by the level of living they provided. They were judged by the myth "that endows a moneymaking man with sexiness and virility, and is based on man's dominance, strength, and ability to provide for and care for 'his' woman" (Gould, 1974, p. 97). The good provider became a player in the male competitive macho game. What one man provided for his family in the way of luxury and display had to be equaled or topped by what another could provide. Families became display cases for the success of the good provider.[13]

Thus the male sex role heaved to the pressures of the machine age. New attributes and new ways of defining masculinity became necessary. Consequently, males began to place greater emphasis on their wages, sexual conquests, and acquired goods as proofs of their masculinity.

For centuries men had contributed in tangible ways first to the group and then to the family. The industrial system ended all of that and created a new man— the paid laborer—whose major contribution to the family was his wages. Men could no longer sign their mark on an individual piece of craftsmanship or watch proudly as a field of grain ripened in the summer's sun. In the factory men could only do menial and repetitive jobs that gave little expression to their creativity. Males quickly began to equate their manhood with the amount of money paid them. The more money a male earned, the more successful he was thought to be. Forget what the work entailed, that was of little consequence. The important feature was the sum of money earned, which finally became a major measure of a man's masculinity.[14]

According to Judeo–Christian tradition, women were considered to have lusty, sensual passions, while men were thought to be more predisposed to reason and logic. Women, the Old Testament stated, epitomized human weakness and wanton sexuality. Men, so the biblical story told, were made in the image of God and above the baser sexual element. However, needing additional support for their masculinity after the move to industrialize, men co-opted the sexual sphere for themselves and placed women on a pedestal of virtuous modesty. Men's drastic turnaround from sexual reserve to sexual license found the new working class male "involved not only in more and earlier sexual activity, but possibly greater male assertiveness, with proof of manliness not just in begetting children but in dominating the female partner."[15]

One other feature of the changing male sex role that resulted from industrialization was the inordinate value placed on material goods. This new symbolization of a man's success caused sociologist Thorstein Veblen to coin the phrase "conspicuous consumption" to capture the new spirit of a man's worth and value in terms of highly visible and valued objects.[16]

Industrialization also influenced women's lives and their sex role. Once again let us refer to Jessie Bernard's analysis of the good-provider role, but this time stress its impact on women:

> As a psychological and sociological phenomenon, the good-provider role had wide ramifications for all our thinking about families. It marked a new kind of marriage. It did not have good effects on women: The role deprived them of many chips by placing them in a peculiarly vulnerable position. Because she was not reimbursed for her contribution to the family in either products or services, a wife was stripped to a considerable extent of her access to cash-mediated markets. By discouraging labor force participation, it deprived many women, especially affluent ones, of opportunities to achieve strength and competence. It deterred young women from acquiring productive skills. They dedicated themselves instead to winning a good provider who would "take care of" them. The wife of a more successful provider became for all intents and purposes a parasite, with little to do except indulge or pamper herself. The psychology of such dependence could become all but crippling.[17]

CONTEMPORARY VIEWS ON THE PROVIDER ROLE

By the early twentieth century, the good-provider role was firmly embedded in the nation's psyche. But all was not to remain placid. Everything seemed to come apart on one fateful day in 1929 when the stock market crashed. Few events of a nonaggressive nature have had such chilling consequences on peoples' lives as did the Great Depression of the 1930s. Not only did millions of men lose their jobs, but they lost something even more important—they lost their self-respect as men and a primary means of validating their masculinity.[18] Because of the importance attached to the good-provider role, unemployed men suffered a form of psychological emasculation.

After a decade of unemployment, World War II returned a sense of masculinity to countless men. After the war and with the economy turned around, men once again wrapped themselves in the mantle of the good-provider role. Women, after a liberating stint as "Rosie the Riverter," returned once again to their kitchens.

Blame it on the war or the new invention called television or women's growing restlessness, but the good-provider role was never the same after World War II. From 1946 to 1965 a gradual erosion began to undermine the social values that supported men in their role as sole provider for the family. The change in—some call it the threat to—the male's provider role began to show itself in several areas: the growing number of women in the work force, a reevaluation of leisure time, and a completely different outlook and value system concerning work itself.

During the last thirty years, women have entered the labor force in unprecedented numbers. About twenty-five percent of all married women between the ages of fifteen and fifty-four were gainfully employed outside the home in 1950. This figure had more than doubled, to over fifty-five percent, by 1978, and it will probably increase to two out of every three women by 1990.[19] The reasons why millions of women are leaving the home for the workplace are as varied as the women themselves, but two reasons stand out. First, families with two incomes are better able to handle the spiraling inflation that has become the norm. The addition of a second paycheck is more often than not the only means for keeping a family's standard of living at nearly the same level as it was only a decade earlier. Second, a paycheck conveys more than mere monetary value; it also has the symbolic value of giving its bearer a sense of worth and dignity. Women have discovered the lesson that men have known for so long: Our society tends to value people and their activities in proportion to their earned income.

Historically, most people have not had the luxury of leisure time built into their life-style. Twelve- to fourteen-hour work days were the norm less than a hundred years ago. Little time was left for more than a few amenities around the home. But leisure-time activities have become a way of life during these last decades of the twentieth century. Nowadays, a majority of men report that they receive more personal satisfaction from their leisure activities than they do from their work.[20] In fact, some men go so far as to forsake their family and work responsibilities for the pursuit of amateur sports.[21] A whole new subculture has arisen in the past decade or so—a subculture of ball-playing men who live only for the macho camaraderie that they find on the field and in the local tavern.

Probably the most serious threat to the male's provider role is the impersonalization found in so many of today's highly technological jobs. In the past a man's work was an integral part of his identity as a man. A man would normally introduce himself in the context of his work; for example, a usual greeting went something like this: "Hi, I'm Dave Smith, I'm the football coach over at Jefferson High," or "I'm the produce manager at the A&P," or "I'm a social worker with Children's Services." After the name, there came an identifying label—a work label. A man's identity, social standing, and value to his social group were all tied up in the announcement of his work. But this has changed. Today many jobs provide little or no meaning in the way of identity to the person who performs them. Sociologist Peter Berger notes this changing feature of the work–man relationship in the following passage.

> Work provided the individual with a firm profile. This is no longer the case with most workers in industrial society. To say "I am a railroad man" may be a source of pride, but the pride is as precarious as the occupational title. To say "I am an electroencephalograph technician" means nothing to most people to whom it is said. To say "I am an addressograph operator means nothing for a different reason, not because people do not understand what kind of work it entails, but because it is next to impossible to derive any sort of self-identification from such an occupation, not even the self-identification with the oppressed proletariat that sustained many workers in earlier phases of industrialism.[22]

The growing number of working couples, the increasing emphasis on leisure pursuits over working activities, the "depersonalization" of work itself, and other factors will eventually bring an end to the male's good-provider role.

However, men are still charged with being a success. Daily, hundreds of thousands of men awake, fumble into their jogging suits, and go for a run; then they shower, shave, and adjust their suits and ties; after a long day at the office, they put on a softball uniform. Each change of clothing brings its own unique challenge for success—lose that midrift spread, close another deal, put the ball over the center-field bleachers. In fact men are more concerned with the achievement of success in the 1980s than they were in the late 1960s and 1970s. Just over a decade ago, young men seemed more concerned with finding meaning in their lives than with earning a buck. Today young men are once again clutching for the gold ring in the business sector. We are witnessing a rebirth of the success ethic. Nowhere is the push for success more obvious than in the number of self-help books that line the shelves of almost every bookstore. Their message is simple and somewhat ominous.

NICE GUYS FINISH LAST

Although former baseball coach Leo Durocher never wrote a book on success, he did win more than his share of games. He once uttered a phrase that has made him one of the "quotable notables" in the success literature, "Nice guys finish last." If nice guys finish last, then what does it take to be a winner, a success in the world today? If we browse around in a bookstore, perhaps we will find the answer in the self-help section. There they are, so prominently displayed and with titles that almost jump off the shelves with the promise of revealing the real "secrets" of success. Here are just a few current titles: *Winning Through Intimidation, Looking Out for Number One,* and *Power! How to Get It, How to Use It.* If we pick up any one and scan the table of contents, we soon get the feeling that being a success is no easy task. It's a jungle out there in the competitive world, and one has to be up to the biggest challenge of one's life. Let us select just one book and see how we, too, can become a success. This one was on the *New York Times* best-seller list—a sure sign of success in the book trade. It was written by Michael Korda and bears the not-so-subtle title *Success!*

Michael Korda can speak knowingly about success, he has already had a fair amount of it in his young life. Raised in a prominent family, Korda attended prestigious schools, authored several bestselling books, and is now senior editor for one of the larger publishing houses in New York. His book *Success!* maintains that one can achieve success by following certain basic principles.[23] Here is a brief synopsis of some of Korda's major points.

Lesson #1: Let Your Energies Flow Success comes to those who work for it. (Although the majority of anecdotes in the book are about successful men, Korda believes that women can also profit from his discussion.) Success and all its trappings (fame, money, status, promotions, perks, others' envy, and so on) are the

Elements of the Male Sex Role

pot of gold at the end of the rainbow for the hard worker. This first lesson fits neatly with the social expectations that men must do something or work at something, preferably something difficult, risky, or possibly even dangerous to prove themselves real men.

Lesson #2: Controlled Paranoia Korda's second lesson stresses that a man should be wary of others, and that means everybody, when it comes to reaching for success. The basic premise here is that no one really wants a man to be a success, at least not too much of a success. People love it when someone fails, and they are downright envious when someone succeeds. We see evidence of this in the public's insatiable appetite for gossip and tales of successful people's undoings. Even one's friends and loved ones are at least ambivalent if not unhappy when a man succeeds too well at something. For example, a wife may initially encourage her husband to go after a job promotion, but what happens after he gets it? She may become moody, withdrawn, and upset because he must travel more and work longer hours. Because many people prefer that others remain as they are, too much success may disrupt a relationship. Thus a man should learn to trust primarily only himself in his climb to success.

Lesson #3: Good Ole Machiavelli More often than not, people must deceive others to get ahead in the cold world of business. As Korda sees it, if others in the business "jungle" are after the same promotion that you want, rest assured that they are not going to move aside or give way just because you are such a nice guy. All's fair in the business world. The quicker one learns how to manipulate and control others for one's own benefit, the better able that person will be to move ahead of the competition.[24] To use other people's strengths and cash in on their weaknesses can only help in one's quest for success. Of course Korda does not suggest putting hemlock in a colleague's martini, but anyone seeking success should be aware that his colleague is after the same promotion or new client. In other words, get him before he gets you!

Lesson #4: Don't Fret Fear of failing and fear of succeeding are the double-edge sword most men carry with them. On the one hand, a man is expected to be a winner in the everyday competition of life if he is to prove himself a real man. Failure is one of the worst catastrophes that could beset a man. On the other hand, men fear success as well. (Since the late 1960s, much has been made in the psychological literature about women's supposed fear of success. But more recent psychological research suggests that men are likely to fear success as much as if not more than women do.[25]) When opportunities come along, many men undermine their chances of succeeding. Doubts and fears are more devastating to a man's success than any competition he may face from his colleagues. According to Korda, the hackneyed cliché, "Nothing ventured nothing gained," should be the motto each man subscribes to if he truly wants to be a success.

Of course, there is much more in Korda's book on how to become a success. What we have here may sound rather ruthless to some, but we should not forget that success in the competitive world is, for the most part, quite ruthless. Countless men are fired, passed over, transferred, or moved laterally into dead-end jobs every day by other men who want to dispose of the competition. Korda's presentation on how to get ahead is pretty tame when one hears some of the horror stories in almost any business enterprise. For all of the people who want to get ahead, to become a success, there are only so many slots. Whoever goes for big stakes has to play to win.

Is becoming a success worth it? Even though men are expected to relish success above all else as proof of their masculinity, success has it price. Addison Steele, another book editor, puts the issue this way:

> Have you seriously considered the cost of getting ahead? The cost to your health? To your peace of mind? To your private life?
> Have you weighed the potential gains of such a sacrifice? Will the corporate advancement make you rich? Will it make you happy? Can such advancement be guaranteed to take place? Are there circumstances you can't control no matter how you comport yourself? Will the next rung be fulfilling or will it merely be a stepping-stone to the one after that? Is there an end to the treadmill?[26]

These questions may be difficult for most men to answer. Some men may not wish even to think about them. But a few men are beginning to jump ship, to get off the treadmill of success, so to speak, and are choosing a less success-oriented life-style by turning their back on the nine-to-five work cult.

DROPPING OFF THE TREADMILL

In the nineteenth century, Washington Irving penned a classic tale about Rip Van Winkle, who stole away to a mountain and slept for twenty years. Irving's tale may be one of the first written accounts of an American man who avoided the responsibilities of his provider role. Few men go to such lengths as Rip Van Winkle did to avoid work, but such avoidance was even a problem during the early years of the industrial revolution. It was not always easy to get men to make the transition from farmer to factory worker. During the nineteenth century,

> . . . mill owners and empire builders in the United States . . . complained that their straw bosses had to pull the workers out of the saloons every Monday—"Blue Monday"—to get them back on the job. There were too many holidays, too many feast days; at work, the spinners and tracklayers tended to daydream and chatter. It was increasingly difficult to get a full seventy hours of work out of them every week.[27]

A plausible explanation for some of this early "mutinous" behavior is that males were not used to the regimentation that came with the new factory system. For centuries men had labored as farmers in concert with seasonal changes. Once a farmer became a factory worker, it mattered little what season of the year it was. Day after day, week after week, and month after endless month, the same job had to be done. Little wonder then that some men were prompted now and then to lay off and spend time in saloons in the company of other men. Where better could men who faced so many social changes feel more secure, more masculine than in the company of other men? After a few drinks and some ritual boasting, a man could always prove his masculinity in a "friendly" fight. Working in the factory took some getting use to. But getting use to factory work men did.

By the end of the nineteenth century, the good-provider role vis-a-vis the factory worker was an integral part of the sex role of most males. To realize just how deeply men had identified with their work, we need only read of the personal devastation that befell a majority of men who were unemployed during the Great Depression.[28] A man without a job lost more than a paycheck. He lost not only his family's but also his own respect for his manhood. As we noted earlier, the prosperous years that began with World War II found men once again aligning their masculinity with their work. During the early 1950s sociologists Nancy Morse and Robert Weiss, both of the University of Michigan's Survey Research Center, found that over eighty percent of the working men they surveyed stated that they would continue to work even if they came into unexpected wealth.[29] Work gave these men a powerful sense of worth, purpose, meaning, and possibly most important, a sense of manliness. Mere wealth alone could not substitute for all of this. However, America was headed for a change by the early 1960s.

Stereotypes like myths take a long time to change and/or disappear. The stereotype of the working male leaving home every morning with either lunch pail or attaché case in hand is beginning to falter. A small but growing number of men are starting to challenge this masculine ideal by asking, "Do I want to work at the same job for the rest of my working years?" "Do I want to report to the same boss and push the same papers from one pile to the next forever?" or "Do I really want to climb higher up the work-success ladder?" (see "To Climb or Not to Climb: A Quiz"). The idea that men without work will crumble, will feel their masculinity shatter as many did during the depression era is becoming a late-twentieth-century myth. Being without work, without a socially acceptable means to validate one's masculinity is no longer as devastating for some men as it once was. Professional and blue collar workers alike are finding that unemployment does not necessarily make a man less masculine.[30]

How is it that something as ingrained in the American value system as the work ethic has fallen on such hard times? Why is it that some men are beginning to question the value of climbing the ladder of success? The answer may be that more and more men define work in negative rather than positive ways. The climb for these men is considered dull, shallow, meaningless, and dis-spiriting rather than exciting, creative, and in-spiriting. Work has lost many of its pleasure-giving features. Once again, Addison Steele puts his finger on a core problem of contemporary work as so many men feel it:

> How refreshing it would be if people could just take pleasure—keen, immediate pleasure—in the work they are presently involved with, instead of always being concerned with climbing, climbing, climbing. Climbing is so hard on the nervous

TO CLIMB OR NOT TO CLIMB

1. Day-to-day happiness is extremely important to me.
   (a) Agree strongly
   (b) Agree moderately
   (c) Disagree moderately
   (d) Disagree strongly
2. I can dissemble pretty well when I have to.
   (a) Agree strongly
   (b) Agree moderately
   (c) Disagree moderately
   (d) Disagree strongly
3. I am envious of friends who are more successful than I am.
   (a) Agree strongly
   (b) Agree moderately
   (c) Disagree moderately
   (d) Disagree strongly
4. I am terribly concerned about what other people think of me.
   (a) Agree strongly
   (b) Agree moderately
   (c) Disagree moderately
   (d) Disagree strongly
5. I think it's a good idea always to "look busy" at the office.
   (a) Agree strongly
   (b) Agree moderately
   (c) Disagree moderately
   (d) Disagree strongly
6. I would not be overjoyed to give up a windowless office that was cool and comfortable for a hot, uncomfortable corner office with a window.
   (a) Agree strongly
   (b) Agree moderately
   (c) Disagree moderately
   (d) Disagree strongly
7. It is much simpler to answer one's own phone rather than letting a secretary do it.
   (a) Agree strongly
   (b) Agree moderately
   (c) Disagree moderately
   (d) Disagree strongly

Source: A. Steele, *Upward Nobility* (New York: Times Books, 1978), pp. 6-9.

8. I have an expensive life-style, and I don't want to give it up.
   (a) Agree strongly
   (b) Agree moderately
   (c) Disagree moderately
   (d) Disagree strongly
9. I am leery of making sacrifices for anything unless I can be assured of positive results.
   (a) Agree strongly
   (b) Agree moderately
   (c) Disagree moderately
   (d) Disagree strongly
10. Leisure activities bore me; I would much rather be at the office.
   (a) Agree strongly
   (b) Agree moderately
   (c) Disagree moderately
   (d) Disagree strongly

SCORING

Award yourself the following number of points for each answer:
Question 1: a–0; b–1; c–2; d–3
Question 2: a–3; b–2; c–1; d–0
Question 3: a–3; b–2; c–1; d–0
Question 4: a–3; b–2; c–1; d–0
Question 5: a–3; b–2; c–1; d–0
Question 6: a–0; b–1; c–2; d–3
Question 7: a–0; b–1; c–2; d–3
Question 8: a–3; b–2; c–1; d–0
Question 9: a–0; b–1; c–2; d–3
Question 10: a–3; b–2; c–1; d–0

EVALUATION

Score 0–10 points: If you tried to climb too high on the corporate ladder, you would be likely to fall off and break both your legs. Very probably, you already know this about yourself. You are too straightforward, too uncalculating, and too much your own person to want to make the necessary compromises to get ahead. Your main ambition is to be happy and fulfilled. You have interests outside your work. You are, according to Michael Maccoby's breakdown of organizational types, a "craftsman," not a "gamesman" or "jungle fighter."

Score 11–20 points: You have a certain amount of healthy ambition, but it is not overwhelming, and there are certain sacrifices you are not prepared to make to bring about your goals. You are at a disadvantage when you try to compete with the more political people in your company. You can't lie as well as they can, you are careless about your corporate image, and, in the middle of a boring meeting, you sometimes find your mind drifting to thoughts of mountain-climbing in the Himalayas or the tennis match you won against the club champion. If *you* try to climb too high on the corporate ladder, you may not notice when one of your co-workers starts sawing away at the very rung upon which you are perched.

Score 20–30 points: You are a corporate in-fighter and very good at it. Such activity fits your temperament and psychology. It is *you* everyone else has to watch out for. Whatever rung you are on now, you are going higher. Recommended readings for you are Michael Korda's *Power* and *Success!*, Michael Maccoby's *The Gamesman,* and Robert J. Ringer's *Winning Through Intimidation.* Quite probably, you have already read them.

system. I have known personally too many, driving, executives—mostly men in their late thirties and early forties—who have had crippling and sometimes fatal heart attacks. I have had lunches with too many colleagues who were nursing an ulcer or a spastic colon. And I have seen too much needless fear, as evidenced by hands trembling in a meeting, backs that suddenly go into spasm at the sight of a closed door, and voices that either slide into the upper register or disappear completely when the boss leaves a note on the desk saying, "Please drop by my office right away."[31]

For many men, work is no longer enjoyed for its own sake. Competitive work, which most think of as a means to success and achievement, has become perverted in some men's minds. On this point, S. A. Miller has suggested that both men and women need to redefine their notions of success and achievement if they are to cope more effectively with the social changes facing each sex in the near future. In proposing a new conception of success and achievement, Miller writes,

While I am strongly of the mind that success drives should be banked and other humanitarian urges encouraged, I don't accept that all of the drive for success or achievement is pernicious or undesirable. This drive is exciting and can be fulfilling. It is a great danger to be avoided when it becomes all embracing or when it is a success without a content that is both personally and socially satisfying or beneficial.

It should be made easier to do interesting and useful things, to feel a sense of accomplishment. As in military strategy, a "sufficing" level of achievement rather than a maximum level of security or position should be sought. Being "number one" should not be the goal; rather, high competence should be enough for both men and women. I have seen many talented people blighted in their work by number-oneism when they probably would have done outstanding and useful work by adopting a high-competence performance criterion.[32]

Elements of the Male Sex Role

SOME CLOSING COMMENTS

We have seen in this chapter that a male is expected to be a success, to be a winner at everything he does, no matter if he is at work, at play, or in bed. A real man is a success at *everything*. The problem is that such an expectation is impossible. At last, some men are questioning the value of the success-at-all-costs male sex role expectation. One critic of men's obsession with success is William Malcomson who points out that success may be, of all things, a failure experience.

> Middle-aged men like me are hooked on the myth of success. We are enslaved, bound, trapped, by this myth. I have been programmed to succeed or give up the whole thing. Failure is not acceptable, not permitted—if you want to be a man. And this is what we who are products of the thirties and forties want to be—men. Not persons, *men.*
>
> The myth of success, American version, is, to put it in its simplest form, that if you work hard enough, you will "make it." You will succeed in what you do, if you care enough about succeeding. Think positively about the possibility of your success, and you will be a success. Being a success means having a good job that provides security for your wife and children. It means doing what you want to do and making good at it. It means doing well in your job, in your home life, in bed, and in the eyes of other men and women, and in God's eyes.
>
> This is our trap. For when you experience success, and I have experienced it—fully, happily, and with a great deal of excitement—you find out that it is a failure experience, it is binding, it is enslaving. Not necessarily in the short run. Not for years, sometimes. But then it comes, slowly, creeping up on you when you are alone at night or in some airplane flying to another conference. You have opened the door of success, and you are not meeting yourself, you are looking at someone else. This is the failure experience—that has haunted me through the years since I heard Ross Snyder of Chicago Theological Seminary say, "Look at yourself and ask if someone else is living your life." That is the problem with success. Someone else is living your life. Another standard, another image, is defining your life. It is the male image—the image of masculine success. You are living that image; you are not living *you.* This is the bondage. Freedom comes only when *you* begin living your life.[33]

SUGGESTED READINGS

Korda, M. *Success!* New York: Ballantine, 1977.
Lefkowitz, B. *Breaktime: Living Without Work in a Nine to Five World.* New York: Hawthorn Books, 1979.
Malcomson, W. *Success Is a Failure Experience.* Nashville: Abingdon Press, 1976.
Steele, A. *Upward Nobility.* New York: Times Books, 1978.

9

Of clenched fists and flexed biceps:

THE AGGRESSIVE ELEMENT

The differences between boys and girls are defined in terms of violence. Boys are encouraged to rough-house; girls are taught to be gentle ("ladylike"). Boys are expected to get into fights, but admonished not to hit girls. (It is not "manly" to assault females — except, of course, sexually, but that comes later.) Boys who run away from fights are "sissies," with the implication that they are queer. As little boys become big boys, their education in violence continues. The leadership in this country today consists of such little boys who attained "manhood" in the approved and heroic violence of World War II. They returned to a society in which street and motorcycle gangs, fast cars, and fraternity hazing confirmed the lessons of war — one must be tough and ready to inflict pain in order to get ahead. Lucy Komisar[1]

In the preceding chapter we discussed the significant place the achievement of success has in the male sex role. In America as in other postindustrial countries, success is often obtained by a competitive struggle among men who desire similar goals. Frequently, when competition gets out of hand and men go too far in their quest for success, some have been known to inflict pain, injury, and even worse on a competitor. That brings us to the third element in the male sex role—aggression.

With respect to the other four elements in the American male sex role, aggression possesses a couple of unique features. First, America is one of the few postindustrial countries in which aggression is still seen as a desirable and "manly" characteristic. Many young American boys are actively encouraged to get out there and aggressively show "what they're made of" against other boys. Consequently, in some groups, an aggressive boy is thought of as more masculine than one who shuns aggressive behaviors. Second, most people think males rather than females are prone toward aggressive and even violent behaviors. Physical aggression is one of the few social behaviors in which scientists see a distinct sex difference (see Chapter 6).

In this chapter we will first analyze aggression and the part it plays in American culture, especially for men. Surprisingly, aggression is both denounced as a significant social problem and applauded as a masculine attribute. Then we will deal more specifically with men's aggression and violence against other men and against women.

THE ANOMALY OF AGGRESSION

Aggression and violence are unsettling social features of human behavior that, on the one hand, excite and stimulate Americans and, on the other, repulse and horrify them. As proof of this cultural quandary, let us think about some examples of various aggressive and violent behaviors. Aggression fills the pages of America's history with military events that either stir people's patriotism (the exploits of the early freedom fighters at Bunker Hill and their twentieth-century descendents at Iwo Jima) or cause public consternation (the unconscionable tragedies at My Lai and Kent State). There is an almost electrifying excitement among the crowds at boxing matches or hockey games as people scream for blood. Later these same people decry violence on their city streets. A majority of Americans report that they favor some form of control over handguns, and yet their elected officials refuse to legislate against handguns because of the "reprisals" from a small but vocal gun lobby. It is as if Americans cannot make up their minds about aggression. To most of the civilized world, America is a cultural paradox when it comes to our ambivalence over aggression.

Part of the problem lies in the fact that many Americans do not have a clear and unequivocal definition of the word "aggression." In the minds of most Americans, the soldiers at Iwo Jima and My Lai clearly acted in decidedly aggressive and even violent ways against other human beings. Certainly, most people would agree that aggression occurred when John Hinckley reached out from a crowd and shot President Reagan or when Lee Harvey Oswald waited alone and then shot President Kennedy. But what can we say of a defensive guard who lands a bone-rattling tackle against a scrambling quarterback, or a dynamic salesperson who goes after a reluctant customer, or a young man who persists in trying to get a date with an indisposed coed? Are these actions aggressive? We need to differentiate between aggressive behavior and assertive behavior.

Leonard Berkowitz, professor of psychology at the University of Wisconsin and a reputed authority on aggression, suggests that the term "aggression" should be applied only to those behaviors in which there is a clear *intention* to cause either physical or psychological harm, injury, or worse to another person.[2] According to Berkowitz's definition of aggression, the dynamic salesperson or determined male suitor should be considered assertive and not aggressive. Berkowitz also differentiates between two types of human aggression, namely, *emotional aggression* and *instrumental aggression*.[3] Emotional aggression occurs in response to a specific emotion such as anger, fear, hatred, or frustration. For example, if a man strikes another in anger that is a case of emotional aggression. Instrumental aggression, on the other hand, occurs when the intention to harm another is *secondary* to yet another more important goal. For example, when the defensive guard just mentioned tackled—and hurt—the quarterback in order to prevent a possible touchdown pass, the guard was displaying instrumental aggression. The aggression inherent in the tackle was aimed primarily at preventing a touchdown, not at hurting the quarterback.

How widespread is aggression in our culture? The fact is aggression and violence are nearing epidemic proportions in the United States. According to a recent Federal Bureau of Investigation's *Uniform Crime Reports,* an aggressive or violent crime is committed in the United States every thirty-one seconds. This means that somewhere in this country *a human being is assaulted, robbed, raped, or murdered every thirty-one seconds!*[4] Other statistics indicate that the United States is one of the most violent nations on earth. If we exclude many of the newly emergent and politically unstable Third World countries and some of the repressive Central and South American countries that seem constantly beset with bloody revolutions, we cannot find a more violent society than America. If we compare the United States with other countries with similar stable governments and sound economics, America stands out in the minds of many as a gigantic parody of the "shoot-'em-up Wild West." For example, Americans kill one another over ten times more frequently than do the citizens of Austria, Australia, Sweden, Poland, and France, and almost twenty times more frequently than do the citizens of Norway, Spain, Greece, and Denmark.[5]

Why is the United States so violent? Once again we suggest that part of the problem is linked to America's ambivalent feelings about aggression. On the one hand, Americans decry the breakdown of law and order and fear the upsurge of violent crimes in the streets. Yet they turn around and admire the machismo of the gunslingers on their television sets and flock to theaters to sit in voyeuristic

"He didn't like his present much, but I made him take it."

darkness as directors strive for gruesome realism in the various ways a body can be destroyed. Some of the most popular heroes on America's televison and movie screens have been aggressive and violent men. Take, for example, men like Marshall Dillon on the long-running TV show *Gunsmoke;* Matt never flinched in a gun fight. Or take John Wayne's countless action movies in which the aggressive actions of red-blooded, two-fisted men were extolled or Sam Pechinpah's celluloid paeans to violence for violence sake in such movies as *The Wild Bunch* and *Straw Dogs,* or the numerous Hollywood actors like Clint Eastwood and Charles Bronson who have made violence and aggression their trademark. Americans clearly have a love–hate relationship with aggression and violence. And yet there is another feature that encourages aggression in America—the male sex role.

American boys and men are expected to be aggressive toward others on supposedly *appropriate occasions.*[6] Most American males, however, do not see themselves as violent or aggressive. Still, we find many parents of young boys encouraging their sons not to back down from a fight, especially if a bully starts it.[7] In terms of the male sex role, a boy should always be ready to defend himself against others in a *masculine* way. The boy who runs away when someone else picks a fight is thought of as a sissy by many parents and peers alike. As boys grow older, many go out for team sports in school. In football, for example, the aggressive lessons continue when a coach spurs on his helmeted charges with peppery advice like, "Get out there and make the other team bleed" or "Don't be afraid to hurt the other guy; it's all part of the game!" At times it seems that the goal in some high school games is to inflict injury rather than to score points. For those young men who drop out of school, there is always a street gang in which aggression and violence form central values among gang members. A common practice among many street gangs is to have a new recruit perform a certain number of violent acts in order to win full membership in the gang and thus be seen as a macho male.[8]

Initially, little boys are cautioned against hurting little girls. Girls, boys are told, are weak and soft and therefore should be cuddled not cudgelled. But somewhere along the path to adulthood, some males come to believe that "women like it when you're a little rough." Some men seem to think of aggression against women as part of the male's right to dominate and control women.

Another lesson in male aggression comes with the belief that a man has a right—some might insist a duty—to seek revenge in aggressive and violent ways if he or his have been violated. Even the Bible allows for such aggressive behavior with its prescription of "an eye for an eye." Consequently, many men believe that a man wronged is a man who must retaliate in kind if he is to be considered a man again. The majority of men who sat through Charles Bronson's portrayal of a New York City architect-turned-midnight-vigilante in the movie *Death Wish* (and more recently *Death Wish II*) applauded the mayhem and destruction Bronson wrought on others. Somehow violence is seen as a cleansing experience for a man who has himself been victimized.

Given all of the lessons in the male sex role with respect to aggression, a real man is expected to act aggressively only on those occasions when another male starts a fight or pushes him too far or to show his dominance over a woman. With the pressures to conform to the aggressive element of their sex role, men, and their exaggerated sense of rugged individualism and penchant for competition, make fertile ground for flowering aggressive behavior.

MEN AGAINST MEN

Thus far we have noted that because aggression is an important element in the American male's sex role, boys and men are expected to inflict pain and injury on one another when the situation warrants it. But what kinds of situations call for the intentional harming of another person? Is it enough of an inducement when a neighborhood bully calls you a name, when someone carelessly kicks sand in your face, when someone cuts back too soon into your lane after passing you, or when someone intends to harm you? These situations and countless others are enough inducement for many American men to fight. "Turning the other cheek" is something taught little boys and girls in Sunday school, but real men know down deep that such soppy counsel is really for girls and sissies.

Are American males really as aggressive and violent as movies and television would have us believe? Setting aside the statistics on violent crimes noted earlier, is the average American male likely to resort to aggression or even violence to "solve" a problem? Could it be that a few violent criminals give law-abiding

Table 9.1

	Almost always	Sometimes	Hardly ever	Never
A. The police should let it go, not do anything.	☐	☐	☐	☐
B. Police should make arrests without using clubs or guns.	☐	☐	☐	☐
C. Police should use clubs, but not guns.	☐	☐	☐	☐
D. The police should shoot, but not to kill.	☐	☐	☐	☐
E. The police should shoot to kill.	☐	☐	☐	☐

Source: M. Blumenthal et al., *Justifying Violence: Attitudes of American Men* (Ann Arbor: Institute for Social Research, The University of Michigan, 1972), p. 26.

American males a bad name? The average American male certainly would not inflict physical harm or injury on another intentionally unless in the *gravest* of circumstances. Or would he?

In the summer of 1969, a research team headed by Monica Blumethal and associated with the University of Michigan's Institute for Social Research completed an in-depth survey of American men's attitudes on the use of violence.[9] A representative group of 1,374 American men between the ages of sixteen and sixty-four made up the sample. The men were asked a series of questions, presented with numerous scenarios, and then asked how they thought each situation should best be handled. Here we will highlight only a few of the study's numerous findings, which form a fascinating glimpse into what American men think and feel about the use of violence.

To discover the men's attitudes toward the use of violence, the researchers developed a series of social situations or scenarios and then asked each male to indicate the amount of control the authorities, that is, the police, should take to remedy or contain the problem at hand. It was thought that the amount of control favored in each of several scenarios would accurately reflect in a general way the males' attitudes about violence and its use as a control mechanism.

For the first scenario, a researcher presented the following social situation.

> There have been times when gangs of hoodlums have gone into a town, terrified people, and caused a lot of property damage. How do you think the police should handle this situation?

After hearing the situation, each man was handed a card that listed several options that the police could use to control the public disturbance. Without any further assistance, each man was requested to indicate his preference for each option (see A, B, C, D, and E of Table 9.1). The percentage distribution for the "hoodlum" scenario is presented in Table 9.2.

Table 9.2 Percentage of Respondents Reporting How the Police Should Handle Hoodlum Gangs (all respondents; N = 1,374)

	Almost always	Sometimes	Hardly ever	Never	Total
A. The police should let it go, not do anything.	7%	6%	6%	81%	100%
B. Police should make arrests without using clubs or guns.	28	52	9	11	100
C. Police should use clubs, but not guns.	18	62	11	9	100
D. The police should shoot, but not to kill.	20	44	23	13	100
E. The police should shoot to kill.	5	27	24	44	100

Source: M. Blumenthal et al., *Justifying Violence: Attitudes of American Men* (Ann Arbor: Institute for Social Research, The University of Michigan, 1972), p. 28.

These men strongly believed in some form of police action. Eighty-one percent of them strongly opposed the option that police should let the disturbance just blow over. Four out of every five men in the sample wanted the police to step in and do something to end the disturbance. We could infer then that American men firmly believe in the idea that some form of action is desirable in dealing with situations involving social disturbance. When it comes to what kinds of actions the police should take, the men sampled presented some interesting dilemmas. When it comes to the use of force, eighty percent regarded the use of clubs as appropriate "almost always" or "sometimes." Sixty-four percent saw no problem with shooting "but not to kill." And thirty-two percent felt that shooting "to kill" was acceptable "sometimes." This last figure is most unnerving. One out of every three men sampled believed that killing another human being was an acceptable way to deal with a disruptive social situation. Is it any wonder that so many public quarrels between and among men end in a shooting?

The men in the sample were also asked to indicate their feelings about various police actions in ghetto riots and campus disturbances. Recall that in the late 1960s, America went through a series of social spasms that rocked many of our social institutions. The civil rights movement was running into opposition, and blacks were growing more and more agitated by the lack of any real progress in their quest for equal treatment. Adding still further to the volatile racial situation, a majority of blacks were housed in poverty and humiliation in this country's inner cities. Across America the conditions were ripe and the ghettos exploded with the crackle of gunfire and burning buildings. Furthermore, the Vietnam conflict continued to escalate, and opposition spilled onto many college campuses. Students protested with marches and sit-ins, and the National Guard and police became strange additions to the academic scene.

Elements of the Male Sex Role

Table 9.3 Percentage Responses to How the Police Should Handle Ghetto Riots
(all respondents; N = 1,374)

	Almost always	Sometimes	Hardly ever	Never	Total
A. The police should let it go, not do anything.	3%	9%	11%	77%	100%
B. Police should make arrests without using clubs or guns.	30	51	10	9	100
C. Police should use clubs, but not guns.	15	65	12	8	100
D. The police should shoot, but not to kill.	14	47	22	17	100
E. The police should shoot to kill.	4	26	19	51	100

Source: M. Blumenthal et al., *Justifying Violence: Attitudes of American Men* (Ann Arbor: Institute for Social Research, The University of Michigan, 1972), p. 30.

Using the same "controlling" options that had been presented in the hoodlum scenario (Table 9.1), the sample of men indicated their attitudes toward how the police should deal with ghetto rioters and student protesters. The percentage distributions for these two situations are presented in Tables 9.3 and 9.4.

The men in the sample felt much the same way about ghetto rioters as they did about marauding hoodlums. Once again, action is the key word in the minds of most American men. The sample strongly supported stopping the rioters with minimal force (eighty-one percent favored arrests without clubs or guns "almost always" or "sometimes"). The remaining categories (C, D, and E) showed the sample holding favorable attitudes toward stronger, even lethal, control options in about the same degree as expressed toward the hoodlums. How American men can perceive hoodlums and rioting ghetto residents in comparable ways is an interesting sociological question.

When it comes to campus disturbances, there is an apparent moderating trend in the sample's responses. In the first place, almost nine out of ten men, or eighty-seven percent, felt that arrests should be made "without using clubs or guns." Furthermore, a substantial shift in attitudes comes in the categories D and E, where there is greater resistance to the use of lethal weapons. However, forty-eight percent of the sample believed that shooting "but not to kill" was appropriate at least some of the time. (The ironic feature of category D is many people's belief that a gun can be fired into a crowd and not possibly kill!) What is undoubtedly the most chilling feature of the survey is that almost one out of every five men, or nineteen percent, felt that shooting to kill was an appropriate way to control student demonstrators at least some of the time. How prophetic that

Table 9.4 Percentage Responses to How the Police Should Handle Student Disturbances (all respondents; N = 1,374)

	Almost always	Sometimes	Hardly ever	Never	Total
A. The police should let it go, not do anything.	4%	12%	14%	70%	100%
B. Police should make arrests without using clubs or guns.	38	49	6	7	100
C. Police should use clubs, but not guns.	16	60	15	9	100
D. The police should shoot, but not to kill.	16	32	25	27	100
E. The police should shoot to kill.	3	16	19	62	100

Source: M. Blumenthal et al., *Justifying Violence: Attitudes of American Men* (Ann Arbor: Institute for Social Research, The University of Michigan, 1972), p. 31.

less than a year after this survey was concluded four students were killed and ten were wounded at Kent State University. When one of the respected townspeople was asked his opinion about the student killings, he remarked,

> We feel that the Guard did exactly what they are sent in to do: To keep law and order. Frankly, if I'd been faced with the same situation and had a submachine gun, there would not have been fourteen shot, there probably would have been 140 of them dead, and that's what they need.[10]

Why did the men in this survey place such emphasis on doing something even if the action resulted in another's injury or even death? The answer, at least part of it, lies in the way men define their sex role. First and foremost, a man must do something to prove himself a man. Only women and fearful men would sit idly by and do nothing in a public disturbance, or at least that is what many men think. Perhaps American boys and men have watched too many movies and television shows in which a man grabs for his gun when there's trouble. No self-respecting man would just wait for the trouble to blow over. No matter the sociological or psychological causes for the obsession for action, the results are usually the same—men aggress against each other in frightful ways.

MEN AGAINST WOMEN

Earlier we noted how American parents often encourage their sons to be aggressive with other boys but warn their sons against hurting girls. However, as boys grow into manhood, something happens to the earlier lessons in appropriate masculine behavior and the prohibition against hurting females loses some of its

Elements of the Male Sex Role

force. All of a sudden, or so it may seem, women who were once considered off-limits for male aggression now become prime targets of it. We will discuss two of the more sordid features of aggression as an element of the male sex role: rape and marital violence or, as it is commonly referred to, wife-beating.

RAPE

Rape is legally defined as the "carnal knowledge of a female forcibly and against her will." A somewhat less legalistic definition but more to the point of our discussion is one provided by Susan Brownmiller in her book *Against Our Will*. She writes that rape occurs when "a woman chooses not to have intercourse with a specific man, and the man chooses to proceed against her will."[11]

Rape is the fastest-rising violent crime listed in the FBI's *Uniform Crime Reports*. In the decade from 1968 to 1977, *reported* rape cases jumped from 15.9 per 100,000 population to 29.1 per 100,000.[12] During 1977 alone, over 63,000 cases of rape were reported by the FBI. The most shocking feature of these statistics is that rape is considered by many experts in crime statistics to be one of the *least* reported violent crimes. The best available estimates suggest that for every one reported rape case there are anywhere from three to ten unreported cases. The conservative estimate of three means that over a quarter of a million women were forcibly raped in the United States in 1977!

But the impersonal figures tabulated in neat columns tell little about the reality and depth of human suffering and degradation that accompany the rape victim for the rest of her life. And what of the man, the rapist who forces a woman to have intercourse against her will? Why would a man rape? Some suggest that men rape because they are driven by a powerful and natural sexual urge, or because they are psychologically disturbed and consequently forced to rape by sheer strength of uncontrollable pathological impulses, or because they feel a sense of insecurity or doubt about their masculinity, or because rape is an extreme extension of the aggressive element of the male sex role.

The notion that rape is a normal and natural consequence of men's powerful sexual urges is ridiculous. Little more than two hundred years ago, women were believed more prone to sexual passion and lust, and men were viewed as more disposed to reason and logic, not sexuality. Any explanation of rape based on such a recent historical flip-flop in what constitutes male and female sexuality certainly cannot now be expected to explain why men have raped for centuries.

Many laypeople and some social scientists believe that a rapist must be suffering from some form of psychological disturbance in order to commit such a serious crime against another person. In these people's minds, the rapist is acting out some pathological sexual impulse. The prevalence of what is called the *pathological perspective* of rape owes much to the work of a nineteenth century physician, Richard von Krafft-Ebing. In 1886 Krafft-Ebing's major work *Psychopathia Sexualis* was published. Quickly, it became the standard text throughout Europe on sexual aberrations. Mirroring the widespread belief of his day, Krafft-Ebing viewed the rapist as a deranged imbecile, that is, a person with a very low intellectual capacity, who suffered from a serious lack of impulse control. In the following passage taken from *Psychopathia Sexualis,* Krafft-Ebing emphasizes the psychological causes of the rapist's behaviors.

> The crime of rape presumes a temporary, powerful excitation of sexual desire induced by excess in alcohol or by some other condition. It is highly improbable that a man morally intact would commit this most brutal crime. Lombrosco considered the majority of men who commit rape to be degenerate, particularly when the crime is done on children or old women. He asserts that, in many such men, he has found actual signs of degeneracy.
>
> It is a fact that rape is very often the act of degenerate male imbeciles, who, under some circumstances, do not even respect the bond of blood.[13]

The scientific evidence is sorely lacking for this contention that rapists suffer some form of demented thought pattern or are generally of lower intelligence than other criminals convicted of serious violent crimes such as murder.[14] We can suggest, however, that rapists who brutalize, mutilate, or even kill their victims either before or after raping them, as in the cases of the Boston Strangler and Jack the Ripper, are probably psychologically disturbed in the most severe sense. In these extreme cases, rape is only one violation, although admittedly a most serious violation, in a sequence of bizarre and disturbed actions.

A third and very popular explanation of men's sexual violence against women is the suggestion that the rapist's violent behaviors stem from a poorly developed or insecure male sex role identity.[15] Recall that many social scientists consider the development of a male's sex role identity to be an extremely risky and failure-prone psychological undertaking (see Chapter 6). Many things supposedly can go wrong in a young boy's life, especially in his relations with his mother, that may cause the boy, and later on the adult man, to feel confused over his masculine identity. Consequently, such a male may be driven to strike out against women in extreme and violent ways. In the final analysis, this perspective on rape blames women for men's violent sexual behaviors. If women as mothers would not cause so much confusion in their sons' minds about their male sex role identity there would be fewer rapists.[16]

Rather than look for some clinical evidence of a compelling psychological syndrome or some deep-seated, basic insecurity in the rapist's sex role identity, we might better look more closely at the male sex role itself, especially the aggressive element. First of all, we must clearly understand that rape is not an act of sex or wanton lust. *Rape is an aggressive act perpetrated on another to show the dominance and power of the rapist.*[17] This fact becomes patently clear when we find that rape in prisons is generally viewed as one of the most brutal ways in which a male prisoner demonstrates his power and dominance over another male prisoner.

In a patriarchal society like America, males are taught certain values about how the sexes should relate both sexually and nonsexually. A majority of American males come to accept the notion that males are inherently superior to females. Pushing the view of male superiority even further, many men believe that

COMMON MYTHS ASSOCIATED WITH RAPE

Myths concerning female rape victims:

Most women like being treated roughly or even aggressively.

Most women fantasize about being raped.

If a woman says no to a man's sexual advances, she really means yes and the man should persist.

It is impossible to rape an unwilling woman.

Many women tease men sexually and thus deserve to be raped.

Women who are raped usually provoked it by the way they dressed or where they were (for example, dark streets or alleys).

Most women who are raped are young and attractive.

Myths concerning male rapists:

Most rapists are perverts or degenerates.

Most rapists are men who have psychological problems with their masculine identity.

Most rapists are strangers to their victims.

A man cannot be raped.

A husband cannot rape his wife.

women should submit to men's wills and be dominated by them. These basic beliefs in men's natural superiority and rightful dominance over women set the stage, so to speak, for rape. Furthermore, certain myths or misconceptions about women's and men's sexuality and rape have grown in people's minds over time (see "Common Myths Associated with Rape"). Add to the ideology of male supremacy and certain myths about rape the social expectations that pressure men to act aggressively as proof of their masculinity, and we have a volatile atmosphere conducive to rape. From this perspective, rape occurs not because some males are driven by powerful sexual urges, mental illness, or insecure sex role identity but rather, to a large degree, because of society's sexist views about women and the sex role expectations placed on men to be aggressively dominant over women. On this point Diane Russell notes that

> Rape is not so much a deviant act as an over-conforming act. Rape may be understood as an extreme acting-out of qualities that are regarded as super masculine in this and many other societies: aggression, force, power, strength, toughness, dominance, competitiveness. To win, to be superior, to be successful, to conquer—all demonstrate masculinity to those who subscribe to common cultural notions of masculinity, i.e., the *masculine mystique*. And it would be surprising if these notions of masculinity did not find expression in men's sexual behavior. Indeed, sex may be the arena where these notions of masculinity are most intensely played out, particularly by men who feel powerless in the rest of their lives, and hence, whose masculinity is threatened by this sense of powerlessness.[18]

The Aggressive Element

MARITAL VIOLENCE

When it comes to marital violence, or wife-beating, many people turn a blind eye and a deaf ear. It is as if there exists an unspoken rule that what goes on between a wife and a husband is nobody else's business. But certainly this could not extend to marital violence, could it? Surely, if people saw a husband physically abuse his wife in public, most would step in and get involved, wouldn't they? In a recent study, a male and female staged an argument in a public restaurant that ended with the female's being slapped.[19] When during the course of the argument the female made it clear that she did not know the male who hit her, several witnesses came to her assistance. However, when the spectators were led to believe that the couple were married, most of the spectators refused to become involved. Furthermore, in a national survey, nearly *twenty-five percent of the women* questioned thought that marital violence was a normal and even a necessary part of marriage, and approximately thirty percent of the males sampled viewed marital violence as a good feature of marriage.[20] Thus marital violence appears to be an almost acceptable cultural norm and probably much more common than most people would like to believe.[21]

How widespread is marital violence in our society? Like rape, marital violence is an underreported crime. However, the following statistics taken from Del Martin's *Battered Wives* give us a glimpse at the extent of marital violence in the United States.

> In Detroit, 4,900 wife-assault complaints were filled in 1972. In New York, 14,167 wife-abuse complaints were handled in Family Court throughout the state during the judicial year 1972–73. "Legal experts think that wife-abuse is one of the most underreported crimes in the country—even more underreported than rape, which the FBI estimates is ten times more frequent than statistics indicate. A conservative estimate puts the number of battered wives nationwide at well over a million," states Karen Durbin. Using the New York court statistics and the "ten times" formula to account for the cases that dropped by the wayside or were never reported, 141,670 wife-beatings could have occured in New York State alone. If we can take this kind of guesswork a step further and consider that wife-battering is probably even more underreported than rape, and that there are fifty states in the Union, Durbin's estimate of "well over a million" could be conservative.
>
> In 1974, Boston police responded to 11,081 family disturbance calls, most of which involved physical violence. At the end of the first quarter of 1975, 5,589 such calls were received—half the previous year's figure in one-quarter time. (As an aside to these figures, Boston City Hospital reports that approximately 70 percent of the assault victims received in its emergency room are known to be women who have been attacked in their homes, usually by a husband or lover.)[22]

Again we find the age-old legacies of patriarchy, this time serving as the foundation for the wife-beating phenomenon. Ever since Roman times and earlier, women have been considered the property of men. A daughter's life was completely in her father's hands as was a wife's. For centuries English Common Law

Elements of the Male Sex Role

Abraham Bosse, The Dictatorial Husband, *1633.*   *Source: The Bettmann Archives.*

recognized a husband's right to "domestic chastisement" of a wife who displeased him. Even though wife-beating is no longer sanctioned by law, many men—at least nearly a third sampled in a national survey—believe that marital violence is an acceptable feature of marriage. It seems that as long as women are seen as secondary citizens with little or no power, there will always be a number of men who feel it part of their male role to abuse sexually and physically the women they live with. Rape and wife-beating are two of the more sinister and disturbing features we find in male–female relations. Why men should find it necessary to commit such forms of human degradation and cruelty on women is a major concern among several segments of society.

SOME CLOSING COMMENTS

In this chapter we saw that American society appears ambivalent toward aggression. In one breath, Americans decry the mayhem brought on by aggression in the streets, and in another, American parents encourage their sons to act aggressively in order to prove themselves manly. We noted also that American males believe that action is preferable to nonaction in the case of a public disturbance.

A large percentage of males go so far as to condone aggressive action even to the point of killing others to restore public calm. Finally, we witnessed male aggression against females in the form of rape and wife-beating. It seems that rape and marital violence can best be understood in relation to the presence of sexist ideology and the male sex role's expectation of male aggression.

Aggression is a valued feature of the male sex role. It seems reasonable to suggest that aggression is more likely to be condoned in those societies where there is a basic inequality between various groups. Aggression is one means by which one group controls and retains its power over other groups (for example, whites over blacks and males over females). If America is ever to become a society in which all people are truly equal, all aggression must be condemned not condoned. Only when females gain total equality as human beings will the aggression that is expected of males cease to be necessary in order for them to prove themselves real men.

SUGGESTED READINGS

Brownmiller, S. *Against Our Will*. New York: Simon & Schuster, 1975.
Chesler, P. *About Men*. New York: Simon & Schuster, 1978.
Martin, D. *Battered Wives*. San Francisco: Glide Publications, 1976.

10

Of bulging codpieces and spent condoms:
THE SEXUAL ELEMENT

A common myth in our culture deals with the supposed sexual differences between men and women. According to this bit of fantasy, female sexuality is complex, mysterious, and full of problems, while male sexuality is simple, straightforward, and problem-free.

Bernie Zilbergeld[1]

While we may be mature in years, sexual maturity is a long, complicated process not systematically linked to physiological and chronological development. In fact, in modern societies, the individual's sexual self is the least and last explicitly developed dimension of self.

Jean Lipman-Blumen[2]

For most men, few other activities can be as exciting or anxiety provoking, as fulfilling or deflating, as stimulating or disturbing, as amusing or guilt producing as *sex* can be. Obviously, anytime we deal with a human feature as socially complex and as personally volatile as sex, we are bound to encounter all kinds of difficulties and problems. Several points need clarification before we begin our discussion.

In the first place, given the social expectations, demands, and prohibitions that surround sex in general and male sexuality in particular, we should not be surprised to find that some social scientists have included sexuality in their discussion of the male sex role while others have not. Recall that in the remarks at the beginning of this section Michael Cicone and Diane Ruble found "interest in sex" to be a central trait in the designation of "typical male," while Robert Brannon, in his fourfold typology, did not include sexual expectations as a distinct element of the male sex role.[3] Given the significance that sex plays in the adolescent's life and the preoccupation most adult men have with sex and their sexual performance in comparison to other men's, male sexuality can be dealt with as an element in the male sex role.

Second, we must be clear about what we mean by the word "sex." *Sex* here means much more than what goes on between two people in bed. Sex includes everything that has an *erotic* component and takes place between people or with only one person. In other words, sex covers a wide range of behaviors, thoughts, and feelings. For example, the sexual element can be found in a loving glance between two people, a kiss on the cheek, an intimate fondling of one's own or another's body, or even an erotic fantasy about another person. *Male sexuality* designates all of the sexual features that involve men. Thus the sexual element in the male sex role is more than a collection of behaviors and techniques; it also includes a man's frame of mind, emotions, and expectations regarding all erotic situations.

This chapter covers a wide range of issues. We will begin by looking at the early psychosocial foundations of male sexuality—how parents treat their son, how they show affection toward him, and how he shows his feelings, especially love, toward others. These and many other basic interactions form a boy's early experiences in his developing sexuality. As a boy matures, he faces adolescence, that period in life when sexual urges, feelings, and social expectations for sexual expressions become increasingly focused on some form of genital expression. Later on, the male will likely settle into a pattern of sexual expression which may or may not be made more difficult by a series of sexual myths that burden a majority of males.

Next we will examine several clinical problems that many men face at some time or other. We will describe various male sexual dysfunctions and some of their underlying causes. We will also look at what is becoming a major problem affecting male sexuality today, a lack of interest in sexual expression.

Finally, we will examine what may seem to be an anomaly in our coverage of male sexuality: sexual abstinence. Sexual abstinence, or asexuality as some call this social phenomenon, is being touted by some men and woman as an opportunity for self-examination. Some men claim sexual abstinence allows them a measure of freedom from the pressures and expectations of their intimate relationships.

RITES OF PASSAGE

In recent years male sexuality has received considerable press attention. Two notable examples of the new wave of journalistic investigation are Gay Talese's *Thy Neighbor's Wife* and Nancy Friday's *Men in Love.* Talese gives his readers a rather intimate, inside look at the extensive goings-on of a number of males engaged in a variety of sexual activities and exploits. To hear Talese tell it, sexual practices are no longer bounded by bedroom walls or strict prohibitions—if they ever were.

Nancy Friday provides the reader with a rare look into one of the most intriguing and least understood facets of male sexuality, the male sexual fantasy. To conjure up a mental image and to populate that cerebral picture with people and activity is a decidedly human ability that gives considerable pleasure. In *Men in Love,* we read that a considerable portion of male sexuality resides in the mind, where a male can weave and spin images of his own glorious and fulfilling sexual exploits. In anecdotal form, Friday presents a large number of sexual fantasies gathered from over three thousand men. Two notions expressed in Friday's book are especially noteworthy for our present discussion. First, many men seemingly have a much more vivid and satisfying sexual life in their fantasies that they do in real life. Second, a male's present sexual fantasies can be used to cover up real or imagined past hurts or rejections. On this last point, Friday provides an interesting speculative note at the end of her book.

> Here at the end of these pages, I find that my years of research have confirmed something even the most uninstructed woman takes as given: Inside every male is a denied little boy.
> He loved his father, but was taught to show that love only through mindless imitation of his father's mindless imitation of *his* father's Victorian authoritarianism.
> He loved his mother, but feared her power.
> The male principle in society says he is expected to be tough and domineering with women, always in control, and sexually voracious. The female principle is the opposite; when he approaches women, he carries with him all his unconscious memories of mother's awesome powers of retaliation and rejection.
> How can he handle the fear and rage that sex means for a man under these conditions? He can't stop, doesn't want to stop, being a man. The frustration is blamed on women, *goddamn them!* Maybe the best thing to do is turn your back on them and forget the whole problem. In the end, it is the man's relentless desire for women that keeps him from his surrender. Fantasies are invented. At least for a sexual moment, magic is called in, reality altered, the perceived nature of women changed; the conflict healed.
> Fantasies are the triumph of love over rage.[4]

Elements of the Male Sex Role

"We'll have to stop meeting like this, Irene. My den mother is getting suspicious."

BOYS NEED LOVING TOO

We have mentioned on several occasions that little boys are expected to be independent and self-sufficient. The ways of teaching these traits are numerous and varied, but research in childrearing generally suggests that little boys are treated more roughly, given more severe physical punishments, and encouraged more often to hold back their feelings of affection and caring than are little girls. On the average, little boys receive less hugging, holding, cuddling, kissing, caressing, and fondling than little girls do. The underlying message of most parenting practices for little boys seems to be, "You really don't need to be fussed over like little girls do. And anyway, we don't want you growing up to be a sissy."

But there is a problem with all of this "toughening up." The little boy is denied some of the warm, caring affection that only close, loving human contact can provide. In a sense, the American way of raising a boy creates the "denied little boy" of which Friday speaks. Not only are denied little boys more apt to engage in human sexual fantasies rather than in genuine and fulfilling human sexuality, as Friday contends, but depriving boys of loving and affectional human contact early in life may have other, more serious consequences, not the least of which is poor sexual adjustment. To make a point on this matter, let us review the research on affectional deprivation among rhesus monkeys. (Obviously, we cannot research affectional deprivation among humans for many reasons not the least of which would be ethical concerns.)

Harry Harlow and his colleagues at the University of Wisconsin have observed some intriguing behavioral problems brought on as a consequence of affectional deprivation among rhesus monkeys.[5] Monkeys raised in isolation in Harlow's laboratories act in disturbed ways when they are later introduced to normally raised monkeys. One of the observed disturbances relates to sexual behaviors. When a male monkey raised in isolation is put with a sexually receptive (in heat), normally raised female monkey, the male does not mate and apparently cannot be taught how to mate successfully. As strong a lure as a sexually receptive female monkey is, the male apparently cannot overcome the earlier influences of social and emotional deprivations that he suffered in isolation.

We must be cautious when drawing any inference about human behaviors based on monkey behaviors. After all, human males are not monkeys. However, Harlow's work provides us with some interesting avenues of speculation about the *possibility* of how depriving a little boy of emotional and loving treatment early in his life may cause him some difficulties in his sexual life later on. Even though we should not go too far in our comparison of Harlow's findings and human sexual difficulties, one thing is definite: All little boys need as much love, gentle and kind reassurance, and loving physical contact as little girls need. The problem is that most boys do not get this.

CLOSE SEXUAL ENCOUNTERS OF A WONDROUS KIND

Boys, like girls, are curious creatures and seemingly have their hands in and on everything from a very early age onward. The first object of a boy's curiosity is his own body. This curiosity is a natural and beneficial feature in the early development of his sexuality. As a boy grows older, he soon learns that by stimulating his genitals he can cause an extremely pleasurable and satisfying sensation. Any self-stimulation that leads to erotic pleasure or arousal is call *masturbation.* In the words of James McCary, a leading expert in human sexuality, masturbation is "a means of self-discovery and sensory awareness."[6] Many parents, however, do not look upon their son's masturbatory behavior as one of the first natural steps in his developing sexuality. Some parents believe that masturbation is evil and sinful, and some even suggest to their errant son that masturbation can cause serious mental and physical deterioration. (There is absolutely *no* scientific evidence that masturbation causes blindness, hair growth on the palms, brain damage, or any other debilitating physical illness!) Because masturbatory behavior is prohibited in most American homes, young boys often learn to sneak their sexual pleasures behind a locked bathroom door or under the bedsheets in the dark of night. Consequently, their early sexual feelings and experiences become bound up with "shameful" thoughts and prohibited pleasures. A young boy soon learns that sex in general and his sexuality in particular are something to hide and be ashamed of.

MASTURBATION: DIFFERENT VIEWS

Masturbation is an intrinsically and seriously disordered act.
   Vatican Declaration on Sexual Ethics, 1975
Don't knock masturbation. It's having sex with someone I deeply love.
   Woody Allen
It was at the end of my freshman year of high school—and freshman year of masturbating—that I discovered on the underside of my penis, just where the shaft meets the head, a little discolored dot that has since been diagnosed as a freckle. Cancer. I had given myself *cancer.* All that pulling and tugging at my own flesh, all that friction, had given me an incurable disease. And not yet fourteen! In bed at night the tears rolled from my eyes. "No!" I sobbed. "I don't want to die! Please—no!" But then, because I would very shortly be a corpse anyway, I went ahead and jerked off into my sock. I had taken to carrying the dirty socks into bed with me at night so as to be able to use one as a receptacle upon retiring, and the other upon awakening.
   Philip Roth

Source: Reprinted in B. Strong, S. Wilson, M. Robbins, and T. Johns, *Human Sexuality,* 2d ed. (St. Paul: West Publishing Company, 1981).

Nevertheless, by early adolescence, most young males have masturbated at least once. In one survey, over sixty percent of the males sampled reported that they had masturbated by the age of thirteen.[7] For the teenage male, then, masturbation plays a significant role in his growing awareness of his sexual self. This feature was noted in a recent book on human sexuality:

> Masturbation is the only sexual outlet for many adolescents. Because the accepted form of sexual behavior involves a partner of the opposite sex, masturbation may be viewed as a sign of sexual failure. This negative social value obscures the fact that self-masturbation is a means of erotic self-discovery and of erotic fulfillment, and that it is an important part of the psychosexual development of most adolescents. It teaches them how their bodies respond, providing a biologically healthy substitute for sexual intercourse during a period when young people are developing emotionally.[8]

Masturbation is only one feature of a young male's developing sexuality. As he ventures out from under the bedsheets, he soon encounters others for whom his sexual urges draw him into some kind of sexual relationship. The first intimate kiss and the faultering touch of another person's genitals are momentous events for most young males. However, before too many years, the earlier apprehensions and anxieties give way to various sexual activities such as heavy petting, oral–genital stimulation, and sexual intercourse. Depending on social influences such as family values and standards, religious training, amount of education, and peer pressures, by the time a young male reaches college age, he will have engaged in most of these intimate sexual activities.[9] By the early twenties, most young males probably think of sex as one more element—albeit an important element—of their expanding sex role.

MYTHS AND MALE SEXUALITY

By the time a young male reaches early adulthood, he probably thinks he knows just about everything there is to know about sex. Over the years, he has told or listened to almost every "dirty" joke there is, he has seen almost every centerfold printed in the last several years, he knows who is supposed to be an easy lay at school, and, of course, he has done just about everything himself at least once. What more can a male learn about sex? Unfortunately, most young men fall prey to a whole series of half-truths, partial prefabrications, and downright misconceptions about male sexuality. To set the record straight, we will now review some of the more persistent myths that cloud various features of male sexuality.

Myth #1: The Other Guy's Is Better Almost every male thinks that other males' sexual experiences are better than his or at least that other males are having fewer problems in their sex lives than he is. Not surprisingly, the basis for such thinking stems from the lack of frank and open discussion about personal sexual matters among most males. Even though males talk a great deal about sex, they rarely if ever discuss their own sexuality with other people, especially other males. Most young men learn very early never to talk about their doubts, confusions, or ignorance of sexual matters, for to do so would make them appear less masculine in the eyes of others—or so they think. When a man has a problem or question about sexuality, he tends to see himself as the only one with such a concern.

Myth #2: Sex Is Just Like Falling Off a Log As noted at the beginning of this chapter, psychologist Bernie Zilbergeld contends that most men view their sexuality as "simple, straight-forward, and problem-free." Women and not men are suppose to be burdened with all kinds of sexual problems and hang-ups. Magazine articles and books abound telling women how to deal with this kind of sexual dysfunction or that kind of sexual disturbance. Female sexuality is no easy matter if we are to believe everything we read. As for male sexuality, little is written and even less said (at least, among men) about the possibility that male sexuality may not be problem-free. One of the first holes punched in the myth of problem-free male sexuality came in 1976 when the popular magazine *Psychology Today* published the results of an extensive survey of its readership. More than 52,000 people participated in the survey. Surprisingly, more than half of the males, fifty-five percent to be exact, reported dissatisfaction with their sex lives.[10] Over forty percent of the males surveyed reported various specific sexual problems such as premature ejaculation and trouble reaching orgasm. Thus the belief that male sexuality is free of problems is nothing more than a myth that most men carry around in their heads.

Elements of the Male Sex Role

Myth #3: A Man Can't Get Enough Sex Most men believe in the idea that there is no such thing as too much sex. To suggest otherwise, that a man—a real man—may want to say "no" or "that's enough," is just plain balderdash. Down deep most men revel in a story of some Don Juan with an insatiable sexual appetite. Sometime or other, most men have fantasized themselves in a harem full of nubile women, where they single-handedly satisfy each and every woman's sexual needs. To refuse sex is something only a woman or a pansy would do. Psychologist Herb Goldberg believes that one of the reasons men are in such a present-day fix over their sexuality is their inability or unwillingness to say NO to sex.[11] A man's sexuality is not like some machine that can be switched on at anytime and run for hours. The penis will not stand erect just because someone barks "attention."

Myth #4: Men Run the Sex Show Even in these days of supposed sexual liberation and equality, the average man would find something quite unsettling in the thought of a woman walking over to him, looking him straight in the eyes, and announcing, "Your place or mine?" Women may be in boardrooms and salesrooms, but there is still one room to which they are suppose to follow man's lead, to be subordinate to a man, and that is the bedroom. Most men believe themselves responsible for everything sexual: the initiation, the setting, the foreplay, and finally orgasm itself for both partners. In *David Meyer Is a Mother,* author Gail Parent parodied some of the frustrations and fears that beset her main character, David Meyer, when he encountered several "new women."

> After my unfortunate experiences with Monica and Kathleen, I thought my suffering was behind me. No, the sexual revolution was here—off the pages of the magazines and onto the sheets.
>
> There was a Janet something, who told me, as we were undressing, that the last guy she slept with got it up for her five times in one night. There was a Lila Feffer, who told me, as we were undressing, that she takes nude Polaroid shots of all the guys she makes it with. No wonder Polaroid stock has taken a dive. There was a Helen Plotkin, who asked, while we were undressing, "Do you believe in kinky sex?" I graduated from high school in the late fifties. Helen, to me it's kinky if the girl gets on top. In each case, I repeated the Monica Steinberg trip. I bailed out before I had the chance to find out if I could make it with these girls. Trying to make it sound like their fault, I dressed quickly and always remembered to put on my shorts.
>
> I tried to sort it out. Obviously, not every woman in the world (or Southern California) was going to be a problem. I had just come up against several within a very short time span and the whole situation was intensified. "You're a very nice, attractive guy," I told myself. "You were supposed to be a real lady-killer when you grew up. What happened?"
>
> I also told myself that I really had nothing to worry about. There were millions of women who were just sweet, old-fashioned girls and didn't care if they came or not. Every year *Playboy* has a new Miss January and a brand-new Miss April. There must be millions of girls who will tickle my back and never ask for anything in return. I didn't really want them, though. I wanted the new woman, like I wanted the new clothes and the new house and the new Mercedes and the *New York Times* delivered to my door. I'm a hip guy with a mustache. I don't wear undershirts. I can't all of a sudden start falling in love with Wacs. I left my wife Frances because she couldn't keep up. I want the girls with the long hair and loose tits and jeans. They just scare the shit out of me, that's all.

"What's the worst thing that can happen?" I asked myself.

The worst thing that can happen is that I take one of these hip, beautiful, liberated women to bed and I can't get it up. I can't get it up! You hear me? She tells a few of her friends. Soon around every corner there's someone laughing at my failure. The whole world gets hysterical at my limpness because we live in hard times and people need something to laugh about. Then, as never before, everyone unites against me—men, women, blacks, whites, yellows, greens, people of all countries, all religions. Arab and Jew finally have a common cause—laughing at David Meyer's member. Everyone in the world chips in and takes out a full-page ad in the L.A. *Times*. It simply reads: DAVID MEYER CAN'T GET IT UP, and there's a black border around the page. That's the worst thing that can happen," I answered myself.[12]

Myth #5: Sex Is All That Counts Probably the most insidious sexual myth of all is the belief that sex is all that really matters when it comes to a relationship with another person. All that business about wanting to be with someone just for the sake of being near, of sharing some tender moments, maybe just a simple touch or a loving caress is just so much hokum. A man wants one thing, and you spell it S–E–X. No wonder many women think that men are out for only one thing—many men are because they think they should be. The problem for a man who sees a woman only as a sex object, a piece, some tail, or whatever other demeaning phrase is used to describe women is that he misses the opportunity of knowing another person as a human being much like himself. Believing that sex is all that counts keeps men separated from full human contact.

These sexual myths keep men from seeing sexuality as it really is. Men come to believe so many illusory notions about sex and their sexuality that many of them never really experience one of the most exquisite of human experiences. Many men were "denied little boys" who never really experienced the basic loving human contacts that make for healthy sexuality later on. Little boys who were shunned and toughened up never really learn to differentiate the sexual myths and fantasies from the reality of loving and caring human relationships. Consequently, many men end up experiencing any one of several sexual dysfunctions.

SEXUAL DYSFUNCTIONS AND OTHER HEADACHES

To hear some men tell it, the only problem they have with sex is not finding enough willing partners. The real truth, the sad and painful truth that is emerging more and more from sex therapy clinics, however, is that many men suffer from various sexual dysfunctions. In this section we will discuss several clinical sexual dysfunctions (erectile insufficiency, premature ejaculation, and retarded ejaculation) and two other sexual problems that are receiving more attention of late (the Don Juan complex and lack of sexual interest). We will conclude the section with a consideration of some of the underlying causes for these male sexual problems.

Elements of the Male Sex Role

IMPOTENCE

Few sexual problems are as devastating to a man as his inability to achieve or sustain an erection long enough for successful sexual intercourse. For many men the idea of not being able to "get it up" is a fate worse than death. The sexual dysfunction commonly known as *impotence,* or what clinicians now prefer to label as *erectile insufficiency,* can take any one of three forms: organic, functional, or psychological.

Organic impotence occurs when a defect, injury, or disease affects the genital structures, the reproductive system, or the central nervous system itself, for example, as in cases of spinal-cord injuries. *Functional impotence* is the result of a failure in the musculature, blood circulation, or nerves related to the penis. Excessive alcohol or drug intake is the major cause for this usually temporary form of impotence. The last and by far the most common form of impotence is psychological. *Psychological impotence* usually occurs when an emotional reaction such as fear, depression, or grief acts as an inhibitor to normal erectile functioning. Prolonged or even permanent impotence is generally psychological in origin and usually requires some type of sex therapy for its relief.

PREMATURE EJACULATION

Premature ejaculation occurs when a man ejaculates before his partner has a satisfactory sexual experience. A basic problem with this sexual dysfunction and one that causes many men much anxiety is determining how long is long enough in withholding ejaculation. In Kinsey's pioneering work in male sexuality, which was completed in the late 1940s, seventy-five percent of the men interviewed reported that they ejaculated within two minutes of their beginning sexual intercourse. Is withholding ejaculation for two minutes premature or not? Remember, the issue is not really one of time but rather of the partner's satisfactory sexual experience. Psychologist Bernie Zilbergeld makes this point when he recounts a client's purported problem of premature ejaculation.

> We'll never forget the man who called himself a premature ejaculator even though fairly regularly he lasted for forty-five minutes of vigorous thrusting. We know he lasted this long because his partner confirmed it. Actually, she had never been orgasmic in intercourse and had no desire to become so. She much preferred shorter intercourse because she sometimes became so sore through almost an hour of thrusting that she could barely sit down the next day. That had little influence on the thinking of our client, who was convinced that she would have orgasms if only he could last an hour.[13]

Clearly, premature ejaculation is a problem that both parties should work out together.

RETARDED EJACULATION

It is also possible that a man may have sexual intercourse with a willing partner and not be able to ejaculate until very late or even at all. This is known as *retarded ejaculation* or *ejaculatory incompetence*. We know about women who do not experience orgasm. But men? Such a problem runs contrary to all we know about, or at least think we know about, male sexuality. Because people hear so little about this condition many think that this sexual dysfunction is rare. As one group of researchers in abnormal psychology put it,

> In fact, relatively few cases of ejaculatory retardation or incompetence are seen by sex therapists, but our own clinical experience suggests that the problem is much more widespread than this observation would seem to indicate. It appears that many men are too embarrassed by the problem even to contemplate therapy for it.[14]

The next two sexual dysfunctions are opposite sides of the same coin. The first, the Don Juan complex, is not a problem of deficiency or insufficiency as are the sexual dysfunctions we have just discussed but rather a "hyperfunction" problem. The second, a problem reported by a growing number of men, is the lack of interest or desire in sexual matters.

THE DON JUAN COMPLEX

Some men believe that to have sex with a different woman every night would be anything but a problem. To be a real-life Don Juan is a fantasy for many macho males. But there is a growing awareness that a man who looks upon women as just so many sexual conquests is a man with a definite sexual problem—one called the *Don Juan complex*.

> The Don Juan . . . is a man who cannot make an emotional investment in his relationships with women. Over compensation for insecurity, an obsessive need to prove masculinity, even hidden hostility toward women—any or all can drive a man from bed to bed without ever finding any real satisfaction. The he-man mask is in absolute control here; the only way a man can throw it off is to release his internal self. This is rarely easy. Dr. Rubin [author of *Compassion and Self-Hate*] writes: "It is particularly difficult to make even initial inroads in a man who is very immature and full of macho confusions. It must be remembered that an undeveloped infantile mentality is essentially a selfish one, which desires all kinds of feeding and knows little or nothing of sharing or giving."[15]

LACK OF SEXUAL INTEREST

A recent survey conducted by *Redbook* magazine found that the most common sexual complaint for both men and women was a "lack of desire for sex."[16] This problem probably afflicts a majority of men at various times when the pressures of work, family, or some other demands squelch their normal interest in sex. Again, however, how long a time frame of "lacking interest" is sufficiently long enough for this to be a true sexual dysfunction? Probably, the best gauge is a

Elements of the Male Sex Role

personal one. When a man feels that his lack of sexual interest is troublesome either for himself or for his partner, then he is probably suffering from a sexual dysfunction.

CAUSES OF SEXUAL DYSFUNCTIONS

What can we say of the millions of men who suffer from sexual dysfunctions? Is there a common denominator, a common culprit, so to speak, lurking behind these varied sexual disturbances? Probably no more than ten percent are caused by biological, physical, and chemical impairment. It seems likely that 90 percent or more of men's sexual dysfunctions are psychological in origin. Take, for example, the case of a widowed man who reported that he was unable to sustain an erection.

> A sixty-year-old man came over a thousand miles to see us. His wife of thirty-two years had died less than a year before and, while he had had a few erections by himself since then, he did not get one on the few occasions when he had gone out with a woman. He wanted to get married again but felt it be impossible until he was capable of having erections with a partner. The man was clearly depressed and we asked who or what turned him on. He couldn't think of anyone or anything. Upon questioning, he admitted that he had not felt sexually aroused since his wife died. We tried some sexual fantasies with him and they failed to evoke any interest. The same was true of erotic literature and movies. Nothing elicited the slightest degree of sexual interest, and yet he was convinced he should be able to get an erection. Needless to say, his goal was somewhat unrealistic. Not until he finished mourning for his wife was he able to get aroused and erect again.[17]

Why does a sixty-year-old man who has lost his wife and sexual partner of over thirty years think that he *should* be able to have an erection so soon after such a personal loss? Could it be that he and countless other men like him suffer various sexual dysfunctions because they are trying to live up to some set of inane expectations of masculinity, such as, the notion that their penis is an instrument immune from the everyday problems, anxieties, and fears that besiege us all? Three common psychological conditions can lead to various sexual dysfunctions and are especially revealing of how deeply ingrained are men's erroneous views of their purported sexual capabilities. These conditions are sexual anxiety, performance anxiety, and an excessive need to please a partner.

Sexual Anxieties As we have already noted, there are few fears that can upset a man as quickly as the fear of failure in the sexual realm. A man who fails in sex is by many men's standards an impotent, powerless, and an emasculated man. Even if there is sound reason for failure, many men will be consumed immediately with fear or anxiety over their future sexual adequacy and ability. For example, here a group of researchers explains how a one-time incident of impotence may lead to long-term impotence simply because of a man's excessive anxiety over sexual functioning.

If a man fails to experience an erection—because of drinking, drugs, fatigue, lack of interest, pressure from his partner or any number of reasons—anxiety and fear are a fairly common set of responses. Potency cuts to the very center of a man's identity; to be impotent is, in some sense, for most men, to be less a man. Many men can dismiss these episodes of non-erection for what they are: simply non-erection related to various factors. But if the man is particularly anxious about his sexuality or has repeated failures in responding with an erection, he may actually become impotent; a cycle of panic and resulting impotence begins, causing more panic and more failure. Some men respond to an occasional erectile failure with calm, knowing such failures are normal, while others react with panic, unaware that such failures are normal.[18]

Performance Anxieties Performance anxieties are similar in many respects to sexual anxieties. When fear of failure over *future* sexual activities underlies sexual anxieties, not being able to meet one's own or someone else's *current* sexual expectations forms the basis of performance anxieties. For example, a husband arrives home from work to find his wife in an amorous mood. Even though he is not sexually aroused himself, he believes the male sexual myth that a man *should* be able to have sex "at the drop of a hat." Consequently, in bed he experiences an erectile failure. Here is a man who believes it unmanly to say no to sex and suffers the consequences of an uncooperative penis. The outcome for this self-imposed expectation is a temporary sexual dysfunction. However, a larger problem may loom in the background, depending on how he handles this first erective failure. If he becomes upset and anxious over this experience, it could lead to a vicious and self-perpetuating cycle of future erective failures; in other words, the preceding inhibition of sexual anxieties could prohibit future satisfactory sexual experiences. If, on the other hand, the man can accept this one-time failure as a sign that he had better communicate his own arousal state to his wife and forget the myth of the ever-ready sex machine, the occasion may have a salutary effect on the sex life of both partners.

Excessive Need to Please a Partner After sex, many women are greeted with innumerable questions about their just-completed sexual experience. "Did you have an orgasm?" "How many times did you come?" "Could you feel me inside you?" "Was it as good for you as the last time?" A man who expresses a genuine concern over his partner's sexual satisfaction is showing a mature and healthy aspect of his personality, but a man who acts like he is gathering data for a sexual survey on the modern woman is showing an immature obsession over failure. For such men, the notion of masculinity is somehow tied up with how well they accommodate a woman in bed. Sex techniques and orgasm counts become enmeshed in their definition of manhood. If, for some reason, a woman should mention that the sexual experience was not what it could have been, the eager beaver will feel like a failure. He may become depressed, fearful, and anxious over his performance, which could set him up for a future sexual dysfunction such as erectile failure. Women often sense this feature in a man's questions and begin to play the game of "let's not bruise his fragile ego." These women begin to say what they think the man wants to hear, and the relationship suffers from an infusion of dishonesty and gamesmanship.

Elements of the Male Sex Role

Other psychological factors can also adversely affect a man's sexuality. A man's self-concept may be so poor and lacking in self-respect or esteem that he will not even try to engage in sexual relationships. Another negative factor that affects some men is discord or trouble in the relationship itself. For example, many married couples abstain from all sexuality because of a seething hostility or antipathy for each other.

The important point to keep in mind is that a man's expectations, attitudes, and emotions all directly relate to how well he functions as a sexual person. The idea that successful and satisfying sex is ninety percent mental and only ten percent physical is a truth many men never seem to grasp.

Up to this point, we have dealt with the developing aspects of male sexuality and some of the problems that can afflict men. Next we will discuss sexual abstinence, or celibacy, as it relates to a growing number of males.

ARE THERE ANY CELIBATES IN THE HOUSE?

The subject of *celibacy,* the conscious refraining from sexual activity for a specific time period, may seem out of place in this discussion of the sexual element of the male sex role. However, a brief discussion of celibacy, or sexual abstinence, seems pertinent because a few men have found sexual abstinence a part of their male experience. We are not talking here of the historic vow of celibacy required of Roman Catholic priests and nuns and other religious groups. We are talking about those men who have chosen sexual abstinence as a means of personal reflection or a temporary sexual halt for any number of reasons, such as an all-encompassing work project. But before we examine this modern version of celibacy, let us look back some two thousand years to its historical roots.

Our present-day views on sexuality, as we have noted in other chapters, owe much of their heritage to early Judeo–Christian traditions. Celibacy owes it legacy to one man, the Christian apostle Paul. Paul preached that a life of total sexual abstinence was a loftier and more spiritually accurate portrayal of the life to come. Even so, Paul conceded that for those Christians "too weak" to live a celibate life, marriage was the only alternative (it was "better to marry than to burn"). However, all sexual expression outside of marriage was strictly forbidden because it did not have a procreative end but rather a pleasure-seeking purpose. Paul's disparaging views on all sexuality became the cornerstone of the Christian ethos that developed over the ensuing two thousand years.

For approximately the first thousand years after Paul's pronouncements against sex, the Christian sexual prohibitions were applied equally to male and female Christians. Both sexes were expected to abstain from all sex unless they were married and then only to have sexual intercourse for the purposes of conceiving another soul for heaven. During the medieval period, however, the birth of the chivalric code brought about a transformation in sex roles. Women were viewed as pure, unblemished, earthly representatives of the Virgin Mary and placed on a pedestal. Men, on the other hand, were seen as more influenced by their nature to baser wants and needs, especially those of sexual gratification. Over the next several centuries, the double standard came to be an expected part of human sexual relationships. Women were expected to surrender to only one man, while men were expected to conquer as many women as possible. Women lost status after they lost their virginity, while men gained respect in the eyes of their male cohorts for their sexual achievements. As time passed, male celibacy or long-term sexual abstinence became associated with various harmful physical ailments, leading one nineteenth-century medical writer to note,

> Protracted celibacy is a violation of physical laws. Where the secretion of the semen is not discharged through the natural passages, it must be absorbed into the body in a decomposed state, to clog up the system, impart impurities in the blood, and derange the action of the lungs and the heart.[19]

Consequently, the double standard's exhortation that men are to have sex frequently and with many women (while women are expected to keep themselves for only one man) became an integral part of the male sex role. However, the double standard has shown signs of weakening in this century. The emphasis on the pleasurable aspects of sex and safer and more reliable forms of birth control have allowed women a greater measure of sexual freedom, yet many men seem to hold ambivalent views about sexuality, especially about premarital sex. On the one hand, a large majority of adult men think premarital sex is a violation of the moral code.[20] On the other hand, the masculine ideal calls for men to be sexually knowledgeable before marriage. In a study of college males conducted by sociologist Mirra Komarovsky, males who were virgins reported more "personal problems" and "hang-ups" than males who were not virgins. Komarovsky described the conflict for male virgins in this way:

> A [college] senior, who is still a virgin in the liberal subculture of our campus, has failed to live up to his own and his peers' ideal of masculinity. This relative failure to attain the norms of a given age-sex role may damage his self-esteem or lower his status among his peers. But, as conveyed by the phrase, "poverty is not a crime," this is not the kind of deviance that provokes moral outrage.[21]

Virginity and sexual abstinence are not the norms in most male circles. Young men and older ones, too, as we have stated, are expected to be sexually active if they are to be considered real men. Fortunately for the virginal or abstinent male, these conditions do not show. A virginal college student can boast to his roommate about his sexual activities and the roommate may never be the wiser. More than a few males have done so!

Talk of virginity and sexual abstinence runs counter to the much touted sexual freedom of the last several decades. Many believe that we are in the midst of a sexual revolution. People—males and females, young and old—are more and more expected to put aside their sexual hang-ups and traditional moral precepts and encounter one another in the leveling arena of the bedroom. But with all of the talk of sexual involvements, why are some men and women opting for a period of sexual abstinence? What can come from such a period except maybe frustration and loneliness? Perhaps because sex is so open, so expected, so available in most social circles, some people are turning to abstinence as a way to reflect on what is going on within themselves. For some people, sexual abstinence may be the secular equivalent of a religious retreat where men or women can get to know themselves better and sort out some of their own priorities. One normal and healthy man who spent eight months in a celibate state described the experience in this way:

> It was generally a good time for me. I spent lots of time by myself, part of which was devoted to thinking about past relationships. I also spent time with friends, enjoying their company and sharing many of my feelings with them.
> The people who knew I wasn't having sex acted a bit strangely, continuously asking how I could do it. It was as if they thought I were performing some miraculous feat. Men were much more surprised than women. Actually, it wasn't very difficult. At times I was lonely, but it wasn't as difficult as I had anticipated. Sometimes I was aware of missing something, but it usually wasn't sex. What I missed most was sleeping next to someone and the cuddling and playing around in bed. I got lots of hugs from my friends, but nothing could replace the warm sense of snuggling with a lover in bed. And that was really the worst of it.
> Often I felt intense relief when alone. I didn't have to concern myself with anyone else's needs or feelings. Many times it felt very good to know that I didn't have to share my bed with someone. It was my bed and I could take it all up and do anything I wanted to there.
> To say I learned a lot is a cliché but nonetheless true. I learned about myself and relationships and, surprisingly, about myself and sex. I realized for the first time how often I had not gotten what I wanted in sex because I had been so busy trying to be nice and considerate. And I saw how the resentment I had accumulated during such occasions spilled over into other parts of my relationships. Another important thing I learned was that my need for solitude was much greater than I had ever imagined. I enjoyed my own company and needed some quiet time each day to be with me. This turned out to be quite useful in later relationships: I could get more of my alone time when I wanted it, thus making it easier for me to really be with my partner when I was with her.[22]

Whether celibacy will catch on is anyone's guess. Some argue that celibacy, or as the chic are calling it, *asexuality,* is found mainly among career-oriented males and females.[23] One social scientist sees celibacy as a viable alternative for more and more people who want more out of their relationships than casual sex.[24] It is possible that in the future more men will opt for celibate relationships before they make a long-term commitment. It sounds strangely familiar, like a repackaging of the old moral precept that sex must be reserved for people who are willing and able to accept more than a passing responsibility for their relationships.

SOME CLOSING COMMENTS

Far too many American men think of their sexuality almost solely in terms of a variety of physical activities "below the waist." In fact, a man's sexuality may be better understood in terms of specific mental activities "above the waist." Rather than his penis, a man's mind is his most erotic organ.[25]

To a large degree many of the sexual problems that men face nowadays and their consequent concerns over their masculinity vis-á-vis sexuality can be better understood in relation to what a man thinks about, not what he does with his genitals. Many men undermine potentially satisfying and enjoyable sexual encounters because they allow negative thoughts to intrude into their consciousness: "What if I can't please my partner?" "What if I can't get an erection, or if I can and I come too quickly or not at all?" "What if my partner doesn't really care for me or is comparing me to someone else?" Such thoughts have caused more than a few men to develop self-doubts about their masculinity.

Males and females are by nature sexual creatures. It should go without saying that sex can be one of the most pleasurable aspects of their makeup. However, far too many males, because of the sexual element of the male sex role, place unrealistic sexual demands on themselves, only to hamper the full range of their sexual potentialities. Most males would do better, sexually speaking, if they would stop trying to prove themselves more masculine through sex and learn to relax, that is to turn off their negative and self-denigrating thoughts and expectations and learn to accept and enjoy their sexuality.

SUGGESTED READINGS

Friday, N. *Men in Love*. New York: Dell, 1981.
Julty, S. *MSP: Male Sexual Performance*. New York: Dell, 1975.
Zilbergeld, B. *Male Sexuality*. Boston: Little, Brown, 1978.

11

Of little toughies and stalwart frontiersmen:
THE SELF-RELIANT ELEMENT

If you can keep your head when all about you
Are losing theirs and blaming it on you,
If you can trust yourself when all men doubt you,
But make allowance for their doubting too;
If you can wait and not be tired by waiting,
Or being lied about, don't deal in lies,
Or being hated, don't give way to hating,
And yet don't look too good, nor talk too wise:

If you can dream — and not make dreams your master;
If you can think — and not make thoughts your aim;
If you can meet with Triumph and Disaster
And treat those two impostors just the same;
If you can bear to hear the truth you've spoken
Twisted by knaves to make a trap for fools,
Or watch the things you gave your life to, broken,
And stoop and build 'em up with the worn-out tools:

If you can make one heap of all your winnings
And risk it on one turn of pitch-and-toss,
And lose, and start again at your beginnings
And never breathe a word about your loss;
If you can force your heart and nerve and sinew
To serve your turn long after they are gone,
And so hold on when there is nothing in you
Except the Will which says to them: "Hold on!"

If you can talk with crowds and keep your virtue,
Or walk with Kings — nor lose the common touch,
If neither foes nor loving friends can hurt you,
If all men count with you, but none too much;
If you can fill the unforgiving minute
With sixty seconds worth of distance run,
Yours is the Earth and everything that's in it,
And — which is more — you'll be a Man, my son!
Rudyard Kipling[1]

We now come to the last element in our overview of the male sex role, self-reliance. Self-reliance implies a certain air or bearing that a man must learn to radiate in all of his activities. Self-reliance is supposedly revealed in how a man walks, talks, and dresses and in the countless ways that he deals with others. Because this element lacks tangible and specific guidelines—unlike the other male sex role elements—it is difficult for a male to master. A young man who is told to act self-reliant on his first job interview wonders just what he should specifically do to accomplish this feat: "How should I act?" "What should I say?" "What should I wear?" In other words, how can he show the interviewer that he is cool, confident, tough-minded, and unflappable? These and many other traits make up the self-reliant element that males are expected to learn and to exhibit.

In this chapter we will first examine several of the characteristics considered to be essential features or building blocks of self-reliance. We will then move into the world of make-believe, into the celluloid fantasy created in motion pictures to focus on archetypal male heroes who epitomize the tough, self-reliant element. Finally, we will examine some of the activities and antics of athletes, soldiers, and politicians, members of three professions that foster the image of self-reliance more strongly than most other professions do.

THE PRECARIOUS POSTURE

Many people may be dismayed to learn that a vast number of men harbor a large number of fears, the kinds of fears that cause men's palms to sweat and stomaches to churn. Even though the male mystique downplays this purportedly unmanly emotion, the fact remains that men do fear. The most nagging fears that prick men's minds are generally related to the expectations that make up the male sex role. Many men, for example, fear that in some slight way or in some unconscious action they may reveal themselves as feminine and thus unmanly. As one man relates, even the way a man stands with arms akimbo can be a cause for fear of being seen as feminine by others.

> I was out by the mailboxes talking with my nextdoor neighbor, a football coach, whom I respected enormously. We were standing there talking. I had my hands on my hips. He said jokingly that I was standing a woman's way, with my thumbs forward. I was 27 years old and I had never really thought about the best way to stand with my arms akimbo. But now, whenever I find myself standing with thumbs forward I feel an effeminate flash, even when I'm alone, and I quickly turn my hands around the other way.[2]

Besides their ever-present fear of lurking femininity, many men secretly fear that after all of the years they spend in the competitive struggle at work, they will receive only a pat on the back and an inflation-eroded pension as the final signs of their success. Some men spend countless hours and expend considerable energy worrying about the possible meanings of other people's behaviors. A man stews that his boss did not speak when they passed in the hallway, the head office is sending one of those collegebred know-it-all, knife-you-in-the-back management trainees to his office, or his secretary smirked at him after a gossip session at the water fountain. He constantly fears the worst, no matter how slight the signal.

Still other men fear the improbable occasion on which they will be found out to be dyed-in-the-wool, leg-shaking, knee-knocking cowards. These men fear that some day they will find themselves in a crowded place where they unintentionally nudge some terrifying hulk who immediately asks for redress. Sensing a life-threatening experience, they envision themselves bolting for the nearest exit, leaving a room full of laughing and jeering onlookers. On the other hand, some men mask their fear of violence by imagining themselves meeting the same challenge by delivering a devastating blow that sends the hulk sniveling to his corner. No matter what the scenario, most men fear any occasion on which they might be called upon to fight.

And what of those men who fear that some day they will be found not to be as sexy as they pretend to be? In the minds of many men, the fear gnaws that some day after a particularly satisfying love-making experience a voice will whisper from the other pillow, "Is that the best you can do?" A woman can sense this fear in her partner when he questions how good he was in comparison to her former lovers. No man wants to think that his sexual performance pales in comparison to others. But a majority of men fear it all the same.

Men fear many other things ranging from aging, baldness, and excess weight to a loss of virility. Men not only fear, they are scared that others may discover their fear. Thus men learn to hide their fears behind a precarious posture, an air of cool confidence, a stance of toughness and self-reliance. The lessons in self-reliance begin early and last for most of a man's life.

Little boys are told from their early years onward that they are not suppose to fear, not suppose to be scared of things that they have little or no control over. As the years go by and the boys become men, the not-supposed-to-fear message is incessantly played over and over until a strange transformation takes place. The message that "men are not supposed to fear" becomes embedded in men's minds as "men do not fear." Thus most men come to believe that other men actually do not have fears. For those men who do have fears—the vast majority of men—a cover is necessary; an image of self-reliance becomes a kind of ruse to hide behind.

The air of self-reliance and toughness is not something that a boy learns quickly or easily. For the most part, the lessons begin in the home, where the boy learns the posture of self-reliance from his father or possibly other male figures. The first lessons deal with simple behaviors, the how-to's of acting like a man. By and large, these early lessons concentrate on what behaviors are expected of males. Behaviors as simple as how to sit or how to wear a towel in a locker room are part of the prescribed style of manly behavior. One man recounts such an early lesson:

> When I was a kid I was sitting on the sofa reading and my legs were crossed, right knee draped over left. My father said, "You're sitting like a girl!" and demonstrated

Elements of the Male Sex Role

"No thank you, Stacy. Not while I'm on duty."

the right way: He placed his left ankle on his right knee so that his thighs were separated at the immodest masculine angle. For a couple of years after that I thought men were supposed to cross legs left over right, while women crossed them right over left. Or was it the other way? I could never remember which. So rather than make a mistake and do it like a girl, I preferred not to cross my legs at all.[3]

Still another man recalls an incident at the local YMCA:

When I was eight I came out of a YMCA shower with my towel wrapped around my chest. The other boys laughed at me and said, "Hey, he's wearing his towel like a girl!" I had three older sisters at home and that's the way they wore bath towels. How the hell was I supposed to know? I thought everyone wore them that way. I didn't go back to the Y for weeks. But when I returned I wore the towel around my waist.[4]

Obviously, the air of self-reliance and toughness expected of men is more than just how a man sits or how he wears his towel in a locker room. The self-reliant element is more a matter of overall style than merely what a man does. A businessman attempts to create an aura of supreme confidence when he negotiates a contract that could spell life or death for his company. When eerie night sounds invade the campsite, a man musters up a stance of courage for others to take comfort in. A young boy rejects another's offer while he stands his post. Everything that a man does he does to show others he is quietly confident of his abilities. These and countless other situations demand that a male exhibit what psychologist Robert Brannon refers to as "the cultivation of a stoic, imperturbable persona, just this side of catatonia."[5]

Few men if any can bring together all of the features of self-reliance in a single situation. Because of the vastness and scope of this element, we need to turn to the world of make-believe, where life is often portrayed by men who are larger than life. Let us go to the movies where self-reliant and tough men abound and where the average man can sit in darkness and play out the self-reliant element in his mind if not in his life.

MALE HEROES

Before television narcotized the American public, countless millions of young males learned in neighborhood theaters what self-reliance and toughness were all about. For twenty-five or thirty-five cents, boys sat in darkened movie theaters every Saturday afternoon and watched as Randolph Scott acted out the arche-typal Western good guy or as Errol Flynn portrayed a swashbuckling hero in his majesty's naval fleet. Today the large silver screen has been replaced for the most part by the nineteen-inch television screen. Not only have the screens shrunk but so have the male characters. We need to look back for a moment at some of the grand male heroes with whom generations of boys grew up, heroes who pointed the way toward the masculine style of self-reliance and toughness.

Male movie heroes come in all shapes and sizes. Some are unshaven and crude and others are debonair and svelte. Even so, most of them are fiercely indepen-dent, coolly confident, tough, and self-reliant.

Of course, not every male star portrays these highly prized masculine attri-butes. Professor Joan Mellen of Temple University categorizes three types of male heroes. However, the type that is of particular interest to our discussion is the one that she labels the "big bad wolves." These male heroes all portray a certain style of masculinity that the men in the audience know is the mark of a "real man." According to Mellen,

> The indomitable male has populated our films since the last shot of *The Great Train Robbery*, made in 1903, when a sinister-looking gentleman with a fierce handlebar moustache pointed his gun and fired at the audience. To this tradition belong the male stars who are meant to fulfill our purported need for heroes: men who protect the weak, serve justice, defeat evil, and relieve us, men and women alike, of any need to take responsibility for doing those defiant things in our own lives. The Big Bad Wolves include all those "strong," dominant screen males such as William S. Hart, Tom Mix, Douglas Fairbanks, Sr., Gary Cooper, Errol Flynn, Henry Fonda, Alan Ladd, Marlon Brando, Kirk Douglas, Rock Hudson, Paul Newman, Charles Bronson, Steve McQueen, and Clint Eastwood. But they do not include those heroes of comedy who share with us our human vulnerability: Charlie Chaplin, Stan Lau-rel and Oliver Hardy, Buster Keaton, and even the Marx Brothers, powerless de-spite the havoc they wreak. Those heroes of the musical who dance and sing away our pain without overcoming it, led by Fred Astaire and Gene Kelly, are equally not among the Big Bad Wolves, for they fall outside the stereotype of the self-con-trolled, invulnerable, stoical hero who justifies the image of unfeeling masculinity as a means of winning in a world that pounces on any sign of weakness. The co-medians treat as absurd and the musical stars as unreal the harsh world in which male heroes pontificate platitudes such as that invoked by an elderly John Wayne in *The Shootist:* "I won't be wronged, I won't be insulted, I won't be laid a hand on. I don't do these things to others, and I require the same of them."[6]

As we see in Mellen's list of "big bad wolves," Hollywood has created a veritable pack of male heroes who epitomize a particular masculine style. Take any one of the wolves and their movies and what do we usually find in their performance: a quiet strength, courage, independence, cool confidence, toughness, and self-reliance. More often than not, we find the heroes pitted against an enemy or fighting for a cause in which the odds are decidedly against them. For example, in the classic Western *High Noon,* a quiet and stoical marshal played by Gary Cooper is called upon to save his town from the ravages of three desperate gunslingers. The townspeople abandon the marshal and behave in cravenly and cowardly ways. (No heroes among that lot!) Mellen refers to *High Noon* as a classic paean to male strength and notes that even the movie's theme song reverberates the message of male courage and strength: "If I'm a man, I must be brave . . . else lie a coward in my grave."[7]

Few movie heroes, however, have captured the element of toughness and self-reliance as did Humphrey Bogart. Bogart was not particularly handsome or dashing like Clark Gable or Errol Flynn, but he conveyed a masculine style in a way few others could match. Mellen notes this quality in Bogart's film *Casablanca:*

> The hero who discovered his masculinity in the commitment to defeat fascism was most brilliantly and consistently played by Humphrey Bogart. And in no Bogart character are manliness and political commitment conjoined with more verve and flair than in his Rick of *Casablanca* (1942). . . .
> What grants this crude exercise in political propaganda its appeal is its association with Bogart's supreme style, *savoir-faire,* and romantic sophistication. His every gesture is cool and knowing, bespeaking an immense knowledge of the ways of the world. If Gable exuded a sense of unquenchable energy, Bogart expects the worst at any instant and lives for the moment. He is beyond being shocked: "I don't mind a parasite," he says in *Casablanca;* "I object to a cut-rate one." He is, paradoxically, a more powerful male than any of his predecessors because he is so cynical about his own or anybody else's capacity to create a world free of corruption and evil-doing. Tough and shrewd, he knows that life at any moment may trap him; if, despite this, we feel safe with him, it is because no event, however outrageous, seems to come as a surprise.[8]

Men in their late thirties and forties grew up with flickering images of Bogart, Flynn, and the other big bad wolves to show them the way in which a "real man" is supposed to act. During the late 1960s and 1970s, a new generation of male stars such as James Coburn, Robert Redford, Burt Reynolds, Jack Nicholson, and Charles Bronson had taken over the role of the male hero. Even though the names had changed, the message was still the same: Be cool, confident, independent, tough, and self-reliant. However, one male superstar whom we could hardly call a big bad wolf is the bespectacled Woody Allen. Allen's characters portray the deep-seated anguish most men feel in the faltering attempts to be something they are not. Allen, the iconoclast on as well as off the screen, depicts the anxiety, pain, and frustration felt by millions of American men who do not quite meet the high standards set by Hollywood's big bad wolves. Allen's movies have become a kind of cinematic happening in which the average guy's strivings and failures at being a "real man" are shown in comic pathos. Even though most of Allen's characters fall short of the ideal, the dream is still the same: Be a big bad wolf. As Mellen points out,

> Woody Allen's comedies about the puny neurotic male in glasses attempting to be a man in a culture glorifying John Wayne and Humphrey Bogart have honest moments despite Allen's failure to transcend the values of Wayne. He is the small man who, protestations and irony aside, aspires to be six feet tall and strong.[9]

Probably no other Woody Allen film shows the negative impact of the average man's attempt at reaching for an unrealistic self-reliant and tough image as well as *Play It Again, Sam*. Again, Mellen notes that

> What is marvelous about *Play It Again, Sam* is its open acknowledgement that most men are secretly tortured by not being Bogart. If the film does not quite admit the harms engendered, it still shows how devastating the image has been. Men have been drilled in this culture to believe that one must be as self-assured as the hero of *Casablanca*. "Who am I kidding," mourns film buff Alan (Woody Allen) after yet one more screening of *Casablanca*, a film to which he is addicted. "I'm not like that and I never will be." Depressed, divorced, and a movie critic, hence even more a victim of Hollywood's values than most men, after watching the Bogart film once again he is overwhelmed by a sense of his own worthlessness. For the first time in American movies, Hollywood admits on screen to the psychological damage and suffering it has caused the American male in imposing so unreal a definition of masculinity.[10]

Even though Woody Allen's character captures the self-doubts and pains experienced by the average guy, his films implicitly endorse the strong and self-reliant male image. The message comes through, albeit somewhat less forcefully than the average Hollywood version: Don't imitate others but rather be yourself—still strong and self-reliant, however—and you will be rewarded with beautiful and sexy heroines. Allen wants others to accept him—something less than the Bogart figure—but his women must still be cut out of the mold of one part Ingrid Bergman and two parts Lauren Bacall. The double standard of sexual acceptability lives on even in the films that parody the male ideal of the big bad wolf.

Are there any realistic film portrayals of how men really are, of how they really feel about the Superman expectations? For the most part, the answer is no. Hollywood has a vested interest in stereotypes, and it has capitalized on men's dreams and wishes to live, at least for a few hours, in a world that is somewhat larger than life and certainly more exciting than their own. However, every now and then a film comes along that pictures men in a different light, in a way that includes not only the clichés but also the anguish and pain perpetuated by the stereotypes. Again, Mellen comments on just such a film:

> One small study, however, is worthy of mention because it so directly attacks the issue of male identity and the masculine role in our society. *Men's Lives* (1975), by Josh Hanig and Will Roberts, is a documentary film which explores masculinity in America by tracing the male growing-up process from boy scout camp to factory.

"I'm not going to work ten to twelve hours and come home and scrub floors," asserts a male factory worker, arguing that women should remain at home. But the consciousness of the young filmmakers themselves offers the hope of change. . . .

Any film honest about challenging the traditional male role must propose alternative images of masculinity. In *Men's Lives* we visit a ballet class in which a boy and a girl practice the same steps. They are equally graceful. The boy, about sixteen, admits that his friends call him a "sissy," and that even his parents are embarassed by his dancing. The boy insists that a man is someone who stands up for what he thinks is right, regardless of what other people think. He has been accused of homosexuality because he is not physically large and does not play football, the continuing group standard for manhood in this culture.

The old stereotypes are with us in full force. A high school football player exclaims,"I like to kill. I like to kill opponents," echoing a conditioning order in army basic training. . . . One boy discloses that his car makes him feel nice and girls "think it gives you strength to handle a car like that." Sexual repression produces such projection and surrogate sexual gratification. A male teacher pompously asserts that those boys who are not enraged when they lose will be failures in life: and we perceive the origin of the football player's pleasure in physical combat. A boy confides that there are two kinds of girls, one's steady girlfriend and the quick pickup, as if he had formed his conceptions straight out of films like *My Darling Clementine,* which enshrines with rigid insistence the double standard and the dichotomy between "good," or passively dependent, and "bad," or autonomous and sexually free, women.

Men's Lives, in its mélange of *cinéma vérité* interviews with boys and men, recapitulates the history of the American film. Each dreadful cliché, from "without competition, there's nothing" to "a man needs to be in control," has been celebrated as a truth in decades of the popular arts from film and pulp novel to comic strip and television. All the while, filmmakers Hanig and Roberts discover that most men in our society see themselves as inadequate, not as supermen but as failures because supermen are the standard. The image of the invulnerable male perpetuates itself. It provides men with an outlet in fantasy through which they can feel briefly masculine, but as with a heroin high, when the narcotic of vicarious living and its exhilaration recede, the reality is all the more demoralizing. Thus even the masculine mystique perpetuates the sense of men's own unworthiness by its impossibility, requiring ever more intense fantasies of indomitable strength. Real-life men in this film lament they can never allow other men to know them well for fear of appearing vulnerable. . . .

Men's Lives suggests that so long as aggressiveness and competitiveness rule the economic life of our society, men will have to cultivate these tendencies in order to survive in it.[11]

Films such as *Men's Lives* are not money-making, box-office attractions, but male heroes such as Charles Bronson and Clint Eastwood are. Many males pressured by the cultural stereotype of the strong, silent, and self-reliant male image will continue to flock to films glorifying violence, sexual conquest, and the indomitable self-reliant masculine image even though the stereotype has been cracked and some men are turning against the fantasized image of the "real man."

Hollywood's version of the supermale is only one force that influences the strong and self-reliant element. Other cultural roles support this image and in some ways have a more insidious effect on young men's perceptions of what is expected of them. Let us turn our attention now to three very different aspects of American life.

THE ATHLETE, THE SOLDIER, AND THE POLITICIAN

Today males have few opportunities to exhibit the full complement of attributes that go to make up the tough and self-reliant element. No longer can a man step out onto a sun-drenched, dusty street, as did Gary Cooper in *High Noon,* and display a manly sense of fierce determination and quiet courage in the face of potentially lethal odds. Neither can most men jet to some exotic spot and coolly liquidate some archetypal fiend all the while satisfying the sexual needs of a bevy of international beauties, as does Roger Moore in the James Bond movies. Such exploits exist only in the minds of movie producers and the millions of males who can only fantasize such masculine roles. In fact, today there are few arenas in which a man can test his tough and self-reliant mettle in ways that will shore up his sense of masculinity. If contemporary males are finding it more and more difficult to prove themselves real men solely in terms of their physical strength as some social scientists claim,[12] then where can men find the opportunity to exhibit and, probably more importantly, to practice being tough and self-reliant? We suggest that the roles of the athlete, the soldier, and the politician still afford men opportunities to test their self-reliance.

JERSEYS AND SHOULDER PADS MAKE THE MAN

"Sport in American society," write social scientists Peter Stein and Steven Hoffman, "is a prominent masculine rite. Every boy has to wrestle with the all-pervasiveness of athletics. The development of athletic ability is an essential element in becoming a 'man'; sports is the training ground for 'the traditional male role.' "[13]

Almost every adult male can remember the times out on the school playground when a group of boys huddled together to choose sides for a game of softball or football. Usually the two most athletically gifted boys acted as rival team captains who set about the serious task of choosing from the group of anxious players the members for the two opposing teams. As each captain picked his team, the waiting boys grew more solemn. The initial hollering and gleeful merriment quickly gave way to a type of deathwatch. Each boy silently prayed, "Please, God, let me be picked next." Finally, the last two or three unselected boys stood mute across from the two almost complete teams. The captains would begin haggling over who would take scrawny Joey or dumpy Peter. After what seemed an interminable wait, Joey and Peter were selected begrudgingly by each captain. The first-round choices made it because of their proven athletic skills. Joey and Peter were picked simply because they were there. Little will ever exceed the pain and anguish of being a Joey or a Peter. To be seen by one's peers as a bumbler, an athletic klutz is an experience as unsettling and depressing as anything that can befall a young boy. Surprisingly, the boy who didn't know the answer to one of the teacher's questions or who got a failing grade on a written assignment actually gained status in the young males' pecking order. But the boy who couldn't catch an infield fly or run for a gain on a football field was a nobody. Yes, sports and athletic prowess permeate all young boys' lives in some way.

Elements of the Male Sex Role

Competitive sports such as baseball, basketball, and football are considered by many Americans as activities that build character and give a young man a leg up on his climb toward manhood. Competitive sports emphasize the winning ethic as well as physical strength, endurance, toughness, independence, emotional insensitivity, and self-reliance. Everything a young man needs to learn about the real world can be learned in athletic competition, or so say most coaches and sports boosters. Certainly, one advantage of athletic involvement is recognition and approval by one's peers, as James Coleman notes in his analysis of high school athletics.[14] But we can still ask, are there trade-offs for this "manly" training, negative consequences that the athletic male accrues that may possibly be harmful to an adult man? This is the question that Peter Stein and Steven Hoffman asked a small group of athletic and nonathletic college males.

The primary focus of Stein and Hoffman's research was what is commonly referred to as *role strain* as it affects the male athlete in high school and in college. Stein and Hoffman borrowed heavily in their analysis of role strain from the research of sociologist Mirra Komarovsky, who defined role strain as the "felt and latent difficulty in role performance and perceived paucity of rewards for role conformity."[15] In other words, some males may experience personal anxiety and anguish because they do not measure up or have the necessary personality characteristics required to perform certain roles. For example, scrawny Joey and dumpy Peter may have experienced role strain because they did not have what it takes to "make it" as athletes in their peer group. Furthermore, both Joey and Peter may have felt less masculine because of their being seen by the other boys as not having the necessary attributes to perform the role of athlete. In their interviews with athletes, Stein and Hoffman found considerable evidence for role strain, if not at the high school level then most assuredly at the college level of athletic involvement. Here are the highlights of some of their more interesting findings.

First of all, several athletes mentioned the lack of rewards, the lack of recognition by others for their contribution to the team's achievements. Competitive sports such as baseball and football tend to reward the few superstars, the flashy players whom the media and the fans largely fawn over. But what of the average team player? What are his rewards for the hours of practice and his determination to give athletics his all? As Stein and Hoffman write,

> Our interviews suggest the importance of distinguishing between internal and external rewards. The available rewards operate in the dominant context of a star system which is based on high rewards for a few at the expense of the many. Superstars receive publicity, prestige, and glamour for performance, while teammates oftentimes feel devalued in their own performance. In . . . three sports, the average players reported that even though they performed well they felt overshadowed by the team's superstar. They sometimes felt contempt and envy toward the better-recognized players. The players reported feeling good about their performance when values predominating the team were such that every member gained recognition for his contribution.[16]

Most dedicated high school athletes spend three to four hours a day in some form of practice. From August until late November, there is football practice; from December to March, there is basketball; and from March to May, there is baseball. Even so, the rewards and recognition from peers seem sufficient compensation for such arduous endeavors. Consequently, over the years, the young athlete absorbs certain role values such as unemotionality and toughness. However, once the athlete moves on to college, these values can cause role conflict in interpersonal relationships, for example, between male athletes and others, especially girlfriends. Again, Stein and Hoffman note this potentially negative consequence of the athletic role:

> With a shift to college, more of the athletes experienced conflict due to their dates' expectations of different personality traits. Women they dated expressed a preference for greater openness, a sharing of feelings, more verbal communication, more sensitivity to feelings, moods, and nonverbal gestures.
> The focus was on relating to each other and the men felt forced to reevaluate the characteristics stressed in their athletic role. They began to experience strain and conflict between these competing expectations. This role strain involved both interpersonal conflict with dates and some intrapsychic tension involving the surfacing of feelings about themselves and their athletic roles and heterosexual dating roles.[17]

One other interesting feature of the role strain phenomenon that occurs among many college athletes is what Stein and Hoffman term the "overload of role obligations." As we just suggested, most high school athletes give themselves almost entirely to sports. However, in college a large number of other activities push in on the athlete's time. There are academic pressures if the athlete wishes to remain in college or to go on for advanced training in a professional or graduate school. Social obligations increase as the athlete probably begins to devote more spare time to one particular intimate relationship. These and other competing activities draw from the time, energy, and dedication the athlete once devoted to sports. Some of the athletes in Stein and Hoffman's study wished that they had been less dedicated to sports earlier because of the relatively few payoffs that sports has for the male athlete who does not wish to make sports a life-long career.

Of course, athletes are not the only ones to experience role strain. The nonathletic sample in Stein and Hoffman's study also noted how sports and its values and expectations either directly or indirectly affected them:

> The role of nonathlete is rife with role strain. The child who is weaker and not well coordinated is chosen less and less often and begins to accept the definition of nonathlete. This development occurs through the early and middle grade-school years when his personality is being shaped. He experiences more and more role strain as his emerging personality does not fit the role of boy–athlete, terms which are closely linked in that age group. The men who did not play ball as children reported that the process of self-definition as a nonathlete was gradual but definite. There was an initial casting of roles (athletes and nonathletes) which became more rigidly defined with each sports contest. Less skillful boys became labelled as nonathletes by the other children.[18]

Elements of the Male Sex Role

Thus we see that sports, especially competitive team sports, extract a considerable toll on all boys, the athletes and nonathletes alike. Yet most Americans see sports as a valued means whereby the young male gains in those virtues that will better prepare him for the competitive and tough adult world. As Stein and Hoffman's analysis points out, a majority of boys suffer at the very least some personal discomfort and at the most considerable anguish when the role expectations imposed by the sports ethic clash with those behaviors and values considered necessary for fitting in and getting along in the adult world. It is no longer enough for a young man to learn only how to block pain or how to shut off all emotion in order for him to live an interpersonally and intrapersonally satisfying life.

In order to avoid leaving the impression that all sports are somehow bad or evil, let us close this section with the conclusion that Stein and Hoffman drew after their insightful analysis.

> We do not mean to imply that positive experiences do not take place in sports. In fact athletes do learn, in varying degrees, to cooperate, compromise, and compete with peers. They learn strategic thinking, physical dexterity, and coordination. They learn competency and mastery of a skill. These functions can be very helpful to a person in leading a more productive adult life.
>
> Our research leads us to ask the question of how sports can be organized so as to allow all participants to benefit from its crucial developmental functions, while minimizing the role strain for both athletes and nonathletes. We can speculate that the optimum condition for successful modern male-role performance is related to some group of athletic experiences of a less competitive and more cooperative nature. The introduction of these values into male–male relationships through sports may result in their eventual introduction in other areas of social interaction. Cooperation, sharing, and compromising without suffering loss of self-esteem are hopeful aspects of change in the athletic role and in the male role.[19]

YOU'RE IN THE ARMY NOW

Most adult men who grew up in the late 1940s and 1950s can probably remember the childhood times when they and their buddies played war. The backyard, rag-tag army gained a degree of credibility with the paraphernalia that the boys accumulated from various sources. One boy had a regulation army canteen and cartridge belt purchased from the local army–navy surplus store, while another sported a real steel army helmet pirated from his dad's old trunk in the attic, and a third had an imitation, but genuine-looking M–1 rifle purchased at Woolworth's. The boys spent hours crawling belly-fashion through bushes and locked in mortal combat with tenacious German or Japanese armies. On Saturday afternoons, boys could sit and learn new battle strategies from Hollywood's version of war games. The screens blazed into action as combat-toughened heroes such as John Wayne, Audie Murphy, and a cast of lesser known actor–soldiers defeated America's enemies. But boys grow up, and for millions of young men the backyard war games and cinematic portrayal of the glory of war finally end when the young men become real soldiers.

In America the military is second only to athletics in being portrayed as a social institution that makes real men out of boys. Recruiting posters are a good example of the military's claim of such masculinizing effects—for instance, "Join the Marines and become a man." As with sports, the military stresses the physical side of a young man's development as the primary validation of his masculinity.[20] At the heart of the military's view of masculinity is the role of the combat soldier. Not surprisingly, much of what is expected of the soldier, especially the combat soldier, is taken directly from what is expected of all "real" men, either civilian or military. Commenting on this core of masculine values and manly expectations, Samuel Stouffer and his associates write,

> The codes according to which a combat unit judged the behavior of its members, and in terms of which conformity was enforced, differed in their generality. Perhaps the most general was one drawn largely from civilian culture but given its special interpretation in the combat situation: Be a man. Conceptions of masculinity vary among different groups, but there is a core which is common to most: courage, endurance, and toughness, lack of squeamishness when confronted with shocking or distasteful stimuli, avoidance of display of weakness in general, reticence about emotional or idealistic matters, and sexual competency.[21]

As we can see in Stouffer's comment, the expectations for the young soldier are much the same as for his civilian counterpart and can be summed up with the same injunction: Be a man. But "be a man" takes on special significance for the soldier. All of the elements in the male sex role of which we have spoken are exaggerated in the military. It is not enough just to avoid feminine behaviors; a soldier is taught total contempt for all women except his mother and possibly the one special girl back home. Women are to be used and abused for the soldier's pleasure. Success in the sense of being the best at whatever he does is ingrained in the soldier. Competition among individual soldiers, squads, platoons, and divisions is part of military training. Aggression not only means being ready to fight but also being ready to kill. (We tend to forget that the primary mission of a soldier is *to kill* the enemy.) A soldier also hears the not-so-subtle message that sex is one of the soldier's basic prerogatives. The notion of the soldier's use of his penis as a weapon comes through in the cadence learned by most recruits as they hold their rifle in one hand and their crotch in the other and yell,

Sir: This is my rifle
      This is my gun
      This is for fighting
      This is for fun!

Likewise, the pressures to be tough, confident, and self-reliant are extreme for the soldier. Some argue that all of this is good for a young man, he gains a sense of personal security in knowing that he can do pretty much whatever he sets his mind to. The military builds character and the end product is a better, more competent man. Boys enter the military, but after a masculinizing hitch, they leave as men—or so many Americans think.

Such a view does not find support in one man's reminiscences of his military training.

> I went into the Army like a lot of people do—a young scared kid of 17 told he should join the Army to get off probation for minor crimes. At the time the Army sounded real fine: three meals, rent-free home, adventure and *you would come out a man.* (It's amazing how many parents put this trip on their kids.)
>
> In basic training I met the dregs of the Army. (Who else would be given such an unimportant job as training "dumb shit kids"?) These instructors were constantly making jokes such as "don't bend over in the shower" and encouraging the super-masculine image of "so horny he'll fuck anything." People talked about fucking sheep and cows and women with about the same respect for them all.
>
> Not many 17-year-olds could conform to such hard core experience. You're told the cooks were gay (pieces of ass for your benefit). The "hard core" sergeants with all these young "feminine" bodies (everyone appears very meek, i.e., feminine, when constantly humiliated, by having his head shaved and being harassed with no legitimate way of fighting back) were always dunghole talking ("your ass is grass and Jim's the lawnmower").
>
> These "leaders" are the *men;* that pretty much makes you the "pussy's"—at the very most "boys." You have to conform to a hard core, tough image or you're a punk. And I began to believe it because of my insecure state of mind, which was so encouraged in training. I was real insecure, so I wanted to be a superman and went Airborne, which, unlike most of the Army, is more intense and worse than basic training. The pressures of assuming manhood are very heavy.
>
> Not only are you hard, you're Airborne hard—sharp, mean, ruthless. You have to be having an impressive sexual life or a quick tongue to talk one up. You've got to be ready to fight a lot because you're tough and don't take shit from anyone. All these fronts were very hard for me to keep up because they contradicted everything I felt. I didn't feel tougher than anyone. I was very insecure about my dick size and ability to satisfy women.
>
> All I had was my male birthright ego. I stayed drunk to be able to struggle through the barroom tests of strength and the bedroom obstacle courses. The pressures became heavier and stronger, requiring more of a facade to cover up the greater insecurity. To prove I was tougher I went looking for fights and people to fuck over. To prove I was "cock strong" I fucked over more women and talked more about it. I began to do all the things I was most insecure about doing, hoping that doing them would make me that "real man."
>
> Having survived the initial shock of such a culture I became very capable in such required role-playing as toughest, meanest, and most virile—the last meaning of a cold unreproachable lover (irresistible to women and unapproachable by other men).[22]

There is no reason to think that this man's experiences are unique. The military strips a young man of his previous identity and through a process of indoctrination creates a person who can follow orders and kill another human being if the situation warrants it. All the hoopla of making boys into men is more of a public-relations gimmick than a real concern of the military establishment. Rather than instilling character and ideals, the military seems more concerned with puffery and braggadocio.

The macho male image. *Source: U.S. Marine Corps Art Collection.*

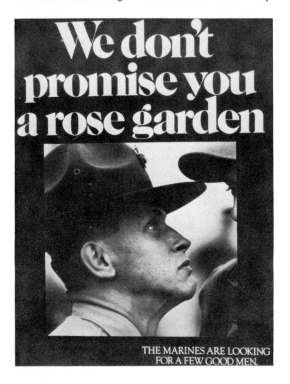

We don't promise you a rose garden

THE MARINES ARE LOOKING
FOR A FEW GOOD MEN.

However, since 1973, with the introduction of the All Volunteer Armed Forces (AVAF), the military has changed its public image somewhat. No longer are there as many recruiting posters picturing the soldier in battle gear challenging the young man to become a real man in the tradition of John Wayne taking enemy strongholds. Today the message is that the military is one of the few places where a young male or female can gain valuable and potentially marketable skills. As William Arkin and Lynne Dobrofsky point out in their analysis of contemporary military socialization,

> As a result of the AVAF, today we find becoming a man being defined in terms of learning an occupation or a skill, but basically the recruitment message of turning a boy into a man has only added the traditional work ethic dimension of masculinity, which equates masculinity with productivity, occupation, and breadwinning. This shift does not change one of the primary objectives of the military, that of turning boys into (fighting) men, but rather it attempts to widen the military appeal. As the result of the negative publicity that was spotlighted by Vietnam, this new appeal further represents a typical peacetime pattern where the masculine warrior appears superfluous to the population.[23]

Elements of the Male Sex Role

One of the more pressing problems facing the modern military establishment is what to do with the female soldier. For many people—civilian and military alike—the presence of women in the military contradicts the idea of the military as one of the last all-male bastions. If women in the military can do everything that men can do with the exception of taking part in combat—a prohibition supported more by social convention than real evidence that women cannot perform effectively in combat—what particular masculinizing validation do men receive for their manhood by serving in the military? Again, Arkin and Dobrofsky respond to this thorny issue:

> The influx of women in all traditional male occupations, with the exception of combat, can only serve to challenge the military socialization in masculinity since the military has yet to develop a female warrior model. Military women tend to represent a neutered or "little brother" role model. But whether a feminine or little brother model of socialization is used for women, it is questionable if the military model of masculinity can be preserved when shared.[24]

We can only speculate on how the growing presence of women will affect the long-held military traditions that support the masculinizing process. One thing seems certain: The military will change the women who enter the service in far greater ways than the women will change the military. Let us now look at politics and politicians as another example of the extreme emphasis on toughness and self-reliance in the male sex role.

"MY FELLOW AMERICANS . . ."

In the fall of 1960 Vice President Richard M. Nixon lost the American presidency to John F. Kennedy. In 1962 Nixon lost his bid for the governorship of California. Nixon, a beaten man with little or no political future, snarled to the press after his gubernatorial loss, "Well, gentlemen, you won't have Nixon to kick around anymore." The end result of Nixon's public sniveling was that people saw him as weak, ineffectual, unreliable, and unworthy of the public's confidence. A question often asked about Nixon was, "Would you buy a used car from this man?" Nixon's public image during the early 1960s was decidedly at its nadir. And yet only six years later, after an extensive remaking of his public image, Nixon was elected President of the United States.[25] President Nixon like the mythical risen phoenix was seen as determined, confident, courageous, tough, and self-reliant. In other words, Nixon had become a man's man.

It goes without saying that politicians are extremely conscious of their public image. And probably there is no facet of their image that they are more concerned about than being seen as hypermasculine in the sense of toughness. A politician who is thought weak, feminine, or cowardly does not win votes. In a real sense, politics is a masculine endeavor by its rigid adherence to masculine attributes, especially the one of toughness. As the author I. F. Stone put it, "The first rule of this small boy statecraft [his term for Washington politics] is that the leader of the gang, like the leader of a tribe, horde, or nation, dare not appear 'chicken.' "[26]

For our analysis of the politician and the emphasis on toughness, we will borrow heavily from author–lawyer Marc Feigen Fasteau's book *The Male Machine,* which was published in 1974. Fasteau devotes an entire chapter to the Vietnam conflict and writes about how the leading politicians throughout the Vietnam era were deeply concerned with their image of toughness.

John Kennedy is not often linked with the Vietnam conflict. However, Kennedy laid the groundwork for America's involvement in Vietnam. In the following passage, Fasteau comments on Kennedy's view of personal toughness.

> The connection between the war and the cult of toughness has not been prominent in the flood of writings about Vietnam, but the evidence is there, subtler in the Kennedy Administration and more blatant under Johnson and Nixon.
>
> There was the Kennedy emphasis on personal toughness. An excessive desire to prove this quality had taken early root in John Kennedy and showed itself first through wild recklessness in sports that led to frequent injuries. This need was demonstrated again in the famous PT-boat incident during his Navy career. Kennedy's bravery in rescuing a shipmate after his boat was rammed and bringing the survivors to safety is well known. But during this rescue, some of his actions appear to reveal the same straining after heroics. . . . Later, sharing his brother's values but being more outspoken, one of the first things Robert Kennedy would want to know about someone being considered as a Kennedy advisor or appointee was whether he was tough. If he was—on to other questions; if not, he lost all credibility.
>
> This attitude was reflected in the counterinsurgency fad that so captivated the Kennedy Administration. Americans, excellent specimens both physically and mentally, would be trained to be the Renaissance men of the twentieth century. They would be able to slit throats in Asian jungles, teach the natives in their own language how to use democracy and modern technology to improve their lives, and would quote Thucydides in their reports. President Kennedy once had the entire White House press corps flown to Fort Bragg, North Carolina, to watch an all-day demonstration of ambushes, counterambushes, and snake-meat eating. The Special Forces epitomized, much more clearly than any civilian engaged in the messier business of politics, the ideals of the Kennedys. They were knowledgeable, they were progressive, up-to-date, they would do good, but above all they were tough, ready to use power and unaffected by sentiment.[27]

With Kennedy's assassination, Lyndon Johnson inherited Vietnam. One of Johnson's most trusted advisors was Secretary of Defense Robert McNamara. McNamara had been president of the Ford Motor Company and brought to Washington a tough, no-nonsense approach to all problems. Fasteau's analysis of McNamara's role in the Vietnam conflict reads as follows:

> McNamara's role, on the other hand, was tragic. He had great drive, an incredibly organized intelligence, and a strong commitment to public service. And he had deeply humane and liberal impulses—and what goes with them, a strongly held ethical framework. But this side of his personality was compartmentalized, walled off from his professional life. In this tension, he exemplified the *best* in American public men and, in the end, the war tore him apart. He could not bring the humane side of himself to bear in thinking about the war. Instead, the cult of toughness went unchallenged as the unarticulated major premise of all the systems analysis, war gaming, and policymaking. For all his other sensitivities, he was as much a victim of it

as the others. His spontaneous response in a hostile confrontation with a group of students after a speech at Harvard in November 1966 was to shout at them that he was tougher than they were—although that had nothing to do with the issue in dispute.[28]

President Lyndon Johnson was haunted by the specter of Vietnam each and every day of his presidency. The senator from Texas who became president by dint of an assassin's bullet and was subsequently elected in a bitter campaign against the conservative and hawkish Barry Goldwater was a man of peace who wanted to be remembered for his Great Society programs rather than for some war in Southeast Asia. To end poverty and civil strife and to enhance educational opportunities and racial harmony were the keys to Johnson's political goals, not the unrelenting quagmire of Vietnam. But Johnson possessed a flaw, a personal quirk that caused Vietnam to take precedence over all other matters. Fasteau claims that "he was more openly insecure about masculinity than John Kennedy and often made explicit the connection between these doubts and his decisions of state."[29] Fasteau quotes from David Halberstam's best-selling book *The Best and the Brightest* on how Johnson became overly concerned with how others viewed his masculinity in relation to his actions in Vietnam. Halberstam writes,

He [Johnson] had always been haunted by the idea that he would be judged as being insufficiently manly for the job, that he would lack courage at a crucial moment. More than a little insecure himself, he wanted very much to be seen as a man; it was a conscious thing. . . . [He] wanted the respect of men who were tough, real men, and they would turn out to be hawks. He had unconsciously divided people around him between men and boys. Men were activists, doers, who conquered business empires, who acted instead of talked, who made it in the world of other men and had the respect of other men. Boys were the talkers and the writers and the intellectuals, who sat around thinking and criticizing and doubting instead of doing. . . .

As Johnson weighed the advice he was getting on Vietnam, it was the boys who were most skeptical, and the men who were most sure and confident and hawkish and who had Johnson's respect. Hearing that one member of his Administration was becoming a dove on Vietnam Johnson said, "Hell, he has to squat to piss." The men had, after all, done things in their lifetimes, and they had the respect of other men. Doubt itself, he thought, was almost a feminine quality, doubts were for women; once, on another issue, when Lady Bird raised her doubts, Johnson had said of course she was doubtful, it was like a woman to be uncertain.[30]

Few modern-day politicians have been as concerned with their public image as has Richard Nixon. As noted above, Nixon's reemergence into the 1968 political arena came about as a direct result of the skillful management of his image as a tough and decisive man. Nixon's approach to Vietnam caused some of the most vehement opposition to the war. During the late 1960s and early 1970s, this country became divided in a way not seen since the Civil War. Nixon's preoccupation with a "peace with honor" became the administrative principle that prolonged the fighting beyond any realistic chance for victory. No matter; Nixon was not going to be the first American president to have a military defeat blemish his public office. Again, Fasteau's analysis of Nixon's preoccupation with toughness is revealing:

> Nixon's particular variant of the cult of toughness is, in Garry Wills' phrase, the "cult of crisis," the ultimate embodiment of the self-made man; he is always remaking and testing himself, watching from some disembodied vantage point to make sure his machinery is working. And the test that counts, the action that separates the men from the boys, that allows him to parade his efforts and virtue, and to experience his worth in the marketplace of competition most vividly, is the crisis. This can be seen in "his eagerness, always, to be 'in the arena,' his praise of others for being cool under pressure, for being 'tested in the fires.' " The title and format of Nixon's book, *Six Crises,* also reflects this preoccupation. Each chapter describes a problem he faced, his efforts to deal with it, and the lessons he learned, mainly about his own reactions to pressure. Some of these lessons are quite revealing.
>
> The most difficult part of any crisis, he wrote, "is the period of indecision—*whether to fight or run away.*" But the choice, as he poses it, is not a real choice at all. What self-respecting man, let alone a President of the United States, can choose to "run away"? Even within the limited range of options he posits, he could have used other words—"walk away," "avoid the issue," for example—which encompass the possibility that retreat can be rational and dignified. "Run away" permits none of these overtones; it sounds just plain cowardly. More important, the substance of the issue, what is actually at stake (apart from honor and "credibility"), has dropped from sight. The emphasis is not on the problem at hand, not on trying to determine what objective is worth pursuing at what cost, but on *himself*—on his courage or lack thereof. In his October 26, 1973, press conference, for example, he said of himself in answer to a question about Watergate, "the tougher it gets the cooler I get"; he responded to another question about the Middle East conflict with "when I have to face an international crisis I have what it takes."[31]

We need not focus only on the politicians of a decade or two ago to find ample evidence that toughness plays a decisive role in politics. We can look at a more recent domestic problem to see how the cult of toughness still prevails in the 1980s. When President Ronald Reagan fired the striking air traffic controllers in the summer of 1981, nearly sixty percent of the American public voiced approval of his "tough stand" against the strikers. In a news magazine article published at the time, President Reagan's decisive action was reported as creating a favorable image of the President facing a "full-blown domestic crisis." The article went on to say,

> "He [Reagan] wanted to jut his jaw out," said one senior aide. "He wanted to be tough." Another, happily contemplating the impact of the President's tough talk, said, "Internationally they'll see someone who isn't afraid to take action and who doesn't back down at the first sign of controversy."[32]

As we have seen, the masculine imperative to be tough and self-reliant plays a decisive role in many men's lives. From the young men who scramble out on crisp fall afternoons to practice football to the man who sits in the Oval Office, all heed the voice deep within that continuously urges, "Be a man."

SOME CLOSING COMMENTS

Men for so long have identified certain attributes as essential features of their masculinity and male sex role that most of them can think in no other terms. A man must always act in certain prescribed ways if he is to be judged a real man. If, for whatever reason, he should not play out the prescribed role, he is immediately condemned as being unmanly, as being less of a man. The pressures—self-imposed and otherwise—that come from such rigid role playing take their toll. Even so, most men continue in a never-ending quest to prove to themselves and to others that they are real men—tough and self-reliant to the core.

In this chapter we have suggested that most men act tough and self-reliant to cover up their gnawing fears that others may not think them real men unless they act in certain ways. Hollywood's male heroes or big bad wolves have played an integral part in educating males in those values, ideals, and behaviors that portray a certain masculine style. This style is particularly apparent in the roles of the athlete, the soldier, and the politician.

SUGGESTED READINGS

Fasteau, M. *The Male Machine.* New York: McGraw-Hill, 1974.

Komarovsky, M. *Dilemmas of Masculinity.* New York: Norton, 1976.

Mellen, J. *Big Bad Wolves: Masculinity in the American Film.* New York: Pantheon Books, 1977.

3

SOME ISSUES OF CONCERN TO MALES

The modern American male lives in a world of unprecedented changes and choice. Change itself is nothing new. Cultures are always shifting; people are always discarding old ways, trying new ones. But the pace and intensity of change in today's society are unprecedented, making tremendous demands on the individual's ability to adjust. Myron Brenton[1]

The male experience is much more complex than any one discipline can successfully unravel or the mere enumeration of a set of socially prescribed norms and stereotypes can encompass. What makes an understanding of male experience even more difficult is that it changes subtly from generation to generation, from situation to situation, and even from one male to another. However, some issues seem to capture the attention of a majority of males regardless of their social standing, economic background, or educational level. In this section we have selected several issues that appear to affect a majority of males at some time or another. These are not the only issues of concern to most males, but we think each of them is compelling enough to be included in our discussion of the male experience.

At some time or another, many men find themselves facing questions about their sexual preference. Even though most males prefer females as sexual partners, a significant number of males and females prefer same-sex partners for sexual relationships. In Chapter 12 we will explore the issue of homosexuality. We will explore some of the more common myths that have grown up around the gay community and take a close look at gay relationships in order to better understand the gay individual.

In Chapter 13 we will focus on the issues of power and intimacy in male-female relationships. Males have usually had a majority of power in their relationships with women. However, when there is an imbalance of power in a relationship, there is usually some kind of conflict, either overt or covert, that makes for an uneasy and oftentimes troubled relationship. The nature of the intimate male-female relationship is gaining increasing attention from social scientists as we begin to unravel some of the mysteries surrounding this special human relationship.

In Chapter 14 we will examine the social phenomenon known as the men's movement to see what impact it is having on men's lives in these last decades of the twentieth century.

Some Issues of Concern to Males

12

Of gay men and opened closets:
HOMOSEXUALITY

We have learned, among other things, that the values and experiences of homosexual couples are similar to those of heterosexuals in many ways. Whatever their sexual preferences, most people strongly desire a close and loving relationship with one special person. For both homosexuals and heterosexuals, intimate relationships can — and often do — provide love and satisfaction. But neither group is immune to the perils of relationships — conflict and possible breakup. Whatever their sexual preferences, people in intimate relationships today struggle to reconcile a longing for closeness with a desire for independence and self-realization. Anne Peplau[1]

Few social topics cause males to become more angry, anxious, irrational, and strident in their views than does the subject of homosexuality. This disturbing fact became obvious when the author participated in a classroom discussion on homosexuality and the gay community. As the discussion became more heated, one male student proclaimed that he would "put the lights out" of any male who approached him with sexual overtones. Another male student declared that all homosexuals should be castrated or at least put in prison. Although several other male students voiced no condemnation of homosexuality, not one male student offered any opposing views against his more outspoken and vehement classmates. It was as if the males in that classroom recognized that by taking a more moderate and understanding approach to the topic, they might themselves be labeled gay. In an article on *homophobia,* or the irrational fear and extreme intolerance of homosexuality, Gregory Lehne points out that the threat of being labeled gay is a powerful means whereby males reinforce their own traditional sex role.[2] What was surprising about this classroom discussion is that, in this supposed era of sexual liberation, males still feel the necessity to condemn and vilify a minority of people who happen to have a different sexual preference from the majority.

In this chapter we will take a close look at homosexuals and the homosexual community—hereafter referred to as gays and the gay community—in order to understand the problems gays encounter in the heterosexual or straight world. First, we will briefly review the history of gay people and attempt to put in perspective the reasons why this group has been so systematically condemned and attacked down through the centuries. We also will examine the recent development of the gay liberation movement and its impact on the larger society and on current social attitudes toward homosexuality. Next, we will look at several common myths that have grown up around the gay person and the gay community. We will see that these myths have little if any basis in the real world. Finally, we will examine gay relationships in order to understand how gay people relate socially and sexually to each other.

By presenting the facts about gays and debunking the many myths associated with them, this chapter attempts to provide a basis for our understanding and acceptance of one another as human beings who all have needs to form close, sharing, and loving relationships with others no matter our sexual preference. With a greater understanding of gay relationships, heterosexual males and females may learn something of value for their own relationships. Specifically, the sex roles that primarily structure all male–female relationships are absent for the most part in gay relationships. Possibly, heterosexual couples could learn some new ways of living, loving, and sharing, if they would only try to understand gay couples better.

FROM HATRED TO UNDERSTANDING AND BACK AGAIN

If we are to understand the gay person and the gay community, we must first deal with the hostility, discrimination, and violence that have been heaped on this group for most of the last two thousand years. During this time, homosexuality has been labeled a "crime against nature," "an abomination," and "a sin." Gays and those thought to be gay have been executed, jailed, blackmailed, and in various other ways, persecuted by the "righteous" majority. The most heinous and largest scale antihomosexual violence took place in Nazi Germany, where hundreds of thousands of suspected homosexuals were rounded up and sent off to gas chambers along with millions of Jews and other "undesirables." In America gays have borne such dehumanizing abuses as castration, lobotomy, shock treatment, and assault by roving gangs of macho adolescents out for an evening's fun of "queer-baiting."[3]

THE ROOTS OF ANTIHOMOSEXUAL SENTIMENT

Why have gays warranted such inhuman treatment over the centuries? Part of the answer can be found in an all-too-brief review of the major religious traditions that have influenced Western cultures. The first large-scale attempt to eliminate homsexual practices, a common and accepted sexual variation among many ancient civilizations,[4] occurred within the pre-Christian Jewish community. For both secular and relgious reasons, the Jewish leadership during the fifth century B. C. proclaimed homosexuality an abomination and a defilement of Yaweh's injunction for the Jewish people to increase and multiply (Genesis 8:15–17). As so often happens in any newly fashioned religious movement, the early Christian Church adopted the established Jewish views on sex and sexuality and reinforced the view that any sexual activity outside of marriage was grounds for eternal damnation. The early Christians went a step further in undermining homosexual activity by prescribing that sexual intercourse be permitted for procreative ends only. Sex as a human expression of love, joy, and pleasure-seeking was strictly forbidden even among married couples. A sixth-century pope, Gregory the Great, went so far as to decree that married couples should not befoul "their intercourse with pleasure." Because homosexuality could never serve procreative ends and because it was considered to be only a source of sexual pleasure, homosexuality was doubly vilified by the early church fathers. Consequently, the antihomosexual sentiment and practices instituted in the Judaic and Christian traditions set the stage for most of the Western world's prohibitions and sanctions against homosexuality.

Some argue that another reason for this antihomosexual bias is the purported "dysfunctional" nature inherent in homosexual activity. Their argument goes something like this: If everyone were somehow to turn homosexual overnight (a highly unlikely turn of events and yet one that the opponents of homosexuality fear will happen if homosexuality becomes a socially acceptable sexual preference), the human species would disappear in a few short decades. In a primitive

HOMOSEXUALITY: DIFFERENT VIEWS

If a man also lie with mankind as he lieth with a woman, both of them have committed an abomination: they shall surely be put to death: their blood shall be upon them.

Leviticus 20:13

"The love that dare not speak its name."

Oscar Wilde

"The love that won't shut up."

Mike Nichols

Some people say, "If you have homosexual teachers, you're automatically going to have homosexual students." I don't know about that theory. Because if it were true, today I would be a nun.

Mark Russell

The more we let violence and homosexuality become the norm, the more we'll become such a sick nation that the communists won't have to take over—we'll just give up.

Anita Bryant

How can we explain heterosexual behavior if this too is a learned phenomenon? And if there is homosexual behavior which can be called nonpathological, can it be explained along the same lines? The answer to these questions becomes much more obvious when we reflect upon the reason why heterosexual behavior is the most common form of sexual behavior in our present society. The reason, I think, is very clear. It is because heterosexuality is encouraged and because homosexual behavior is discouraged. Consequently, it is the "natural" thing for young men to prefer girls as sexual objects. One need only reflect upon the content of the popular media to realize that the cues are all around us and that they exist in the most subtle as well as the most gross forms. Men learn heterosexual object-choice because no other object-choice is considered possible for them; that is, they are not allowed to conceive of the possibility that there can be another kind of sexual object other than the opposite sex.

Martin Hoffman

The issue of homosexuality always makes me nervous. . . . I don't have any, you know, personal knowledge about homosexuality and I guess being a Baptist, that would contribute to a sense of being uneasy.

Jimmy Carter

The only unnatural sex act is one that can't be performed.

Alfred Kinsey

Source: Reprinted in B. Strong, S. Wilson, M. Robbins, and T. Johns, *Human Sexuality,* 2d ed. (St. Paul: West Publishing Company, 1981).

society where a high birth rate was necessary to offset a high infant mortality rate, the prevalence of homosexual activity could indeed threaten the viability of the group's future existence. An often repeated example of the negative consequences of the absence of heterosexual activity is the recent diminution of the religious sect known as the Shakers, whose religious beliefs prohibit *all* sexual activity. But this argument is baseless and the Shaker example irrelevant to the discussion when one recognizes the social and technological realities of contemporary society. In fact, in most postindustrial societies where population zero is seen as the only long-term solution to the world's diminishing resources, the number of males and females who abstain from procreative sex either as practicing homosexuals or as life-long celibates may be performing a valuable service. Thus homosexuality in contemporary Western culture can be viewed as a functional alternative sexual preference rather than as a dysfunctional sexual aberration.

A SHORT-LIVED ABOUT-FACE

Prejudicial attitudes and discriminatory practices can only change when their dehumanizing consequences are viewed in the light of public awareness. As in the case of blacks and women, the social movement to win gays their rights as human beings began when gay people came out of the closet and became visible. The beginning of the gay movement started on the West Coast after World War II. Sociologists Martin Weinberg and Colin Williams recount the beginning of the homophile movement in the following passage.

> The first major United States homophile organization was the Mattachine Foundation, established in 1950 in Los Angeles as a secret society to promote discussion groups and educational efforts regarding homosexuality. Eventually the secrecy was dropped, and the organization became charted as a corporation in 1954 in California with the title of Mattachine Society, Inc. The headquarters were soon moved to San Francisco. (In 1955, the Daughters of Bilitis—D. O. B.—was established in San Francisco, independent of Mattachine, as the first all-female homophile organization.) The Mattachine Society also established a number of chapters in cities around the country, but internal schisms within the movement led to their being dropped. Some of these continued as autonomous organizations in the early 1960s, the two main ones being Mattachine of New York (M. S. N. Y.) and Mattachine of Washington. Consequently, Mattachine of San Francisco, though a parent body, no longer controls its offshoots.[5]

The early homophile organizations served primarily as meeting places where gays could find support and comaraderie. Formal discussion groups became a central fixture of these organizations and provided gays an opportunity to talk about their concerns. Counseling services for "troubled" gays were often provided in many of the organizations that sprang up in most large cities.

In general, the 1950s was a decade of quiet involvement by a minority of gays who began coming out of the closet. The 1960s, with the growing social consciousness of various groups' oppressions, found more gays joining different homophile organizations and lobbying for a relaxation in many of the discriminatory laws that had accumulated over the years. The public's first real awareness of the gay community came not from the efforts of one of the formal organizations but rather from an incident of police harrassment in New York City. Weinberg and Williams describe the incident:

> . . . in New York City, the Gay Liberation Front came into existence with an incident on June 28, 1969. The city police made an early morning raid on the Stonewall, a homosexual bar on Christopher Street, a popular cruising area in Greenwich Village. The manager and employees were arrested on the grounds of selling liquor illegally, and the patrons were ordered to leave, which they did. They gathered outside, however, where they were joined by a variety of others who shared their consternation at the raid. On emerging from the Stonewall, the police were pelted with pennies, cans, rocks, and other objects and were driven back into the Stonewall, which was locked from the outside and set afire. The Tactical Police Force (riot police) was summoned, and several hours of street fighting ensued, resulting in many arrests and beatings.
>
> The following night, the more militant homosexuals (under the slogan of "Gay Power") decided to "liberate" Christopher Street. Their activities swelled the crowds again, this time including Black Panthers, "yippies," and "crazies." A riot situation developed, and again the Tactical Police Force was called to clear the streets.
>
> June 28, 1969, and the Stonewall incident became one of the major symbols of the gay liberation movement. On its anniversary one year later, Gay Liberation Day was proclaimed with a march that has been repeated every June to the present; the number of participants has ranged from about five thousand to fifteen thousand. Whatever the merits of the Stonewall event, it was a turning point that brought many disaffected young homosexuals into the mainstream of the homophile movement.[6]

After Stonewall, the gay liberation movement began to demand full and equal rights for those people whose only difference from the majority of Americans was their sexual preference. In 1973 the American Psychiatric Association and in 1974 the American Psychological Association passed resolutions removing homosexuality from the official list of mental disorders. In 1975 the Civil Service Commission, moved by a federal court decision, stated its policy that people could not be denied federal employment because of their sexual preference. For a time, the gay liberation movement looked as if it were at last making real headway in changing the social consciousness and values of the American public. Around the country, various cities and counties passed ordinances prohibiting discrimination against gays in housing and employment. However, a vicious and openly hostile backlash loomed on the horizon.

In 1977 in Dade County Florida, there began a movement to repeal the county's antidiscriminatory housing and employment ordinance. In the forefront of the opposition to the ordinance was Anita Bryant, a beauty-contest winner and popular singer. Bryant warned the Dade County citizenry that if they did not repeal the antidiscriminatory ordinance, they would soon be living in a Sodomlike land. Unexpectedly, the ordinance was repealed overwhelmingly. Bryant went on a national spree, warning all who would listen—and there were plenty—of the dangers of homosexuality.

Increasingly, gays are being accorded freedom and dignity. *Source © Jean-Claude Lejeune.*

Another sign of the reemergent antihomosexual attitudes was the publication of a survey which reported the attitudes of a large sample of psychiatrists and their belief in a relationship between homosexuality and mental illness.[7] The survey represented a dramatic reversal of psychiatric opinion in the 1973 denouncement of homosexuality as a mental disorder. Of the 2,500 psychiatrists surveyed, sixty-nine percent felt homosexuality was a pathological condition, seventy-three percent believed that gay men were less happy than heterosexual men, sixty-percent indicated that gay men were less likely to have mature, loving relationships, and seventy-percent viewed a gay male's problems as stemming from personal conflict rather than from social stigmatization. Notwithstanding all of the scientific evidence to the contrary, the psychiatric community appeared to step back into the nineteenth century.

Thus the decade of the 1970s opened with the hope that gay men and lesbians finally would be accorded a measure of freedom and dignity and closed on a note of hostility and misconceptions among the public and mental health professionals alike. What the 1980s and 1990s hold for those Americans who have a different sexual preference is a matter of great concern for all Americans.

DEBUNKING THE MYTHS ABOUT GAYS

As noted above, gays have been the target of discrimination and persecution in most Western societies during the past two thousand years. A majority of Amer-icans still espouse prejudicial attitudes toward gay people. For example, a ma-jority of adults questioned in a recent national sample believe that gays are responsible for a loosening of our nation's moral fiber and that the acceptance of homosexuality would eventually lead to our civilization's downfall.[8] Many be-lieve the repeated contention that the demise of the Greco–Roman civilizations was based solely on their acceptance of homosexuality. One feature that stands out in any survey of people's attitudes toward gays is how little understanding the general public has about gays as individuals and about the gay community. Consequently, gays like most other minority groups suffer the negative effects of stereotypes, misconceptions, and myths (see "Some Common Myths About Gays"). We will take a close look at several prominent myths pertaining to gays, especially gay males, and present some of the relevant research findings that for the most part debunk these myths.

One myth that persists about gays and heterosexual males alike is that a man is totally and exclusively either heterosexual or homosexual in his sexual preference. As so often is the case, reality does not match this illusion that sexual behaviors, interests, and preferences fit neatly into a dichotomous, either–or category. However, the erroneous view of a dichotomous male sexuality has endured and been supported through centuries of hostility and violence against gays—more frequently and with greater vigor against males than gay females, or lesbians—especially in those countries espousing a Judeo–Christian value system.[9]

Approximately thirty-five years ago, the extent of the "varieties" of male sexual behaviors was systematically reported for the first time. In 1948 Alfred Kinsey and his colleagues at Indiana University published the findings from the first large-scale survey of American males' sexual activities in the monumental *Sexual Behavior in the Human Male*.[10] This work made Kinsey, a professor of biology, both famous for the myth-shattering findings and despised for what some people considered his impropriety in studying such a taboo subject as human sexuality. One of the study's more shocking revelations was that thirty-seven percent of the men interviewed reported having had "some overt homosexual experience to the point of orgasm between adolescence and old age." Thus the commonly accepted belief that only a few men had ever engaged in a homosexual act was shown to be patently false. Another myth-shattering idea presented in Kinsey's work was that sexual preference must be defined along a continuum of sexual behaviors and interests rather than in a strict either–or fashion. To this end, Kinsey introduced a seven-point scale or continuum ranging from 0, indicating exclusive heterosexual behaviors and interests, to 6, indicating exclusive homosexual behaviors and interests (see Figure 12.1). This formulation allowed for a much more precise description of the real varieties of male sexual preferences. For example, a primarily heterosexual male who has had, say, two or three homosexual experiences and now and then fantasizes a homosexual encounter would rank a 1 or possibly a 2 on Kinsey's scale, while a primarily gay male who has had intercourse with a female on a few occasions would probably rate a 4 or 5 on the scale. Kinsey's pioneering work changed the scientific community's view of sexuality and more importantly of male sexual preference. However, the average layperson still believes that sexual preference is an either–or feature of a male's sexual makeup.

To highlight Kinsey's approach toward the continuum of male sexual preference, let us briefly review the controversial research of sociologist Laud Humphreys.[11] As Kinsey suggested, in the real world people's sexual behaviors and interests do not usually fit into mutually exclusive categories. In order to observe a small minority of men who engage in periodic and impersonal homosexual activity, Humphreys acted as lookout to protect the participants who frequented certain men's rooms (referred to as "tearooms" in the gay community) used for sexual activities. As lookout, Humphreys was able to record the license plates of

Figure 12.1 Kinsey homosexual rating scale. *Source: Adapted from Alfred C. Kinsey et al.,* Sexual Behavior in the Human Male *(Philadelphia: Saunders, 1948), p. 638.*

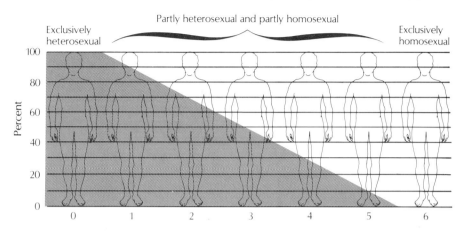

the participants; much later he visited the car owners in their homes on the pretext of being a survey researcher. Humphreys discovered that a large number of the tearoom trade were in fact married family men who were highly respected in their communities. Now what are we to make of these men with respect to their sexual preference? They are certainly not exhibiting what most people assume to be a basic either–or sexual preference. On Kinsey's scale, these men would rank a 2 or possibly even a 3. Humphrey's research dramatically points out the need for viewing homosexuality as existing along a continuum of varying degrees of sexual behaviors and interests.

IT'S ALL A PROBLEM OF SEX ROLE IDENTITY

A common myth that most people believe is that masculinity and homosexuality are mutually exclusive features of a male's personality. Basically, this myth suggests that if a male exhibits a masculine sex role identity (that is, behaves in appropriate sex-typed ways and expresses appropriate sex-typed attitudes and interests), he certainly cannot be homosexual. Many psychologists and psychiatrists have borrowed this myth and suggested that male homosexuality is the result of a disordered or deficient masculine sex role identity.[12] This view of male homosexuality is based on Sigmund Freud's early speculation that male homosexuality stemmed from a boy's "primary feminine identification."[13] Like Freud others have described male homosexuality as a deficiency in masculine identity, using such phrases to describe the nature of male homosexuality as "a flight from masculinity,"[14] "a search for masculinity,"[15] "a confession of masculine failure,"[16] and "a secret longing to play the female's less demanding role."[17] What all of these views have in common is the belief that homosexuality results when a boy develops a feminine rather than a masculine sex role identity.[18]

The idea that male homosexuality is related to a deficient or inadequately developed male sex role identity requires that we accept certain assumptions about male development. Recall that in Chapter 6 we discussed the persistence of certain assumptions about the male sex role, namely the eleven assumptions that make up what Joseph Pleck called the male sex role identity (MSRI) paradigm. Basic to the MSRI paradigm is the assumption that males have an innate psychological need to develop a masculine sex role identity, which according to the MSRI perspective is a risky and failure-prone undertaking for most males. Recall also that in Pleck's analysis of the MSRI, he found little scientific evidence to substantiate the existence for the purported construct of a psychological masculine identity. Furthermore, in a review of the research linking male homosexuality with a deficient male identity, Pleck found little, if any, actual scientific support for such an assumed relationship.[19] Thus the belief that gay males possess a deficient psychological masculine identity is just one more myth hampering an understanding of gay males.

MISOGYNY IS THE ANSWER

Another myth one commonly hears about gay males is that they hate or have an aversion to the opposite sex. According to this myth, all "normal" males are naturally sexually attracted to females and so a male whose sexual preference is for another man must either hate and/or possibly fear the female sex. Again, theoretical speculation to support the antifemale perspective about gay males abounds. For example, Sandor Ferenczi, a staunch advocate of Freud's views, has suggested that gay males approach women "with pronounced antipathy and not rarely with hatred that is badly, or not at all concealed."[20] Others have followed Ferenczi's lead and suggested that gay males hold a "general contempt . . . for females,"[21] or that "only men incapacitated for the love of women by their insurmountable fears and resentments become dependent for gratification upon the escape into homogeneous pairs,"[22] or that homosexuality stems, at least partially, from "the result of covert but incapacitating fears of the opposite sex."[23]

The problem with this line of reasoning is that gay males do not exhibit the purported hatred, fear, or aversion toward females that many theorists attribute to them. As a matter of fact, the research into the feelings, attitudes, and even the physical attraction that gay males have toward females convincingly debunks these notions and shows them to be more akin to myth than to reality. For example, in a series of well-controlled studies, Freund (not Freud) and his colleagues found that gay males were as physically attracted (as measured by their penile erections) by pictures of nude females and descriptions of heterosexual intercourse as were heterosexual males.[24] As for gay males' attitudes toward women in general, Moore and McDonald found that gay males actually held more positive and egalitarian attitudes toward women and their roles than did heterosexual males.[25]

IT'S THE MOTHER'S FAULT

Females are often blamed for many if not most of men's problems. Females also seem to be a favorite "scapegoat" among some social scientists when they explain a male's development and subsequent problems he may suffer.[26] More to the point of our discussion is a popular notion among some theorists that mothers are somehow responsible for their sons' homosexuality. For example, Meyer suggests that the hatred for women that leads to male homosexuality basically stems from a "mother's overprotective and seductive relationship with her son."[27] Others also have linked a mother's domineering, overprotective, and controlling behaviors as essential ingredients causing male homosexuality.[28]

However, in studies dealing with normally adjusted (that is, psychologically healthy) gay males, there is no evidence that mothers were seen as cold, rejecting, domineering, or seductive in their relationships with their sons.[29] Gay males who did perceive their mothers in such negative ways were more likely to exhibit dysfunctional neurotic symptoms. But the same relationship between a male's psychological pathology and his negative views of his mother–son relations were also found in heterosexual males. Therefore, one might conclude that a mother's dominance and control is more likely to be related to a son's psychological health than to his sexual preference. Again, however, we must be wary of falling into the fault-finding trap—this time faulting a mother for her son's psychological adjustment. We could just as well suggest that a male's psychological adjustment is related to his relationship with his father, to his relationships with his peers, or to some other social factors. We should be extremely cautious in blaming any one feature of a man's entire male experience for being the root of all his problems—especially when it is so easy and convenient to blame women.

IT'S ALL IN THE HORMONES

As noted in Chapter 3, many social scientists are looking with interest at the possibility that the male hormone testosterone is an important chemical agent influencing the outcome of the male experience. Thus it should come as no surprise to find some speculating that male homosexuality is the "result of an insufficient proportion of the male sex hormone."[30] In one of the most frequently cited studies bearing on the possible relationship between testosterone levels and homosexuality, Robert Kolodny and his associates studied the levels of plasma testosterone concentrations in thirty gay males and fifty heterosexual males.[31] Overall, Kolodny found no significant differences in testosterone levels between these two groups of college males. However, when Kolodny compared the levels of only those gay males who scored a 5 or 6 on Kinsey's scale (that is, males with exclusively homosexual preferences and interests) with the levels of all heterosexual males, he found the gay males' testosterone levels to be significantly lower than heterosexual males' levels.

Researchers are proving that male homosexuality is not a result of varying hormone levels. *Source:* © *Jean-Claude Lejeune.*

Kolodny's research spurred a series of studies that tried to replicate his findings. Even though some researchers found similar results to Kolodny's,[32] most have been unable to confirm Kolodny's data suggesting that exclusive gay males suffered a deficit of testosterone.[33] In fact, in one study that attempted to replicate Kolodny's findings, the researchers found the plasma testosterone levels significantly *higher* among exclusively gay males than among a comparable group of heterosexual males.[34] Thus the idea that testosterone levels may somehow be linked to homosexuality seems at best a precarious proposition and at worst just another myth, which pretends to explain male homosexuality in terms of a man's chemistry.

JUST LIKE HUSBANDS AND WIVES

Another persistent myth about gay males is the belief that gay couples who live together play out the traditional roles of "husband" and "wife." The stereotypic view of the gay couple pictures one partner acting out the functions of the traditional husband—the primary breadwinner, the active and dominant partner in sexual activity, and the one responsible for all major decisions. The other partner in the relationship is portrayed as the submissive and passive wife, primarily responsible for the household chores, the passive and submissive partner in sex, and more apt to follow the decisions of the other.

Some Issues of Concern to Males

As with the other myths, this one does not stand up to research findings. The idea that one partner is financially responsible for the couple and the other tends to the household chores is just plain nonsense. Actually, most gay couples' live-in relationships find both partners involved in full-time paid employment and sharing the household tasks fairly equally.[35] As for sex, gay couples report a fairly equal give-and-take approach to sex.[36] When it comes to who makes the decisions, gay couples generally espouse a fairly egalitarian approach to decision making.[37] However, the ideal of both partners sharing an equal voice in decisions is not always found in gay relationships—or in most heterosexual relationships for that matter. Researchers have found that the gay partner who has the greater resources of money and education is more apt to have the greater say in the relationship.[38] One thing seems certain: most gay couples who live together stress the ideal of equality and role flexibility to a greater degree than do most heterosexual couples.

YOU CAN SPOT 'EM A BLOCK AWAY

Many people picture a gay male as decidedly effeminate in dress and mannerisms and a lesbian as decidedly macho in dress and mannerisms. The caricatures of a gay male who talks with an affected lisp, walks with a swishing motion, and gestures exuberantly with a limp wrist and of a lesbian who saunters around in a leather jacket and motorcycle boots are all too common. However, researchers find no evidence whatsoever that most gay males and lesbians exhibit these presumed effeminate behaviors and "butch" masculinity, respectively.[39]

THE MISERABLE LOT

Similarly, many people think of gay males as being unhappy, lacking in self-esteem, and being quite disturbed individuals. It would take several pages to list all of the psychological and psychiatric literature that has detailed the pathology associated with homosexuality. The problem with most of this literature, however, is that it has assumed that heterosexuality is a more "natural" and hence healthier aspect of a male's personality. This "heterosexual bias" in most research on homosexuality has caused researchers and theorists alike to assume that all homosexuals were *de facto* psychological cripples.[40] Nevertheless, several studies find little or no evidence that gay males are any more likely to exhibit pathological symptoms than are comparable heterosexual males.[41]

PROTECT THE CHILDREN

During the late 1970s, Anita Bryant and her followers crusaded against gay males and lesbians using as one of their most powerful weapons the idea that the children of the land were in danger of being coerced into homosexuality. Wherever Bryant spoke, she never failed to charge that gays were always looking for young recruits to snare into their homosexual world. One of the major targets of this vicious slander was gay teachers, who were depicted as somehow infusing their classrooms with the sensual lure of homosexuality. Gays were also portrayed as prowling the streets ever watchful for young and impressionable children who could be tempted by the "corrupt and evil" world of homosexuality. Bryant did not seem to care that what she was preaching had little to do with the facts. To the contrary, she seemed more concerned with whipping up the public's sentiment and emotions against all gays. In her attempt to create a strong backlash against gays, she was fairly successful. As a matter of fact, however, gays—as teachers or members of any other profession—do not proselytize their sexual preference to young children any more than heterosexuals do. For example, when gay teachers speak about their goals in the classroom, they talk of creating an environment in which children can learn and think and grow as intelligent, creative human beings.[42] Does that sound like homosexual propaganda? The idea that gays lurk in the shadows or in the hallways or behind desks in our schools, ever watchful for young children whom they can somehow draw into a homosexual life, serves little value except to show just how far some people will go to slander, misrepresent, and mythologize gay people.

THEY'RE ALL ALIKE

Every time a person speaks about some group that he or she has little or no contact with or first-hand knowledge of, that person presents a group stereotype, most often an unflattering one. For example, we overhear two males leaning over their beers at a local tavern as one of them pontificates to the other, "You know about those queers, don't you? Hell, those fags are marching in the capital demanding—get that, *demanding*—equal rights! Why, hell, what they need is to be thrown out of the country or maybe into prison. You know what, those sissies are all a bunch of pansies that should be glad guys like you and me don't just up and beat the hell out of 'em!" Even in less vituperative discussions, most people lump all gays into one category as if they had all come out of some assembly-line punch press. It should go without saying, but researchers have found that gays—like all groups that are easy prey for homogeneous labels (for example, blacks, Chicanos, Asians, and women)—have been found to vary among themselves in every possible way.[43] Most gay males do not fit the stereotype of effeminate hairdressers who lure children, live miserable and disturbed lives, and psychologically speaking, are more likely to identify with females than with males. Clearly, none of the stereotypes that have grown into cultural myths are true for the vast majority of gay people.

There seem to be two reasons why so many myths have grown up around gays and the gay community. First, most heterosexuals have never taken the time to examine their own fears of homosexuality. Second, they have never bothered to learn the fact that just because another person has a different sexual preference does not mean that he or she does not have the same needs, desires, and problems common to *all* human beings. The myths about gays will continue to hold sway in many peoples' minds as long as gays are seen as "deviants" and "unnatural" rather than as human beings who want to find love and intimacy with another human being who happens to be of the same sex.

GAY RELATIONSHIPS

We now turn our attention away from the myths about gay males and focus on that special human phenomenon in which two people seek mutual satisfaction, find acceptance and companionship, and experience sexual gratification, namely, the intimate relationship between two people who happen to be gay. We will focus our discussion in this section on two different and yet interrelated aspects of the intimate gay relationship: the physical (physical aspects of gay sex, frequency of gay sexual contact, and the sexually exclusive versus the sexually open relationship) and the psychological (commitment, satisfaction, and love within a long-term initimate gay relationship). Naturally, we do not mean to imply that any intimate relationship between two people—either gays or heterosexuals—can be so easily reduced into its physical and psychological spheres, but such an admittedly arbitrary division does allow us to understand better the patterns and dynamics of intimate gay relationships.

THE PHYSICAL SIDE OF GAY RELATIONSHIPS

In 1979 famed sex-researchers William Masters and Virginia Johnson published their eagerly awaited physiological study on gay sexual practices, *Homosexuality in Perspective*.[44] Beginning in 1964 and ending in 1968, 176 gays (94 men and 82 women) and 567 male and female heterosexuals performed various sexual activities under the watchful gaze of scientists and movie cameras. As in their previous studies, Masters and Johnson quickly cautioned the reader not to go too far with their findings because of the possibility that people, no matter their sexual preference, may act quite differently in front of an audience than they would behind closed doors. However, Masters and Johnson's study reveals some interesting insights into the varieties and various sexual techniques found among gay and heterosexual couples.

Obviously, many kinds of sexual activities between gays are similar to those between heterosexuals. Almost everyone kisses, caresses, and experiences orgasm to a similar degree. However, setting aside the similarities, Masters and Johnson found several striking differences in the ways gays and heterosexuals went about their sexual activities.

Long-standing gay couples or those who had lived together for at least a year seemed quite in tune with each other's sexual needs, wants, and pleasures. By and large, gay couples engaged in longer periods of sexual foreplay than did heterosexuals and did not seem eager to reach orgasm quickly. During this extended foreplay, many gay couples talked a great deal to each other, giving subtle cues as to what pleased them sexually. When orgasm was reached, it occurred by means of mutual masturbation, fellatio (oral stimulation of the penis), anal penetration, or some combination thereof. A majority of the gay couples reported enjoying a variety of sexual activities and techniques. One interesting piece of information from the study relates how some gay men experienced heterosexual fantasies during homosexual activity. So much for the purported hatred and/or fear of women thought to afflict gay males.

What may be even more enlightening than the fact that gay males do have heterosexual fantasies are some of the study's findings about the heterosexuals' love-making activities. For the most part, the heterosexual men observed by Masters and Johnson seemed almost obsessed with reaching orgasm. In the minds of most of the heterosexual males, sex seemed to be goal oriented; that is, the final objective—their own orgasm—was the most important element of their sexual activity. Sexual foreplay such as prolonged kissing, caressing, and massaging their partner was nearly absent in some heterosexual couples or little more than a series of prescribed motions that had to be performed before the men got down to the real business at hand—penetration and ejaculation. The heterosexual men in this study showed little sensitivity or knowledge for that matter of the "little things" that would excite and stimulate their female partner. Communication between heterosexual couples was considerably less than the communication that Masters and Johnson found in the gay couples. Not surprisingly, heterosexual females also showed little awareness of the varieties of male genital stimulation that could be employed during periods of sexual foreplay. Overall, the lack of communication and the resulting ignorance about his or her partner's likes and dislikes appeared to be a major stumbling block in a majority of the heterosexual couples' sexual activities. Another interesting note about the heterosexual men studied was that several reported having homosexual fantasies during their sexual activity.

Without going too far in generalizing from such small samples that were observed under what most would agree were unnatural conditions, two features stand out about the sexual activities of long-term gay and heterosexual couples. First, gay couples seem more knowledgeable and sensitive when it comes to each other's physical needs and wants than do heterosexual couples. Second, heterosexual men, at least those studied in this research, seem to approach sex with their minds focused primarily on their own orgasm. Little wonder then that many women complain to one another about their husband's callousness when it comes to his wife's sexual needs.

Many people believe gay males are insatiable in their sexual appetites (another myth some people want to perpetuate). The fact of the matter is that gay couples have sexual relations with about the same frequency or maybe a little more than do heterosexual couples.[45] In a sample of gay males studied by researchers Jay and Young, eleven percent of the gays surveyed reported having sex daily with their partners, thirty-eight percent engaged in sexual relations three to four times a week, forty percent one to two times a week, and eleven percent had sex less than once a week.[46] Bell and Weinberg's sample of 574 white gay males presents a wider range of sexual frequencies, with the following percentages: Three percent reported no sexual activity in the past year, three percent only once or a few times in the past year, three percent every other month, seventeen percent two to three times a month, thirty-two percent once a week, thirty percent two to three times a week, thirteen percent four to six times a week, and four percent seven times or more a week.[47] Approximately half of the gay males in both samples reported having sex on an average of one to three times a week. It seems that sex between two people on the average of one to three times per week is not sufficient evidence to suggest that gay males are sexual satyrs.

Does an intimate relationship require that the two parties remain sexually "faithful" to each other? The answer to this question seems to depend on the two parties. Gay males are often portrayed as less committed to the ideal of sexual exclusivity than are heterosexuals and researchers have found this to be the case. In other words, gay males are less likely to remain monogamous in their relationships than are heterosexuals or lesbians for that matter.[48] However, heterosexual husbands are more likely to have more extramarital relations than are their wives.[49] Thus if gay and heterosexual males are more likely to seek sexual relationships outside of their "primary" relationships than are lesbians and heterosexual women, one might conclude that the promiscuity found among gay males is more a factor of their maleness than of their sexual preference. In the words of one gay male;

> Promiscuity is inbred in all boy children, and since most boy children don't find out they're gay until later in life, their promiscuity has nothing to do with their gayness. It has to do with their *male*ness.[50]

In summary, long-term gay couples seem to have an enjoyable and mutually satisfying sex life, with much of the credit going to their ability and/or willingness to communicate with each other about their physical needs and wants and their approach to sexual relations as more than an occasion for an orgasm. Furthermore, the frequency of sexual activity among gay couples appears to fall across a wide spectrum, ranging from daily sexual encounters to over a year's abstinence. Finally, gay males seem less committed to sexual exclusivity in their primary relations but this is more likely a feature of their being socialized males than of their being gay.

THE PSYCHOLOGICAL SIDE OF GAY RELATIONSHIPS

Most would agree that it is much easier to gather data on the frequency of and techniques used in sexual encounters between people than it is to plumb the psychological components (such as personal joy, satisfaction, happiness, commitment, and love) of an intimate relationship. As we have already noted, gay males are thought by many to be bereft of such psychological intangibles in their lives and in their intimate relationships. The myth of the lonely gay male endlessly cruising for quick and impersonal sex still persists. However, research casts serious doubt on such a generalization. In several studies, the percentages of lesbians and gay males reporting their involvement in long-term and personally satisfying relationships approximates seventy-five and fifty percent, respectively.[51] Even so, some people still insist that what gay couples experience certainly is not real satisfaction and love, at least not like that found among many heterosexual couples.

How then does one measure satisfaction and love in a relationship? One way is to ask each person if he or she finds satisfaction, happiness and feelings of loving and being loved with his or her partner. Researchers who have asked gay men and lesbians to respond to such questions have been virtually unable to differentiate between gay couples' and heterosexual couples' responses on various measures of satisfaction, liking, and love in their relationships.[52]

But what about the values thought essential to and the priorities involved in intimate relationships? Do gays have different concerns, values, and personal priorities in their relationships than do heterosexuals? Anne Peplau and several of her associates investigated the values and priorities within gay and heterosexual relationships and found some interesting answers to these questions. During the late 1970s, Peplau studied the responses given by 127 lesbians, 128 gay men, and 65 male and 65 female heterosexuals to a lengthy questionnaire.[53] Peplau asked her samples to rank on a scale from 1 to 9 the importance of certain features associated with personal relationships (see Figure 12.2). Her findings showed some striking similarities and differences between gays and heterosexuals and—what may be more significant to the issue of intimate relationships—between males and females in general, no matter their sexual preference.

The major difference between gays' and heterosexuals' priorities in their relationships revolve around the issue of sexual fidelity or sexual exclusivity. Both heterosexual males and females place significantly greater importance on the value of remaining sexually faithful than do gay men and lesbians. We might explain this difference by noting the not-so-subtle social pressures for sexual faithfulness that are placed on married heterosexual couples by the institutions of marriage and religion. For the most part, gay couples do not "contract" their primary relationships in the same way that most heterosexual couples do. Furthermore, many married heterosexual couples remain faithful—and thus espouse faithfulness as a value—not because of a personal commitment to the relationship but rather, for example, because of the children, joint properties, and the expenses involved in costly divorce settlements. These "barriers" are nearly nonexistent in most gay relationships, and thus gays have fewer presssures to remain sexually faithful other than their own personal inclination to do so.

What may be more significant about Peplau's research is the degree to which the sexes, no matter their sexual preference, differed with respect to certain values and priorities they felt important in their intimate relationships. Most striking among these differences was the generally greater importance females—both

Some Issues of Concern to Males

Figure 12.2 Comparing priorities in love. How homosexual and heterosexual men and women rate the importance of various aspects of a love relationship. The graph bars, based on data from 100 homosexuals and heterosexuals in the author's study, show the average value they gave each statement, on a scale of 1 to 9 (with 1 meaning they placed little importance on it and 9 indicating they value it highly). In general, differences between men and women on the ratings were greater than between homosexuals and heterosexuals.
Source: L. Peplau, "What Homosexuals Want," Psychology Today, *March 1981, p. 32. Ziff-Davis Publishing Company.*

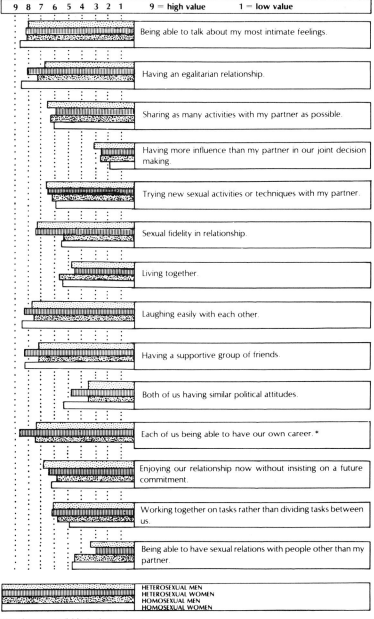

*No data are available for homosexual women

heterosexuals and lesbians—placed on having egalitarian relationships, having a supportive group of friends, sharing similar political attitudes with their partner, and having their own career. Most of these values appear to have a decidedly feminist overtone. (Recall that Peplau gathered her data in the late 1970s and thus most of her female respondents probably had been exposed to feminist issues if not by being involved in the feminist movement itself, then at least through various media presentations.) Feminists have argued that women must have an equal voice in matters relating to their intimate relationships, have their own group of friends and not rely only on their partner as their major conduit to other friendships, and have their own career interests. It would seem, at least among Peplau's female samples, that the feminist perspective has influenced the ordering of priorities in intimate relations among many females.

The one value that all of the groups ostensibly agreed on as a significant one for a loving relationship was being able to communicate intimate feelings to their partner. The ability and willingness to share feelings, thoughts, and concerns was judged by almost everyone in Peplau's study to be an essential ingredient in a loving and involved partnership. What is somewhat surprising about this almost unanimous valuing of communication skills is the fact that in Masters and Johnson's research on sexual intimacies heterosexual couples were lacking in respect to communicating their feelings and desires about sexual matters. It would seem that although most people agree that communication is an extremely important element in an intimate relationship, some are more adept at it than others, at least in certain respects.

SOME CLOSING COMMENTS

Traditionally, most males have felt extremely uneasy and some downright hostile about the issue of homosexuality. The reasons for homophobia among most males are, of course, debatable. Rather than suggest that homophobia springs from some unconscious homosexual urge within males, we tend to think that most males have been taught to hate anything even vaguely feminine as part of the male sex role. Because gay males are often viewed by heterosexuals as being feminine, they become targets for a "real man's" hatred and derision. Furthermore, the social forces reinforcing hatred toward gay people are plentiful; not the least of these is the Judeo–Christian portrayal of gays as wanton and lustful sinners. In addition, a number of other myths have grown up around gays and the gay community. Myths tend to distort and falsify reality, and thus most people do not have a clear understanding of the gay person.

Recent social psychological research has tended to demystify gays and to show them to be human beings whose psychological needs and wants are for all intents and purposes identical to those of heterosexuals. Possibly because of what we have learned recently about gay relationships and their apparent lack of traditionally restrictive male and female roles, heterosexuals would be wise to take a lesson or two from gays in order to improve the relationships between the sexes.

Bell, A., and Weinberg, M. *Homosexualities: A Study of Diversity Among Men and Women.* New York: Simon & Schuster, 1978.

Boswell, J. *Christianity, Social Tolerance, and Homosexuality.* Chicago: University of Chicago Press, 1980.

Freedman, M., and Mayes, H. *Loving Men.* New York: Hark Publishing, 1976.

Silverstein, C., and White, E. *The Joys of Gay Sex.* New York: Crown, 1977.

Tripp, C. *The Homosexual Matrix.* New York: Signet Books, 1975.

Walker, M. *Men Loving Men.* San Francisco: Gay Sunshine Press, 1977.

Weinberg, M., and Williams, C. *Male Homosexuals.* New York: Penguin, 1975.

13

Of unequal power and strained relationships:
POWER AND MALE–FEMALE RELATIONS

In the new code of laws which I suppose it will be necessary for you to make I desire you would remember the ladies, and be more generous and favorable to them than your ancestors. Do not put such unlimited power into the hands of the husbands. Remember all men would be tyrants if they could. If particular care and attention is not paid to the ladies we are determined to foment a rebellion, and will not hold ourselves bound by any laws in which we have no voice, or representation. Abigail Adams[1]

Marriage, to women as to men, must be a luxury, not a necessity; an incident of life, not all of it. And the only possible way to accomplish this great change is to accord to women equal power in the making, shaping and controlling of the circumstances of life. Susan B. Anthony[2]

If there are men who are concerned about their associations with other men—fearing that some may interpret their relations as bordering on the homosexual—there are many more men who are ill at ease about their relations with women. Some suggest that men have always felt uneasy about women and more particularly about male–female affiliations. More often than not men have tended to blame their restiveness over women on the purported mysteries of the feminine mind and makeup. However, in the last decade or so, more and more men have grown apprehensive over certain changes in modern-day male–female relationships. Some men, for example, find themselves uncomfortable when a woman picks up the check in a restaurant or does not wait for a door to be opened. Relations between the sexes are changing, and many men feel more than a vague twinge of anxiety when they consider the changing female role.

In this chapter we will take a critical look at some of the reasons that underlie many men's growing concern over their changing relations with women. We will begin by examining one of the traditional mainstays of male–female alliances, namely, power. First, we will define power and enumerate the different types of power. Next, we will see how men have traditionally been favored with more power in their relations with women and how recent changes in the female's role are beginning to shift the power balance toward women. Finally, we will discuss the institution of marriage and once again find that men have traditionally benefited more from marriage than have women. These changes in power and the recent challenges to the traditional male and female roles in marriage are causing many men concern over their future male sex role.

THE NAME OF THE GAME IS POWER

Power is central in all human relationships, especially those between the sexes. When a wife defers to her husband's choice of a new car or a father finally relents to a mother's insistence that their daughter go off to the state university rather than stay at home and attend the local community college, we can see the everyday uses of power in male–female relations. As it is found in most interpersonal relations, *power* can be defined as "the ability to get another person to think, feel, or do something he or she would not have ordinarily done spontaneously."[3] A person's *use* of his or her power on another is called *influence*. In the interpersonal power game, the person who uses power (influences) is the *influencer* and the person who is affected by the other's power is the *influencee*.

TYPES OF POWER

Six basic types of social power are commonly found in male–female relations: coercive, reward, legitimate, referent, expert, and informational (see "Interpersonal Power").[4] Power can be gained from several different sources. Often a person will have more than one base of power; this is especially true of males in our society.

INTERPERSONAL POWER

Types of Social Power	Interaction Between Influencer and Influencee
Coercive power	Influencer has ability to use threats and/or punishments to force another to comply.
Reward power	Influencer gives positive rewards to induce another's compliance.
Legitimate power	Influencer holds a particular social position or role to which others defer.
Referent power	Influencer is liked or admired by others, and thus others change because of identification.
Expert power	Influencer is thought more knowledgeable in an area, and others defer accordingly.
Informational power	Influencer is able to explain why another should change.

Coercive Power Coercive power involves the threat of punishment or the withdrawal of something of value. Coercive power can be effective only when a person has control over another or has the strength and/or weapons to carry out a threat. For example, when a parent threatens a child with punishment or withdrawal of privileges, usually the parent has control over the child's life and/or the strength to carry out the threat of punishment to ensure the child's compliance with the parent's demands. Sadly, coercive power is a common form of influence in many parent–child and husband–wife relationships. Even though coercive power is relatively easy for those possessing greater strength or control over another to obtain, there are some definite problems in any relationship built primarily on this power base. The relationship between the influencer and influencee will be filled with distrust and either open or hidden conflict. Furthermore, the victim of coercive power will in most instances come to dislike if not despise the coercive person. Often a person subjected to another's coercive control will leave the relationship when the opportunity presents itself. The fact of the matter is that coercive power does not make for a lasting and caring relationship.

Reward Power Reward power involves the dispensing of reinforcements to induce another to change. Rewards or reinforcements can be either material (for example, money) or nonmaterial (for example, praise). Although reward power is generally more effective than coercive power, it also has some drawbacks. If perchance the rewarder loses his or her source of reinforcement, the person who expects the reward may cease to perform the desired behavior. For example, the child who keeps his or her room clean only to get an allowance may let the room become messy if the parents can no longer afford an allowance. Furthermore, rewarding a person for some desired behavior oftentimes does not induce long-term changes in that person's behavior. Reward power is more humane than coercive power, but it often induces a person to change for the wrong reason—only to get a reward, not because the changed behavior is good in and of itself.

Legitimate Power Legitimate power derives from a particular position or role a person occupies. For example, the role of father confers certain authority or power to a man over his children. His influence over his children comes not because of rewards, punishments, or other factors but strictly because he occupies a particular role in relationship to his children. When a child balks at taking out the garbage, with the plaintive, "Why do I have to?" the child is influenced with the words, "Because I'm your father and I told you to do it!" One of the problems with legitimate power is that it tends to put up barriers between the influencer and influencee.

Referent Power Referent power is possessed by people who are admired or liked by others. Most people imitate to some degree or another the behaviors of people they admire. Consequently, the admired person either knowingly or unknowingly has some power over his or her admirers. The son who respects and wants to be like his dad when he grows up is showing the influence the father has over his son.

Expert Power Expert power is found in those people who are thought by others to have expertise in a particular area or subject. For example, a certified mechanic is considered an expert on car maintenance and is therefore able to influence another person when it comes to the subject of cars. The mechanic–father who goes with his son to purchase the son's first car is better able to dissuade his son from buying a "lemon" than is another father who barely knows where to put the gasoline.

Informational Power If "knowledge is power," then a person who uses knowledge and can explain in a credible way why another should do something has informational power. Noteworthy is the fact that informational power differs from expert power. The influencer with expert power needs only to tell another to do something and the other complies because of the presumed expertise of the influencer. The influencer with informational power causes another to change because he or she is able to explain *why* the change is desirable. For example, a father who explains to his daughter's satisfaction the need for her to take difficult science courses in high school to help her get into an excellent university later on is likely to influence his daughter's choice of classes.

Thus far, we have described six types of power. Next we will look at how males and females traditionally have had access to different power bases and how this affects their relationships.

THE SEXES AND THE BALANCE OF POWER

Several factors act as determinants of the amount of power a person holds or can use in his or her relations with others: status, concrete resources, expertise and self-confidence.[5] Males and females traditionally have had differing amounts of power at their disposal. The consequent imbalance of power between the sexes is largely the result of how these determinants relate to each sex.

Status Status is a socially defined position or rank in a society. A person gains status on the basis of possessing certain characteristics (for example, money, titles, beauty) that are prized by the group. A person can either work for and thus earn status (this is known as *achieved status*) or simply have status arbitrarily bestowed by virtue of something he or she has no control over (this is known as *ascribed status*). For example, a student who completes college and gets a BA degree earns achieved status. A person who is exceptionally attractive automatically has ascribed status in a society that values beauty. Societies vary in the kinds of characteristics that they consider valuable, but one characteristic that is prized in nearly every society is being male. These societies place greater value— that is, confer higher status—on their male members than on their female members.

By virtue of the male's greater ascribed status in society, in nearly every situation, males have more legitimate power (power based solely on rank or position) than do women. (An exception to the imbalance in legitimate power is the female's influence over children in the positions of mother and teacher.) When a male and a female are involved in the same activity, the male's activity is usually more highly valued. An example of this is a man's being paid significantly more than a woman for doing the same work. As noted in Chapter 5, Philip Goldberg documented the inequality of legitimate power between the sexes in a study of college women's judgments on academic writing.[6] Recall that Goldberg had two groups of college females read two identical sets of articles, one presumably written by a male and the other presumably written by a female author. The females ranked the presumed male's articles significantly higher with respect to content and style than those supposedly written by the female author. Males, it seems, are the standard or norm by which most people make their judgments of worth or value—even judgments about what is considered as evidencing mental health.[7]

Concrete Resources Obviously a person who possesses or has control over certain resources (such as physical strength, money, sexual favors, and so on) can use them to control others. For example, males are usually physically stronger than females, and some males are inclined to use their strength to control females (coercive power). Furthermore, males in our society are more apt to control money and other valuable commodities, and some males use these resources as rewards to gain control over females (reward power). On the other hand, some females use sexual favors to gain leverage over males (again, reward power). However, on the whole, males have traditionally had more resources and consequently a great number of power bases than females have had.

Some Issues of Concern to Males

Expertise Recall that expert power belongs to those who are believed to possess specialized knowledge and/or skills in a particular field. Once again males tend to be considered as experts in nearly every major field in society (medicine, law, government, science, literature, music, and so on). Even in those fields where females are presumed to have greater experience and knowledge, males are still viewed as experts. A good example of this is found in the area of cooking. Although cooking is traditionally thought of as women's work and one of women's prescribed sex role duties, restaurants are more likely to hire male rather than female cooks and to call these males chefs, not cooks.

Self-Confidence A generalized sense of competence and numerous experiences of success give a person an overall sense of self-confidence. For the reasons outlined above, males tend to possess greater self-confidence in themselves and their abilities than do females. Traditionally, males have been favored in the number of their power bases (coercive, reward, legitimate, expert, and informational) and in the determinants that reinforce a male's use of these bases (higher status, resources, expertise, and self-confidence).

MALE CONCERNS OVER LOST POWER

Females have had fewer opportunities than males have had to exert influence over others. However, in the last several years, a number of shifts in the determinants of power have considerably affected the female's power bases. For example, as more females have entered the job market, they have gained more control over resources such as paychecks, job experience, and marketable skills. Likewise, as more females have entered into various professions, they have gained expertise in areas once viewed as strictly male-dominated fields. We are beginning to witness a certain degree of power equalization between the sexes.

However, not everyone is content with the shift toward a more equal sharing of power. In fact, some males seem concerned or even threatened by it. Perhaps the following anecdote can help to explain why some men feel this way. Arnold Kahn relates the story:

> Imagine a bully in a large sandbox. Whenever another child comes to play in the sandbox, the bully throws sand in his or her face. Imagine that the bully has been doing this for some time. Now, comes a child who understands the arbitrariness of this one individual controlling this large sandbox. This child explains to the bully that it is not good for society for one child to be in this large sandbox, that there is plenty of room for many children to play, and that throwing sand on them is not a nice way to act. Will the bully change his ways? Will he see that by giving up his power and control over the sandbox he will gain friendship and have the opportunity for more fulfilling human interaction? I think the bully will not give in if his whole sense of who he is is based upon his bullying behavior. The bully will not change if he has come to believe it is his right to be a bully, and if by being a bully he feels good about himself. By asking the bully to change one is not only attacking the bully's exercise of power, but attacking the bully's very essence as well. It's not that he likes to bully per se, but that he only feels good and worthy when he does bully, and what's more, he is probably not fully conscious of that fact.[8]

In many respects, males have for centuries been like little bullies throwing sand into the faces of most females who tried to come and play in the sandbox. After bullying for so long, are males apt to move over quietly and welcome females into the sandbox, to begin sharing the buckets and shovels without some resistance? Hardly! Being a bully, even a bully with few friends, has its rewards. The bully has the entire sandbox to himself, every now and then he can experience the exhilaration of pushing another person around, of showing off to all the bystanders just how strong and powerful he really is. For many males, being a bully is fun.

However, the days of the bully–male are limited. A spate of new laws and affirmative action programs are forcing males to own up to the fact that they must make room for females. As more and more females take their rightful places, the once invulnerable all-male power bases will slowly erode. Total equality may be sometime in the future, but it is on the horizon. Some males will hold out; they will kick, scream, and at every available opportunity will continue to throw sand in the faces of the sandbox's new members. But one day even the most ardent male bully will have to share his bucket and shovel with a female who steps in the sandbox and says, "Move over, mister, you're sitting on my space."

INTIMATE MALE–FEMALE RELATIONSHIPS

Intimate relationships between the sexes have long been a favorite subject of poets, playwrights, and novelists; only recently have these special relations captured the attention of social scientists.[9] Intimate male–female relationships are presently in a state of flux. Changing sex roles, greater social acceptance of divorce and serial marriages, changing sexual mores, economic pressures, and greater educational and employment opportunities for females are only a few of the recent social forces shaping new patterns of intimate involvements between the sexes. Some males—and females—find these changes disquieting and uncomfortable. Rather than try to describe all of the ingredients involved in and the various factors affecting intimate male–female relationships, we will focus on a few specific areas, namely, certain values and attitudes underlying intimate relationships, the balance of power in intimate relationships, and the satisfaction and well-being found in intimate relationships.

VALUES THAT BIND AND VALUES THAT SEPARATE

In our society people are raised to value that intense emotional experience characterized by two people's caring, sharing, and yearning for each other, the experience called *love*. Children learn early that the knight will come and kiss awake Sleeping Beauty as their older siblings explore love's mysteries in their first intimate encounters with that special person and as Mom and Dad sit on the front porch sensing the fruits of love in silent reflection. Love is truly a splendid thing or at least something highly valued in most people's way of thinking.

"We're playing house. . . . He's the floor."

For most people true love naturally leads to one of the most important and socially approved intimate relationships: marriage. Love and marriage, if we are to believe the song, go together like a horse and carriage. However, our present-day view on love and marriage is not as ancient a relationship as the joining of a horse with a carriage. Marriages based on love, in fact, were almost nonexistent prior to the seventeenth century.[10] Before the seventeenth century, marriage was the primary social institution that cemented political and economic ties between families, not the natural outcome of two people's intense needs to share their lives together. Nevertheless, today the institution of marriage is the most evident social sign proclaiming the love between two people.

To a large extent, people's views on marriage are shaped by their definitions of sex roles. For example, a male who defines a male's primary responsibilities in marriage as revolving around his "breadwinning" activities will view marriage somewhat differently from one who sees marriage as a partnership in which providing and caretaking of the young are joint undertakings. Generally speaking, males view both the male and female sex roles in a more traditional fashion than females view the two sex roles.[11] In other words, males generally define male and female sex roles as distinct and separate, with females responsible for children and the home and males responsible for the family's economic needs. But what specifically do males and females want from their intimate relationships, especially from marriage? Are their values and priorities different or similar? If they are different, are the differences great enough to cause conflict between males and females? Recent research conducted by Anne Peplau and her colleagues proves enlightening with respect to the values that males and females hold about intimate relationships.

Dyadic Attachment What kinds of personal goals do males and females expect from an intimate relationship like marriage? The most common goals stated by both sexes are affection and companionship.[12] However, researchers have found some differences between the sexes on these two goals with respect to social class.[13] For example, working class husbands tend not to value companionship as much as their wives do.[14]

Anne Peplau, Susan Cochran, and Steven Gordon found that males and females share some values in common and differ in others.[15] Initially, these researchers asked a number of males and females to rank a variety of items on a nine-point scale of desirability or importance (see Figure 12.2, page 257). Some of the items dealt with the mutual sharing of activities and tasks, while others described each partner in an intimate relationship as having a separate life outside of the relationship. After analysing the data, Peplau and her colleagues found that the items fit into one of two categories: dyadic attachment or personal autonomy.

Dyadic attachment refers to those features in a relationship that reflect a person's desire for a close-knit, emotionally secure, and psychologically dependent intimate relationship. A person who feels that a couple should do most things together, should center their lives on each other, and should find most of their social and emotional needs satisfied within the relationship is reflecting and valuing attachment most of all in the intimate relationship. By and large, Peplau found no sex difference in the valuing or devaluing of this feature of togetherness for the respondents' intimate relationships.

Personal Autonomy Personal autonomy refers to a person's desire to have relationships, interests, and activities outside of those found with one's primary partner. For example, a person who desires to have a support group of friends not related to the primary partner and wishes to have a career of his or her own is a person who values his or her own personal autonomy. When it comes to valuing personal autonomy, Peplau and her associates found a slight sex difference in that females in the study generally seemed to value aspects of personal autonomy more than males did. However, rather than suggesting that personal autonomy reflects a basic sex difference, Peplau and other researchers believe that this is related to how males and females define sex roles in general.[16] It seems that males and females who view sex roles in a more open and less restrictive sense are more apt to place greater value on a person's having greater freedom and independence in his or her primary partnership.

Integrating Togetherness and Independence Can a person value features of both dyadic attachment and personal autonomy in the primary intimate relationship? Yes. For example, a female can have a group of friends she enjoys socializing with, a career that demands much of her attention, and a husband with whom she finds many of her emotional, social, and sexual needs met. Many women today have all of these. The problem of integrating togetherness and independence seems to lie in the way society defines the female sex role. Traditionally, women have been expected to center their lives and energies almost

Some Issues of Concern to Males

exclusively on their husbands, children, and activities around the home. The female sex role has promoted the basic value of togetherness over most other values. However, as more women seek careers of their own, along with having a family—as men are expected to do—most people will come to accept the values of togetherness and independence as viable, obtainable, and integrative goals for an intimate relationship.

POWER AND INTIMATE RELATIONSHIPS

As noted earlier, power is a key ingredient in all relationships. When it comes to intimate relationships, who holds more power in the relationship and how do the sexes use their power? Once again, Anne Peplau provides an analysis of how power is distributed in an intimate relationship and how each sex uses its power to influence the other.[17]

The Ideal Versus the Reality of the Balance of Power Males seem less likely to espouse egalitarianism as an important goal for intimate relationships than do females (see Figure 12.2, page 257). Nevertheless, in several studies conducted during the 1960s, researchers concluded that most American couples favored egalitarian relationships as the basis for marriage.[18] Granted, in most marriages, husbands make certain decisions, wives others, and both together still others. But what kinds of decisions do husbands customarily make as opposed to those made by their wives? If a wife controls the time at which supper is served or decides what detergent to use for the family's wash and the husband decides to add another bedroom to the house or trade in the three-year-old car for a new model, are these really the same kinds of decision-making powers? In fact, husbands generally have more power and influence in a marriage than wives do.

Let us examine the following scenario: John and Mary Smith have been married for fifteen years and both have careers. The couple's children, David and Dianne, seem quite happy in the fourth and sixth grades with their many friends. Mary has worked for a stock brokerage firm for the past five years, and John has been a salesperson at a small computer company for the past nine years. The family has a nice home located in a suburb just outside of Boston where all of the Smiths are well-respected and liked by their neighbors. One day Mary's boss tells her that the company has been watching her for over a year and has decided that she is their candidate to head up a new branch office in Denver with a significant increase in her annual salary. Mary goes home that night with the good news, and while at supper, she tells her family that they are heading for Denver!

When the author has presented this scenario in several classes, the reactions have been usually the same from both male and female students. What about the contented husband and children, and how can Mary just assume that the others will want to leave the Boston area for Denver? What about John's career, and what can he do in Denver with no prospects for a job? What about the problem of uprooting the children from their school and all of their friends? A majority of students seem to feel that Mary's potential career advancement does not warrant the uprooting of the Smith family.

But what if John had come home and announced his computer firm was transferring him to another district several states away where he could expect to do better in sales. Would the students feel as adamant about John's uprooting the family? Probably not, because husbands are expected to go where the work is and the family is expected to follow. Husbands, it seems, can make more significant decisions that affect the family than can wives.

But what is the basis for the husband's greater power in marriage? Peplau suggests three factors to account for the imbalance of power that decidedly favors husbands over wives. First, as we noted earlier, males by social convention have more power by virtue of their higher status, and this favored male status accrues to the husband in marriage. Second, males generally have more resources within their marriage (for example, greater income, education, age, and so on) than their wives do, and this gives males an additional edge in the balance of power. Third, females have tended to be more dependent on their husbands for their security than vice versa. Peplau cites Jessie Bernard's analysis of the wife's dependent status as bearing on an egalitarian relation:

> Take a young woman who has been trained for feminine dependencies, who wants to "look up" to the man she marries. Put her at a disadvantage in the labor market. Then marry her to a man who has a slight initial advantage over her in age, income, and education, shored up by an ideology with the male bias. . . . Then expect an egalitarian relationship?[19]

Power Tactics How do the sexes influence each other, especially in those situations where there is a conflict between them? Researchers have found some evidence that the sexes do in fact use different tactics to influence each other in conflict situations. For example, in studies of dating couples and newlyweds, females reported using more indirect or emotional methods such as pouting or becoming silent and withdrawn in order to influence males. Males noted that they were more likely to rely on logical arguments to persuade the female to change her mind.[20] Apparently, there is some truth to the common stereotypic view of females and males in their use of different power tactics in conflict situations.

However, we have noted elsewhere how males are socialized to be less emotionally expressive and taught that they should rely on logical arguments to persuade others. Likewise, females are expected to express their feelings openly. What would people think of a husband who softly cries as he pleads with his wife to let him go bowling with the guys? Why, most would think that he is no man at all. But what of the wife who silently throws the burnt toast at her husband who disagrees with her decision to buy a new coat? That seems totally in character and probably a good way to get the coat if her husband doesn't want his next meal overcooked. How the sexes are raised and how they are taught to deal with conflict seems to play a large role in the sex differences to conflict resolution. Another feature that we should not forget is that pleading, crying, withdrawal, and other emotional displays are more appropriate in conflict situations for the person with less power in the relationship.[21] Relying on displays of emotion is basically a tactic used by children and females (powerless people). The common tactical differences in male-female conflict situations seem related, first, to the socialization of sex role differences and, second, to the relative differences in power found between males and females.

SATISFACTION AND WELL-BEING

When married men get together they often lament about how misunderstood, mistreated, and henpecked they are by their wives. If we were to believe the talk, we would think that marriage was fraught with problems and restrictions and that a married man's lot must be a rather bleak and unhappy one. However, the research into marital satisfaction presents an almost entirely different picture. Overall, researchers have found that husbands and wives agree that marriage provides considerable personal happiness and satisfaction.[22] Despite the fact that many men feel compelled to "bad mouth" marriage, there is some evidence that in certain ways males may benefit from marriage more than females do.

Generally speaking, marriage provides more benefits to an individual than being single, divorced, or widowed, and this is especially true for males. When it comes to personal well-being and mental and physical health, husbands tend to accrue more positive benefits from marriage than do wives.[23] Not all of the causes for this sex difference in marital benefits are fully understood, but we can list several of the more obvious ones.

First, in most traditional (male-dominant) marriages, the husband gains the services of someone—the wife—to cook, clean, and do the daily chores around the house. Although the husband is expected to work outside of the home, after work he often uses the remainder of the day for hobbies and other leisure-time pursuits. In those marriages where both the husband and wife work outside of the home, the wife is still more likely to be responsible for most of the house-work.[24] In most cases the wife who holds a full-time job finds herself strapped with double-duty, and for many wives this can cause distress, frustration, and considerable fatigue. Thus, in most male-dominant marriages and many egalitarian ones for that matter, husbands definitely benefit more than wives.

A second benefit many males gain in marriage is the number of situations in which the wife acts as a kind of socioemotional bridge between her husband and others. For example, many husbands feel so inept or uncomfortable in dealing with special emotional relations such as those with children, parents, or close friends that the wife will act as a personal emissary to convey the husband's feelings to these other people. Because so many males come to believe that they should not show tenderness, caring, and sensitivity, they leave these expressions to their wives to carry out.

One other area in which males benefit more than females do from mariage is that of physical health care. The role of wife and mother includes the expectation of caring for the health and physical well-being of family members. Consequently, many wives express concern over their husband's physical health, often prompting him to take better care of himself than he would if he were single, divorced, or widowed. For many husbands, the first person they turn to with their aches and pains is the ever-present family nurse, who is expected to make it all better. Not surprisingly, wives do not receive the same concern over their health from their husbands.

Although both husbands and wives generally report overall satisfaction with marriage, most husbands accrue more benefits than do their wives.

SOME CLOSING COMMENTS

Many men today are becoming more concerned about their relationships with women. Much of this concern revolves around the issues that are affecting women's lives. As women change their definitions of themselves, their roles, and their goals, men are having to confront many well-established features in their own lives. One of the most serious concerns among men is the change in the balance of power between the sexes. As women gain more resources and expertise and become more self-confident, they are bound to gain more power in their relations with men. For some men this presents a real problem—the loss of power.

When we examine intimate heterosexual relationships more closely, we find still other areas that threaten some men. As women strive to establish more personal autonomy or independence in their lives, their intimate male partners are going to have to confront a change in their male role. As women change, men can no longer be the only focus of women's lives. A man will have to learn to share his female partner with others. For many men this may prove very difficult indeed.

The future of marriage is up for grabs. Many women are likely to begin to assert their needs and to ask more from the marital relationship than they have in the past. Again, this may prove threatening to some men. Males and females will continue to seek each other out for companionship and affection, of course, but men will have to come to grips with new female demands and adjust or continue to feel uncomfortable with what is inevitable—changing male-female relationships.

SUGGESTED READINGS

Bernard, J. *The Future of Marriage*. New York: Bantam, 1972.

Blood, R., and Wolfe, D. *Husbands and Wives: The Dynamics of Married Living*. New York: Free Press, 1960.

Cromwell, R., and Olson, D., eds. *Power in Families*. New York: Wiley, 1975.

Komarovsky, M. *Blue-Collar Marriage*. New York: Random House, 1967.

Lasswell, M., and Lobsenz, N. *Styles of Loving*. New York: Ballantine, 1980.

Pietropinto, A., and Simenauer, J. *Husbands and Wives*. New York: Berkeley Books, 1981.

14

Of clashing values and a questionable future:
WHERE TO FROM HERE?

> *A new civilization is emerging in our lives, and blind men everywhere are trying to suppress it. This new civilization brings with it new family styles; changed ways of working, loving, and living; a new economy; new political conflicts; and beyond all this an altered consciousness as well. Pieces of this new civilization exist today. Millions are already attuning their lives to the rhythms of tomorrow. Others, terrified of the future, are engaged in a desperate, futile flight into the past and are trying to restore the dying world that gave them birth.* Alvin Toffler[1]

With less than two decades left in the twentieth century, people are beginning to look ahead to the next century and to ask what the future holds. With continuous upheavals in social, political, and economic spheres, it is only normal for a person to be concerned about how the changes in these areas will affect him or her personally. What will the institution of the family be like? Will childless couples become the norm? Will a woman become President of the United States? Will husbands stay at home while wives go off to the office? Will men become more submissive if women become more assertive? All of these questions and countless others focus on some of the concerns most people have about the future of sex roles.

There is a basic problem inherent in any attempt to answer these questions. Simply put, there is no way of *knowing* the future. We could do what farsighted social scientists have done by examining past and present trends in the institution of marriage and then projecting these trends into the future.[2] Or, we could examine the works of creative science-fiction writers and read what futuristic possibilities await the sexes in some as yet uncharted alien civilization.[3] But these writers' creative views of the future may have little resemblance to what may actually happen in the year 2001, much less 3001.

In this chapter we will refrain from prognosticating the future of sex roles and, instead, outline some of the social pressures that either push for change or support the status quo in society's sex roles and consider whether real changes in traditional male and female sex roles can occur in the near future. There are, of course, advantages that both men and women have by virtue of the traditional ways of defining sex roles. Some people are genuinely skeptical about the possibility that a majority of men may willingly give up their privileged position, which has accrued from the age-old definitions of masculinity and the male sex role.

CLASHING VALUES AND CHANGING TIMES

Upon occasion most people have been faced with two conflicting or mutually exclusive social pressures. For a time people may refuse to choose either alternative; however, if the pressures are strong enough and people cannot avoid the situation any longer, they may react with anger toward one or both of the pressures. In many respects, contemporary men are faced with a real dilemma in the guise of conflicting social pressures over their sex role.

On the one hand, adult men today were socialized to act in certain ways and to value specific ideals. To be a real man was fairly easy to accomplish and adhere to. At an early age, these men learned that as long as a male did not act feminine, attained some measure of success in work and provided for his family, stood up for his rights when necessary and was willing to fight if need be, showed the proper interest in sex (always), and displayed a tough and self-reliant manner, he was a man. On the other hand, certain segments of society are beginning to undercut these values and introduce new role expectations for the male to live up to. In a real sense, the rules of the game of what it means to be a man are being tampered with. Consequently, it is getting harder to fulfill the male sex role.

We can be more specific about the pressures some men are facing in their lives. Some women are demanding (not requesting) that men act in ways that may make some men uncomfortable—for example, that they be more communicative about their feelings and more open in male–female relations. Some employers are demanding that their male employees learn new skills; for example, many employers expect all of their supervisors to take human relations courses, become proficient in interpersonal communications, accept female bosses, and learn how to be more open and sensitive to their workers' personal needs. What is a male to do when much of what he learned as a boy conflicts with what others expect of him as an adult? Bernie Zilbergeld provides an interesting anecdote about one man's quandary over his interactions with women.

> A woman told us this story about a man she knows. He had always performed small courtesies for women. One day a woman for whom he had opened a door in a large department store loudly lambasted him ("Don't you think I can open my own door, you pig?"), which was quite different from the smiles and thank-you's he was used to. He was embarrassed and gave serious thought to the matter. He decided that the new order was here and he would have to conform—no more courtesies. Things went fine until one day when he was roundly criticized for not offering his seat to a woman on a bus. He thought about this for some time and came to a conclusion: "There's no way of doing things right. If I act the way I was brought up to act, that's wrong. If I don't act that way, that isn't right either. I'm going back to being the same old asshole I've always been and I don't care if it's right or not."[4]

Men, of course are not the only ones experiencing role conflict these days. Women are also finding themselves besieged from different sources about how they should live their lives. Speaking about the social pressures facing countless millions of American housewives, sociologist Myra Marx Ferree has noted,

> The American housewife feels herself to be besieged. On one side stand traditionalists, who tell her that her greatest pleasures come from satisfying the needs of others: making a home for her family, raising healthy children, and pleasing her husband. On the other side stand egalitarians, who tell her that her needs are important, too. A fulfilling career has generally come to mean one outside the home.[5]

As in all battles over changing sex roles, one side paints the image of the housewife as living a life of boredom and servitude while the other glories in the fulfillment and satisfaction of the homemaker. Both positions carry a seed of truth and a sack of falsehoods.

Let us take a closer look at several specific changes that the sexes are encountering. First of all, the institution of the family is radically different from what it was a mere fifty years ago.[6] The popular conception of a typical American family—the "Ozzie and Harriet" version—consisting of a working husband-father, a full-time homemaker-mother, and two children is anything but the norm nowadays. Over fifty percent of all married women now hold full-time jobs outside of the home while still being primarily responsible for the housework. The new version of marriage American style finds couples waiting longer to get married (average age: 24.0 for males, and 21.5 for females) and once married postponing having children for several years if not entirely. Likewise, many people are opting to stay single or, if married, to have more than one spouse in serial fashion "until death do them part."

A second social and economic change bearing on people's sex roles is the breakdown in the traditional division of labor. In the past certain jobs were considered for men only and other jobs for women only. Currently, however, women are taking jobs as coal miners, truck drivers, and factory workers.[7] Men, on the other hand, are moving in greater numbers into nursing and teaching and even encroaching into the once strictly female world of the secretary.[8]

A third change affecting males and females, but especially the latter, is the greater control women have over conception. With the "pill" and other types of contraception, women are now freer to engage in sexual relationships without fear of pregnancy. Consequently, there has been a lessening in the traditional double standard of sexual conduct. A sign of the changing times in sexual relations outside of marriage is found in the numbers of people who accept an unmarried couple's right to live together. In the eighteen- to twenty-nine-year-old group, almost eighty percent of those who know such live-in couples report that the arrangement is okay. Over sixty percent of those between the ages of thirty and forty-four report a favorable attitude toward such couples.[9]

A fourth social change, primarily affecting men, is a decline in the emphasis on the breadwinner role. Because a majority of married women are now members of the paid employment force, the expectation that the husband be the sole provider for his family is no longer as strong an expectation as it once was. What impact the dual-career couple will have on marriage and motherhood remains to be seen.

One last social phenomenon affecting men's and women's roles is not so much a change but rather an addition to the socializing agents that mold the thinking of each sex. For example, up until a few years ago, if a woman wanted to read about the lives of women, she was pretty much confined to the ever-popular romance novel. Today a whole new genre of fictitional literature, called *"feminist literature,"* has developed. Female authors such as Doris Lessing, Rita Mae Brown, Toni Morrison, and Erica Jong tell of strong, competent, and intensely real women struggling in a harsh world and, for the most part, surviving. Men, on the other hand, have not been as fortunate in finding fictional literature that presents anything other than the traditional macho plot. However, we can hope that literature such as John Irving's *The World According to Garp,* a story about a man raised by a feminist mother, is not a solitary literary phenomenon.

One might think that all of these social changes taken together would push men and women inexorably toward a new definition of their masculinity and femininity. But sex roles do not lend themselves to change without some resistance. Next we will discuss some of the resistive forces that keep many people from changing the traditional descriptions and norms thought appropriate for each sex.

Change is uncomfortable! Even though everything and everyone changes, people can become anxious and even belligerent when they are asked to change their long-cherished beliefs, attitudes, and behaviors. There is something soothing, secure, and satisfying when things stay much the same. When it comes to changing something as ingrained as how a person defines his or her sex role, there is likely to be considerable resistance.

A majority of men and women today are being pulled, pushed, tugged, and squeezed by a variety of social forces demanding that women and men act in this or that fashion. Is it any wonder that many people end up like the man in Zilbergeld's anecdote, frustrated, confused, angry, or some combination thereof? As a consequence many people think, "Why change and be condemned when I can stay in my old comfortable rut and, yes, still be condemned, but, at least, comfortable." Many people experience considerable role strain with the inherent conflict between certain sex role expectations and their personality make-up, but is changing to another way of behaving going to be any easier? The answer for most people is definitely no. As we have said, change is uncomfortable, but discomfort is not the only reason that people resist changing their definitions of sex roles. In fact, some definite values accrue to each sex from their respective traditional sex roles: Men hold onto power and women retain security. Let us examine these two so-called advantages in adhering to traditional sex roles.

In analyzing the interactions between the sexes, we find a basic inequality between them, an inequality based on males' having more power as defined by their sex role over their own lives and the lives of women (see Chapter 13).[10] It seems plausible to suggest that many if not most men just plain enjoy having status, power, and control over women. Given the choice, almost anyone would prefer power to powerlessness. Consequently, we can assume that most men are unwilling to change the traditional sex role configuration if all they can see is that they will lose some of their power. Even the ideal of an egalitarian relationship is undesirable to some men because men still would have to surrender some of their traditional power to make male-female relationships more equitable. Many men feel that *any* change in the definition of the sex roles means a loss for them, and they are quick to ask, "What do I gain in the bargain?"

But men are not the only ones digging in their heels, holding the line, so to speak, against any real or significant change in the traditional sex roles. Many women are fighting just as hard as men are. We need only point to the very effective campaign that Phyllis Schlafly and her STOP ERA movement mounted against the ratification of the Equal Rights Amendment. Another example of the female resistance to changing sex roles can be seen in the "feminist backlash literature" as exemplified by Marabel Morgan's *The Total Woman* and Helen Andelin's *Fascinating Womanhood*.[11]

Why would women be against sex role changes that would result in their gaining greater power and a greater voice in their own lives? There is no easy answer to this question. Women have lived for so long in an inferior position that it is a

Some Issues of Concern to Males

wonder that so many women have stepped forward and challenged the entrenched patriarchal system in the first place. Still, a much larger number of women have not challenged the system but appear content to let it continue as it has for well over two thousand years. Old ways take a long time to change. But another factor also contributes to many women's refusal to change. In many ways, women have not gained the educational and economic bases for a complete overhaul of the system of sex roles. A large number of American women are like the black slaves of the pre-Civil War era. Lacking in marketable skills and undereducated for today's technological society, what would these women do if the sex roles changed overnight? Starve? Thus another of the reasons that some women are withholding their support from the feminist movement may be that they feel more secure in their present state. Secure and provided for, these women are dependent on men's traditional role as primary breadwinner.[12] For many women, being dependent on a good provider is presently their only version of the American dream.

We should not think that because men and women are focusing on different issues that their roles are mutually exclusive. A change in how women act will directly affect how men act and vice versa. Too often this fact is overlooked when we talk of changing the system. As social scientists Betty and Theodore Roszak have pointed out, both sexes' roles are interdependent and for the most part supportive of each other. Consequently, the old game of playing masculine and feminine will not change easily (see "He Is Playing Masculine . . . She Is Playing Feminine").

Let us now turn our attention to the fledgling men's movement that supports changes in the traditional male sex role.

CHANGING THE GUARD—OR ARE WE?

As we suggested above men today are caught between two cultures as it were: the one culture—long-established and grounded in history—demands that men act according to traditional patterns of dominance, strength, and power; the other culture—new and as yet uncertain of all of its tenets—decrees that men give up part of their power in favor of sexual equality and learn to permit themselves options once thought unmanly.

Even for men attending college, where new ideas, values, and behaviors are supposedly more a part of everyday life, confusion over the male sex role is readily apparent. A majority of the college men sociologist Mirra Komarovsky interviewed for her book *Dilemmas of Masculinity* reported that they preferred "intellectual" women *but* were quick to add that they did not want their dates to outshine them intellectually. In addition, the college men noted that they wanted their future wives to have their own challenging and exciting careers *but* did not

HE IS PLAYING MASCULINE . . . SHE IS PLAYING FEMININE

He is playing masculine *because* she is playing feminine. She is playing feminine *because* he is playing masculine.

He is playing the kind of man that she thinks the kind of woman she is playing ought to admire. She is playing the kind of woman that he thinks the kind of man he is playing ought to desire.

If he were not playing masculine, he might well be more feminine than she is—except when she is playing very feminine. If she were not playing feminine, she might well be more masculine than he is—except when he is playing very masculine.

So he plays harder. And she plays . . . softer.

He wants to make sure that she could never be more masculine than he. She wants to make sure that he could never be more feminine than she. He therefore seeks to destroy the femininity in himself. She therefore seeks to destroy the masculinity in herself.

She is supposed to admire him for the masculinity in him that she fears in herself. He is supposed to desire her for the femininity in her that he despises in himself.

He desires her for her femininity which is *his* femininity, but which he can never lay claim to. She admires him for his masculinity which is *her* masculinity, but which she can never lay claim to. Since he may only love his own femininity in her, he envies her her femininity. Since she may only love her own masculinity in him, she envies him his masculinity.

The envy poisons their love.

He, coveting her unattainable femininity, decides to punish her. She, coveting his unattainable masculinity, decides to punish him. He denigrates her femininity—which he is supposed to desire and which he really envies—and becomes more aggressively masculine. She feigns disgust at his masculinity—which she is supposed to admire and which she really envies—and becomes more fastidiously feminine. He is becoming less and less what he wants to be. She is becoming less and less what she wants to be. But now he is more manly than ever, and she is more womanly than ever.

Her femininity, growing more dependently supine, becomes contemptible. His masculinity, growing more oppressively domineering, becomes intolerable. At last she loathes what she has helped his masculinity to become. At last he loathes what he has helped her femininity to become.

So far, it has all been symmetrical. But we have left one thing out.

The world belongs to what his masculinity has become.

The reward for what his masculinity has become is power. The reward for what her femininity has become is only the security which his power can bestow upon her. If he were to yield to what her femininity has become,

Source: B. Roszak and T. Roszak, Foreword to *Masculine/Feminine,* ed. B. Roszak and T. Roszak (New York: Harper & Row, 1969,) pp. vii–viii.

> he would be yielding to contemptible incompetence. If she were to acquire what his masculinity has become, she would participate in intolerable coerciveness.
>
> She is stifling under the triviality of her femininity. The world is groaning beneath the terrors of his masculinity.
>
> He is playing masculine. She is playing feminine.
>
> How do we call off the game?

want their wives' careers to interfere with their duties of house and children. Thus men seem to want it both ways: the privileges of the old and the stimulating options of the new (see "I Can Be Open").

When Betty Friedan described "the problem that has no name" in her book *The Feminine Mystique,* women got angry. Women got angry because Friedan held a mirror up before them and forced them to take a long, hard look at themselves and their lives. Women got angry and screamed back at the mirror—NO MORE! Women who had felt alone and alienated all of a sudden felt a kindred spirit, a type of sisterhood with thousands and thousands of other women. The problem that had been one of the best kept secrets was finally exposed in public and women got angry. Friedan described the problem in the following manner:

> The problem lay buried, unspoken, for many years in the minds of American women. It was a strange stirring, a sense of dissatisfaction, a yearning that women suffered in the middle of the twentieth century in the United States. Each suburban wife struggled with it alone. As she made the beds, shopped for groceries, matched slipcover material, ate peanut butter sandwiches with her children, chauffeured Cub Scouts and Brownies, lay beside her husband at night—she was afraid to ask even herself the silent question—"Is this all?"[13]

Angry women began to meet in small consciousness-raising groups (C-R groups) in kitchens and living rooms around the country. Beginning in these small C-R groups, women gathered into larger groups and the women's movement was born. The women's movement became dedicated to changing social structures and public policies that affected women's lives. The women's movement that was spawned in the late 1960s has become one of the most influential social movements of the twentieth century. And all because women got angry. But what about men? Are men becoming angry and not just confused and distressed? Is there a men's movement designed to challenge and to change the system of sexual inequality and redress the imbalance in the male-dominant power structures? What about men's liberation?

There is no single, nationally recognized organization similar to the National Organization for Women (NOW) that people can look to as representing a men's movement. Thus we must look at several different sources in order to try to answer these questions.

"I CAN BE OPEN"

At 22, Bob Amore belongs to a generation still grappling with the transitional roles of the sexes. Like many of his campus contemporaries, he supports most feminist goals as a matter of simple justice. "It seems moronic to me that a women could be working her butt off as hard as a man and not get paid as much," he says. And like many young males, he also harbors some primal notions of the rights of men. A girlfriend paying her own way on a date makes him feel "a little less macho," he says. And a girlfriend driving the car is even worse: "I feel like a little kid being driven around by my mother. When I'm driving, I feel like I'm in control. For one thing, I like the idea that I'm *protecting* her."

As a music and acting major at Northwestern University, Amore is the product of two cultures—the traditional one he grew up in and the liberated one that surrounds him at school. Raised in a Roman Catholic family in Brooklyn, N.Y., he senses that he is more conservative on the issues of the women's movement than some of his friends. But he knows he has become more liberal than his father, a teacher. "I used to copy my father's ideas," he recalls. "I can remember thinking, 'Who do these bra-burning women think they are?' Today, I'm liable to pick up one of their magazines and read through it. I've actually been reading that 'trash' and there are some good things in it. So I've become a lot more open-minded to feminism."

The Upper Hand

Amore's parents divorced when he was a college freshman, and he believes it was due, in part, to his father's being too "overbearing" in the marriage. He is certain he will be more "understanding" toward his own wife when he marries. Yet he is equally convinced of his need to have the upper hand. "I don't think my family would work if I wasn't the head of it in a domineering way," he says. "I think I need it, and I think my wife would have to know I need it." His present girlfriend surely knows: though he doesn't hesitate to do the cooking and cleaning in his own off-campus apartment, when he has dinner at her house, there is not much question about who does the chores. "Oh, I may help her with the dishes," he says, "but in a very chauvinistic way I feel she's the woman and that's her job. Sometimes she likes it, sometimes she hates it."

Amore is aware that his cherished ideas of male and female roles are undergoing a gradual, significant change, but he is still confused. "Intellectually I realize women are taking on different roles but I still like to think of them in a rather traditional sense," he says. "Maybe women really are superior to men, as I heard a psychiatrist say on a TV show. They seem to

Source: David Gelman, *Newsweek,* January 16, 1978, p. 60. Copyright 1978, by Newsweek, Inc. All Rights Reserved. Reprinted by Permission.

cope with strain better and they don't need their egos boosted all the time like we do. Guys still need to hang around together, reinforce each other. That hasn't changed from my dad's time."

Breaking the Barrier

The dawning sense of male hangups helped Amore work through an important decision. As a youngster, he explains, he had been enthralled at performances of the American Ballet Theater, and he harbored a secret desire to be a dancer. But although dancing would have helped him advance his acting ambitions, it struck him as being too "feminine." Instead, Amore says, he went in for sports and weight-lifting. "I guess I considered myself more masculine the more I lifted weights. But recently, I broke down the barrier in myself and started practicing ballet. I'd worked through the whole 'queer' stigma. And I realize now that I had more hangups when I lifted weights than now that I'm dancing. I love it. I look better and feel better—though my father still has a problem with it."

In spite of himself and the covenants of his upbringing, Amore finds the new sexual egalitarianism is having its effect on him. He never would have taken up ballet, he says, except that it has become more acceptable for men who are "straight." And his tensions about masculinity have eased up in other ways as well. "Nowadays I'm still not sure of myself about a lot of things," he says, "But at least I can be open. I can pinpoint my problems, even if I don't know what to do." And just being able to admit that uncertainty separates the new male from the old macho.

ARE MEN CONFUSED AND ANGRY?

Based on research such as that of Mirra Komarovsky conducted with men at Columbia University, we can assume that many men are confused and distressed about what it means to be a man today.[14] Judging by the recent outpouring of literature, the single biggest area of confusion exists in men's sexuality.[15] Books abound on the various sexual problems men are facing in their relationships. But are men angry about the limitations and restrictions posed by their traditional male sex role? This question defies a simple yes or no response. Regional organizations such as the Maryland-based Free Men take a decidedly angry stance when it comes to the so-called men's questions. Executive director of Free Men, Richard Haddad, speaks of the anger men should feel about their restrictive roles, but his message has more of an antifeminist ring than an anger directed at the male-dominant power structure that oppresses men and women alike.[16] One indication of possible anger among some men can be found in courtrooms across the nation. Men are beginning to challenge the old "favoritisms" that often are granted to women in divorce and child-custody cases.[17] Nevertheless, men's confusion over various features of their sex role expectations does not yet seem to have flared into full-fledged anger among most men.

ARE C-R GROUPS COMMON IN MEN'S CIRCLES?

Consciousness raising groups are a relatively recent social phenomenon. Warren Farrell, author of *The Liberated Man,* defines a C-R group as

> . . . a group of persons meeting regularly to develop each other's awareness of alternative ways of overcoming the limitations on our lives that evolved from our view of ourselves as masculine or feminine. The consciousness-raising group creates a subculture which encourages questioning and experimenting in ways that are applicable to one's personal life.[18]

There is no telling how many men in America have attended a C-R meeting and then become regular members of a C-R group. But why would men join a C-R group in the first place? Obviously, men are confused, but have they been alienated, discriminated against in job placement, held back from promotions, sexually harrassed, and the brunt of countless personal indignities from others' words and deeds? Hardly! Then why do men join C-R groups? Psychologists Alan Gross, Ronald Smith, and Barbara Strudler Wallston believe that many of the early men's C-R groups acted as a kind of refuge for worried, anxious, and confused men. According to their analysis,

> Many of the early men's consciousness-raising (C-R) groups were organized by men whose relationships with women had been stressed as women became more dissatisfied with traditional heterosexual relationships. Joining men's groups was one response to relationship stress that often threatened to destabilize marriages and other primary relationships. Some joined seeking support during crises such as loss of child custody. Others were motivated to join after observing benefits obtained by women from women's movement groups that offered support and meaningful friendship not readily accessible to men.[19]

We do not have to stretch our imagination too far to picture an upset husband or distraught lover spending an evening alone while his wife or female intimate attended her C-R group—and asking himself, "What can those women be talking about all evening? Is she (wife or lover) telling them about our sex life? Why does she have to go and waste her time? What the hell is a C-R group, anyway?" As women began to change because of their meetings, the men in their lives had to deal with it. One of the ways they found to deal with it was to start their own C-R groups. Thus in the early 1970s men began to question what it meant to be a man in the company of other men. The C-R phenomenon spread—not as quickly among men as it had among women—and some men joined with other men and began to move into a new consciousness.

Some Issues of Concern to Males

"Your mother's at a lib meeting. Now eat your olives and shut up."

WHAT ABOUT A MEN'S SOCIAL MOVEMENT?

Social psychologists are interested in how influences associated with large-scale social movements such as the civil rights movement and the student movement of the 1960s change people's lives. Social psychologist Muzafer Sherif has provided a list of common characteristics that taken together define a social movement.[20] Sherif's six characteristics can be summarized as follows:

1. A social movement begins when people come together and focus their energies on some perceived inequality or unfair treatment or situation.
2. A social movement includes both those who are directly affected by some inequality or unfair treatment or situation and others who sympathize with these people's plight.
3. A social movement must develop a definite ideology and a structured organization that is identified with the ideology.
4. Change is the sole purpose of a social movement, although personal needs will be filled from participation in the social movement.
5. A social movement must have some method, usually planned, by which change can come about over time.
6. Publicity of the organization's perception of the problems and activities sponsored by the organization are the chief methods used to bring about change.

Taking each of Sherif's six characteristics, let us see how the "fledgling men's movement" fares.

1. *Coming together with a problem.* As we have already noted, some men have joined men-only C-R groups to share their problems and confusions and, more generally, to gain a perspective on the limitations of the male sex role. The first National Men and Masculinity Conference was held in Knoxville, Tennessee in the spring of 1975. Since then, there has been an average of one national men's conference each year devoted to a particular theme (for example, "Men Supporting Men," State College, Pennsylvania; "Straight/White/Male: Wrestling With the Master Culture," Des Moines, Iowa; and "Men & Sexism," Los Angeles, California). With respect to the first criterion for a social movement, men, albeit in small numbers, have joined hands and focused on specific concerns and issues relating to their lives.

2. *Men and their allies.* The second criterion requires not only people who are directly affected by the movement's issues but a gathering of allies as well to create a social movement. In addition to men such as those mentioned in number one above, are there allies in the men's movement? For example, are any women involved in the men's movement? The fact of the matter is that at most national men's conferences women have not always been welcomed participants. Even though Barbara Strudler Wallston was an invited keynote speaker at the Los Angeles men's conference, in the main, women have not been very visible. Nevertheless, there is evidence that a few women have generously provided support for a feminist-based men's movement. Take, for example, the glowing testament written by Gloria Steinem in the introduction to Marc Feigen Fasteau's book *The Male Machine:*

This book by Marc Feigen Fasteau is very, very different. There is honesty on every page, and somehow the reader senses that the change being discussed here is not just theory. It is practice that has been lived and tested by the author himself.

The most obvious proof of this is the author's choice of both viewpoint and example. Yes, this book is about the destructiveness of the sexual caste system and as such, it supports most feminist criticisms of current injustice. But there is none of the usual "let-me-help-you" liberalism that demands gratitude, and probably continued inferiority, in return. On the contrary, the author doesn't attempt to write, sympathetically or otherwise, about the cause of women at all. His viewpoint is his own: that of a male human being looking at the masculine stereotype, and assessing the ways that stereotype has formed or limited him and the men around him. His examples are taken from his own life, from numerous interviews with other men in a variety of jobs and social conditions, and from an analysis of the many institutions and decision-making processes that are crucially influenced by the masculine mystique. It is precisely this self-interest, this frank concern with problems of the male role, that makes him a more trustworthy feminist ally than any mere supporter or sympathizer could ever be. . . .

This book is a complement to the feminist revolution, yet it is one no woman could write. It is the revolution's other half. True, no group of people give up power voluntarily, and therefore women can never relax efforts to overthrow the structures of patriarchal power. But there will be male allies like this one; men who also want a world in which we can shed the crippling stereotypes of sex or race, and become the unique individuals we were born to be.[21]

3. *Ideology and organization.* If there is a prevalent ideology that the men's movement rallies around it is *sexism.* Our society is controlled by males, mainly white and purportedly straight (heterosexual). This is the basic issue that not only the feminist movement but also a smattering of "changing men" are focusing their energies against. This ideological perspective is captured in books such as Jon Snodgrass's anthology *For Men Against Sexism.*[22] As for the organization element, there is no regional or national organization that speaks for the men's movement.

4. *Change.* If, as Sherif claims, change is the sole purpose of a social movement, what change or changes does the men's movement seek? Are men seeking change in the male-oriented power structures, for example? There are just too many privileges and perks that come to most men simply because they are male. Some men who identify with the men's movement are working to change such things as the divorce laws and laws that govern child custody cases, which in many states still favor women. And there are some men who favor the abolishment of the *whole* traditional male role system (see "Berkeley Men's Center Manifesto"). However, most of the men who attend national men's conferences and meet regularly in men's C-R groups appear to be more concerned about finding a forum to ventilate their confusions and distress and gaining other men's support in personal and social areas than about working for a change in political structures.[23]

5. *Method for change.* The feminist movement is most often associated with efforts on behalf of the passage of the Equal Rights Amendment to the Constitution. Feminists have campaigned, lobbied, and generally used every legitimate tactic to accomplish this goal. As for men in the men's movement, there is no evidence of a national method for implementing change with the exception of a few regional groups that are working for changes in the laws mentioned above. How can one expect a method for change when there is no national or general issue or goal save that of personal catharsis?

6. *Publicity.* The men's movement has received little in the way of national exposure. True, Robert Brannon and Joseph Pleck have appeared on the "Phil Donahue Show" to discuss men's lives and their roles. Countless articles and papers have appeared in various and sundry magazines, newspapers, and journals.[24] But for the most part, much of the public is unaware of what may be called a men's movement.

BERKELEY MEN'S CENTER MANIFESTO

We, as men, want to take back our full humanity. We no longer want to strain and compete to live up to an impossible oppressive masculine image— strong, silent, cool, handsome, unemotional, successful, master of women, leader of men, wealthy, brilliant, athletic, and "heavy." We no longer want to feel the need to perform sexually, socially, or in any way to live up to an imposed male role, from a traditional American society or a "counterculture."

We want to love ourselves. We want to feel good about and experience our sensuality, emotions, intellect, and daily lives in an integrated way. We want to express our feelings completely and not bottle them up or repress them in order to be "controlled" or "respected." We believe it requires strength to let go and be "weak." We want to enjoy masturbating without feeling guilty or that masturbation is a poor substitute for interpersonal sex. We want to make love with those who share our love, male or female, and feel it should not be a revolutionary demand to be either gay, heterosexual, or bisexual. We want to relate to our own personal changes, motivated not by a guilt reaction to women, but by our growth as men.

We want to relate to both women and men in more human ways—with warmth, sensitivity, emotion, and honesty. We want to share our feelings with one another to break down the walls and grow closer. We want to be equal with women and end destructive competitive relationships between men. We don't want to engage in ego battles with anyone.

We are oppressed by conditioning which makes us only half-human. This conditioning serves to create a mutual dependence of male (abstract, aggressive, strong, unemotional) and female (nurturing, passive, weak, emotional) roles. We are oppressed by this dependence on women for support, nurturing, love, and warm feelings. We want to love, nurture, and support ourselves and other men, as well as women. We want to affirm our strengths as men and at the same time encourage the creation of new space for men in areas such as childcare, cooking, sewing, and other "feminine" aspects of life.

We believe that this half-humanization will only change when our competitive, male-dominated, individualistic society becomes cooperative, based on sharing of resources and skills. We are oppressed by working in alienating jobs, as "breadwinners." We want to use our creative energy to serve our common needs and not to make profits for our employers.

We believe that Human Liberation does not stem from individual *or* social needs alone, but that these needs are part of the same process. We feel that all liberation movements are equally important; there is no hierarchy of oppression. Every group must speak its own language, assume its

> own form, take its own action; and when each of these groups learns to express itself in harmony with the rest, this will create the basis for an all embracing social change.
>
> As we put our ideas into practice, we will work to form a more concrete analysis of our oppression as men, and clarify what needs to be done in a socially and personally political way to free ourselves. We want men to share their lives and experiences with each other in order to understand who we are, how we got this way, and what we must do to be free.

Judging from Sherif's six categories, we cannot say that what is called the men's movement fulfills all of the requisite characteristics of a full-fledged social movement. As Gross, Smith, and Wallston point out,

> Theoretically at least, the fledgling U.S. men's movement has easy access to money, organizational skills, and other resources traditionially controlled by males, yet in the past decade it has failed to cohere and prosper as a nationally influential movement. In contrast with its frequent comparison, modern feminism, it has not succeeded in significantly altering the fabric of society, in suggesting new legislation, or even in providing an alternative avenue for the personal frustrations of millions of American men. Nonetheless, the men's movement, largely through men's groups, men's conferences, and a few shoestring publications, has directly and indirectly influenced the lives of several thousand men. The men's movement is certainly not a case study of success. . . .[25]

WHAT ABOUT MEN'S LIBERATION?

Many people become puzzled or upset when they hear the phrase "men's liberation." "What do men need liberation from—they have everything already!" snaps a woman who was passed over for a promotion at the office in favor of a man with less education, less training, and less experience than she. "What do we need liberation for?" asks a sales representative who is nursing an ulcer, hasn't made his sales quota for the month, and has visitation rights to his children every other weekend. Obviously, men's liberation is meaningless to these two people. But others see a real need for men's liberation if the world is going to become a better, a saner place for everyone to live in. Author Jack Nichols views the matter of men's liberation as essential:

> A saner society will flower when men liberate themselves from contrived, socially fabricated prohibitions, cultural straitjackets, and mental stereotypes that control and inhibit behavior through arbitrary definitions of what it means to be a man. When it is clear that the worship of the intellect is destructive, as are the idolization of competition, admiration for what is big, and the resort to violence as remedy, men will react differently to one another, with different expectations, priorities, purposes, and awarenesses. Instead of admiring top dogs, domineering masters and bosses, and instead of supporting power coups, they will regard such persons and their activities as anachronistic and counterproductive.[26]

We have looked now at most of the major issues that affect men today. Commencing with the pressures for change as well as the forces for stasis or a continuation of the traditional structures, we have concluded that many men are confused and even distressed over these conflicting strains in their lives. However, we find little evidence that a large number of men are supportive of any real or significant changes in the power structures that dominate our patriarchal society. As for a ground swell of men pushing for liberation from their restrictive images of masculinity or the traditional elements of the male sex role, the evidence is weak at best in some male circles and nonexistent in most others.

A CLOSING COMMENT

In this final chapter of *The Male Experience,* we have found that many men are caught between two cultures: one pushing for change, the other fighting for continuity. As yet there is little evidence of a viable men's movement. Our caution in this chapter is prompted by the knowledge that those who attempt to predict the future are often made to look like fools.

We opened this book by noting a Chinese curse, "May you live in changing times." We close it with the heartfelt wish, "May you be all that you can be."

SUGGESTED READINGS

Carter, L., Scott, A., and Martyna, W., eds. *Women and Men: Changing Roles, Relationships, and Perceptions.* New York: Praeger, 1977.

Dahlstrom, E., ed. *The Changing Roles of Men and Women.* Boston: Beacon, 1971.

David, D., and Brannon, R., eds. *The Forty-Nine Percent Majority.* Reading, Mass.: Addison-Wesley, 1976.

Nichols, J. *Men's Liberation: A New Definition of Masculinity.* New York: Penguin, 1975.

Pleck, J., and Sawyer, J., eds. *Men and Masculinity.* Englewood Cliffs, N.J.: Prentice-Hall, 1974.

Chapter 1: Today's Uncertain Male

1. J. Money and A. Ehrhardt, *Man & Woman, Boy & Girl* (Baltimore: The Johns Hopkins University Press, 1972).

2. J. Rubin, F. Provenzano, and Z. Luria, "The Eye of the Beholder: Parents' Views on Sex of Newborns," *American Journal of Orthopsychiatry* 44 (1974): 512–19.

3. S. Goldberg and M. Lewis, "Play Behavior in the Year-Old Infant: Early Sex Differences," *Child Development* 40 (1969): 21–31.

4. J. Will, P. Self, and N. Datan, "Maternal Behavior and Perceived Sex of Infant," *American Journal of Orthopsychiatry* 46 (1976): 135–39.

5. R. Hartley, "Sex-Role Pressures and the Socialization of the Male Child," *Psychological Reports* 5 (1959): 457–68.

6. J. Williams, S. Bennett, and D. Best, "Awareness and Expression of Sex-Stereotypes in Young Children," *Developmental Psychology* 11 (1975): 635–42.

7. J. Coleman, "Athletics in High School," in *The Forty-Nine Percent Majority,* ed. D. David and R. Brannon (Reading, Mass.: Addison-Wesley, 1976), pp. 264–69.

8. G. Sheehy, *Passages* (New York: Dutton, 1976).

9. R. Gould, "Measuring Masculinity by the Size of a Paycheck," in *The Forty-Nine Percent Majority,* ed. D. David and R. Brannon (Reading, Mass.: Addison-Wesley, 1976), pp. 113–18.

10. N. Mayer, *The Male Mid-Life Crisis* (Garden City, N.Y.: Doubleday, 1978).

11. E. Pleck and J. Pleck, eds., *The American Male* (Englewood Cliffs, N.J.: Prentice-Hall, 1980); and P. Stearns, *Be a Man! Males in Modern Society* (New York: Holmes & Meier, 1980).

12. J. Bachman and M. Jennings, "The Impact of Vietnam on Trust in Government," *Journal of Social Issues* 31, no. 4 (1975): 141–55; E. Ladd, "The Polls: The Question of Confidence," *Public Opinion Quarterly* 40 (1976): 544–52; A. Miller, "Political Issues and Trust in Government: 1964–1970," *American Political Science Review* 68 (1974): 951–72; and J. Mueller, *War, Presidents and Public Opinion* (New York: Wiley, 1973).

13. See M. Baker, *Nam* (New York: Morrow, 1981); P. Caputo, *A Rumor of War* (New York: Holt, Rinehart & Winston, 1977); M. Herr, *Dispatches* (New York: Knopf, 1977); and G. Lewy, *America in Vietnam* (New York: Oxford University Press, 1978).

14. For the history of the women's movement, see B. Deckard, *The Women's Movement* (New York: Harper & Row, 1975); and E. Flexner, *Century of Struggle* (Cambridge, Mass.: Harvard University Press, 1959).

15. J. Freeman, "The Women's Liberation Movement: Its Origins, Structures, Impact, and Ideas," in *Women: A Feminist Perspective,* ed. J. Freeman (Palo Alto, Calif.: Mayfield, 1975), pp. 448–60.

16. Ibid., pp. 451–52.

17. B. Zilbergeld, *Male Sexuality* (Boston: Little, Brown, 1978).
18. For more information on the whole issue of counseling for men, see *The Counseling Psychologist* 7, no. 4 (1978).
19. See, for example, A. Corman, *Kramer vs. Kramer* (New York: New American Library, 1977); J. Heller, *Something Happened* (New York: Ballantine, 1975); G. Parent, *David Meyer Is a Mother* (New York: Bantam, 1977); and P. Roth, *Portnoy's Complaint* (New York: Bantam, 1969).
20. I. Broverman et al., "Sex-Role Stereotypes and Clinical Judgments of Mental Health," *Journal of Consulting and Clinical Psychology* 34 (1970): 1–7.
21. C. Tavris, "Men and Women Report Their Views on Masculinity," *Psychology Today,* August 1977, p. 37.

Section 1: Perspectives on the Male
1. H. Thoreau, *A Week on the Concord and Merrimack Rivers* (Boston: James Monroe, 1849).

Chapter 2: The Historical Perspective
1. W. Durant, *The Story of Civilization: Our Oriental Heritage* (New York: Simon & Schuster, 1954), p. 12. (Originally published, 1935.)
2. P. Stearns, *Be a Man! Males in Modern Society* (New York: Holmes & Meier, 1979), p. 4.
3. E. Pleck and J. Pleck, eds., *The American Man* (Englewood Cliffs, N.J.: Prentice-Hall, 1980), p. 1.
4. See A. Marwick, *The Nature of History* (New York: Macmillan, 1970).
5. E. Davis, *The First Sex* (New York: Penguin, 1972).
6. See, for example, C. Degler, *Is There a History of Women?* (Oxford: Clarendon Press, 1975); M. Hartman and L. Banner, eds., *Clio's Consciousness Raised: New Perspectives on the History of Women* (New York: Harper & Row, 1974); G. Lerner, "New Approaches to the Study of Women in American History," *Journal of Social History* 3 (1969): 53–62; and G. Lerner, *The Female Experience* (Indianapolis: Bobbs-Merrill, 1977).
7. J. Katz, *Gay American History* (New York: Crowell, 1976).
8. See, for example, G. Barker-Benfield, *The Horrors of the Half-Known Life: Male Attitudes toward Women and Sexuality in Nineteenth-Century America* (New York: Harper & Row, 1976); J. Dubbert, *A Man's Place* (Englewood Cliffs, N.J.: Prentice-Hall, 1979); P. Filene, *Him/Her/Self: Sex Roles in Modern America* (New York: Harcourt Brace Jovanovich, 1974); A. Kirshner, *Masculinity in a Historical Perspective* (Washington, D.C.: University Press of America, 1977); E. Pleck and J. Pleck, eds., *The American Man* (Englewood Cliffs, N.J.: Prentice-Hall, 1980); and P. Stearns, *Be A Man! Males in Modern Society* (New York: Holmes & Meier, 1979).
9. For a provocative analysis of woman's role in the evolution of the human species, see Davis's discussion of gynocracy in *The First Sex;* and E. Morgan, *The Descent of Woman* (New York: Bantam, 1973).
10. See J. Mellaart, *Çatal Hüyük: A Neolithic Town in Anatolia* (New York: McGraw-Hill, 1967).

11. See K. Dover, *Greek Homosexuality* (Cambridge, Mass.: Harvard University Press, 1978).
12. Davis, p. 231.
13. E. Pagels, "What Became of God the Mother? Conflicting Images of God in Early Christianity," *Signs* 2 (1976): 293–303.
14. Pleck and Pleck, p. 6.
15. Davis, pp. 286–87.
16. A. Stewart, D. Winter, and A. Jones, "Coding Categories for the Study of Child-Rearing from Historical Sources," *Journal of Interdisciplinary History,* Spring 1975, pp. 687–701.
17. L. Kerber, "Daughters of Columbia: Educating Women for the Republic," in *The Hofstadter Aegis: A Memorial,* ed. S. Elkin and E. McKitrich (New York: Knopf, 1974), pp. 36–59.
18. B. Welter, "The Feminization of American Religion: 1800–1860," in *Clio's Consciousness Raised: New Perspectives on the History of Women,* ed. M. Hartman and L. Banner (New York: Harper & Row, 1974), pp. 137–57.
19. B. Welter, "The Cult of True Womanhood: 1820–1860," *American Quarterly,* Summer 1966, pp. 151–74.
20. E. Flexner, *Century of Struggle* (Cambridge, Mass.: Harvard University Press, 1959).
21. Pleck and Pleck, p. 18.
22. Quoted in P. Filene, *Him/Her/Self: Sex Roles in Modern America* (New York: Harcourt Brace Jovanovich, 1974), p. 79.
23. Filene, pp. 105–6.
24. Pleck and Pleck, p. 27.
25. J. Hantover, "The Boy Scouts and the Validation of Masculinity," in Pleck and Pleck, pp. 285–301.
26. Quoted in Filene, p. 106.
27. C. Crowley and C. Crowley, "Rugby—Gem of Cumberlands," *The Tennessee Conservationist,* December 1963, pp. 14–16.
28. Flexner, p. 131.
29. See, for example, D. Garrison, "The Tender Technicians: The Femininization of Public Librarianship, 1876–1905," in Hartman and Banner, pp. 158–78.
30. E. DuBois, "The Nineteenth-Century Woman Suffrage Movement: Suffrage as a Total Ideology," *Feminist Studies* 3 (1975): 112.
31. M. Komarovsky, *The Unemployed Man and His Family* (New York: Dryden Press, 1940).
32. S. Terkel, *Hard Times: An Oral History of the Great Depression* (New York: Avon, 1970), p. 19.
33. S. Stouffer et al., "Masculinity and the Role of the Combat Soldier," in *The Forty-Nine Percent Majority,* ed. D. David and R. Brannon (Reading, Mass.: Addison-Wesley, 1976), pp. 179–83.

Chapter 3: The Biological Perspective

1. A. Montagu, *The Natural Superiority of Women* (New York: Collier Books, 1974), p. 80.
2. J. Money and P. Tucker, *Sexual Signatures* (Boston: Little, Brown, 1975), p. 38.
3. E. Wilson, *On Human Nature* (Cambridge, Mass.: Harvard University Press, 1978).

4. D. Symons, *The Evolution of Human Sexuality* (New York: Oxford University Press, 1979).
5. J. Pleck, *The Myth of Masculinity* (Cambridge, Mass.: The MIT Press, 1981).
6. A. Rosenfeld, "If Oedipus' Parents Had Only Known," *Saturday Review,* September 7, 1974, pp. 49, 52.
7. See Money and Tucker; and Montagu.
8. Montagu, pp. 82–84.
9. J. Money and A. Ehrhardt, *Man & Woman, Boy & Girl* (Baltimore: The Johns Hopkins University Press, 1972), p. 33.
10. P. Jacobs et al., "Aggressive Behavior, Mental Subnormality, and the XYY Male," *Nature* 208, no. 1 (1965): 351–52.
11. E. Hook, "Behavioral Implications of the Human XYY Genotype," *Science* 179 (1973): 139–50.
12. H. Jones et al., "The Role of the H–Y Antigen in Human Sexual Development," *The Johns Hopkins Medical Journal* 145 (1979): 33–43.
13. J. Money, A. Ehrhardt, and D. Masica, "Fetal Feminization Induced by Androgen Insensitivity in the Testicular Feminizing Syndrome: Effects on Marriage and Maternalism," *The Johns Hopkins Medical Journal* 123 (1968): 160–67; and Money and Ehrhardt, pp. 108–11.
14. Money and Ehrhardt, p. 42.
15. S. Levine, "Sex Differences in the Brain," *Scientific American,* April 1966, pp. 84–90.
16. J. Bremer, *Asexualization: A Follow-Up Study of 224 Cases* (New York: Macmillan, 1959); and C. Hawke, "Castration and Sex Crimes," *American Journal of Mental Deficiency* 55 (1950): 220–26.
17. J. Katz, *Gay American History* (New York: Crowell, 1976).
18. R. Bahr, *The Virility Factor* (New York: Putnam, 1976).
19. H. Persky, "Reproductive Hormones, Moods, and the Menstrual Cycle," in *Sex Differences in Behavior,* ed. R. Friedman et al. (Huntington, N.Y.: Krieger, 1978), pp. 455–66.
20. J. Delaney, M. Lupton, and E. Toth, *The Curse: A Cultural History of Menstruation* (New York: Mentor, 1976).
21. E. Ramey, "Men's Cycles," *Ms.,* January 1972.
22. C. Fox et al., "Studies on the Relationship Between Plasma Testosterone Levels and Human Sexual Activity," *Journal of Endocrinology* 52 (1972): 51–58.
23. C. Doering et al., "A Cycle of Plasma Testosterone in the Human Male," *Journal of Clinical Endocrinology and Metabolism* 40 (1975): 492; and C. Doering et al., "Plasma Testosterone Levels and Psychologic Measures in Men Over a 2-Month Period," in *Sex Differences in Behavior,* ed. R. Friedman et al. (Huntington, N.Y.: Krieger, 1978), pp. 413–31.
24. M. Parlee, "The Rhythms in Men's Lives," *Psychology Today,* April 1978, pp. 82, 85–86, 91.
25. L. Berkowitz, *Aggression: A Social-Psychological Analysis* (New York: McGraw-Hill, 1962).
26. K. Moyer, "Sex Differences in Aggression," in R. Friedman et al., pp. 335–72.
27. E. Maccoby and C. Jacklin, *The Psychology of Sex Differences* (Stanford, Calif.: Stanford University Press, 1974), p. 243.
28. H. Persky, K. Smith, and G. Basu, "Relation of Psychologic Measures of Aggression and Hostility to Testosterone Production in Man," *Psychosomatic Medicine* 33 (1971): 265–77.

29. L. Kreuz and R. Rose, "Assessment of Aggressive Behavior and Plasma Testosterone in a Young Criminal Population," *Psychosomatic Medicine* 34 (1972): 321–32.
30. H. Meyer-Bahlburg et al., "Aggressiveness and Testosterone Measures in Man," *Psychosomatic Medicine* 36 (1974): 269–74.
31. Pleck, p. 170.
32. T. Tieger, "On the Biological Basis of Sex Differences in Aggression," *Child Development* 51 (1980): 943–63.
33. G. Mitchell, "Paternalistic Behavior in Primates," *Psychological Bulletin* 71 (1969): 339–417.
34. A. Ehrhardt and A. Baker, "Fetal Androgens, Human Central Nervous System Differentiation, and Behavior Sex Differences," in R. Friedman et al., pp. 33–51.
35. Ibid., pp. 44–46.
36. Pleck, p. 173.

Chapter 4: The Anthropological Perspective
1. B. Yorburg, *Sexual Identity* (New York: Wiley, 1974), p. 52.
2. See the discussion of early hominid development in D. Johanson and Edey, *Lucy: The Beginnings of Humankind* (New York: Simon & Schuster, 1981); and R. Leaky and R. Lewin, *Origins* (New York: Dutton, 1977).
3. A. Montagu, *The Nature of Human Aggression* (New York: Oxford University Press, 1976).
4. M. Mead, *Sex and Temperament* (New York: Morrow, 1935/1963).
5. Ibid., p. 15.
6. Ibid., p. 135.
7. Ibid., p. 189.
8. Ibid., p. 245.
9. M. Meggitt, "Male-Female Relationships in the Highlands of Australian New Guinea," *American Anthropologist* 66 (1964): 204–24.
10. E. Friedl, "Society and Sex Roles," *Human Nature*, April 1978, p. 70.
11. E. Davis, *The First Sex* (New York: Penguin, 1972); and M. Stone, *When God Was a Woman* (London: Quartet Books, 1976).
12. S. Binford, "Myths & Matriarchies," *Human Nature*, May 1979, pp. 62–66.
13. R. Rohrlich-Leavitt, "Women in Transition: Crete and Sumer," in *Becoming Visible: Women in European History*, ed. R. Bridenthal and C. Koonz (Boston: Houghton Mifflin, 1977), p. 57.
14. M. Rosaldo and L. Lamphere, eds., *Woman, Culture, and Society* (Stanford, Calif.: Stanford University Press, 1974), p. 3.
15. J. Brown, "Iroquois Women: An Ethnohistoric Note," in *Toward an Anthropology of Women*, ed. R. Reitner (New York: Monthly Review Press, 1975), pp. 235–51.
16. Gen. 3:16.
17. L. Tiger, *Men in Groups* (New York: Random House, 1969), pp. 143–44.
18. M. Spiro, *Kibbutz: Venture in Utopia* (Cambridge, Mass.: Harvard University Press, 1956).
19. E. Wilson, *On Human Nature* (Cambridge, Mass.: Harvard University Press, 1978), pp. 91–92.
20. M. Harris, "Why Men Dominate Women," *New York Times Magazine*, November 13, 1977, pp. 46, 115–23.

21. M. Harris, *Cannibals and Kings* (New York: Random House, 1977), p. 57.
22. Friedl, p. 70.
23. L. Hoffman, "Changes in Family Roles, Socialization, and Sex Differences," *American Psychologist* 32 (1972): 644–57.
24. H. Barry, M. Bacon, and I. Child, "A Cross-Cultural Survey of Some Sex Differences in Socialization," *Journal of Abnormal and Social Psychology* 55 (1957): 327–32.
25. S. Freud, "Some Psychical Consequences of the Anatomical Distinction Between the Sexes," in *Standard Edition of the Complete Works of Sigmund Freud,* Vol. 19, ed. J. Strachey (London: Hogarth, 1953). (Originally published, 1925.)
26. K. Horney, *Feminine Psychology* (New York: Norton, 1967), p. 60.
27. B. Bettelheim, *Symbolic Wounds* (New York: Collier Books, 1962).
28. H. Hays, *The Dangerous Sex: The Myth of Feminine Evil* (New York: Pocket Books, 1966).
29. Horney, pp. 133–46.
30. Y. Murphy and R. Murphy, *Women of the Forest* (New York: Columbia University Press, 1974).
31. N. Chodorow, "Family Structure and Feminine Personality," in *Woman, Culture, and Society,* eds., M. Rosaldo and L. Lamphere (Stanford, Calif.: Stanford University Press, 1974), p. 50.
32. R. Burton and J. Whiting, "The Absent Father and Cross-Sex Identity," *Merrill-Palmer Quarterly* 7 (1961): 85–95.
33. S. Kessler and W. McKenna, *Gender: An Ethnomethodological Approach* (New York: Wiley, 1978).
34. M. Garbarino, *Native American Heritage* (Boston: Little, Brown, 1976).
35. R. Lowie, *The Crow Indians* (New York: Farrar & Rinehart, 1935).
36. T. Berger, *Little Big Man* (New York: Fawcett Crest Books, 1964).
37. M. Olien, *The Human Myth* (New York: Harper & Row, 1978).

Chapter 5: The Sociological Perspective
1. E. Maccoby and C. Jacklin, *The Psychology of Sex Differences* (Stanford, Calif.: Stanford University Press, 1974), 373–74.
2. H. Lopata, "Sociology," *Signs* 2 (1976): 165–76.
3. For example, the University of California, San Diego, has developed a Course by Newspaper (CbN) entitled "American Families." See *American Families: A Course by Newspaper Reader,* ed. E. Douvan, H. Weingarten, and J. Scheiber (Dubuque, Ia.: Kendall/Hunt, 1980).
4. L. Hoffman, "Changes in Family Roles, Socialization, and Sex Difference," *Amercan Psychologist* 32 (1977): 644–57.
5. A. Etzioni, "Sex Control, Science, and Society," *Science,* September 1968, pp. 1107–12.
6. B. Forisha, *Sex Roles and Personal Awareness* (Morristown, N.J.: General Learning Press, 1978).
7. J. Rubin, F. Provenzano, and Z. Luria, "The Eye of the Beholder: Parents' Views on Sex of Newborns," *American Journal of Orthopsychiatry* 44 (1974): 516–17.
8. J. Will, P. Self, and N. Data, "Maternal Behavior and Perceived Sex of Infant," *American Journal of Orthopsychiatry* 46 (1976): 135–39.
9. S. Goldberg and M. Lewis, "Play Behavior in the Year-Old Infant: Early Sex Differences," *Child Development* 40 (1969): 21–31.

10. H. Rheingold and K. Cook, "The Contents of Boys' and Girls' Rooms as an Index of Parents' Behavior," *Child Development* 46 (1975): 459–63.
11. Goldberg and Lewis.
12. L. Hoffman, "Early Childhood Experiences and Women's Achievement Motives," in *Women and Achievement: Social and Motivational Analysis,* ed. M. Mednick, S. Tangri, and L. Hoffman (Washington, D.C.: Hemisphere Publishing, 1975), pp. 129–36.
13. W. Lambert, A. Yackley, and R. Hein, "Child Training Values of English Canadian and French Canadian Parents," *Canadian Journal of Behavioral Sciences* 3 (1971): 217–36.
14. L. Weitzman, "Sex-Role Socialization," in *Women: A Feminist Perspective,* ed. J. Freeman (Palo Alto, Calif.: Mayfield, 1975), p. 118.
15. R. Hartley, "Sex-Role Pressures and the Socialization of the Male Child," in *Men and Masculinity,* ed. J. Pleck and J. Sawyer (Englewood Cliffs, N.J.: Prentice-Hall, 1974), pp. 7–8.
16. H. Biller and D. Meredith, *Father Power* (New York: McKay, 1974); F. Dodson, *How to Father* (New York: NAL, 1974); and S. Gilbert, *What's a Father For?* (New York: Warner Books, 1975).
17. The most visible and best organized group lobbying for fathers' rights in child-custody is the national organization called Fathers United for Equal Rights (FUER).
18. See Rubin et al.; E. Goodenough, "Interest in Persons as an Aspect of Sex Differences in the Early Years," *Genetic Psychological Monographs* 55 (1957): 312; M. Rabban, "Sex-Role Identification in Young Children in Two Diverse Small Groups," *Genetic Psychological Monographs* 42 (1950): 81–158; and M. Papenek, "Authority and Sex Roles in the Family," *Journal of Marriage and the Family* 31 (1969): 88–96.
19. D. Lynn, *The Father: His Role in Child Development* (Monterey, Calif.: Brooks/Cole, 1974), p. 80.
20. H. Biller, *Paternal Deprivation* (Lexington, Mass.: Lexington Books, 1974), p. 1.
21. J. Pleck, *The Myth of Masculinity* (Cambridge, Mass.: The MIT Press, 1981).
22. E. Hetherington, "Effects of Paternal Absence on Sex-Typed Behaviors in Negro and White Preadolescent Males," *Journal of Personality and Social Psychology* 4 (1966): 87–91.
23. M. Lewis, "Parents and Children: Sex-Role Development," *The School Review* 80 (1972): 229–40.
24. J. Nash, "The Father in Contemporary Culture and Current Psychological Literature," *Child Development* 36 (1965): 261–97.
25. L. Langway, "A New Kind of Life with Father," *Newsweek,* November 30, 1981, pp. 93–94, 96, 97C, 97E, 97I, 98.
26. J. Gardner, "Sesame Street and Sex Role Stereotypes," *Women* 1, No. 3 (1970): 42.
27. S. Sternglanz and L. Serbin, "Sex Role Stereotyping in Children's Television Programs," *Developmental Psychology* 10 (1974): 710–15.
28. "TV's 'Disastrous' Impact on Children," *U.S. News & World Report,* January 19, 1981, p. 43.
29. M. Long and R. Simon, "The Roles and Status of Women on Children and Family TV Programs," *Journalism Quarterly* 51 (1974): 107–10.
30. L. Busby, "Defining the Sex-Role Standards in Commercial Network Television Programs Directed Toward Children," *Journalism Quarterly* 51 (1974): 690–96.

31. N. Tedesco, "Patterns in Prime Time," *Journal of Communication* 24 (1974): 119–24.

32. G. Gerbner, "Violence in Television Drama: Trends and Symbolic Functions," *Television and Social Behavior* (Washington, D.C.: U.S. Government Printing Office, 1972); and S. Head, "Content Analysis of Television Dramatic Programs," *Quarterly of Film, Radio and Television* 9 (1954): 175–94.

33. J. Bardwick and S. Schumann, "Portrait of American Men and Women in TV Commercials," *Psychology* 4 (1967): 19.

34. A. Courtney and T. Whipple, "Women in TV Commercials," *Journal of Communication* 24 (1974): 110–18.

35. L. Weitzman, *Sex Role Socialization* (Palo Alto, Calif.: Mayfield, 1979), p. 7.

36. L. Heyn, "Children's Books," *Women* 1 (1969): 22–25; M. Key, "The Role of Male and Female in Children's Books—Dispelling All Doubt," *Wilson Library Bulletin* 46 (1971): 167–76; A. Nilsen, "Women in Children's Literature," *College English,* May 1971, pp. 918–26; and J. Tate, "Sexual Bias in Science Fiction for Children," *Elementary English* 50 (1973): 1061–71.

37. L. Weitzman et al., "Sex Role Socialization in Picture Books for Preschool Children," *American Journal of Sociology* 77 (1972): 1125–50.

38. U.S. Bureau of the Census, *Statistical Abstract of the United States, 1980* (Washington, D.C.: U.S. Government Printing Office, 1980), pp. 418–20.

39. *Project on Equal Rights, Stalled at the Start: Government Action on Sex Bias in the Schools* (Washington, D.C.: Department of Health, Education and Welfare, 1978), p. 7; see also D. Shah, "Of Sports, Sex and Money," *Newsweek,* March 16, 1981, pp. 98, 101.

40. D. McGuinness, "How Schools Discriminate Against Boys," *Human Nature,* February 1979, pp. 82–88.

41. P. Sexton, *The Feminized Male* (New York: Random House, 1969), pp. 29–30.

42. Pleck; see also C. Stasz, S. Weinberg, and F. McDonald, *The Influence of Sex of Student and Sex of Teachers on Students' Achievement and Evaluation of the Teacher* (Princeton, N.J.: Educational Testing Service, 1972).

43. L. Serbin et al., "A Comparison of Teacher Responses to the Preacademic and Problem Behavior of Boys and Girls," *Child Development* 44 (1973): 796–804.

44. K. O'Leary et al., "The Effects of Loud and Soft Reprimands on Behavior of Disruptive Students," *Exceptional Children* 37 (1970): 145–55; and P. Brown and R. Elliott, "Control of Aggression in a Nursery School Class," *Journal of Experimental Child Psychology* 2 (1965): 103–7.

45. N. Frazier and M. Sadker, *Sexism in School and Society* (New York: Harper & Row, 1973).

46. M. U'Ren, "The Image of Women in Textbooks," in *Women in Sexist Society: Studies in Power and Powerlessness,* ed. V. Gornick and B. Moran (New York: Basic Books, 1971), p. 326.

47. D. Austin, V. Clar, and G. Fitchett, *Reading Rights for Boys* (New York: Appleton-Century-Crofts, 1971); and S. Zimet, *What Children Read in School* (New York: Grune & Stratton, 1971).

48. "Women on Words and Images," in *Dick and Jane as Victims* (Princeton, N.J.: Educational Testing Service, 1972).

49. D. Bordua, "Educational Aspirations and Parental Stress on College," *Social Forces* 38 (1960): 267.

50. U. Bronfenbrenner, *Two Worlds of Childhood* (New York: Russell Sage Foundation, 1970).
51. B. Fagot and C. Patterson, "An *in vivo* Analysis of Reinforcing Contingencies for Sex-Role Behaviors in the Preschool Child," *Developmental Psychology* 1 (1969): 563–68.
52. B. Whiting and C. Edwards, "A Cross-Cultural Analysis of Sex Differences in the Behavior of Children Aged Three through Eleven," *Journal of Social Psychology* 91 (1973): 171–88.
53. R. Hartley and F. Hardesty, "Children's Perceptions of Sex Roles in Childhood," *The Journal of Genetic Psychology* 105 (1964): 43–51.
54. Quoted in C. Stoll, *Female and Male* (Dubuque, Iowa: Wm. C. Brown, 1979), p. 88.
55. P. Costanzo and M. Shaw, "Conformity as a Function of Age Level," *Child Development* 37 (1966): 967–75.
56. W. Chaze, "Youth Gangs Are Back—on Old Turf and New," *U.S. News & World Report,* June 29, 1981, pp. 46–47.
57. J. McKee and A. Sherriffs, "The Differential Evaluation of Males and Females," *Journal of Personality* 25 (1957): 356–71; J. McKee and A. Sherriffs, "Men's and Women's Beliefs, Ideals, and Self-Concepts," *American Journal of Sociology* 64 (1959): 356–63; and L. Pogrebin, *Growing Up Free* (New York: McGraw-Hill, 1980).
58. 1 Cor. 11:7–9.
59. H. Lopata, *Occupation: Housewife* (New York: Oxford University Press, 1971); and A. Oakley, *The Sociology of Housework* (New York: Pantheon, 1974).
60. P. Goldberg, "Are Women Prejudiced Against Women?" *Trans-Action* 5 (1968): 28–30.
61. *Gallup Opinion Index,* Report No. 128, March 1976 (Princeton, N.J.: The Gallop Poll Organization), p. 45.
62. Bureau of the Census, p. 511.
63. Ibid., p. 422.
64. U.S. Congress, Senate, Committee on Labor and Human Resources, *Sex Discrimination in the Workplace, 1981,* 97th Cong. (Washington, D.C.: U.S. Government Printing Office, 1981), pp. 398–99.
65. E. Goffman, *The Presentation of Self in Everyday Life* (Garden City, N.Y.: Doubleday, 1969).

Chapter 6: The Psychological Perspective

1. J. Kennedy, Commencement Address, Yale University, New Haven, Conn., June 11, 1962.
2. I. Broverman et al., "Sex-Role Stereotypes: A Current Appraisal," *Journal of Social Issues* 28, No. 2 (1972): 59–78; M. Cicone and D. Ruble, "Beliefs about Males," *Journal of Social Issues* 34, No. 1 (1978): 5–16; S. Fernberger, "Persistence of Stereotypes Concerning Sex Differences," *Journal of Abnormal and Social Psychology* 43 (1948): 97–101; J. McKee and A. Sherriffs, "Men's and Women's Beliefs, Ideals, and Self-Concepts," *American Journal of Sociology* 64 (1959): 356–63; and P. Rosenkrantz et al., "Sex-Role Stereotypes and Self-Concepts among College Students," *Journal of Consulting and Clinical Psychology* 32 (1968): 287–95.
3. L. Terman, *Genetic Studies of Genius,* Vol. 1 (Stanford, Calif.: Stanford University Press, 1925).

4. L. Terman and L. Tyler, "Psychological Sex Differences," in *Manual of Child Psychology,* 2nd. ed., ed. L. Carmichael (New York: Wiley, 1954), Chapter 19.

5. E. Maccoby and C. Jacklin, *The Psychology of Sex Differences* (Stanford, Calif.: Stanford University Press, 1974).

6. One subject omitted from Maccoby and Jacklin's review of sex differences is human communications. For those interested in an excellent overview of this subject, see B. Eakins and R. Eakins, *Sex Differences in Human Communication* (Boston: Houghton Mifflin, 1978).

7. Quoted in R. Morgan, ed., *Sisterhood is Powerful* (New York: Vintage Books, 1970), p. 36.

8. H. Witkin et al., *Personality Through Perception* (New York: Harper & Row, 1954); and H. Witkin et al., *Psychological Differentiation* (New York: Wiley, 1962).

9. D. Broverman et al., "Roles of Activation and Inhibition in Sex Differences in Cognitive Abilities," *Psychological Review* 75 (1968): 23–50; and Mary Parlee's rejoinder in *Psychological Review* 79 (1972): 180–84.

10. U.S. Bureau of the Census, *Statistical Abstract of the United States, 1980* (Washington, D.C.: U.S. Government Printing Office, 1980), p. 628.

11. Maccoby and Jacklin, pp. 89, 91.

12. Ibid., 113–14.

13. S. Jourard, *The Transparent Self* (New York: Van Nostrand, 1964); S. Jourard and P. Lasakow, "Some Factors in Self-Disclosure," *Journal of Abnormal and Social Psychology* 56 (1958): 91–98; M. Komarovsky, *Blue-Collar Marriage* (New York: Random House, 1967); and M. Komarovsky, *Dilemmas of Masculinity* (New York: Norton, 1976).

14. P. Cozby, "Self-Disclosure: A Literature Review," *Psychological Bulletin* 79 (1973): 73–91.

15. V. Sermat and M. Smyth, "Content Analysis of Verbal Communication in the Development of a Relationship: Conditions Influencing Self-Disclosure," *Journal of Personality and Social Psychology* 26 (1973): 332–46.

16. Quoted in K. Deaux, *The Behavior of Women and Men* (Monterey, Calif.: Brooks/Cole, 1976), p. 58.

17. Quoted in Morgan, p. 36.

18. S. Goldberg and M. Lewis, "Play Behavior in the Year-Old Infant: Early Sex Differences," *Child Development* 40 (1969): 21–31.

19. Maccoby and Jacklin, p. 196.

20. I. Janis and P. Field, "Sex Differences and Personality Factors Related to Persuasibility," in *Personality and Persuasibility,* ed. I. Janis (New Haven, Conn.: Yale University Press, 1959).

21. S. Asch, "Studies of Independence and Conformity: A Minority of One Against a Unanimous Majority," *Psychological Monographs,* 1956, *70* (Whole No. 416).

22. F. Sistrunk and J. McDavid, "Sex Variable in Conforming Behavior," *Journal of Personality and Social Psychology* 17 (1971): 200–207.

23. J. Pleck, "Men's Power with Women, Other Men, and Society: A Men's Movement Analysis," in *The American Man,* ed. E. Pleck and J. Pleck (Englewood Cliffs, N.J.: Prentice-Hall, 1980), p. 421.

24. R. Parke and S. O'Leary, "Mother-Father-Infant Interaction in the Newborn Period: Some Findings, Some Observations, and Some Unresolved Issues," cited in Maccoby and Jacklin, p. 221.

25. Maccoby and Jacklin, pp. 230–33.
26. A. Bandura, "Influence of Models' Reinforcement Contingencies on the Acquisition of Imitative Responses," *Journal of Personality and Social Psychology* 1 (1965): 589–95; M. Harris, "Mediators Between Frustration and Aggression in a Field Experiment," *Journal of Experimental Social Psychology* 10 (1974): 561–71; M. Harris, "Field Studies of Modeled Aggression," *Journal of Social Psychology* 89 (1973): 131–39; J. Hokanson and R. Edelman, "Effects of Three Social Responses on Vascular Processes," *Journal of Personality and Social Psychology* 3 (1966): 442–47; and S. Taylor and S. Epstein, "Aggression as a Function of the Interaction of the Sex of the Aggressor and the Sex of the Victim," *Journal of Personality* 35 (1967): 473–86.
27. S. Freud, *Three Essays on the Theory of Sexuality* (New York: Avon, 1905/1965).
28. For criticism of Freud's view of female psychology, see K. Millet, *Sexual Politics* (London: Abacus, 1971); and S. de Beauvoir, *The Second Sex* (New York: Vintage, 1974).
29. For another view of female psychosexual development, see K. Horney, *Feminine Psychology* (New York: Norton, 1973); for a comprehensive overview of Freud and other neo-Freudians and their views on female psychology, see J. Williams, *Psychology of Women* (New York: Norton, 1977).
30. A. Bandura and R. Walters, *Social Learning and Personality Development* (New York: Holt, Rinehart & Winston, 1963).
31. W. Mischel, "A Social-Learning View of Sex Differences in Behavior," in *The Development of Sex Differences,* ed. E. Maccoby (Stanford, Calif.: Stanford University Press, 1966), pp. 56–81.
32. L. Kohlberg, "A Cognitive-Developmental Analysis of Children's Sex-Role Concepts and Attitudes," in Maccoby, p. 83.
33. Ibid., p. 89.
34. Ibid., p. 95.
35. J. Money and P. Tucker, *Sexual Signatures* (Boston: Little, Brown, 1975), pp. 91–92.
36. S. Fling and M. Manosevitz, "Sex Typing in Nursery School Children's Play Interests," *Developmental Psychology* 7 (1972): 146–52; and L. Lansky, "The Family Structure Also Affects the Model: Sex-Role Attitudes in Parents of Preschool Children," *Merrill-Palmer Quarterly* 13 (1967): 139–50.
37. B. Fagot and G. Patterson, "An *in vivo* Analysis of Reinforcing Contingencies for Sex Role Behaviors in the Preschool Child," *Developmental Psychology* 1 (1969): 563–68.
38. J. Pleck, *The Myth of Masculinity* (Cambridge, Mass.: The MIT Press, 1981), pp. 51–62.
39. Ibid., pp. 62–65.
40. T. Kuhn, *The Structure of Scientific Revolutions* (Chicago: University of Chicago Press, 1962).
41. Pleck, 1981, pp. 4–5.
42. L. Terman and C. Miles, *Sex and Personality* (New York: McGraw-Hill, 1936); H. Gough, "Identifying Psychological Femininity," *Educational and Psychological Measurement* 12 (1952): 427–39; and D. Brown, "Sex-Role Preference in Young Children," *Psychological Monographs,* 1956, *70*(14, Whole No. 421).

43. D. Miller and G. Swanson, *Inner Conflict and Defense* (New York: Holt, Rinehart & Winston, 1960); H. Biller, "A Multiaspect Investigation of Masculine Development in Kindergarten Age Boys," *Genetic Psychology Monographs* 78 (1968): 89–138; and D. Lynn, *Parental and Sex Role Identification: A Theoretical Formulation* (Berkeley, Calif.: McCutchan, 1969).

44. K. Franck and E. Rosen, "A Projective Test of Masculinity-Femininity," *Journal of Consulting Psychology* 13 (1949): 247–56.

45. J. Gonen and L. Lansky, "Masculinity, Femininity, and Masculinity–Femininity: A Phenomenological Study of the Mf Scale of the MMPI," *Psychological Reports* 23 (1968): 183–94; and S. Bem, "The Measurement of Psychological Androgyny," *Journal of Clinical and Consulting Psychology* 42 (1974): 155–62.

46. W. Farrell, *The Liberated Man* (New York: Random House, 1974); and H. Goldberg, *The Hazards of Being Male* (New York: Nash, 1976).

47. Pleck, 1981, p. 9.

Section 2: Elements of the Male Sex Role

1. M. Cicone and D. Ruble, "Beliefs about Males," *Journal of Social Issues* 34, no. 1 (1978): 11.

2. R. Brannon, "The Male Sex Role: Our Culture's Blueprint of Manhood, and What It's Done for Us Lately," in *The Forty-Nine Percent Majority,* ed. D. David and R. Brannon (Reading, Mass.: Addison-Wesley, 1976), p. 12.

Chapter 7: The Antifeminine Element

1. K. Millett, *Sexual Politics* (London: Abacus, 1971), p. 51.

2. G. Liddy, *Will* (New York: Dell, 1980), p. 51.

3. H. Hays, *The Dangerous Sex* (New York: Pocket Books, 1966), p. 1.

4. Quotations taken from "Know Your Enemy: A Sampling of Sexist Quotes," in *Sisterhood Is Powerful,* ed. R. Morgan (New York: Vintage Books, 1970), pp. 33–38.

5. J. Bernard, *The Female World* (New York: The Free Press, 1981), p. 11.

6. For a history of misogynist attitudes, see V. Bullough, *The Subordinate Sex* (New York: Penguin, 1974).

7. R. Eisler, *The Equal Rights Handbook* (New York: Avon, 1978).

8. M. Komarovsky, "Cultural Contradictions and Sex Roles: The Masculine Case," *American Journal of Sociology* 78, no. 4 (1973): 873–84; and M. Komarovsky, *Dilemmas of Masculinity* (New York: Norton, 1976).

9. J. Doyle and R. Shahade, "College Males' Academic Field and Attitudes Toward Women," *Psychological Reports* 40 (1977): 1089–90.

10. J. Doyle, "Attitudes Toward Feminism—Forty Years Later," *Sex Roles* 2 (1976): 399–400.

11. B. Yorburg and I. Arafat, "Current Sex Role Conceptions and Conflict," *Sex Roles* 1 (1975): 135–46.

12. P. Goldberg, "Are Women Prejudiced Against Women?" *Trans-Action* 5, no. 5 (1968): 28–30.

13. S. Kossen, *The Human Side of Organizations,* 2nd ed. (San Francisco: Canfield Press, 1978), p. 306.

14. R. Unger, *Female and Male Psychological Perspectives* (New York: Harper & Row, 1979), p. 436.

15. J. Footlick, D. Camper, and P. Clausen, "Women's Issue of the '80s," *Newsweek,* June 22, 1981, pp. 58–59.
16. J. Laws, "Work Motivation and Work Behavior of Women: New Perspectives," in *Psychology of Women: Future Directions of Research,* ed. J. Sherman and R. Denmark (New York: Psychological Dimensions, 1978).
17. P. Samuelson, *Economics,* 10th ed. (New York: McGraw-Hill, 1976), p. 790.
18. B. Bass, J. Krussell, and R. Alexander, "Male Managers' Attitudes Toward Working Women," *American Behavioral Scientist* 15 (1971): 221–36.
19. V. Schein, "The Relationship Between Sex Role Stereotypes and Requisite Management Characteristics," *Journal of Applied Psychology* 57, no. 2 (1973): 95–100.
20. J. Laws, "The Psychology of Tokenism: An Analysis," *Sex Roles* 1 (1975): 51–67.
21. S. Bem and D. Bem, "We're All Nonconscious Sexists," *Psychology Today,* November 1970, pp. 22, 24, 26, 115–16.
22. I. Broverman et al., "Sex-Role Stereotypes: A Current Appraisal," *Journal of Social Issues* 28, no. 2 (1972): 59–78.
23. L. Ellis and P. Bentler, "Traditional Sex-Determined Role Standards and Sex Stereotypes," *Journal of Personality and Social Psychology* 25 (1973): 28–34.
24. N. Henley, *Body Politics: Power, Sex, and Nonverbal Communication* (Englewood Cliffs, N.J.: Prentice-Hall, 1977).
25. J. Balswick and C. Peck, "The Inexpressive Male: A Tragedy of American Society," *The Family Coordinator* 20 (1971): 363–68.
26. L. Etheredge, *A World of Men: Private Sources of American Foreign Policy* (Cambridge, Mass.: The MIT Press, 1978); and M. Fasteau, *The Male Machine* (New York: McGraw-Hill, 1974).
27. W. Farrell, *The Liberated Man* (New York: Random House, 1974), pp. 71–72.
28. S. Jourard, "Some Lethal Aspects of the Male Role," in *Men and Masculinity,* ed. J. Pleck and J. Sawyer (Englewood Cliffs, N.J.: Prentice-Hall, 1974), p. 26.
29. L. Tiger, *Men in Groups* (London: Nelson, 1970).
30. M. Fasteau, *The Male Machine* (New York: McGraw-Hill, 1974), p. 14.
31. G. Lehne, "Homophobia among Men," in *The Forty-Nine Percent Majority,* ed. D. David and R. Brannon (Reading, Mass.: Addison-Wesley, 1976), p. 79.
32. Quoted in J. Wagenvoord and P. Bailey, *Men: A Book for Women* (New York: Avon, 1978), pp. 269–70.
33. R. Brannon, "The Male Sex Role: Our Culture's Blueprint of Manhood, and What It's Done for Us Lately," in David and Brannon, pp. 18–19.

Chapter 8: The Success Element
1. R. Brannon, "The Big Wheel: Success, Status, and the Need to Be Looked Up To," in *The Forty-Nine Percent Majority,* ed. D. David and R. Brannon (Reading, Mass.: Addison-Wesley, 1976), p. 89.
2. J. Nichols, *Men's Liberation: A New Definition of Masculinity* (New York: Penguin, 1975), p. 91.
3. I. Berlin, *Theater Arts,* February 1958.
4. J. Millan and B. Hinds, *If I Quit Baseball, Will You Still Love Me?* (New York: Sheed and Ward, 1976).

5. See, for example, C. McClintock and S. McNeel, "Reward and Score Feedback as Determinants of Cooperative and Competitive Game Behavior," *Journal of Personality and Social Psychology* 4 (1966): 606–13; D. Messick and W. Thorngate, "Relative Gain Maximization in Experimental Games," *Journal of Experimental Social Psychology* 3 (1967): 85–101; and A. Scodel et al., "Some Descriptive Aspects of Two-Person, Non-Zero-Sum Games: I," *Journal of Conflict Resolution* 3 (1959): 114–19.

6. R. Helmreich and J. Spence, "The Secret of Success," *Discovery, Research and Scholarship at the University of Texas at Austin* 2, no. 2 (1977): 4–7.

7. M. Rosenbaum, "Cooperation and Competition," in *Psychology of Group Influence,* ed. P. Paulus (Hillsdale, N.J.: Erlbaum, 1980).

8. D. Johnson et al., "Effects of Cooperative, Competitive, and Individualistic Goal Structures on Achievement: A Meta-Analysis," *Psychological Bulletin* 89 (1981): 47–62.

9. L. Miller and R. Hamblin, "Interdependence, Differential Rewarding, and Productivity," *American Sociological Review* 28 (1963): 768–78.

10. M. Sherif et al., *Intergroup Cooperation and Competition: The Robber's Cave Experiment* (Norman: University of Oklahoma Book Exchange, 1961).

11. J. Bardwick, "Men and Work." Unpublished paper, 1973, p. 12.

12. A. Toffler, *The Third Wave* (New York: Bantam, 1981).

13. J. Bernard, "The Good-Provider Role: Its Rise and Fall," *American Psychologist* 36, no. 1 (1981): 4.

14. R. Gould, "Measuring Masculinity by the Size of a Paycheck," in *Men and Masculinity,* ed. J. Pleck and J. Sawyer (Englewood Cliffs, N.J.: Prentice-Hall, 1974), pp. 96–100.

15. P. Stearns, *Be a Man! Males in Modern Society* (New York: Holmes & Meier, 1979), p. 44.

16. T. Veblen, "Conspicuous Consumption," in David and Brannon, pp. 118–22.

17. Bernard, p. 2.

18. M. Komarovsky, *The Unemployed Man and His Family* (New York: Dryden Press, 1940).

19. R. Smith, ed., *The Subtle Revolution* (Washington, D.C.: Urban Institute, 1979), p. 14.

20. D. Yankelovich, "The New Psychological Contracts at Work," *Psychology Today,* May 1978, pp. 46–47, 49–50.

21. H. Stein, "The Glory Boys," *Esquire,* February 1981, pp. 36–40, 42–43, 46–48.

22. P. Berger, "Some General Observations on the Problem of Work," in *The Human Shape of Work,* ed. P. Berger (New York: Macmillan, 1964), p. 215.

23. M. Korda, *Success!* (New York: Ballantine, 1978).

24. See R. Christie and F. Geis, *Studies in Machiavellianism* (New York: Academic Press, 1970).

25. Helmreich and Spense.

26. A. Steele, *Upward Nobility* (New York: Times Books, 1978), p. 5.

27. B. Lefkowitz, *Breaktime* (New York: Hawthorn Books, 1979), p. 38.

28. Komarovsky; and S. Terkel, *Hard Times: An Oral History of the Great Depression* (New York: Avon, 1970).

29. N. Morse and R. Weiss, "The Function and Meaning of Work and the Job," *American Sociological Review* 20 (1955): 191–98.

30. Lefkowitz, pp. 42–47.

31. Steele, p. 6.
32. S. Miller, "The Making of a Confused, Middle-Aged Husband," in Pleck and Sawyer, p. 51.
33. W. Malcomson, *Success Is a Failure Experience* (Nashville: Abingdon Press, 1976), pp. 11–12.

Chapter 9: The Aggressive Element

1. L. Komisar, "Violence and the Masculine Mystique," in *The Forty-Nine Percent Majority,* ed. D. David and R. Brannon (Reading, Mass.: Addison-Wesley, 1976), p. 203.
2. L. Berkowitz, *Aggression: A Social-Psychological Analysis* (New York: McGraw-Hill, 1962).
3. For another perspective on aggression, see K. Moyer, "Kinds of Aggression and Their Physiological Basis," *Communications in Behavioral Biology* 2 (1968): 65–87.
4. Federal Bureau of Investigation, *Crime in the United States: Uniform Crime Reports, 1977* (Washington, D.C.: U.S. Government Printing Office, 1978).
5. U.S. Bureau of the Census, *Statistical Abstract of the United States, 1978* (Washington, D.C.: U.S. Government Printing Office, 1978).
6. L. Minturn and W. Lambert, *Mothers of Six Cultures* (New York: Wiley, 1964).
7. R. Sears, E. Maccoby, and H. Levin, *Patterns of Child Rearing* (Evanston, Ill.: Row, Peterson, 1957).
8. W. Chaze, "Youth Gangs Are Back—on Old Turf and New," *U.S. News & World Report,* June 29, 1981, pp. 46–47.
9. M. Blumenthal et al., *Justifying Violence: Attitudes of American Men* (Ann Arbor: Institute for Social Research, The University of Michigan, 1972).
10. J. Michener, *Kent State: What Happened and Why* (New York: Random House, 1971), p. 446.
11. S. Brownmiller, *Against Our Will* (New York: Simon & Schuster, 1975), p. 8.
12. Federal Bureau of Investigation, p. 37.
13. R. von Krafft-Ebing, *Psychopathia Sexualis* (New York: Putnam, 1965), pp. 544–45.
14. S. Griffin, "Rape: The All-American Crime," *Ramparts* 10 (1971): 26–35.
15. W. Blanchard, "The Group Process in Gang Rape," *Journal of Social Psychology* 49 (1959): 259–66.
16. D. Abrahamsen, *The Psychology of Crime* (New York: Columbia University Press, 1960).
17. See Brownmiller; and A. Medea and K. Thompson, *Against Rape* (New York: Farrar, Straus & Giroux, 1974).
18. Quoted in J. Pleck, *The Myth of Masculinity* (Cambridge, Mass.: The MIT Press, 1981), p. 146.
19. M. Straus, "The Marriage License as a Hitting License: Social Instigation of Physical Aggression in the Family." Paper presented at the meeting of the American Psychological Association, Chicago, September 1975.
20. M. Straus, "Normative and Behavioral Aspects of Violence Between Spouses: Preliminary Data on a Nationally Representative USA Sample." Paper presented at the Conference on Violence in Canadian Society, Ottawa, March 1977.
21. M. Straus, "A Sociological Perspective on the Prevention and Treatment of Wife-Beating," in *Battered Women,* ed. M. Roy (New York: Van Nostrand Reinhold, 1977).
22. D. Martin, *Battered Wives* (San Francisco: Glide Publications, 1976), pp. 11–12.

Chapter 10: The Sexual Element

1. B. Zilbergeld, *Male Sexuality* (Boston: Little, Brown, 1978), p. 3.
2. J. Lipman-Blumen, "Dilemmas of Sex," in *American Families*, ed. E. Douvan et al. (Dubuque, Iowa: Kendall/Hunt, 1980), p. 183.
3. M. Cicone and D. Ruble, "Beliefs About Males," *Journal of Social Issues* 34 (1978): 11; and R. Brannon, "The Male Sex Role: Our Culture's Blueprint of Manhood, and What It's Done for Us Lately," in *The Forty-Nine Percent Majority,* ed. D. David and R. Brannon (Reading, Mass.: Addison-Wesley, 1976).
4. N. Friday, *Men in Love* (New York: Dell), p. 541.
5. H. Harlow, "The Nature of Love," *American Psychologist* 13 (1958): 673–85; H. Harlow and M. Harlow, "Social Deprivation in Monkeys," *Scientific American,* November 1962, 137–47; and H. Harlow and R. Zimmerman, "Affectional Responses in the Infant Monkey," *Science* 130 (1959): 421–23.
6. J. McCary, *Human Sexuality,* 2nd ed. (New York: Van Nostrand, 1979), p. 183.
7. M. Hunt, *Sexual Behavior in the 1970's* (Chicago: Playboy Press, 1974).
8. B. Strong et al., *Human Sexuality,* 2nd ed. (St. Paul: West Publishing Company, 1981), pp. 235–36.
9. G. Kaats and K. Davis, "The Dynamics of Sexual Behavior of College Students," *Journal of Marriage and the Family* 32 (1970): 390–99; and M. King and D. Sobel, "Sex on the College Campus: Current Attitudes and Behavior," *Journal of College Student Personnel* 16 (1975): 205–9.
10. "Your Pursuit of Happiness," *Psychology Today,* August 1976, p. 31.
11. H. Goldberg, *The Hazards of Being Male* (New York: Nash, 1976).
12. G. Parent, *David Meyer Is a Mother* (New York: Bantam, 1977), pp. 15–16.
13. Zilbergeld, p. 213.
14. J. Coleman, J. Butcher, and R. Carson, *Abnormal Psychology and Modern Life,* 6th ed. (Glenview, Ill.: Scott, Foresman, 1980), p. 532.
15. J. Wagenvoord and P. Bailey, *Men: A Book for Women* (New York: Avon, 1978), p. 189.
16. L. Sarrel and P. Sarrel, "Sex Problems We Don't Talk About—and Should," *Redbook,* February 1981, p. 142.
17. Zilbergeld, p. 62.
18. Strong, p. 260.
19. Quoted in Wagenvoord and Bailey, p. 193.
20. I. Reiss, *The Social Context of Premarital Sexual Permissiveness* (New York: Holt, Rinehart & Winston, 1967).
21. M. Komarovsky, *Dilemmas of Masculinity* (New York: Norton, 1976), p. 126.
22. Quoted in Zilbergeld, pp. 153–54.
23. A. Bell, "Asexuality: Everybody's Not Doing It," *The Village Voice,* January 23, 1978, pp. 1, 20.
24. G. Brown, *The New Celibacy* (New York: McGraw-Hill, 1978).
25. J. Steinhart, "The Most Erotic Part of Your Body," in *Human Sexuality,* ed. O. Pocs (Guilford, Conn.: Dushkin, 1982), pp. 50–52.

Chapter 11: The Self-Reliant Element

1. Quoted in *The Forty-Nine Percent Majority,* ed. D. David and R. Brannon (Reading, Mass.: Addison-Wesley, 1976), pp. 163–64.
2. Quoted in J. Wagenvoord and P. Bailey, *Men: A Book for Women* (New York: Avon, 1978), p. 44.
3. Ibid., p. 44.
4. Ibid., p. 42.
5. R. Brannon, "The Male Sex Role: Our Culture's Blueprint of Manhood, and What It's Done for Us Lately," in David and Brannon, p. 25.
6. J. Mellen, *Big Bad Wolves: Masculinity in the American Film* (New York: Pantheon, 1977), pp. 4–5.
7. Ibid., p. 228.
8. Ibid., p. 141.
9. Ibid., p. 336.
10. Ibid., p. 337.
11. Ibid., pp. 343–45.
12. J. Gagnon, "Physical Strength, Once of Significance," in David and Brannon, pp. 169–78.
13. P. Stein and S. Hoffman, "Sports and Male Role Strain," *Journal of Social Issues* 34, no. 1 (1978): 136.
14. J. Coleman, "Athletics in High School," in David and Brannon, pp. 264–69.
15. M. Komarovsky, *Dilemmas of Masculinity* (New York: Norton, 1976), p. 9.
16. Stein and Hoffman, p. 142.
17. Ibid., p. 144.
18. Ibid., p. 147.
19. Ibid., p. 149.
20. J. Pleck, "The Male Sex Role: Definitions, Problems, and Sources of Change," *Journal of Social Issues* 32, no. 3 (1976): 155–64.
21. S. Stouffer et al., "Masculinity and the Role of the Combat Soldier," in David and Brannon, p. 179.
22. Anonymous, "Life in the Military," in *Men and Masculinity,* ed. J. Pleck and R. Sawyer (Englewood Cliffs, N.J.: Prentice-Hall, 1974), pp. 127–28.
23. W. Arkin and L. Dobrofsky, "Military Socialization and Masculinity," *Journal of Social Issues* 34, no. 1 (1978): 154–55.
24. Ibid., p. 167.
25. J. McGinniss, *The Selling of the Presidency, 1968* (New York: Simon & Schuster, 1969).
26. I. Stone, "Machismo in Washington," in Pleck and Sawyer, p. 131.
27. M. Fasteau, *The Male Machine* (New York: McGraw-Hill, 1974), pp. 163–64.
28. Ibid., p. 172.
29. Ibid., p. 172.
30. Ibid., p. 173.
31. Ibid., pp. 180–81.
32. T. Morganthau et al., "Who Controls the Air?" *Newsweek,* August 17, 1981, p. 18.

Section 3: Some Issues of Concern to Males
1. M. Brenton, *The American Male* (Greenwich, Conn.: Fawcett Premier Books, 1966), p. 33.

Chapter 12: Homosexuality
1. L. Peplau, "What Homosexuals Want," *Psychology Today,* March 1981, pp. 28–29.
2. G. Lehne, "Homophobia Among Men," in *The Forty-Nine Percent Majority,* ed. D. David and R. Brannon (Reading, Mass.: Addison-Wesley, 1976), pp. 66–88.
3. See V. Bullough, "Homosexuality and the Medical Model," *Journal of Homosexuality,* 1 (1974): 99–110; and J. Katz, *Gay American History* (New York: Crowell, 1976).
4. W. Durant, *The Life of Greece* (New York: Simon & Schuster, 1939).
5. M. Weinberg and C. Williams, *Male Homosexuals* (New York: Penguin, 1975), pp. 40–41.
6. Ibid., pp. 53–54.
7. H. Lief, "Sexual Survey #4: Current Thinking on Homosexuality," *Medical Aspects of Human Sexuality,* November 1977, pp. 110–11.
8. E. Levitt and A. Klassen, "Public Attitudes Toward Homosexuality: Part of the 1970 National Survey by the Institute for Sex Research," *Journal of Homosexuality* 1, no. 1 (1974): 29–43; see also M. Storms, "Attitudes Toward Homosexuality and Femininity in Men," *Journal of Homosexuality* 3, no. 3 (1978): 257–63.
9. Katz.
10. A. Kinsey, W. Pomeroy, and C. Martin, *Sexual Behavior in the Human Male* (Philadelphia: Saunders, 1948).
11. L. Humphreys, *Tearoom Trade* (Chicago: Aldine, 1970).
12. I. Bieber et al., *Homosexuality* (New York: Basic Books, 1962).
13. S. Freud, "Three Essays on the Theory of Sexuality," in *The Standard Edition of the Complete Psychological Works of Sigmund Freud,* Vol. 7, ed. J. Strachey (New York: Macmillan, 1953). (Originally published, 1905.)
14. A. Kardiner, "The Flight from Masculinity," in *The Problem of Homosexuality in Modern Society,* ed. H. Ruitenbeek (New York: Dutton, 1963), pp. 17–39.
15. C. Socarides, *The Overt Homosexual* (New York: Grune & Stratton, 1968).
16. L. Ovesey, *Homosexuality and Pseudohomosexuality* (New York: Science House, 1969).
17. H. Ruitenbeek, ed., *The Problem of Homosexuality in Modern Society* (New York: Dutton, 1963).
18. D. Brown, "The Development of Sex-Role Inversion and Homosexuality," *Journal of Pediatrics* 50 (1957): 613–19; P. Fisher, *The Gay Mystique: The Myth and Reality of Male Homosexuality* (New York: Stein and Day, 1972).
19. J. Pleck, *The Myth of Masculinity* (Cambridge, Mass.: The MIT Press, 1981), pp. 73–76.
20. S. Ferenczi, "The Nosology of Male Homosexuality," in Ruitenbeek, pp. 3–16.
21. Kardiner, in Ruitenbeek, pp. 17–39.
22. S. Rado, "An Adaptational View of Sexual Behavior," in Ruitenbeek, pp. 94–125.
23. J. Meyer, "Individual Psychotherapy of Sexual Disorders," in *Comprehensive Textbook of Psychiatry—II,* ed. A. Freedman, H. Kaplan, and B. Sadock (Baltimore: Williams & Wilkins, 1975).

24. K. Freund et al., "Heterosexual Aversion in Homosexual Males," *British Journal of Psychiatry* 122 (1973): 163–69; K. Freund et al., "The Phobic Theory of Male Homosexuality," *Archives of General Psychiatry* 31 (1974): 495–99; and K. Freund, R. Langevin, and Y. Zajac, "Heterosexual Aversion in Homosexual Males: A Second Experiment," *British Journal of Psychiatry* 125 (1974): 177–80.

25. R. Moore and G. McDonald, "The Relationship Between Sex-Role Stereotypes, Attitudes Toward Women and Male Homosexuality in a Non-Clinical Sample of Homosexual Men." Paper presented at Canadian Psychological Association, Toronto, 1976.

26. N. Chodorow, "Family Structure and Feminine Personality," in *Woman, Culture, and Society,* ed. M. Rosaldo and L. Lamphere (Stanford, Calif.: Stanford University Press, 1974); and D. Dinnerstein, *The Mermaid and the Minotaur* (New York: Harper & Row, 1976).

27. Meyer.

28. Bieber; and J. Snortum et al., "Family Dynamics and Homosexuality," *Psychological Reports* 24 (1969): 763–70.

29. G. Robertson, "Parent-Child Relationships and Homosexuality," *British Journal of Psychiatry* 121 (1972): 525–28; and M. Siegelman, "Parental Backgrounds of Male Homosexuals and Heterosexuals," *Archives of Sexual Behavior* 3 (1974): 3–18.

30. A. Karlen, *Sexuality and Homosexuality: A New View* (New York: Norton, 1971).

31. R. Kolodny et al., "Plasma Testosterone and Semen Analysis in Male Homosexuals," *New England Journal of Medicine* 285, no. 21 (1971): 1170–74.

32. R. Pillard, R. Rose, and M. Sherwood, "Plasma Testosterone Levels in Homosexual Men," *Archives of Sexual Behavior* 3, no. 5 (1974): 453–57.

33. D. Barlow et al., "Plasma Testosterone Levels in Male Homosexuals: A Failure to Replicate," *Archives of Sexual Behavior* 3, no. 6 (1974): 571–75; L. Birk et al., "Serum Testosterone Levels in Homosexual Men," *The New England Journal of Medicine* 289, no. 23 (1973): 1236–38; P. Doerr et al., "Plasma Testosterone, Estradiol, and Semen Analysis in Male Homosexuals," *Archives of General Psychiatry* 29 (1973): 829–33; and G. Tourney and L. Hatfield, "Androgen Metabolism in Schizophrenics, Homosexuals, and Normal Controls," *Biological Psychiatry* 6, no. 1 (1973): 23–36.

34. K. Brodie et al., "Plasma Testosterone Levels in Heterosexual and Homosexual Men," *American Journal of Psychiatry* 131, no. 1 (1974): 82–83.

35. A. Bell and M. Weinberg, *Homosexualities: A Study of Diversity Among Men and Women* (New York: Simon & Schuster, 1978).

36. J. Harry, "On the Validity of Typologies of Gay Males," *Journal of Homosexuality* 2 (1976): 143–52; and M. Saghir and E. Robins, *Male and Female Homosexuality* (Baltimore: Williams & Wilkins, 1973).

37. J. Harry, "The 'Marital' Liaisons of Gay Men," *The Family Coordinator* 28, no. 4 (1979): 616–21; and J. Spada, *The Spada Report: The Newest Survey of Gay Male Sexuality* (New York: New American Library, 1979).

38. J. Harry and W. DeVall, *The Social Organization of Gay Males* (New York: Praeger, 1978).

39. J. DeLora and C. Warren, *Understanding Sexual Interaction* (Boston: Houghton Mifflin, 1977); J. Gagnon, *Human Sexualities* (Glenview, Ill.: Scott, Foresman, 1977); J. Gagnon and W. Simon, *Sexual Conduct: The Social Sources of Human Sexuality* (Chicago: Aldine, 1973); and C. Warren, *Identity and Community in the Gay World* (New York: Wiley, 1974).

40. S. Morin, "Heterosexual Bias in Psychological Research on Lesbianism and Male Homosexuality," *American Psychologist* 32 (1977): 629–37.
41. T. Clark, "Homosexuality as a Criterion Predictor of Psychopathology in Nonpatient Males," *Proceedings of the 81st Annual Convention of the American Psychological Association* 8 (1973): 407–8; and S. Hammersmith and M. Weinberg, "Homosexual Identity: Commitment, Adjustment, and Significant Others," *Sociometry* 36 (1973): 56–79.
42. M. Trent, "On Being a Gay Teacher: My Problems—and Yours," *Psychology Today,* April 1978, p. 136.
43. Bell and Weinberg; T. Clark and R. Epstein, "Self Concept and Expectancy for Social Reinforcement in Noninstitutionalized Male Homosexuals," *Journal of Consulting and Clinical Psychology* 38 (1972): 174–80; and Morin.
44. W. Masters and V. Johnson, *Homosexuality in Perspective* (Boston: Little, Brown, 1979).
45. L. Peplau and S. Gordon, "The Intimate Relationships of Lesbians and Gay Men," in *Gender Roles and Sexual Behavior: The Changing Boundaries,* ed. E. Allgeier and N. McCormick (Palo Alto, Calif.: Mayfield, 1981).
46. K. Jay and A. Young, *The Gay Report* (New York: Summit, 1977).
47. Bell and Weinberg.
48. Bell and Weinberg; J. Harry and R. Lovely, "Gay Marriages and Communities of Sexual Orientation," *Alternative Life Styles* 2 (1979): 177–200; and K. Plummer, "Men in Love: Observations on Male Homosexual Couples," in *The Couple,* ed. M. Corbin (New York: Penguin, 1978), pp. 173–200.
49. M. Hunt, *Sexual Behavior in the 1970's* (New York: Dell, 1974); Kinsey et al.; and A. Pietropinto and J. Simenauer, *Husbands and Wives* (New York: Berkeley, 1979).
50. Cited in M. Mendola, *The Mendola Report: A New Look at Gay Couples* (New York: Crown, 1980), p. 55.
51. Peplau and Gordon.
52. Ibid.
53. Peplau.

Chapter 13: Power and Male-Female Relations

1. A. Adams, *Letters to John Adams, 1776.*
2. S. Anthony, Speech on Social Purity, 1875.
3. P. Johnson, "Women and Interpersonal Power," in *Women and Sex Roles,* ed. I. Frieze et al. (New York: Norton, 1978), p. 302.
4. J. French and B. Raven, "The Bases of Social Power," in *Studies in Social Power,* ed. D. Cartwright (Ann Arbor: Institute for Social Research, The University of Michigan, 1959); and B. Raven and A. Kruglanski, "Conflict and Power," in *The Structure of Conflict,* ed. P. Swingle (New York: Academic Press, 1970).
5. J. Tedeschi, B. Schlenker, and S. Lindskold, "The Exercise of Power and Influence: The Source of Influence," in *The Social Influence Process,* ed. J. Tedeschi (Chicago: Aldine, 1972).
6. P. Goldberg, "Are Women Prejudiced Against Women?" *Trans-Action* 5, no. 5 (1968): 28–30.
7. See I. Broverman et al., "Sex Role Stereotypes and Clinical Judgments of Mental Health," *Journal of Consulting and Clinical Psychology* 34 (1970): 1–7.

8. A. Kahn, "The Power War: Male Response to Power Loss Under Equality." Paper presented at the meeting of the American Psychological Association, Montreal, September 1980, p. 11.

9. Z. Rubin, *Liking and Loving: An Invitation to Social Psychology* (New York: Holt, Rinehart & Winston, 1973).

10. L. Stone, *The Family, Sex and Marriage in England: 1500–1800* (New York: Harper & Row, 1977).

11. J. Doyle and R. Moore, "Attitudes Toward the Male's Role Scale (AMR): An Objective Instrument to Measure Attitudes Toward the Male's Sex Role in Contemporary Society," *JSAS Catalog of Selected Documents in Psychology* 8 (1978): 35–36; and J. Spence and R. Helmreich, "The Attitudes Toward Women Scale: An Objective Instrument to Measure Attitudes Toward the Rights and Roles of Women in Contemporary Society," *JSAS Catalog of Selected Documents in Psychology* 2 (1972): 66.

12. G. Levinger, "Task and Social Behavior in Marriage," *Sociometry* 27 (1964): 433–48.

13. B. Farber, "An Index of Marital Integration," *Sociometry* 20 (1957): 117–18.

14. L. Rubin, *Worlds of Pain* (New York: Basic Books, 1976).

15. L. Peplau and S. Gordon, "Women and Men in Love: Sex Differences in Close Relationships," in *Women, Gender and Social Psychology,* ed. V. O'Leary, R. Unger, and B. Wallston (Hillsdale, N.J.: Erlbaum, in press).

16. S. Parelman, "Dimensions of Emotional Intimacy in Marriage: Gender and Sex-Role Influences," cited in Peplau and Gordon.

17. Peplau and Gordon.

18. R. Blood and D. Wolfe, *Husbands and Wives: The Dynamics of Married Living* (New York: The Free Press, 1960); and R. Centers, B. Raven, and A. Rodriguez, "Conjugal Power Structure: A Re-examination," *American Sociological Review* 36 (1971): 264–78.

19. Cited in Peplau and Gordon.

20. T. Falbo and L. Peplau, "Power Strategies in Intimate Relationships," *Journal of Personality and Social Psychology* 38 (1980): 618–28; and H. Raush et al., *Communication, Conflict and Marriage* (San Francisco: Jossey-Bass, 1974).

21. See H. Kelley et al., "Sex Differences in Comments Made During Conflict Within Close Heterosexual Pairs," *Sex Roles* 4 (1978): 473–91.

22. N. Bradburn, *The Structure of Psychological Well-Being* (Chicago: Aldine, 1969); A. Campbell, P. Converse, and W. Rodgers, *The Quality of American Life* (New York: Russell Sage Foundation, 1976); and G. Gurin, J. Veroff, and S. Feld, *Americans View Their Mental Health* (New York: Basic Books, 1960).

23. J. Bernard, *The Future of Marriage* (New York: Bantam, 1972); and W. Gove, "The Relationships Between Sex Roles, Mental Illness and Marital Status," *Social Forces* 51 (1972): 34–44.

24. J. Robinson et al., "Sex-Role Differences in Time Use," *Sex Roles* 3 (1977): 443–58.

Chapter 14: Where To from Here

1. A. Toffler, *The Third Wave* (New York: Bantam, 1981), p. 9.

2. J. Bernard, *The Future of Marriage* (New York: Bantam, 1972).

3. See, for example, U. Leguin, *The Left Hand of Darkness* (New York: Ace Books, 1969).

4. B. Zilbergeld, *Male Sexuality* (Boston: Little, Brown, 1978), p. 312.

5. M. Ferree, "The Confused American Housewife," *Psychology Today,* September 1979, p. 76.

6. A. Skolnick and J. Skolnick, eds., *Family in Transition* (Boston: Little, Brown, 1977).

7. S. Cowley et al., "Women at Work," *Newsweek,* December 6, 1976, pp. 68–70, 73–76, 81.

8. "As Men Move in on Women's Jobs," *U.S. News & World Report,* August 10, 1981, pp. 55–57.

9. I. Robertson, *Sociology,* 2nd ed. (New York: Worth, 1981), p. 369.

10. R. Unger, "Male Is Greater Than Female: The Socialization of Status Inequality," *The Counseling Psychologist* 6 (1976): 2–9.

11. M. Richmond-Abbot and N. Bishop, "The New Old-Fashion Womanhood," *Human Behavior,* April 1977, pp. 64–69.

12. J. Bernard, "The Good Provider Role: Its Rise and Fall," *American Psychologist* 36 (1981): 2.

13. B. Friedan, *The Feminine Mystique* (New York: Dell, 1970), p. 11.

14. M. Komarovsky, *Dilemmas of Masculinity* (New York: Norton, 1976).

15. See F. Caprio, *The Sexually Adequate Male* (Hollywood: Wilshire Books, 1974); S. Julty, *MSP: Male Sexual Performance* (New York: Dell, 1975); and S. Silber, *The Male: From Infancy to Old Age* (New York: Scribner's, 1981).

16. R. Haddad, *The Men's Liberation Movement: A Perspective* (Columbia, Md.: Free Men, 1979).

17. See J. Ornstein, *The Lion's Share: A Combat Manual for the Divorcing Male* (New York: Times Books, 1978); and *Newsweek,* December 8, 1980, pp. 50–54.

18. W. Farrell, *The Liberated Man* (New York: Random House, 1974), p. 217.

19. A. Gross, R. Smith, and B. Wallston, "The Men's Movement: Personal vs. Political," in *The Politics of Social Movements,* ed. J. Freeman (New York: Longmans, in press). The quotations cited here and later are taken from a prepublication draft of the article, pp. 9–10.

20. M. Sherif, "On the Relevance of Social Psychology," *American Psychologist* 25 (1970): 144–56.

21. G. Steinem, Introduction, in M. Fasteau, *The Male Machine* (New York: McGraw-Hill, 1974), pp. xiii–xv.

22. J. Snodgrass, ed., *For Men Against Sexism* (Albion, Calif.: Times Change Press, 1977).

23. Gross, Smith, and Wallston.

24. See K. Grady, R. Brannon, and J. Pleck, *The Male Sex Role: A Selected and Annotated Bibliography* (Rockville, Md.: National Institute of Mental Health, 1979); *Men's Studies Bibliography,* 3rd ed. (Cambridge, Mass.: Massachusetts Institute of Technology, 1977); and J. Harrison, "Men's Roles and Men's Lives," *Signs* 4, no. 2 (1978): 324–36.

25. Gross, Smith, and Wallston, p. 1.

26. J. Nichols, *Men's Liberation: A New Definition of Masculinity* (New York: Penguin, 1975), pp. 317–18.

Adam, 75–76, 150
Adams, Abigail, 260
Aeneas, 26
Agamemnon, 25
Allen, Woody, 201, 219–20
Andelin, Helen, 278
Anthony, Susan, 260
Ardrey, Robert, 76
Arkin, William, 228–29
Athena, 25

Baker, A., 64
Bandura, Albert, 125
Bardwick, J., 98, 167
Basu, G., 63
Bell, Alan, 255
Berger, Peter, 171
Berger, Thomas, 83
Berkowitz, Leonard, 182
Berlin, Irving, 162
Bernard, Jessie, 151, 169–70, 270
Bettelheim, Bruno, 80
Biller, Henry, 95
Bloch, Marc, 23
Blumenthal, Monica, 185
Bogart, Humphrey, 219
Bonaparte, Napoleon, 119
Boston Strangler, 190
Brannon, Robert, 144–45, 160, 162, 197,
    217, 287
Brenton, Myron, 236
Bronson, Charles, 183–84, 219, 221
Brown, Rita Mae, 277
Brownmiller, Susan, 189
Bryant, Anita, 241, 243, 251–52

Carmichael, Stokely, 150
Carter, Jimmy, 241
Chodorow, Nancy, 81
Cicone, Michael, 144, 197

Clarke, Arthur, 11
Cleaver, Eldridge, 151
Clytemnestra, 25
Coburn, James, 219
Cochran, Susan, 268
Coleman, James, 223
Cook, K., 92
Cooper, Gary, 219, 222
Corman, Avery, 15
Costanzo, P., 105

Darwin, Charles, 67
David (a fictional character), 4–9
Davis, Elizabeth Gould, 23, 73
Dillon, Matt, 183
Dobrofsky, Lynne, 228–29
Doering, C., 62
Donahue, Phil, 287
Durant, Will, 22
Durbin, Karen, 192
Durocher, Leo, 172

Eastwood, Clint, 183, 221
Ehrhardt, A., 64
Elizabeth I, 29
Etziona, Amitai, 90
Eve, 27–28, 75–76, 81, 150

Fagot, Beverly, 103
Farrell, Warren, 156–57, 284
Fasteau, Marc, 119, 159, 230–32, 286
Febvre, Lucien, 23
Federal Bureau of Investigation (FBI), 182,
    189, 192
Ferenczi, Sandor, 248
Flynn, Errol, 218–19
Fox, C. A., 62
Freud, Sigmund, 79, 122–24, 127, 129, 134,
    247–48

Freund, K., 248
Friday, Nancy, 198–99
Friedan, Betty, 13, 43, 281
Friedl, Ernestine, 73, 78–79

Gable, Clark, 219
Gardner, Jo Ann, 97
Goldberg, Herb, 203
Goldberg, Philip, 106, 264
Goldberg, Susan, 92, 119
Goldwater, Barry, 231
Gordon, Steven, 268
Gregory the Great (6th century pope), 240
Gross, Alan, 284, 289
Guinevere, 28

Haddad, Richard, 283
Halberstam, David, 231
Hamlet, 29
Hardesty, F., 105
Harlow, Harry, 200
Harris, Marvin, 78
Hartley, Ruth, 93, 105
Helen of Troy, 25
Heller, Joseph, 15
Henry VIII, 29
Hetherington, E. Mavis, 95
Hinckley, John, 182
Hoffman, Abbie, 151
Hoffman, Martin, 241
Hoffman, Steven, 222–25
Homer, 25
Horney, Karen, 79–80
Hughes, Sir Thomas, 40
Humphreys, Laud, 246–47

Irving, John, 277
Irving, Washington, 174

Jacklin, Carol, 63, 88, 114–19, 121
Jack the Ripper, 190
James, William, 163
Jay, K., 254
Jesus Christ, 26–28

Job, 150
Johnson, Lyndon, 230–31
Johnson, Virginia, 253, 258
Jong, Erica, 277
Jourard, Sidney, 119, 157, 161

Kahn, Arnold, 265
Kennedy, John F., 13, 112, 182, 229–31
Kinsey, Alfred, 205, 241, 246–47
Kipling, Rudyard, 150, 214
Kirk, Grayson, 151
Kohlberg, Lawrence, 127–29
Kolodny, Robert, 249
Komarovsky, Mirra, 210, 223, 279, 283
Komisar, Lucy, 180
Korda, Michael, 172–74
Kossen, Stan, 152
Krafft-Ebing, Richard von, 189
Kreuz, L., 63

Lamphere, Louise, 74
Lancelot, 28
Lear, 29
Lehne, Gregory, 159, 239
Lessing, Doris, 277
Levine, S., 59
Lewis, Michael, 92, 119
Liddy, G. Gordon, 148, 155
Lipman-Blumen, Jean, 196
Little Horse, 83
Lombardi, Vince, 164
Long, Michele, 97
Lorenz, Konrad, 76
Luria, Z., 91
Luther, Martin, 150
Lynn, David, 94–95

Macbeth, 29
McCary, James, 200
Maccoby, Eleanor, 63, 88, 114–19, 121
Maccoby, Michael, 177–78
McDavid, John, 120
McDonald, Gary, 248
Machiavelli, 173
McNamara, Robert, 230
Malcomson, William, 179
Martin, Del, 192
Marx Ferree, Myra, 276
Masters, William, 253, 258

Mead, Margaret, 69–73
Meggitt, Mervyn, 72–73
Mellen, Joan, 218–20
Meyer, David, (a fictional character), 203
Meyer, J., 249
Michelangelo, 29
Miller, S. A., 178
Millet, Kate, 148
Minnow, Newton, 96, 99
Mischel, Walter, 125
Money, John, 48, 56–57, 128–29
Montagu, Ashley, 48, 52
Moore, Robert, 248
Moore, Roger, 222
Morgan, Marabel, 278
Morris, Desmond, 76
Morrison, Toni, 277
Morse, Nancy, 175
Murdock, G., 70
Murphy, Audie, 225
Murphy, Yolanda and Robert, 80
Muskie, Edmund, 156–57

Newman, Paul, 137
Nichols, Jack, 162, 289
Nichols, Mike, 241
Nicholson, Jack, 219
Nixon, Richard, 229, 231

O'Leary, S. E., 121
Olien, Michael, 83
Orestes, 25
Oswald, Lee Harvey, 182

Pandora, 27, 148
Parent, Gail, 15, 203
Parke, Ross, 121
Parlce, Mary Brown, 62
Patterson, Gerald, 103
Paul the Apostle, 27, 106, 150, 209
Pechinpah, Sam, 183
Peplau, Ann, 238, 256, 258, 267–70
Persky, H., 63
Piaget, Jean, 127
Plato, 26
Pleck, Elizabeth, 22, 36, 39
Pleck, Joseph, 22, 36, 39, 63–64, 95, 101,
          113, 120, 131, 134, 138, 140–41,
          248, 287

Pope Clement, 27
Provenzano, F., 91

Ramey, Estelle, 62
Reagan, Ronald, 182, 232
Redford, Robert, 137, 219
Reynolds, Burt, 219
Rheingold, H., 92
Ringer, Robert, 178
Rohrlich-Leavitt, R., 74
Roosevelt, Teddy, 39
Rosaldo, Michelle, 74
Rose, R., 63
Rosie the Riverter, 170
Roszak, Betty and Theodore, 279
Roth, Philip, 15, 201
Rubin, J., 91
Ruble, Diane, 144, 197
Russell, Diane, 191
Russell, Mark, 241

Samuelson, Paul, 153
Santanyana, George, 45
Schein, Virginia, 154
Schlafly, Phyllis, 108–9, 278
Schopenhauer, Arthur, 115
Schumann, S., 98
Scott, Randolph, 218
Seneca, 150
Serbin, Lisa, 102
Seton, Ernest Thompson, 40
Sexton, Patricia, 101
Shakespeare, William, 29
Shaw, M., 105
Sherif, Muzafer, 285–87, 289
Shettles, Landrum, 50, 52
Simon, Rita, 97
Sistrunk, Frank, 120
Skinner, B. F., 124
Slocum, Bob, (a fictional character), 15
Smith, K., 63
Smith, Ronald, 284, 289
Snodgrass, Jon, 287
Snyder, Ross, 179
Sophocles, 123
Stearns, Peter, 22
Steele, Addison, 174–75
Stein, Peter, 222–25
Steinem, Gloria, 286
Stone, Gregory, 105

Stone, I. F., 229
Stone, Merlin, 73
Stouffer, Samuel, 226
Strudler Wallston, Barbara, 284, 286, 289

Talese, Gay, 198
Tennyson, Alfred, 14
Terkel, Studs, 42
Terman, Lewis, 114
Thoreau, David, 20
Tiger, Lionel, 76–77, 158
Toffler, Alvin, 274
Tolstoy, Leo, 150
Tucker, Patricia, 48, 56–57, 128–29
Tyler, Leona, 114

Unger, Rhoda, 153
U'Ren, Marjorie, 102

Van Winkle, Rip, 174
Veblen, Thorstein, 170

Virgil, 25–26
Virgin Mary, 28, 30

Walters, Richard, 125
Watson, John, 124
Wayne, John, 136–37, 141, 183, 225, 228
Weinberg, Martin, 242–43, 255
Weiss, Robert, 175
Weitzman, Lenore, 93, 99
Williams, Colin, 242–43
Wilson, Edward, 77
Witkin, Herman, 115–16

Yahweh, 75, 240
Yorburg, Betty, 66
Young, A., 254

Zeus, 25
Zilbergeld, Bernie, 196, 202, 205, 276, 278

Abolition movement
    impact on female role, 39
Aeneid, 26
Affectional deprivation among boys, 199–200
Aggression, 181–84
    in America, 182–84
    in classrooms, 102
    definition of, 182
Androgyny, 135
Androsperm, 50
Anlagen, 54
Annales, 23
Antihomosexual sentiment, 240–45
    by psychiatrists, 243–44
Apgar scores, 91
Arapesh, 70–72
Athletics, 7
    athletic programs, 100, 120

Behaviorism, 124
Best and the Brightest, The, 231
Big bad wolves, 219–21
Bourgeois male ideal, 30
Boy Scouts of America, 40

Career options, 100
Casablanca (film), 219
Castration
    anxiety, 61
    homosexuals and, 61
Chivalric male ideal, 28–29
Choctau Indians, 74
Christianity
    change in human values, 26
    influence on sex roles, 27
    views toward homosexuality and, 27–28
Chromosomes, 4, 49–54
Cognitive-developmental theory of sex role
    development, 127–30

Competition
    as a world view for men, 163–68
Conception
    imbalance in sex ratio, 50–51
Consciousness-raising groups, 281, 284
    rap groups and the women's movement,
        13–14
Couvade, 80
Creek Indians, 74
Crow Indians
    berdache, 83–84

Daughters of Bilitis (DOB), 242
David Meyer Is a Mother, 203
Democratic National Convention (Chicago,
    1968), 12
Dependency
    in childhood, 68
    in classrooms, 102
Dilemmas of Masculinity, 279
Doctrine of the Spheres, 38
Don Juan Complex, 206
Draft resistance, 12
Dyadic attachment, 268–69

Educational system, 100–103
Electra complex, 123–24, 127
Embryo
    ambisexual stage, 4, 54
Emotional constipation, 156–57
Emotional incompetence, 156
Epic male ideal, 25–26
ERA, 13
Evolution, 67

Fascinating Womanhood, 278
Fathering, 93–95

Fears
among men, 15–16
of success, 173–74
Federally Employed Women's Organization, 13
Female sex role
in colonial times, 37
in the 19th century, 40–41
Feminine Mystique, The, 281
Feminized Male, The, 101
Feudalism, 28
and dualistic view of women, 28–29
Follicle stimulating hormone (FSH), 58–59
For Men Against Sexism, 287
Freud's views
on masculinity-feminity, 134
on sex role development, 122–24, 129–30

Gender identity, 3, 17–18, 128–29
Genetic sex, 50
Genital tubercle, 55–58
Golden age of matriarchy, 73–74
Good provider role, 41–43, 168–72
Gynocracy, 24
Gynosperm, 50

Hermaphrodite, 55
High Noon (film), 219, 222
History
impact of gay movement on, 24
redefinition of, 23
Homophobia, 239
Homosexuality
either-or perspective of, 246–47
fear of, 159–61
and hormones, 249–50
myths about, 245–53
and psychological disturbance, 251
and sex role identity, 247–48
and traditional marriage roles, 250–51
Homosexuality in Perspective, 253
Homosexuals
appearance of, 251
and children, 251–52
compared to heterosexual couples, 255–58
incidence of sexual activity among, 254–55
and misogyny, 248
and mothers, 249

Hopi Indians, 74
H-Y antigen, 54
Hypothalamus, 58

Impotence, 205
Incest, 77
Independence
in children's play, 93
as outcome of punishment, 93
Industrial revolution
effects on male sex role, 10–11
Interstitial cell stimulating hormone (ICSH), 58–59
Iroquois Indians, 74
Israeli kibbutz, 77

Kent State University, 12, 188
Klinefelter's syndrome (XXY), 53
Kuma, 72

Labioscrotal swelling, 55–58
Lack of sexual interest among men, 206–7
Leydig cells, 58–59
Liberated Man, The, 284
Literature
feminist, 277
image of troubled male, 15–16
Little Big Man, 83

Mae Enga, 72
Male bond, 76–77, 158
Male dominance
avoidance of feminine identification and, 79, 81
biological explanation of, 76–78, 81
envy of women and, 79–80
fear of women and, 79–80
Freud's views on, 79
Judeo-Christian explanation of, 75–76, 81
psychological explanation of, 79–81
socioeconomic explanation of, 78–79, 81
as a universal cultural feature, 73
Male Machine, The, 230, 286

Male sex role
    and aggression, 183–84
    American aristocracy and, 37
    American versions of, 36–44
    anthropological perspective of, 21
    biological perspective of, 21
    and breadwinner role, 163
    and competition, 163–68
    elements of, 144–46
    and emotional expression, 155–58
    emphasis on physical activity and,
        39–40
    expectations of, 3, 17, 144–46
    historical perspective of, 20
    and homosexual men, 255
    influence of peers on, 6, 95
    influence of teachers on, 6, 102
    influence of television on, 6, 96–99
    influence of textbooks on, 102–3
    modern views of, 136–38
    parental expectations and, 5
    psychological perspective of, 21
    resistance to change of, 9–10
    self-reliant element of, 215–18
    sociological perspective of, 21
    and success, 163
    traditional views of, 136–37
Male Sex Role Identity Paradigm, (MSRI),
    131–35
Male sexuality
    myths of, 202–4
Marital violence, 192–93
Marriage
    benefits for men, 271–72
Married Women's Acts, 38
Masculinity
    dominance as sign of, 10
    short hair and, 9–10
Masturbation, 60, 200–201
Matriarchal rule, 73–74
Matrilineality, 74
Mattachine Society, 242
Men in Groups, 76
Men's liberation, 289–90
Men's Lives (film), 220–21
Men's movement, 285–89
Menstruation
    cycles, 58
    women's emotions and, 61
Mid-life crisis, 8
Misogynous beliefs (see: sexism)

Mohave Indians, 83
    alyha, 84
    hwame, 84
Mullerian duct, 55
    Mullerian-inhibiting substance, 55
Mundugumor, 70–72
Mundurucú people, 80
    and female dominance, 80

Naked Ape, The, 76
National Organization for Women (NOW),
    13, 281
Natural Superiority of Women, The, 152
Navajo Indians
    nadle, 83
Nineteenth Amendment to the Constitution,
    13, 41

Observational learning
    and sex roles, 125
Oedipus complex, 123–24, 127
On Aggression, 76
On the Origins of Species, 67

Patriarchy, 23–24
    in early Christianity, 27
    19th century challenge against, 34
    in Puritan thought, 36
Peers, 95, 120
    as socializing agents, 103–5
Penis envy, 124
Pentagon Papers, The, 12
Personal autonomy, 268–69
Phaedrus, 26
Pituitary gland, 58
Power
    between the sexes, 264–65
    concern among males, 265–66, 269–71
    types of, 261–63
Premature ejaculation, 205
Primogeniture, 29, 37, 40
Psychology of Sex Differences, The, 144
Puberty, 59
    and male secondary sex characteristics,
        59–60

Rape, 189–91
  definition of, 189
  incidence of, 189
  and masculine identity, 190
  myths about, 191
Reinforcement, 124
Renaissance male ideal, 29
Retarded ejaculation, 206
Rod-and-frame test, 115–16
Role strain
  among athletes, 223–25
  among nonathletes, 224–25
Rugby, Tennessee, 40

Self-disclosure, 119, 157–58
Self-reliant element
  role of athletics, 222
  role of the politician, 229–32
  role of the soldier, 225–29
Seneca Falls Convention (1848), 12–13, 39
Sex and Temperament, 70
Sex chromosomes, 50–54
Sex differences, 92, 113–22
  an aggression, 102, 121–22
  and analytical cognitive styles, 116
  and creativity, 118
  and dependency, 102, 119–21
  and global cognitive style, 116
  and hyperactive label, 101
  and independence, 92–93
  and intellectual abilities, 114–18
  and nurturant behaviors, 121
  and quantitative ability, 116–17
  and self-disclosure, 119
  and social differences, 118–22
  and types of punishment, 93
  and verbal abilities, 115
  and visual-spatial abilities, 115–16
Sex hormone binding globuline, 61
Sexism, 105–9, 149–55
Sex-linked diseases, 52
  hemophilia as an example of, 52
Sex reassignment, 128–29
Sex role development
  changes in, 275–79
  and childrens' bedrooms, 92
  and fathers' role, 91, 94–95
  among Indians, 82–83
  and mothers' role, 92–93
  and teachers' impact, 102

Sex role stereotypes, 113–14
  before birth, 91
  in childrens' books, 99
  on television, 97–99
  in textbooks, 102–3
Sex Role Strain (SRS) Paradigm, 138–41
Sex therapy, 15
Sexual abstinence, 209–11
Sexual interests, 7
Sexual problems, 15
  anxieties, 207–8
  performance anxiety, 208
Social institutions
  interdependence between sex roles and,
    11–12
Socialization
  among Arabs, 89
  definition of, 89
  in Japan, 89
  Israeli kibbutz and, 89
Socializing agents, 89
  parents as, 90–96
  peers as, 103–5
Social learning theory
  and sex role development, 124–30
Sociobiology, 77–78
Spiritual male ideal, 26–28
Subincision, 80
Success
  signs of, 8
Suffragette movement, 41
Supermale syndrome (XYY), 53

Tchambuli, 70, 72
Technology
  male sex role and, 10–11
Television
  as socializing agent, 96–99
Territorial Imperative, The, 76
Testosterone, 4, 21, 54–59
  cycles of, 61–62
  and depression in men, 62
  and emotionality, 61–62
  male aggression and, 62–63
  nurturant behaviors and, 64
  postnatal effects and, 6–7
  sex drive and, 60–61

Tests
    Buss-Durkee Hostility Inventory, 63
    masculinity-femininity (M-F), 134–35
    Multiple Affect Adjective Checklist, 62
    projective, 135
Three Essays on the Theory of Sexuality,
    123
Title IX of the Educational Amendment of
    1972, 100
Total Woman, The, 278

Urethral fold, 55–58

Values
    males over females, 90–91
Vietnam, 12, 230

Will Wimbles, 40
Wolffian duct, 55
Women's Equity Action League, 13
Women's movement, 12–14
    experimental group, 13–14
    rap groups, 13–14
    traditional group, 13–14
World According to Garp, The, 277

39, 714

39, 714

Doyle, James A.

The male experi-
ence

DATE DUE		
FEB 2 7 1985		
Nov 24	DEC 2 2 1995	
APR 1 4 1987	DEC 1 4 1995	
FEB 1 5 1988	APR 0 6 1997	
OCT - 4 1988	APR 0 2 1997	
OCT 1 8 1988		
NOV 1 1988		
NOV 1 5 1988		
DEC 1 1988		
DEC 1 5 1988		
APR 1 7 1991		
APR 1 9 1994		